THE
ILLUSTRATED ENCYCLOPEDIA
OF
WORLD
HORSE RACING

FOREWORD BY
Steve Cauthen

WHSMITH
EXCLUSIVE
· BOOKS ·

Foreword

A competition or a race has always had universal appeal. And when that race also involves the finest horses in the world, the appeal is irresistible.

Anyone who knows horse racing, from the immensely wealthy owners, or jockeys like myself, to the average race-goer, is drawn to the common ground of the race-track where all that matters is a knowledge of and a love of horses. It is the same all over the world, for horse racing is both a great draw and a great leveller.

This book is a fascinating look at what for me is both work and pleasure. Here are the great horses of the calibre of Red Rum and Shergar, famous owners such as The Queen Mother and Baron Guy de Rothschild, jockeys like Fred Archer and Sir Gordon Richards, trainers including Dick Hern and Peter Cazalet, and superb courses all over the world from Goodwood to Randwick and Aqueduct. Not only are they part of history, but part of the folklore of racing as well.

I've never seen a book on horse racing that covers so much in one volume, from history and betting to breeding and major records. The Illustrated Encyclopedia of World Horse Racing *brings to the reader the flavour, variety, and, yes, love of the greatest sport in the world. I feel very privileged to be a part of it.*

Steve Cauthen

House Editor Dorothea Hall
Editor Richard Dawes
Art Editor Gordon Robertson
Picture Research Moira McIlroy
Production Controller Tom Helsby

Produced exclusively for W H Smith Limited
by Marshall Cavendish Books Limited
58 Old Compton Street
London W1V 5PA

Typeset by J&L Composition Ltd, Filey, North Yorkshire
Printed and bound by Dai Nippon, Hong Kong

ISBN 1 85435 199 0

Contents

Famous jockey Sir Gordon Richards went to St Moritz for the ice sport of curling. The Swiss go there to race!

The History of Horse Racing

The competitive urges of man and horse made it inevitable that the former would race the fleet-footed steed he had captured and domesticated for use in battle. But gradually the horse was transformed from an instrument of war to an object of pleasure, prized for its competitive spirit and stamina.

Chariot racing gave way to ridden races and the exhilaration of the occasion attracted spectators eager to support their favourites. That support frequently involved money and the resultant motivation to breed fast animals precipitated the evolution of the sophisticated thoroughbred known throughout the world wherever racing takes place.

John Sturgess's painting, The Derby Favourites, *features (from left to right) the 1896 Derby winner Persimmon, with St Frusquin and Regret.*

What we know of Ancient Greece suggests a preference for chariot racing rather than ridden races. Homer, for example, referred to riding as a gymnastic display of no practical value. In this respect, horse racing, like so many sports, served as a training ground for war. It is inconceivable that those fearless and fearsome mounted warriors, the Mongols, who, along with the Hyksos (the latter around 1500 B.C.) were principally responsible for introducing the horse to Europe and North Africa, neglected to race their charges, although no hard evidence attests to the fact. The India of the Rig-Veda and Homer's Greece begin to offer a clearer picture. The Greek horse, standing about 10½ hands, was obtained from the Libyans and made its competitive debut at the 25th Olympiad of 680 B.C. in the quadriga or four-horse chariot race. Thirty-two years later the first ridden races appeared in the programme of Olympic events. The contestants rode bareback with the aid of a rudimentary bit.

The origins of racing

The Greek debt to Libya was an early demonstration of the influential role North

A Greek amphora of about 500 B.C. depicting a horse race. It was given as a prize at such events.

Africa would play in the evolution of the thoroughbred and the development of horse racing. Spain was importing horses from Morocco by 400 B.C.; farther east, the Romans acquired the taste from the people of Thurii. According to Strabo, the first race was proclaimed by Romulus immediately after he founded Rome. By the reign of Tarquinius Priscus, 260,000 racegoers could squeeze into the Circus Maximus to enjoy the sport. However, the emphasis still lay upon the chariot, the armoured car of its day.

As the power of Rome spread throughout Europe, so did horse racing. In the wake of the Claudian invasion of Britain in A.D. 43 there is evidence of racing at Caerleon, Dorchester, Netherby, and Silchester, until the picture once again grows murky with the onset of the Dark Ages. Nevertheless, although details may be lacking, one can be quite sure that horse racing in the accepted sense of the term, had been incorporated into European society by the dawning of the Middle Ages.

The venue for medieval racing was the fair, a periodic gathering which mingled business and pleasure. At Smithfield market in the late twelfth century, trials were held between the horses assembled for sale. In 1370, at Sémur in the Côte d'Or, races were organized at the annual fair held on the Thursday after Pentecost. The Irish raced their hobbies (racing ponies) at the Aenach, or fair, the most notable being the Aenach Colmain on The Curragh. The races often matched two contestants. Occasionally the rivalry extended to factions of the community, as in the famous Palio (originally an embroidered cloak) of Siena, first mentioned in 1238, in which the race is contested by the wards of the city during the Feast of the Assumption in August.

One particularly longstanding English fair was the Roodee or Roodeye, held on the banks of the Dee outside Chester. In 1540, or thereabouts, a silver bell, value 3s. 4d. was offered for competition at the direction of the mayor and his corporation. A milestone had been reached: England was starting down a road which eventually led to it presenting the recognizable sport of horse racing to the world. More than any other factor, the success of that journey depended upon, and resulted from, the development and gradual refinement of the horse into the racing machine we now call the thoroughbred.

The thoroughbred

Although the term 'thro-bred' did not appear in print until 1713, some 25 years after the importation of the Byerley Turk, the first of the three renowned Arab stallions from whom all today's thoroughbreds descend, the English horse had experienced earlier injections of foreign blood. There was reputedly an Arab stallion in Scotland as early as 1121, which would probably have been mated with the native Galloways, racing ponies of no more than 13 hands. Henry VIII certainly imported North African Barbs, which were stabled alongside his hunters and hobbies at Greenwich and at the Royal Stud at Eltham. Queen Elizabeth I founded a new stud at Tutbury and frequently raced: at Croydon in 1574 and Salisbury in 1585, for example. At her death in 1601 racing was also taking place at Carlisle, Richmond, and Boroughbridge. Elizabeth's successor James I bought an 'Arabian' for £154 and as a result of his regular hunting trips across Newmarket

Heath, established a royal stable there. We read of a horse race at Newmarket on 19 March 1619. His son Charles I likewise favoured Newmarket for races, and in 1634 a Gold Cup was contested there. Elsewhere, famous racing venues such as Doncaster (1600), Lincoln (1617), and Epsom (1640s) were being mentioned. At Kiplingcotes in Yorkshire a set of rules, covering subscriptions, weights, and fouls was adopted in 1619.

However, it is Charles II whose name will forever be linked with the development of Newmarket as a racing centre. Charles had raced at Epsom one year after his restoration and made his first visit to Newmarket in 1666. His stays sometimes lasted three weeks, so he built a palace. He watched training gallops as well as the races and actually won the Newmarket Town Plate in 1675. Such Plates involved four heats over 4 miles (6.5 km) carrying 12 stone (76 kg). The racers, needing to be big and strong, were usually older animals. In other words, neither race nor racers bore much resemblance to their modern counterparts. But all that would change within 100 years of 'Old Rowley's' death in 1685.

The first great horses

The importation of the Byerley Turk (1689), the Darley Arabian (1704) — from whose male line some 90 per cent of modern thoroughbreds descend — and the Godolphin Arabian (1729) began to alter the appearance and conformation of the racehorse; John Cheny's matchbook (1727) served to provide a centralized record of results and was the forerunner of James Weatherby's Racing Calendar (1773). At the Star & Garter, Pall Mall, in or around 1750, the Jockey Club was founded to lend leadership and authority to the sport. On the track, developments were no less dramatic and far-reaching. The first two-year-old raced in 1769, and the first Classic for three-year-olds, the St Leger, was won by Allabaculia in 1776 and was followed by the Oaks (1779), Derby (1780), 2,000 Guineas (1809), and 1,000 Guineas (1814). The first important handicap race, Ascot's Oatlands (1791), course bookmakers (c.1790), the General Stud Book (1791), and organized steeplechasing (1811) were just round the corner. By 1800 there were 83 tracks — York was established in 1709, Ascot in 1711 — and 536 horses in training, 25 per cent of them two- and three-year-olds. It would be misleading to state categorically that the format of English racing had been firmly established but the roots of the modern sport are by now clearly distinguishable.

Racing personalities

The history of English racing since 1800 is dominated by the exploits of those pre-eminent figures who imposed their personalities upon the game. Administrators such as Lord George Bentinck, whose reforms in the early decades of the nineteenth century eliminated so many of the corrupt practices infesting the Turf, and Admiral Henry Rous, the prince of handicappers, whose weight-for-age scale of 1850, contained in his book *Laws and Practice of Horse Racing*, remains largely intact to this day. Trainers, from Robert Robson and record Classic winner John Scott, Mat Dawson and John Porter, Alec Taylor and Fred Darling to Noel Murless, Dick Hern, and Henry Cecil, who have

This engraving is of a chariot race, revived at Padua, Italy, in 1866. It is believed that the ancient Greeks also preferred racing chariots to riding horses.

gradually transformed the task of preparing a racehorse from one of prolonged galloping and sweating into something approaching a fine art, involving all the technical expertise of the computer age. The knights of the pigskin: Buckle, Fordham, Archer, Donoghue, Richards, Piggott. Riding styles may change, from the upright, long-legged grip of Archer to the bottom-high perch of Piggott, but the true horseman's empathy with his mount and that God-given, all-crucial will-to-win are just the same.

What of the horse at the heart of it all? He has changed, too, and is now a more specialized, sleeker, altogether faster species than in Richards's or Archer's day. Although it remains invidious to make comparisons between vastly different eras, it is quite likely that the English champion of 1986, Dancing Brave, is as superior to Ormonde and St Simon as Rous believed those two Victorian titans were to Flying Childers, Highflyer, and Eclipse, the first great racehorses to tread the English Turf (whom Rous thought would be pressed to win a £50 plate) and that these in turn surpassed the original Arab imports. Indeed, in 1885, an Arab champion called Asil (receiving 4½ stone/28.5 kg) was thrashed 20 lengths over 3 miles (4.8 km) by Iambic, whom St Simon humiliated by a distance in the Ascot Gold Cup of 1884 over 2½ miles (4 km). What would Archer have made of starting stalls (1965) or the photo-finish camera (1947) and its younger brother the all-seeing Camera Patrol (1966), which would surely have spotted some of his more nefarious tactics? Or the tantalizing prospect of amassing even more winners by riding at evening meetings (1947) or the pleasure of competing against lady riders (1975)? How would Rous have reacted to betting shops (1961), computerized handicapping (1973) or a sponsored Derby (1984)? Of course, not all of these innovations were English in origin but it has been towards England that other countries have looked when establishing their own racing systems.

Irish racing

The development of Irish racing was severely curtailed by the Great Rebellion of 1688–90. In the aftermath of James II's removal no Catholic was allowed to own a horse worth more than £5, though such a Draconian law in the land of the horse provoked considerable abuse. The Irish had raced their hobbies since time immemorial, and by 1739 racing was again so widespread that it was made illegal to run for any plate worth less than £20. Ireland's Newmarket Heath was The Curragh (Gaelic for horses' courses), a similarly wide expanse of lush turf atop a limestone base, which both drained well and put calcium into the bones of young stock. The Irish Turf Club was founded in 1790 when 18 courses — some using the strands or beaches — were listed in Mr Pat Sharkey's *Irish Racing Calendar*. One can gauge the standard of racing by the fact that 16 of the all-important King's Plates were to be found in the annual programme.

However, Ireland's unique contribution to the world of horse racing was to invent the steeplechase. As elsewhere, match races were commonplace but the one arranged in 1752 between Mr Edmund Blake and Mr O'Callaghan involved 4½ miles (7.2 km) of natural country from Buttevant Church to the spire of St Leger Church in County Cork. This potentially lethal sport proved extremely popular. 'A sort of racing for which the Paddies are particularly famous,' wrote one English visitor, 'in which, unless the rider has pluck and his prad goodness, they cannot expect to get well home.' Betting frequently concerned the number of falls in addition to the identity of the winner. No wonder: one race on St Patrick's Day, 1813 at Rathangan, in County Roscommon, took place over a distance of 6 miles (9.6 km) and included six five-foot (1.5 m) walls and several yawning ditches.

By 1809 another contemporary was safely able to assert that the 'Irish [horses] are the highest and the steadiest leapers in the world.' This handsome tribute was amply endorsed by the lengthy list of Irish-bred horses to triumph in the Grand National, steeplechasing's sternest test since its inception in 1839. Sixteen winners have also been trained in Ireland, Mathew (1847) being the first, L'Escargot (1975) the most recent, although two of the best Irish-bred National

The great stallion St Simon, from a painting by Percy Earl. St Simon sired the winners of 17 Classics before he died at the age of 27.

heroes, if not the best, Manifesto and Golden Miller, were trained in England. Manifesto was bred by Henry Dyas near Navan and ran in eight Nationals between 1895 and 1904. He won in 1897 and 1899 (carrying a record 12 stone 7 lb/79.5 kg) and finished third in 1900, 1902, and 1903 under the crippling burdens of 12.13 (82 kg), 12.8 (80 kg), and 12.5 (78.5 kg).

Golden Miller was born on Laurence Geraghty's Pelletstown farm 15 miles (24 km) north-west of Dublin, in County Meath. Trained by Basil Briscoe for the Hon Dorothy Paget, he won the 1934 race in record time with 12 stone 2 lb (77 kg) but, so it was believed, took such an aversion to the obstacles that he failed to complete his three subsequent Nationals. 'The Miller' also won five consecutive Cheltenham Gold Cups, a race increasingly acknowledged as the Blue Riband for chasers, and holds the unique distinction of winning the National and Gold Cup in the same year. The only other horse to ever win both events is his fellow countryman L'Escargot.

A great chaser

Fittingly, Ireland can also claim the greatest chaser of them all — Arkle. His owner, the Duchess of Westminster, would never risk her beloved horse at Aintree, so the National does not figure in his 22 victories (from 26 starts) over fences. Only six horses finished in front of him in a steeplechase and of those just his great English-trained, but Irish-bred, rival Mill House was giving him weight (5 lb/2.25 kg). That day, in the Hennessy Gold Cup of 1963, a vital slip on a patch of mud was said to have been the cause of defeat. On the other days it was quite simply the weight Arkle was asked to concede. In his last 19 races he never carried less than 12 stone (76 kg), and handicappers were forced to frame two sets of weights for races in which he was entered — one for use if he ran and one for use in his absence. Apart from Mill House, no horse beat Arkle at less than 21 lb (9.5 kg) and only at that difference in his last race at Kempton, after he had covered some 2½ miles (4 km) with a fractured pedal bone in his off-fore hoof.

Nevertheless, one must not make the mistake of undervaluing the Irish flat-racer. Since Bob Booty won King's Plates at Warwick and Lichfield in 1808, plenty of Irish-bred champions, such as Harkaway, Barcaldine, Ard Patrick, Pretty Polly, and The Tetrarch have crossed the Irish Sea to achieve fame and glory on English tracks, and as long as Ireland continues to produce intuitive horse-masters like Paddy Prendergast and Vincent O'Brien her success is assured. O'Brien's six Epsom Derbys highlight a shift in the balance of international Turf power which has steadily gathered momentum since World War II, because five of those winners were bred in North America. The Virginian colonists, who had no horses in 1607, for example, were exporting them by 1688. Horse racing was about to receive a fresh impetus.

Until Cortes reintroduced the horse in 1519, the American continent's knowledge of the species was restricted to eohippus, whose 11-inch-high (28 cm) fossilized form has been identified in rocks 45 million years old. Cortes landed with 11 stallions and five mares; in 1541 his compatriot Hernando De Soto lost some horses on an expedition up the Mississippi. Native American stock was on its way. Farther north and east English colonists lost little time indulging in the sport of horse racing. On the capture of New Amsterdam, Sir Richard Nicolls laid out a track on Salisbury Plain, Long Island, in 1665, and presented a silver cup to be contested each spring and autumn.

Early racing in America

The colonies set about acquiring English blood. Bulle Rock, a son of the Darley Arabian, was the first, imported into Virginia by Sam Gest in 1730. Others soon followed. Spark, inbred to the Darley Arabian, was bought by Maryland's governor, Sam Ogle, in 1747; Childers, a son of Flying Childers, was introduced by John Tayloe to his Mount Airey Stud in 1751; Janus, a grandson of the Godolphin Arabian, arrived in 1757. However, the most influential of all the early stallion imports was Diomed, the inaugural Derby winner of 1780. Ignominiously labelled a stud failure, he was bought as a 21-year-old for 50 guineas in 1798 by Colonel John

The Darley Arabian, painted by D. Dalby. The original painting was once owned by Henry Darley at Aldby Park, Yorkshire.

Diomed, winner of the first Epsom Derby, in 1780, was owned by Sir Charles Bunbury, the leading figure of the Turf at that time. Diomed was exported to the USA at the age of 21, and from him stemmed many of that country's greatest horses.

Hoomes, yet before his death in 1808 Diomed had created through his son Sir Archy the dominant American male line of the nineteenth century, which culminated in Boston and Lexington (Diomed's great-great-grandson).

As the frontier was pushed west of the Appalachians after the War of Independence, the horse expressed perfectly the young nation's desire to get things done in a hurry. By 1800 Dr Redmond Dillon Barry, formerly a surgeon in the British Navy, had brought Bluegrass from his native Ireland to the limestone country near his new farm at Gallatin on the Tennessee–Kentucky border. Within 40 years Kentucky possessed more racetracks (17) than the original colonies of Virginia (13), Maryland (3), and the Carolinas (16). Interstate rivalries became cut-throat, none more so than that between Kentucky and Virginia. The latter, on account of its early initiatives, still regarded itself as the premier racing state. The result was a period characterized by keenly fought match races — the best of three heats over 3–4 miles (4.8–6.4 km). In other words, very much in the style of the English Plates.

North–south rivalry

The first matches of renown were those in the 1820s between Tennessee's champion Haynie's Maria and a succession of challengers backed by the future President, General Andrew Jackson. Then, in 1823, on the recently constructed, artificial dirt track

of the Union Course, Long Island, in front of 60,000 people, New York's American Eclipse, representing the North, took on Virginia's Sir Henry, upholding the honour of the South at $10,000 a side. Sir Henry won the first heat, but after a change of jockey American Eclipse prevailed in the other two. Durng the next ten years there were 30 North–South matches of this kind, resulting in 17 victories for Dixie.

Probably the best horse to race in America before the Civil War was the Virginian Boston (named after a game of cards), who won 40 of his 45 races between 1836 and 1842. At the height of his fame his owners baited England with a $50,000 challenge to produce a faster horse, only to receive a polite refusal. After serving 42 mares in the spring of 1841 Boston came back into training and in May 1842 was matched with the brilliant northern mare Fashion, who broke the four-mile (6.4 km) world record in the first heat and went on to win the second easily. Boston returned to stud, where his offspring included Lexington (16 times champion sire) and Lecomte, who fought out three memorable duels in 1854 and 1855. With the scores even at one each, Lecomte's owner wagered $25,000 that Lexington could not lower his horse's record of seven minutes 26 seconds for the four miles. On 2 April 1855, carrying 103 lb (45.5 kg) Lexington beat the clock by more than six seconds at New Orleans' Metairie racetrack. Less than a fortnight later, Lexington defeated Lecomte in the Jockey Club Purse and was then retired.

Yet, of all the many match races, 'the most gallantly contested, as well as the most beautiful race ever seen in this country,' according to *The Spirit of the Times*, was that between the mares Fashion and Peytona on 13 May 1845. Spectators began the 12-mile (19 km) trek from New York to the Union Course well before dawn. Seventy thousand saw the South's unbeaten Peytona, receiving 5 lb (2.25 kg) for her two years, defeat Fashion two–nil.

Match racing

The match race has remained more of a fixture on the American Turf than anywhere else. Though not strictly speaking a match, the head-to-head between Parole, Ten Broeck, and Tom Ochiltree at Pimlico in 1877 prompted the solitary occasion on which Congress has been adjourned in order to witness a sporting event. Well into the twentieth century, matches were arranged to settle old scores or establish once and for all who was the real champion — for example, Man O' War v. Sir Barton (1920), War Admiral v. Seabiscuit (1938), Whirlaway v. Aslab (1942), Armed v. Assault (1946), Swaps v. Nashua (1955).

American racing began to change in the years following the Civil War. The pendulum swung away from the stamina-laden four-milers (6.4 km) towards the speed horse, which has ultimately come to epitomize the

North American breed. Of course, long ago the colonists were wont to run their 'quarter' horses down any convenient stretch of turnpike, so in that respect the quest for speed was nothing new, but with the founding of those races which were eventually designated the American Triple Crown, this trend was given unequivocal support. To win the Belmont Stakes (1867), Preakness Stakes (1873), or the Kentucky Derby (1875), no horse had to travel more than 1½ miles (2.4 km). Furthermore, as American tracks developed into uniform, one-mile (1.6 km) ovals, considerable early pace was necessary to secure position before negotiating the first of the tight bends. Much of this speed was bred into American mares by the importation of English and European stallions. Horses such as Leamington (imported in 1865, sire of the first American Derby winner, Iroquois), Star Shoot (1901, sire of the first American Triple Crown winner, Sir Barton) and Rock Sand (1906, maternal grandsire of Man O' War) continued the work of Diomed, for example, while the dollar has lured Bull Dog (sire of Citation, the first dollar 'millionaire'), Nasrullah (sire of Bold Ruler, Nashua, and Never Bend, and thus the grandsire of Secretariat and Mill Reef), Ribot, Sea Bird, and many others.

Anti-betting laws

As American racing organized itself around the turn of the century (the Jockey Club of New York, American racing's parent body, dates from 1894) on such cornerstones as August Belmont II, Leonard Jerome, William Whitney, and the Lorillard brothers, the power of the dollar and the pioneering spirit of a new nation were always liable to prove a trail-blazing and often unbeatable combination. There have been hiccups. The twin blows of anti-betting legislation, which destroyed racing in New York for two years before World War I, and the Jersey Act of 1913 (repealed 1949), which contentiously excluded so many American-bred animals from the General Stud Book just when so many were collecting important English events (and consequently assuming significance at stud) marked the nadir of American racing fortunes.

But, taken as a whole, America has given world racing a great deal in the twentieth century. Notable are the technical innovations (the photo-finish, starting stalls), international jamborees (the Washington DC International, the Breeders' Cup), and a revolutionary style of riding, with talented exponents of it too numerous to mention, as indeed are the number of outstanding horses. Two centuries after Bulle Rock's transatlantic voyage it is the Europeans who are now on the receiving end. In 1970 Northern Dancer became the first American stallion to be champion sire in England without ever having raced or stood here. Furthermore, in the 1987 season there were 2,146 North American-bred runners in England, Ireland, France, and Italy, of which 942 won.

Lexington was a record breaker on the racecourse and, at stud, he was America's champion sire 16 times.

Admiral Henry Rous was the most powerful figure in English racing in the second half of the nineteenth century. His advice to owners: 'Keep yourself in the best company and your horses in the worst'.

Expatriate influence

The English expatriates on the eastern seaboard of America were not alone in spreading the gospel of English racing. Others sailed south and east from England. By 1797 Cavalry Regiments were racing at Green Point Common, in the Cape Province of South Africa, and two years later the English stallion Rockingham left the Cape for Australia. On 15, 17, and 19 October 1810 the first official race-meeting on the Australian continent took place at Hyde Park, Sydney. Despite the problems created by the aridity which prevails over much of the country, Australia has more racecourses (606) than any other country in the world and is second only to the USA in the size of its thoroughbred population. By the 1820s the sport was well established on a regular basis. Sydney's Randwick opened for business in April 1833 and was surrounded by nine other tracks within a 100-mile (160 km) radius. Seven years later Flemington held its inaugural meeting in Melbourne, while 1842 saw the formation of the Australian Jockey Club.

Besides copying the English structure, Australian racing also benefited at first hand from the flair of Henry Rous who, as a Captain, was stationed in New South Wales during 1827–8 and imported Emigrant, a potent factor in establishing some of the most enduring Australian families. The first Classic was the Australian St Leger, run at Home Bush in 1841 and won by Eleanor, but although the Victoria Derby was introduced in 1855 and the AJC Derby in 1861, Australia has maintained a tradition, unique among the world's premier racing nations, of attaching more significance to the handicap as a measure of ability. Even today 40 per cent of her Group 1 contests are run under handicap conditions and Australia's richest, greatest, and most prestigious event, the Melbourne Cup, since 1861 religiously started at 2.40 p.m. on the first Tuesday of November at Flemington, is a discretionary handicap over 2½ miles (4 km). Accordingly, to be considered a champion in Australia, a horse must prove itself in handicap company and it is no coincidence that the two undisputed paragons of Australian Turf history, Carbine and Phar Lap (both New Zealand-bred), triumphed in the Melbourne Cup under monstrous weights. Eighty-five thousand packed Flemington in 1890 to see Carbine defy 10 stone 5 lb (66 kg) and set a record time in spite of splitting a heel in running. Fifty years later only slightly fewer (72,358) watched the 'Red Terror', Phar Lap, carrying 9 stone 12 lb (62.5 kg), justify odds-on favouritism for the only time in the Cup's history. Like so many Australasian champions, Phar Lap was a gelding, but no gelding anywhere in the world (with the possible exception of his American counterpart of the 1950s and 1960s, Kelso) has surpassed his reputation.

The Australasian scene

Australian-bred horses earned recognition for their speed, a trait accentuated by the arrival in 1950 of Star Kingdom, the fastest two-year-old performer ever to enter the continent. He became champion sire five times. His great grandson Kingston Town (another gelding) won 14 Group 1 races, including three consecutive W. S. Cox Plates (the country's principal all-aged middle-distance championship) to become the idol of racegoers in the 1980s, but he just lacked sufficient stamina to win a desperate finish for the Melbourne Cup of 1982. By contrast, horses bred in New Zealand, which is to Australia as Ireland is to England, and reared outside under natural conditions, are chock-full of stamina. In addition to Carbine and Phar Lap, New Zealand produced Tulloch who, in 1957, brought off for the first time in a century the Classic treble of AJC, VRC, and QTC Derbys, although he also failed (carrying 10 stone 1 lb/64 kg) to land the Melbourne Cup.

It may not be too fanciful or chauvinistic to claim that the tentacles of English influence had, by the 1980s, penetrated every corner of the racing world. Organized racing was recognized in Germany (1822, Doberan), Hungary (1827, Pest), Italy (1837, Florence and Naples), Russia (1825, Lebodan), India (1812, Calcutta), Japan (1861, Yokohama), Argentina (1821, Buenos Aries), and Hong Kong (1884). Even the French, those perennial foes whose love of the horse at Crécy and Agincourt had cost them dear, needed an Engishman (albeit French-born and resident), the noted eccentric Lord Henry Seymour, to found the French equivalent of the Jockey Club, in 1833. During that decade barely 60 horses contested the 14 days of racing at Paris (on the Champ de Mars, site of the Eiffel Tower), Chantilly, and Versailles.

Pretty soon, however, the importation of English Derby winners Cadland, Dangerous, and Mameluke reflected the conscious attempt at anglicization. The resilient turf of Chantilly became the favoured training grounds and the stables rang to the noise of *le head-lad*, *le stable-boy*, and *le jockey*. A magnificent new course was laid out on a previously barren plain in the Bois de Boulogne. Longchamp opened in 1857 and after consulting Admiral Rous, the authorities announced its principal race as the Grand Prix de Paris, with a prize of FF100,000 (half from the City of Paris and half from the major rail companies), far exceeding any of the French Classics. The domination of French racing by the English (Seymour had won the first three French Derbys) was completed when 12 of the first

two dozen Grands Prix fell to English-trained horses.

But the traffic was not all one way. The initial French winners of English Classics, Fille de l'Air (1864 Oaks) and the mighty 'Avenger of Waterloo', the 1865 Triple Crown winner Gladiateur, were both trained in England, but Camelia's 1,000 Guineas victory of 1876 was the genuine article even if her trainer was an Englishman.

The future of horse racing

As thoroughbred racing gallops towards its tricentennial, with some 2,000 tracks in operation and over 300,000 horses in training, the Sport of Kings shows signs, in places, of becoming the Sport of Sheikhs. The Arab world which bequeathed racing its three founding fathers — the Byerley Turk, the Darley Arabian, and the Godolphin Arabian — currently nurtures horse lovers more interested in acquiring prime horseflesh than selling it. In addition, not only are more and more of the choicest yearlings and elite races falling into Arab hands throughout Europe, but also the domestic sport in Kuwait, Bahrain, and especially Saudi Arabia, is on the increase. Already one English Classic winner, Bruni, has been exported to stand at stud in Kuwait. Has the wheel turned full circle? Therein lies one illustration of what Rous termed 'the glorious uncertainty of the Turf'.

Arab owners are making deep inroads into European racing, but they also enjoy their sport at home, as seen at this track in Saudi Arabia.

Breeding

Over the years, the breeding of racehorses has changed dramatically from being an expensive pastime for rich individuals to the multi-million, multi-national business it is today.

What promotes this kind of financial involvement, in a science with very little guarantee of success, is the hope of producing a champion.

Thanks to the Weatherby family, historical documentation of every thoroughbred, through the publication of the General Stud Book, has given pedigree students the opportunity to put their theories to the test in their quest to breed a true champion.

Students and theories abound but no one in the history of the thoroughbred has been as successful as Federico Tesio, responsible for such great horses as Ribot and Nearco. He has consistently produced good racehorses out of fairly cheap mares – in fact, Nearco has proved to be the most powerful influence in the thoroughbred during the sixties and seventies, principally through the prolific sire of sires Northern Dancer.

Few of the leading sires presently standing in either North America or Europe lack a preponderance of Nearco blood, but history encourages the small breeder to think that he will breed the next champion.

*Three Arab stallions from which every thoroughbred racehorse is descended. The Byerley Turk (**top**) and the Darley Arabian (**bottom**) are both from original paintings by John Wootton. The Godolphin Arabian (**centre**) is from the original painting by George Stubbs.*

The breeding of racehorses has exercised a powerful fascination through the centuries. Some breeders have proved more successful than others, but, the fact remains, breeding is not an exact science and it is the possibility of producing a champion from very humble origins that has driven breeders to devote their lives to striving for such an end.

Breeding thoroughbreds could not have taken place without records being kept and it is the historical evidence of past generations that has intrigued pedigree students and allowed the continuation of successful families. The publication of the first 'General Stud Book' by James Weatherby in 1791, and the appearance of subsequent volumes up to the present day, ensured that every pedigree was recorded back to the founding members of the thoroughbred breed.

Every thoroughbred can be traced back to one of three individuals, the Darley Arabian, the Byerley Turk, and the Godolphin Arabian. The first of these was bought for James Darley in 1704 and was the great-great-grandsire of Eclipse, born in 1764, unbeaten in 26 races, and founder of one of the greatest sire lines.

The Byerley Turk was acquired by Captain Robert Byerley when fighting against the Turks in 1687 and became his charger when he commanded the Sixth Dragoon Guards. He was the great-great-grandsire of Herod, who was foaled in 1758 and was the originator of another line which can still be traced

back to him. The Godolphin Arabian was initially owned by the King of France and bought by Edward Coke in 1729, then to become the property of Lord Godolphin. He was the grandsire of Matchem, foaled in 1748 and propagator of the third and final line, which is still in existence today.

The Herod line

In looking at these three great lines, let us start with the two that have the least influence on the present-day thoroughbred – the Herod and Matchem lines. By the end of last century the former was almost extinct in England, although it was thriving in France. Since then, however, it has made a dramatic reappearance in England through the very successful sire Ahonoora and the 1969 Derby winner Blakeney.

Herod sired two very good sons, Woodpecker and Highflyer. Highflyer, born in 1774, was owned by Richard Tattersall, founder of the famous auction house, and was unbeaten in 12 races. He sired Sir Peter Teazle, who won the Derby for the 12th Earl (the founder of the great race) and in time produced two lines through Walton and St Pauls. The Walton line was responsible for two Derby winners in Cremorne and Macaroni, while the St Pauls line produced the Derby winners Wild Dayrell and Kisber. However, the foremost member of the family was the filly Formosa, sired by Buccaneer. Formosa won the 1,000 Guineas, the Oaks, and the St Leger. Unfortunately, the Highflyer line became extinct in this country early this century.

The Woodpecker line, principally through the post-war Boussac empire remains intact. Woodpecker, through Buzzard, was the grandsire of the very useful brothers Castiel, Selim, and Rubens. The second of these was the sire of Sultan, who bred three Classic winners, notably Bay Middleton, who won the 2,000 Guineas and the Derby. Bay Middleton, who stood at stud for Lord George Bentinck, sired the brilliant The Flying Dutchman. The Flying Dutchman won 15 of his 16 races, including the 1849 Derby, the St Leger, and the Ascot Gold Cup, being the first horse to win all three races. His only defeat came at the hands of Voltigeur in the Doncaster Cup in 1850, but in a match the following year he beat him by a short head when 11 lb (5 kg) better off.

The Flying Dutchman took up stud duties in France and can be traced back through the Boussac families. Bruleur was a sixth-generation descendant of The Flying Dutchman, and while not a brilliant race horse, he had a big impact on the breed in France. He was beaten in the French Derby but proved a very useful stayer, winning the French St Leger and the Grand Prix de Paris. His greatest contribution to racing, however, was siring Ksar, twice winner of the Prix de l'Arc de Triomphe, and proving the

The Godolphin Arabian, one of three sires to whom all thoroughbreds can be traced.

most powerful force in post-World War II French middle-distance breeding. Ksar sired Tourbillon, who gave Marcel Boussac his second French Derby in 1931 and went on to prove very influential in his racing empire.

Although Boussac was having tremendous success in France, his first Classic winner in England came with Djebel, a son of Tourbillon, in the 1940 2,000 Guineas. Djebel then went on to win the Prix de l'Arc de Triomphe and in turn sired many notable winners, including Arbar, who won the Ascot Gold Cup, and My Babu, winner of the 2,000 Guineas, who sired Our Babu, another winner of the same race. But it was Djebel's son Clarion III who was responsible for the revival of the line in England, for he was the grandsire of Lorenzaccio, the winner of the Champion Stakes, who sired Ahonoora.

Out of Helen Nichols, a winner but dam of only one other winner, Ahonoora started life as a handicapper by winning the Stewards' Cup at Goodwood for trainer Frankie Durr, but went on to win the William Hill Sprint Championship at York. Since going to stud in 1980, Ahonoora has proved very successful – Park Appeal, the winner of the Cheveley Park Stakes and Don't Forget Me, the winner of the English and Irish 2,000 Guineas, are among the total of 58 winners sired to the end of the 1987 season.

Perhaps the most exciting Herod line traces back to Castiel, the full brother of Selim. Castiel sired Thormanby, who won 14 races, including the Derby and the Ascot Gold Cup, and is a direct descendent of Roi Herode, who was imported to England from France in 1909 in an attempt to revive the Herod line.

Although the mission failed, it looked as if it had worked when Roi Herode sired the brilliant The Tetrarch. Bought by Major Dermot McCalmont as a yearling for 1,300 guineas, The Tetrarch was a brilliant two-year-old, unbeaten in seven races, and proved himself at stud by siring the winners of six Classics from Four Course, winner of the 1,000 Guineas, to Salmon Trout. The latter was one of three winners of the St Leger and sired King Salmon, who won the Eclipse and the Coronation Cup but was subsequently exported to Brazil. But while The Tetrarch proved himself at stud, none of his progeny excelled and the line seems to have died out in England.

The Matchem line

The second great line, that of Matchem, is at present only just surviving. Matchem sired Conductor, whose fifth-generation descendant Melbourne sired the most potent member of the line, West Australian. Melbourne sired four Classic winners – Sir Tatton Sykes, winner of both the 2,000 Guineas and the St Leger, Camezon, winner of the 1,000 Guineas, Blink Bonny, who won the Derby and the Oaks, and West Australian, born in 1850, winner of the 2,000 Guineas, the

Derby, and the St Leger. The latter also earned the distinction of being the first winner of the Triple Crown.

The influence of West Australian spread to both sides of the Atlantic with two different lines. In the USA the family was responsible for producing the greatest pre-war race-horse, Man O'War. 'Big Red', as he was known throughout the country, won 20 of 21 races, including the Preakness and the Belmont Stakes, his only defeat coming in the Sanford Memorial Stakes as a two-year-old. Man O'War's most successful son in the USA was War Admiral, who won the American Triple Crown – the Preakness Stakes, the Kentucky Derby, and the Belmont Stakes. Unfortunately, 'Big Red's' stud career was severely hampered by Samuel Riddle, his owner, who restricted the champion to only 25 mares a year. Even so, while Riddle's policy did not offer the champion a chance to fully influence himself on the breed, he was still very visible in the pedigrees of such winners as Sir Ivor, Buckpasser, and Arts and Letters.

Man O'War's influence on the Matchem line in England came from his son, War Relic, who sired the very fast Relic, the winner of five of his seven races. Relic was imported to France by François Dupré and from his daughter Reliance produced the Classic winners Match III, Relko, and

The Byerley Turk, great-great-grandsire of Herod, was ridden by his owner, Captain Robert Byerley, in a cavalry charge at the Battle of the Boyne, in 1690.

Proud mother Spiletta with her foal, Eclipse. The chestnut colt became a great racehorse and the sire of three Epsom Derby winners.

Reliance II. However, after six seasons at stud in France, Relic was taken to England, where he sired Pieces of Eight, winner of the Eclipse and the Champion Stakes, as well as Buisson Ardent, who won the Middle Park and the French 2,000 Guineas. Buisson Ardent was responsible for Roan Rocket, the winner of five races, including the St James's Palace Stakes and the Sussex Stakes. Later, Roan Rocket proved very successful at siring precocious two-year-olds.

Another son of War Relic who influenced the line in England was Intent, whose grandson In Reality, the winner of 14 races, including the Pimlico-Laurel Stakes, sired Known Fact, who was born in 1977. Trained by Jeremy Tree, Known Fact won the Middle Park and gave the now all-powerful Khalid Abdullah his first Classic winner in the 1980 2,000 Guineas.

While the progeny of West Australian was thriving in America, their counterparts in England were also producing good racing stock. His son Salem bred Barcaldine, winner of the Derby and the St Leger, while his great-grandson Hurry On, trained by Fred Darling and unbeaten in six races, including the St Leger, was the modern progenitor of the Matchem line.

Hurry On's son Precipitation, winner of the Ascot Gold Cup, produced three Classic winners – Chamoissaire, winner of the St Leger, Airborne, winner of the first post-war Derby and the St Leger, and Premonition, winner of the St Leger. Chamoissaire continued the line by siring the St Leger winner Cambrener and the double-Classic winner Santa Claus, whose stud career only lasted

five seasons before he died of a blood clot. Unfortunately, he failed in that time to produce a worthy successor and the line has since died.

The most successful son of Precipitation was Sheshoon. He was an out-and-out stayer who won the Ascot Gold Cup, but after ten years at stud he suddenly became very popular and headed the European list of sires in 1970, largely because of the efforts of his son Sassafras, who beat the then unbeaten Nijinsky in the Prix de l'Arc de Triomphe. Sheshoon's first offspring to win a Classic was Mon Fils, who won the 1973 2,000 Guineas at 50–1. Neither Sassafras nor Mon Fils has been particularly successful at stud and it looks as if the Sheshoon line is also in danger of extinction.

The Eclipse line

The Eclipse line has had the greatest impact on the modern thoroughbred, for nearly every successful family is descended from one of the many lines that have developed in the past 150 years. Eclipse was one of the greatest horses ever to have raced. Sir Theodore Cook wrote of Eclipse:

'His excellence was not only owing to the races he won, but even more clearly to the astonishing ease with which he won them, and to the fact that in addition to his undoubted speed and stride, he possessed sound wind, an ability to carry heavy weight, and an endurance over long distances which could never be thoroughly tested, for its limit was never reached.'

But it was through just two of Eclipse's sons, Pot8os and King Fergus, that the Eclipse line grew into the most powerful sire line that exists. Pot8os was named after a rather amusing spelling error by his lad, who was told to write 'Potato' on his door but wrote 'Potoooooooo' instead. Pot8os was the grandsire of Whalebone, who sired Camel and Sir Hercules. Another son of Whalebone was Defence, who was the great-grandsire of Gladiateur, a brilliant racehorse who won the 1865 Triple Crown and the Ascot Gold Cup the following year. Tragically, Defence died early in his stud career and what almost certainly would have been another good line did not survive.

Camel sired the very good stayer Touchstone, who won the St Leger, the Ascot Gold Cup, and the Doncaster Cup twice. Touchstone bred five Classic winners, including Orlando, winner of the Derby, but was exported to the USA, where the line continues to the present day. However, the line has recently reappeared in England via Teenoso, winner of the 1983 Derby and the King George VI and Queen Elizabeth Stakes the following year. Teenoso was by Youth, winner of the French Derby, who was by the very successful American sire Ack Ack.

It was Newminster, winner of the St Leger, who continued the line in England, siring Hermit and Lord Clifden. Hermit, who cost 1,000 guineas as a yearling, won the Derby at 100–1 and was a phenomenal success at stud, being leading sire for seven consecutive seasons. Nevertheless, the line died out in England, although it continued in France. Lord Clifden, winner of the St Leger, sired Hampton, the winner of 20 races and sire of Ladas, winner of the 1894 2,000 Guineas and the Derby at the very short price of 9–2-on. It was Ladas's son Bay Ronald, winner of the Hardwicke, who was the great grandsire of one of the most influential sires in the history of British racing, Hyperion, who is discussed later.

Bay Ronald sired Dark Ronald, the Princess of Wales's Stakes winner and sire of Son-In-Law. Owned by Sir Abe Bailey, Son-In-Law won two Jockey Club Cups and was the sire of Bosworth, who won the St Leger and the Eclipse. It was his great-grandson Herbager (French Derby winner) who was responsible for this line's continuation in England through his three sons, Sea-Hawk II, Appiani II, and Grey Dawn II.

The sons of Herbager

All three sons raced in France, but in an attempt to revive the Son-In-Law line in Britain, Sea-Hawk II and Appiani II were exported to Ireland. While standing in Ireland, Sea-Hawk II sired Bruni, winner of the St Leger, and Appiani II sired Star Appeal, winner of the Prix de l'Arc de Triomphe and the Eclipse Stakes. Grey Dawn II, champion two-year-old in France in 1964, sired Dunbeath, winner of the Futurity Stakes at Doncaster and now at stud in Newmarket.

Whalebone's other son Sir Hercules was responsible for the development of a far larger collection of Eclipse lines. Sir Hercules sired Irish Birdcatcher, who was the great-grandsire of Isonomy, the winner of two Ascot Gold Cups, Epsom, Goodwood, and Doncaster Cups as well as the Cambridge-shire Stakes. Isonomy, while having a rather 'stout' racing career lacking an element of brilliance, proved very successful at stud – his son Gallinule sired the brilliant Pretty Polly, the winner of 22 of her 24 races, including the 1,000 Guineas, the Oaks, and the St Leger.

Another of Whalebone's sons was the Triple Crown winner of 1891, Common, trained by the great John Porter, who produced the colt for his racecourse debut in the 2,000 Guineas. But it was Isinglass who was the mainstay of the family, following a racing career where he was beaten in only one of his 12 races and won the Triple Crown for his owner Colonel Harry McCalmont.

Isinglass's son John O'Gaunt, although beaten in both the 2,000 Guineas and the Derby, sired the great Swynford, winner of the St Leger, the Eclipse, and the Coronation Cup, to list but a few of his victories. Swynford proved a prolific sire of both good colts and fillies. Keysoe (St Leger), Ferry

(1,000 Guineas), and Tranquil (1,000 Guineas and St Leger) were all Classic-winning fillies, while Swynford's colts included Sansovino (Derby) and Blandford.

Blandford had a tremendous influence on the thoroughbred during the interwar years. He sired a host of good winners, including Bahram, winner of the Triple Crown in 1935, Blenheim, winner of the Derby, and Windsor Lad and Trigo, winners, respectively, of the Derby and the St Leger. The two St Leger winners did not have good stud careers, the only notable individual by Windsor Lad being Windsor Slipper, the winner of the Irish 2,000 Guineas, the Derby, and the St Leger. Blenheim, on the other hand, sired Mahmoud, winner of the Derby in record time for the Aga Khan, and Donatello II, winner of the Italian Derby and sire of both Alycidon and Crepello.

Alycidon won the Ascot Gold Cup and his full brother Acropolis, winner of the Great Voltigeur Stakes, became the grand-sire of Sagaro, one of the greatest stayers seen this century and the only horse to win three Gold Cups. Crepello raced only five times but won the 2,000 Guineas and the Derby. He had a significant influence on the Blandford line, being champion sire once in 1969, having earlier produced Busted, who numbered among his victories the King George VI and Queen Elizabeth Stakes and the Eclipse. By the end of the 1987 season Busted had sired the winners of over 850 races, for prize money of more than £4.5 million. However, his two most successful sons are Bustino and Mtoto.

Pretty Polly, a brilliant daughter of Gallinule, included three Classics in her 22 triumphs.

Bustino, owned by a great character in British racing, Lady Beaverbrook, and trained by Major Dick Hern, won the St Leger and Coronation Cup. But the race he will always be remembered for is his epic dual with the Derby winner Grundy in the 1975 King George VI and Queen Elizabeth Stakes when he went down by a short head. Bustino has already made his mark at stud, siring over ten Group winners – most notably Paean, winner of the Ascot Gold Cup. Mtoto, an outstanding-looking individual trained by the young Newmarket trainer Alex Stewart is, at the time of writing, still racing and has every chance of proving himself an exceptional older horse.

Bahram, who ran in the colours of the Aga Khan and was trained by Frank Butters, sired both Persian Gulf and Big Game. Big Game, winner of the 2,000 Guineas, was leading sire in 1948 but unfortunately proved a far better sire of fillies than colts. Ambiguity, winner of the Oaks, and Queenpot, winner of the 1,000 Guineas, are to his credit, but there is no notable son. Persian Gulf's descendants, by contrast, are still in evidence, although Parthia, the only Derby winner he sired, was exported to Japan in 1968.

We must go right back to Irish Birdcatcher to discover another very large branch of the Eclipse family. In 1842 The Baron, the son of Irish Birdcatcher, was born and he was responsible for another great racehorse, Stockwell, the winner of 11 races, including the 2,000 Guineas and the St Leger. Stockwell then went on to establish himself as one of the great sires, leading the table on no fewer than six occasions and siring the winners of seventeen Classics, including Blair Athol, winner of the Derby on his racecourse debut, and Lord Lyon, winner of the Triple Crown.

But it was Stockwell's son Doncaster, winner of the 1872 Derby, who continued the line. He sired the 1880 Derby winner Bend Or, whose great-great-grandson Phalaris is responsible for the most powerful and influential sire lines in the history of the thoroughbred.

The progeny of Ormonde

Bend Or, by siring the 1886 Triple Crown winner Ormonde, could have been responsible for another very efficient side of the family. Ormonde, trained by John Porter, was something of a freak. Brilliant as he was as a racehorse, he was desperately unsound in his wind and then proved a disaster at stud, producing only sixteen foals in eleven years and giving little chance to further the line. However, one of his sons was the beautifully bred Orme, out of Angelica, a full sister to St Simon. Orme's son Flying Fox, once again trained by John Porter and winner of the 1899 Triple Crown, had a major influence in America through his great-grandsons Sir Gallahad III and Bull Dog. These were brothers by Teddy, winner of the 'Epreuve de Selection' (substituted for the French Derby). Sir Gallahad III sired the American Triple Crown winner Gallant Fox, while Bull Dog's grandson Citation won the American Triple Crown.

In Europe a fourth-generation descendent of Teddy, Tantième, was to become one of the most influential sires of the 1950s and 1960s. Tantième, the winner of two Prix de l'Arc de Triomphe, sired the full brothers Match III and Reliance II, both exceptional horses. Match III won the French St Leger, the King George VI and Queen Elizabeth Stakes, and the Washington DC International but, tragically, died early in his stud career. Reliance II won the French Derby and the French St Leger. Tantième was the grandsire of Relko, a three-quarters brother to the two just mentioned. Relko was the winner of the French 2,000 Guineas, the Derby, the French St Leger, and the Coronation Cup and sire of Relkino, winner of the 1977 Benson and Hedges Gold Cup.

Phalaris was by the five-times leading sire Polymelus (Prince of Wales Stakes, Champion Stakes) who was by Cyllene, sire of four Derby winners. Phalaris won 16 races during World War I and sired the winners of over 400 races, including the full brothers Sickle and Pharamond II, both exported to America. The latter was the sire of Silly Season, winner of the Champion Stakes, and in America of Buckpasser, a tough horse

Ascot has probably never staged a greater race than the King George VI and Queen Elizabeth Stakes duel between Grundy (nearest camera) and Busted's son, Bustino.

who won 25 of his 31 races and became a highly sought-after sire.

Sickle was the great-grandsire of Native Dancer, winner of 22 of his 23 races, failing only to complete the American Triple Crown when he was defeated in the Kentucky Derby. He then followed his highly successful racing career by stamping himself a sire of international repute. He sired Dan Cupid, whose son Sea Bird II took the racing world by storm in the mid-1960s and is still considered by some to have been the greatest horse to have raced in Europe, winning seven of his eight races, including the Derby and the Prix de l'Arc de Triomphe. His stud career did not match his performance on the racecourse, his best son being the American stallion Little Current. However, his daughter Allez France was unquestionably a brilliant filly, winning the French 1,000 Guineas, French Oaks, Prix de l'Arc de Triomphe, Prix Vermeille, and the Prix Ganay twice.

Mixed ability

Native Dancer was also the sire of Atan, who was the winner of a very humble five-furlong (1 km) race worth just $2,600. But Atan sired Sharpen Up, who was responsible for the full brothers Kris and Diesis, whose respective victories included the Sussex Stakes and the Dewhurst and who are both highly successful at stud; Sharpo, champion sprinter in Europe in both 1981 and 1982; and the brilliant filly Pebbles, winner of the 1,000 Guineas, the Champion Stakes, the Eclipse Stakes, and the Breeders' Cup Turf at Aqueduct, New York.

Another very influential son of Native Dancer was the Champion American two-year-old Raise a Native, whose son Exclusive Native was sire of the 1978 American Triple Crown winner Affirmed. Raise a Native is also the sire of Mr. Prospector, champion older sprinter in America in 1974 and sire of winners of nearly 1,000 races and $22.7 million, including Conquistador Cielo, winner of the Belmont Stakes, Provida, winner of the Prix de la Forêt, and Hello Gorgeous, winner of the Futurity Stakes at Doncaster.

Another very successful branch of the Phalaris family resulted from his son Fairway, owned by Lord Derby and trained by Frank Butters, and winner of 12 races, including the St Leger. He was leading sire four times in the late 1930s and mid 1940s and one of his sons, Fair Trial, born in 1932 and leading sire in 1950, was sire of Palestine, winner of the 2,000 Guineas for the Aga Khan and sire of Pall Mall, winner of the 2,000 Guineas for Queen Elizabeth II.

Fair Trial also sired Blue Peter, a dual Classic winner with the 2,000 Guineas and the Derby to his name, as well as the Eclipse in 1939, but it was Petition who had the biggest influence on this side of the family. He was leading sire in 1959 and in that year his daughter Petite Etoile won the 1,000 Guineas and followed that with the

Coronation Cup the next year. Petition's son Petingo, winner of the St James's Palace Stakes was responsible for English Prince (Irish Derby), Fair Salinia (Oaks, Irish Oaks), and the ill-fated Troy, winner of the 1979 Derby, but tragically died of a twisted gut after just three years at stud.

Petition was grandsire of Queen's Hussar, winner of the Sussex Stakes and sire of the brilliant Brigadier Gerard, owned and bred by John Hislop and trained by Major Dick Hern to win 17 of his 18 races, including the 2,000 Guineas.

Fairway was the grandsire of the Prix de Moulin winner Great Nephew, sire of two champion racehorses, Grundy and Shergar. Grundy won the 1975 Derby and beat Bustino in an epic dual in the King George VI and Queen Elizabeth Stakes the same year, but after a not very worthwhile stud career in England was exported to Japan. Shergar, owned by the Aga Khan, had one of the easiest victories in the Derby in the history of the race and followed it by winning the Irish equivalent. His career at stud was eagerly awaited, but tragically lasted only one season before he was kidnapped from the Ballymany Stud. His disappearance remains a mystery.

But it was Phalaris's son Pharos, born in 1920 and winner of the Champion Stakes, who had a staggering influence on the post-war thoroughbred, being the sire of Nearco.

Having gone thus far through the family of Eclipse, we must now turn back to his son

Petite Etoile, brilliant daughter of Petition, won 14 races. They included the 1,000 Guineas and Oaks, but she was a bitter disappointment at stud.

King Fergus, founder of the St Simon line. Winner of the St Leger and nineteen other races, he was the great-great-grandsire of Voltaire, winner of the Doncaster Cup and sire in 1847 of Voltigeur, who won the Derby and the St Leger for Lord Zetland. Voltigeur's son Vedette was the grandsire of one of racing's most famous horses, St Simon.

St Simon was never beaten and his victories included the Epsom Derby, Goodwood Cups, and the Ascot Gold Cup. He was leading sire nine times, seven of which were in consecutive years between 1890 and 1896. He sired brilliant colts and fillies, among them the winners of all five Classics in 1900. It was his two sons Persimmon and Rabelais who carried the St Simon line through to the present day. Persimmon, owned by the Prince of Wales and trained by Richard Marsh, won nine races, including the Derby, the St Leger, and the Ascot Gold Cup, and at stud was leading sire four times. He was sire of Sceptre, winner of four Classics in 1902 – the 1,000 Guineas, the 2,000 Guineas, the Oaks, and the St Leger.

Persimmon's great-grandson Prince Rose was the founder of three further lines still to be found today. His son Prince Chevalier, winner of the French Derby, was the grandsire of Charlottown, who was the winner of the Derby in 1966.

Prince Bio's outstanding son was Sicambre, winner of the French Derby and grandsire of the St Leger winner Athens Wood. Sicambre was also, via Diatome, the grandsire of the Irish Derby winner Steel Pulse and grandsire, through another of his sons Phaeton, of Vitiges, winner of the Champion Stakes.

Impact in the USA

However, it was Princequillo who proved very influential in the USA, principally through his very good son Round Table, who was voted 'champion grass horse' for three consecutive years before becoming a very good sire in the USA, leading the American sires table in 1972. Round Table's best runner in Britain was Artaius, winner of the Eclipse and Sussex Stakes.

Rabelais, the Goodwood Cup winner, was the grandsire of Cavaliere d'Arpino, winner of the Gran Premio di Milano and sire of Bellini, winner of the Italian Derby. Bellini's son Tenerani, also winner of the Italian Derby and the Goodwood Cup, was sire of one of racing's greats – Ribot.

He was bred by Signor Federico Tesio, who was known as 'the Wizard of Dormello' on account of his amazing track record at the St Andrea Stud. Exceptional horses Tesio might have bred, but none to match Ribot, who was unbeaten in 16 races and whose victories included the King George VI and Queen Elizabeth Stakes and the Prix de l'Arc de Triomphe twice.

Ribot's stud career took place in three different countries – one season in England,

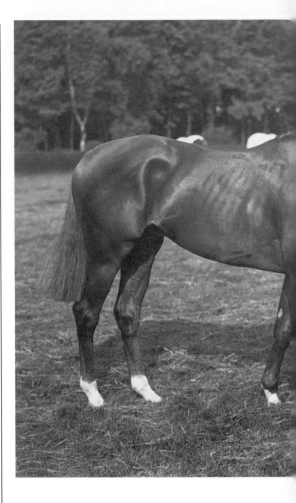

a spell in Italy, and then to Kentucky, where he stayed until his death in 1973. He was leading sire three times in Britain during the 1960s, being responsible for the full brothers Ribocco and Ribero, winners of the Irish Derby and St Leger, Boucher, winner of the St Leger, and Ragusa, his most successful son in Britain. Ragusa won the Irish Derby, the St Leger, and the King George VI and Queen Elizabeth Stakes and was sire of Morston, owned and trained by Arthur Budgett at Whatcombe, near Lambourn, and winner of the 1973 Derby.

Ribot's influence was felt mainly in America, where he sired Arts and Letters, the winner of 23 races, and Tom Rolfe, sire of both Hoist The Flag and Run The Gantlet. Hoist The Flag was sire of Alleged, twice winner of the Prix de l'Arc de Triomphe and a prolific sire of winners, including Leading Council, winner of the Irish St Leger, and Law Society and Sir Harry Lewis, both winners of the Irish Derby.

Run The Gantlet, winner of the Washington DC International, died in 1986, having sired the winners of 575 races and over $5 million. In Britain these include Commanche Run (St Leger) and Ardross, twice winner of the Ascot Gold Cup.

The Hyperion line

Lord Derby's Hyperion, by Gainsborough out of Selene by Chaucer was an extremely useful racehorse who went on to have a very marked effect on the development of the

and the Prix de l'Arc de Triomphe and sire of Altesse Royale, a brilliant filly who won the 1,000 Guineas, the Oaks, and the Irish Oaks. The Queen's champion was also responsible for Aurelius, the 1961 St Leger winner, and St Paddy, a dual Classic winner, including the Derby and the St Leger, and sire of Connaught, the Eclipse Stakes winner; Purnell, winner of the Irish St Leger and now standing at stud in Brazil; and, most recently, Jupiter Island, out of the brilliant mare Mrs Moss, winner of the Hardwicke Stakes.

Vaguely Noble is a good example of a champion with a pedigree suggesting a degree of mediocrity. He was by the unsuccessful sire Vienna (by Aureole) but quickly established himself as a champion by winning the Observer Gold Cup. The death of his breeder, Major Lionel Holliday, forced the sale of Vaguely Noble at the December Sales in 1967 and caused a sensation when knocked down to Robert Franklyn for 136,000 guineas, then a record for any horse sold at auction.

The following year Vaguely Noble showed that he was a bargain by winning the equivalent of his purchase price and ending the season by winning the Prix de l'Arc de Triomphe. He was syndicated to stud in America but led the sires' table in 1973 and 1974 in Britain, being responsible for the multi-winner Exceller, the Derby winner Empery, and the brilliant filly Dahlia, winner of 13 races, including the Irish Oaks, the King George VI and Queen Elizabeth Stakes twice and the Washington DC International. All of these horses were owned by the Texan Nelson Bunker Hunt.

Although Hyperion was a middle-distance performer, he injected plenty of speed into the family and a number of branches of the family are predominantly sprinters. He sired the champion sprinter Abernant, grandsire of Absalom, winner of the Vernons Sprint Cup at Haydock Park and was grandsire of Tudor Minstrel, winner of the 1947 2,000 Guineas.

Tudor Minstrel's three sons, Will Somers, Tudor Melody, and Sing Sing have all established further lines. Will Somers, who died in 1980, sired Balidar, sire of Bolkonski, winner of the 2,000 Guineas. Tudor Melody, a brilliant two-year-old, was sire of the Queen Elizabeth II Stakes winner Welsh Pageant, while Sing Sing was responsible for a number of very fast horses, notably Jukebox, Song, and Mummy's Pet, all popular sires with breeders of precocious horses.

The Nearco line

Such has been the influence of Nearco on the post-war thoroughbred that it is difficult to know where to start. He was, surprisingly, leading sire only twice, although he proved to be a prolific sire of sires, his most influential sons being Nearctic, Nasrullah, Royal Charger, Dante, and Mossborough. Mossborough was the sire of Ballymoss, trained by the great Vincent O'Brien, who over the

thoroughbred, principally in Britain but also throughout the world. He won the Derby and the St Leger in 1933 and quickly went on to prove himself at stud, leading the sires' table on six occasions and being sire of numerous Classic winners, including Owen Tudor (the Derby), Sun Chariot (1,000 Guineas, Oaks, and St Leger), Sun Stream (1,000 Guineas, Oaks), and Godiva (1,000 Guineas, Oaks).

Hyperion's influence has tended to be concentrated in Great Britain, but it was the exportation of his son Aristophanes to Argentina that ensured the international growth of the family. Aristophanes was to sire the great Forli, champion in Argentina before being sent to the USA, where he completed his racing career and then stood at stud in Kentucky.

Forli sired eleven crops and over 30 Stakes winners, including Forego, twice 'horse of the year' in the USA, and Thatch, champion three-year-old in England in 1973 and sire of Thatching, champion older sprinter in Europe in 1979, and Tommy Way, winner of the Italian Derby.

Hyperion was sire of Aureole, owned by Queen Elizabeth II, and undoubtedly his best son, winning the King George VI and Queen Elizabeth Stakes and the Coronation Cup in 1954. But Aureole will be remembered by many for finishing second in the Derby in Coronation Year, 1953. Aureole was champion sire in 1960 and 1961 and was sire of Saint Crispin III, winner of the Eclipse

next 25 years did extremely well with the family. Ballymoss was an exceptional racehorse who won the Irish Derby and the St Leger to name but two of his races and was the sire of H. J. Joel's Royal Palace, the winner of the 2,000 Guineas, the Derby, the Coronation Cup, the Eclipse Stakes, and the King George VI and Queen Elizabeth Stakes. However, the line has more or less disappeared as Royal Palace failed to sire a good son, although he has proved a highly successful sire of brood-mares and fillies, notably Dunferline, who won the Oaks and the St Leger in the year of the Silver Jubilee of her owner, Her Majesty the Queen.

Nearco's son Dante won the substitute Derby at Newmarket in 1945 and was the sire of Darius, winner of the 2,000 Guineas. Darius's son Derring-Do was not only a top-class miler but a very good sire, responsible for a number of individuals who have stamped themselves as sires of note. Three of his sons won Classics – High Top, winner of the 2,000 Guineas and sire of Top Ville (French Derby), Colorspin (Irish Oaks), and Circus Plume (the Oaks); Roland Gardens, winner of the 2,000 Guineas; and Peleid, winner of the St Leger. Derring-Do was also the sire of Dominion, who is proving to be a very good sire, generally of two-year-olds.

Royal Charger, born in 1942, was exported in 1953 to America, where this branch of the family thrived. He was the grandsire of Hail

to Reason, winner of the Preakness Stakes and sire of Roberto, who won the 1972 Derby, beating Rheingold a by short head before going on to win the Benson and Hedges Gold Cup and the Coronation Cup. At stud Roberto has sired the winners of over 600 races, including Al Tulaq (Grand Prix de Paris), Touching Wood (St Leger and Irish St Leger), and Celestial Storm (Princess of Wales Stakes). Royal Charger was also the grandsire of Sir Gaylord, sire of both Sir Ivor and Habitat.

Sir Ivor, trained and ridden by the then invincible team of Vincent O'Brien and Lester Piggott, won the 2,000 Guineas, the Derby, and the Champion Stakes in England and the Washington DC International in America. At stud he sired the brilliant Ivanjica.

Habitat, again ridden by Lester Piggott, but trained at Blewbury by Fulke Johnson Houghton, was a brilliant miler and a very successful sire at stud, being champion first-crop sire of 1973 and champion two-year-old sire on four occasions. However, he was a far better sire of fillies than of colts and was responsible for Rose Bowl (Champion Stakes) and Flying Waters (1,000 Guineas, Champion Stakes). His most significant son was Double Form, winner of the King's Stand and the Prix de l'Abbaye de Longchamp and sire of the fine sprinter Double Schwartz.

A great sire of sires

Nearctic was responsible for Northern Dancer, probably the most famous sire of sires in the history of the thoroughbred. Northern Dancer was champion three-year-old in both Canada and the USA in 1964 and was the sire of the winners of more than 1,400 races and more than a staggering $25.5 million. He was the sire of Nijinsky (the winner of the Triple Crown in 1970), The Minstrel (Derby, King George VI and Queen Elizabeth Stakes), El Gran Señor (Irish Derby), Northern Trick (Prix Vermeille), Sadler's Wells (Irish 2,000 Guineas, Eclipse Stakes), Secreto (Derby), Lomond (2,000 Guineas), Shareef Dancer (Irish Derby), Northern Baby (Champion Stakes), Storm Bird (Dewhurst Stakes), and Lyphard (Prix de la Forêt) to name but a few of his progeny. They in turn have been tremendous sires – Nijinsky, for example, has sired the winners of nearly 1,000 races worth a total of $25 million. Lyphard has sired the winners of more than 700 races and more than $18 million, including the brilliant Dancing Brave, champion three-year-old in Europe in 1986.

Racing does not generally lend itself to certainties but one is that the Northern Dancer line will remain the most influential sire line for a very long time.

Nasrullah, following a spell at stud in Ireland, where he was leading sire in 1951, was exported to America and led the sires' table on five occasions, proving to be a major influence on the American thoroughbred in the 1960s. He raced in England and won the

Winner of England's Triple Crown, Nijinsky went to stud in Kentucky. Vincent O'Brien, who trained him, has taken many of Nijinsky's sons back to Ireland.

Champion Stakes and before being exported sired four Classic winners, including Never Say Die, winner of the Derby and the St Leger, and sire of the 1962 Derby winner Larkspur. Grey Sovereign, another of Nasrullah's sons, was the grandsire of Wolver Hollow, winner of the Eclipse and sire of Wollow, winner of the 2,000 Guineas, the Sussex Stakes, and the Benson and Hedges Gold Cup.

American influence

But it was in the USA that Nasrullah had his most significant influence. His son Bold Ruler was leading sire for seven successive years and was responsible for Bold Lad (Ire), Secretariat, and Boldnesian. Bold Lad (Ire), a very good two-year-old in Britain, became a top sire of fast horses, notably Never So Bold (champion older sprinter in Europe in 1985), Daring Display (Prix Morny), Waterloo (1,000 Guineas), and Ballad Rock, sire of Chief Singer, winner of the Sussex Stakes. Boldnesian's claim to fame was that by producing Bold Reasoning he became the grandsire of Seattle Slew, winner of the American Triple Crown.

But when we think of Triple Crown winners it is Secretariat, Bold Ruler's greatest son, who springs to mind. He was a brilliant racehorse, a hero known throughout America as 'Big Red', winning a total of 16 races.

Blushing Groom quickly established himself at stud, following a racing career in France in which he won seven races, including the French 2,000 Guineas. A son of Red God, a very fast two-year-old, Blushing Groom failed to stay beyond a mile (1.6 km), a point not lost on those who had syndicated him for $6 million before the Epsom Derby. But he soon proved himself at stud and has sired the winners of more than 1,000 races, including Rainbow Quest, a very good, tough racehorse who won the Coronation Cup and the Prix de l'Arc de Triomphe on the disqualification of Sagace; Al Bahathri (Irish 1,000 Guineas); and Green Dancer, winner of the Prix Lupin.

The strongest branch of the Nasrullah family is without doubt that of Never Bend, champion two-year-old in America. With the siring of Mill Reef and Riverman the line has established itself as one of the most powerful in the world. Mill Reef, owned by one of racing's most sporting owners, Paul Mellon, and trained by Ian Balding, was brilliant and as a three-year-old won the Derby, the Eclipse, and the King George VI and Queen Elizabeth Stakes. Tragically, he broke his leg as a four-year-old when preparing for a second attempt at the Prix de l'Arc de Triomphe. At stud Mill Reef was champion sire in 1978 and has sired such notable horses as Shirley Heights (already very successful at stud, his son Slip Anchor winning the Derby in 1986), Reference Point, who won the Derby, and Glint of Gold, who won the Grand Prix de Paris. Mill Reef died in 1986

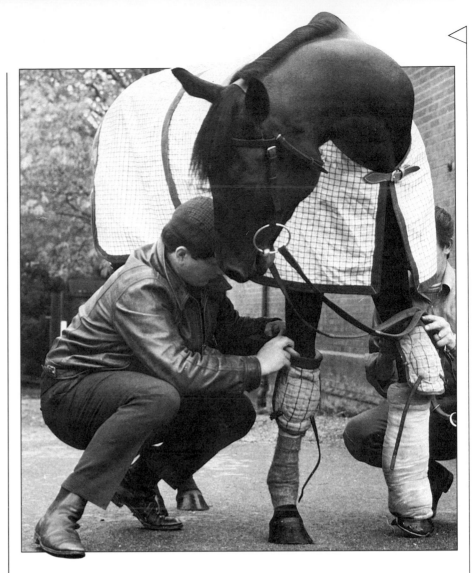

but all the evidence suggests that the line will thrive.

Riverman, winner of the French 2,000 Guineas, stands at Gainsway in Kentucky and has proved as successful at stud as Mill Reef, with a predominance of good winners in France, notably Detroit (Prix de l'Arc de Triomphe), Gold River (Prix Royal Oak, Prix Cadran, Prix de l'Arc de Triomphe), Irish River (French 2,000 Guineas), and the brilliant mare Triptych, trained by P. Biancone and David O'Brien, winner of the Irish 2,000 Guineas, the Champion Stakes, the Matchmaker International at York, the Phoenix Champion Stakes, and the Prix Ganay.

The General Stud Book

The breeding industry inevitably relies on the historical record of pedigrees, but clearly, if it is to be of any use, this information must be authentic. This fact was certainly not lost on the originator of the General Stud Book, James Weatherby. He went to Newmarket in 1770 as Keeper of the Match Book, compiled in 1773 its successor, the Calendar, and two years before he died produced his first General Stud Book. Before the publication of the first General Stud Book in 1791 pedigree records were sketchy – there were inconsistencies and, with no official documentation, were open to falsification.

Weatherby, the founder of the family

Mill Reef, here still wearing the plaster on the fractured leg that ended his brilliant racing career, recovered to become a great stallion.

firm still responsible to this day for all the administrative requirements of the Jockey Club, felt there must be some standardization of families. His criteria for inclusion in his Stud Book were based on some one hundred mares of the latter part of the seventeenth century bred to the Arabian stallions and their descendants. He had little historical evidence on which to base his work, relying on a few private stud books and early racing results. However, his listing of mares with their pedigree and yearly record at stud, plus details of sire, sex, and colour, was subsequently found to be reasonably accurate.

A continuing record

Following the death of James Weatherby, his nephew took over the task of compiling the General Stud Book and since then the pedigree of every thoroughbred has been recorded. Volume I appeared in 1808 but not until Volume II, published in 1822, was the word 'thoroughbred' mentioned. This occurred in the description of the breeding of Copenhagen, the Duke of Wellington's charger at Waterloo.

The publication of further volumes was erratic. For example, Volume III appeared in 1832, Volume IV in 1840 – a gap of eight years – while Volume V was published in 1845. However, after Volume VI, published in 1849, subsequent volumes appeared every four years, with the introduction of Irish Mares in Volume XX (1905).

The General Stud Book's strict adherence to the requirements for admission and the dogged denial by its compilers that other countries were capable of producing good racehorses brought about a series of crises. The first major blow came in 1865 when Gladiateur, bred in France, won the Triple Crown. The situation was aggravated by a substantial increase in horses imported from France, Australia, and America. The result was a modification of the preface to Volume XVIII, published in 1897:

'The importation of a number of mares bred in the United States of America and in Australia, a few of which will remain at stud in this country, may have some effect on the stock bred here, but the pedigrees of these horses, though accepted in the Stud Books of their own country, cannot in all cases be turned back to the thoroughbred stock exported from England, from which they all claim to be and from which, no doubt, they mainly are descended; these animals are, therefore, in those cases, marked with reference to their own "Stud Books".'

Soon things went from bad to worse. Anti-betting legislation in America at the turn of the century resulted in a huge influx of American-bred horses to Britain. The 'knock-on' effect was dramatic, with, in some respects, just cause. The first American Stud Book was published in 1868 by Colonel Saunders D. Bruce, whose interpretation of the term 'thoroughbred' was very much more relaxed than that of the British, as the preface to the first volume indicated:

'without wishing to take the responsibility of fixing a standard for the bloodstock of the United States, the general custom has been followed of calling those thoroughbreds that have an uncontaminated pedigree for five generations. Some of our most distinguished families on the American Turf cannot be traced this far, and they have been embodied in this work, their claims being recognised by everyone familiar with the subject; and their exclusion would have wrought manifest injustice.'

Not only were the requirements for entry far less stringent, but the Colonel's need of funds and constant support from the major breeders resulted in huge numbers of bogus pedigrees until Volume VII, published in 1898, when the New York Jockey Club took over. With so many American-bred horses in Britain, the Jockey Club was forced to step in and the outcome was what became known as the 'Jersey Act of 1913'. Lord Jersey, then Senior Steward, added a note to Volume XII:

'No horse or mare can, after this date, be considered as eligible for admission unless it can be traced without flaw on both sire's and dam's side of its pedigree to horses and mares themselves already accepted in earlier volumes of the Book.'

Such was the stringency of the rules that Britain was soon in danger of being left behind as a leading producer of thoroughbreds, mainly because of the French. The latter won the 1914 Derby with 'the half-bred' Dunbar II and, chiefly through the Boussac empire, with the two very successful stallions Tourbillon and his son Djebel (both non-qualifiers) made frequent visits to England, rarely going home unrewarded. But it took victories in two Classics in 1948 to force a further change. The preface of Volume XXXI, published in 1949, read:

'Any animal claiming admission from now onwards must be able to prove satisfactorily some eight or nine crosses of pure blood, to trace back for at least a century, and to show such performances of its immediate family on the Turf as to warrant the belief in the purity of its blood.'

It was fortunate that such a compromise was made as there was a sudden glut of Classic winners, who, before the thirty-first Volume, would have not qualified for entry!

The most recent change came about in 1970 with the publication of Volume XXXVI. Conditions for entry now offered two alternatives: the appearance of the whole family in the General Stud Book or a combination of either 'thoroughbred' crosses with racing performances. However, it was not the conditions of entry that surprised the breeding industry but the announcement by Peter Weatherby (his family having reserved the right of both entry and disqualification) that while the very good racemare Lavant was technically not eligible he was nevertheless to exercise the right to admit her and her progeny to the Stud Book. It was a move greatly appreciated by the breeding industry, since Lavant was the dam of both So Blessed and Lucasland, who were both winners of Newmarket's July Cup.

Breeding theories

With such an emphasis on personal preference the breeding of racehorses is permeated by a variety of opinions and theories. For many breeders, the financial considerations are foremost, but for the large commercial breeder the benefit of hindsight regarding other breeders' theories, and successes and failures, is paramount when planning a breeding policy.

Before we look at some of the particular theories and ideas about breeding, a few general points should be brought out about the 'top' and 'bottom' sides of a pedigree. It must be remembered that, to put it simply, it is performance on top, pedigree on the bottom. A well-known phrase connected with choosing a colt is: 'he doesn't have a stallion's pedigree'. It suggests that while the individual might prove a very good racehorse the lack of a fashionable pedigree will jeopardize his career at stud. Conversely, a well-bred colt who becomes a champion is very likely to become a leading sire during the following years.

Therefore, a colt, if he is to have a future at stud, must be proven on the racecourse. The same does not apply to the 'bottom' side – the dam. Nearly every filly who races will end her days in the paddocks, a practice which allows for more scope for the unexpected. But the commercial breeder is very much more interested in pedigree than in performance on the dam's side. A badly bred filly who proves useful on the racecourse is unlikely to have the same broodmare value (unless successful at stud) as a well-bred filly who proves useless on the racecourse.

Inbreeding and outcrossing

The term 'inbreeding' means the duplication of a name, normally a stallion's, in both the top and bottom half of a pedigree. The purpose of inbreeding is to exaggerate the genetic make-up of the duplicated name in an attempt to bring out the best racing qualities and improve the likelihood of breeding a champion. The method used to describe the intensity of 'inbred blood' is numerical. For example, '3 × 4 to Northern Dancer' means that Northern Dancer appeared in the third generation on the top side and the fourth on the bottom. Clearly, the closer to the individual the duplication appears the more likely it is that the genes

Stallion boxes at Ireland's famous Coolmore Stud.

Federico Tesio was one of the world's greatest breeders. He had a 'feel' for the business and a flair for choosing good mares.

will have some influence. However, it must not be forgotten that it is not just the favourable genes that might be exaggerated.

An 'outcross' occurs when there is no immediate duplication of blood. Outcrossing is frequently used when there is a preponderance of one family in either side of a family, so that an injection of new blood is required in an attempt to not ruin the family. Outcrosses tend to be subject to fashion, principally due to 'nicks' – the combination of two totally unrelated bloodlines producing winning stock. Such families have in the past proved very expensive, although some have produced a number of winners. An example is the Nasrullah–Princequillo cross, the most notable product of this cross being Mill Reef.

Federico Tesio

'The Wizard of Dormello' was undoubtedly a genius, having bred on his farm Dormello, near Lake Maggiore in Northern Italy, such great horses as Nearco, Tenerami, Botticelli, and Ribot from relatively modest mares.

Tesio never professed to have any theories on breeding, but treated each mare as an individual and looked for a sire by using the yardstick of his own impressions as to performance and conformation. However, during some 50 years as a breeder he felt he needed to 'put the best to the best' and used all the leading sires in England and France. And yet his skill was more than that. He had a natural ability to choose and find good mares – for example, Cutnip, whom the trainer bought for £100 and who was the

grandam of Nearco. Furthermore, Tesio was a very tough and meticulous worker.

Tesio's farm was spread over a large area, and its variety of altitudes allowed a good choice and growth of grass. Its size also offered greater opportunities for isolation if the stud contracted a virus. Tesio was also a great believer in the natural courses of events – he therefore never irrigated his paddocks and moved his horses south, near to Rome, in winter. He was never afraid of selling stock, and this produced a large turnover which allowed him to experiment. To sum up Tesio's achievement, it was his supernatural 'feel', his thoroughness, and his willingness to be imaginative that together made him one of racing's greatest breeders.

The Influence of Villier and Verola

Colonel J. Villier first propounded the idea of dosages and 'chefs-de-race'. The latter are stallions who have stamped themselves as influential in the development of the racehorse. Colonel Villier submitted three series of 'chefs-de-race', the first from the early nineteenth century, the second from the middle of that century, and the third from the latter part. He went on to suggest that the 'chefs-de-race' were necessary in definite proportions in the make-up of a racehorse, a consideration which, of course, influences the choice of breeding stock.

The Italian Dr Francesco Verola expanded on Villier's initial observations, producing a further series of 'chefs-de-race'. These were then broken down into five classes – 'brilliant', 'intermediate', 'classic', 'stout', and 'professional'. 'Brilliant' implied both speed and stamina and an 'index of consistency' was established by dividing the total number of appearances 'chefs-de-race' made in each class by the number made in the 'brilliant' class. Nearco had one 'chef-de-race' in the brilliant class, two in the intermediate, and three in the stout, giving him an index of consistency of five divided by one – five.

Commercial aspects of the breeding industry

It is only in the last 20 or so years that the breeding industry has become highly commercialized. In the past the great owners tended to control the major families, breeding predominantly their own stock, but since World War II the emphasis has gradually changed from the production of home-breds to buying yearlings at the sales.

Some of the great names associated with the commercial market since the war are Nelson Bunker Hunt, Robert Sangster and, in the last ten years, the tremendous involvement in the bloodstock industry of the Arabs, notably the Maktoum family. The effect of this buying power throughout the industry has been substantial, resulting in stallion syndications going 'through the roof' and therefore ridiculous prices being paid for yearlings at the sales.

The production of the commercial yearling is a very different matter from that of its home-bred equivalent. The commercial breeder has initially to evaluate the future trends, looking for potentially fashionable stallions for his mares. As the industry is sufficiently fickle to alter its opinion over the course of a season, the commercial breeder has a natural preference to go to for a 'first-season sire' who, in the absence of hindsight, tends to command good prices if backed up by a good racing career. Home-bred foals, by contrast, are generally given plenty of time and the owner is not under the same pressure as his commercial counterpart, who has to produce his individual to be sold some 15–18 months after birth.

The commercial breeder, driven by a hurried programme, is faced with a dilemma. While he wants his yearlings to look as big and as well as possible at the sales, to catch the eye of the big buyer and so achieve a better price, he must also look to the longer term. An over-produced yearling is prone to weakness and, to a lesser extent, problems of temperament, both of which factors may affect its racing performance. While the commercial breeder is looking for the best possible price at the sales, he is also mindful of the fact that the individuals he submits at the sales should go on to perform well on the racecourse if they are to enhance both the name of the breeder and the horse's family.

The international state of racing is such that what has happened in Britain is even more pronounced in the USA. A brief look at the syndication values of stallions over the last 20 years shows what an impact the bloodstock industry has had generally. Sir Ivor was syndicated for $2 million in 1968, while a year later Vaguely Noble was syndicated for a staggering $5 million. Nijinsky's syndication to America was £2.5 million, but it was during the late-1970s that the overall market reached an all-time high, with Seattle Slew being syndicated for $12 million and Affirmed for $17 million.

A comparison with the syndication of stallions in Britain shows that the British market lags far behind and yet still commands very good prices. For example, Mill Reef was syndicated for £2 million in 1973 and his son Shirley Heights for nearly £2 million in 1978. A more recent illustration of how buoyant the market remains is Kalaglow, winner of the King George VI and Queen Elizabeth Stakes in 1982, who was syndicated for nearly £5 million.

The enormous syndications have inevitably been reflected in the yearling prices. In America the leading yearling sales take place at Keeneland, in Kentucky, during July and then at Saratoga, north of New York. The yearling average in 1973 was $51,283, reaching a record in 1984 of $486,902, although the figure fell in 1987 to $320,391. The British equivalent is the Highflyer Sales (formerly the Houghton Sales) at Newmarket. In the ten years 1977–87 the average rose from 14,167 guineas to a record high of 96,710 guineas. This went slightly against the US trend, although the previous high had been in 1984 when the average was 92,520 guineas, only to fall in 1985 and 1986.

During the early 1980s Robert Sangster and his syndicate dominated the international bloodstock scene, buying on both sides of the Atlantic and having a major involvement in Australia. Their beeding empire was centred at Coolmore in Ireland, but by the mid-1980s the Arabs had surpassed all expectations, buying the best available and building up such a wealth of stock that Sangster began to look small. However, not to be outdone, in 1985 he bought at Keeneland a half-brother to Seattle Slew for a record $13.1 million.

One of the consequences of this feverish buying has been the emergence of a new commercial breed – 'the pinhooker', a bloodstock commodity broker named after his equivalent in Kentucky's tobacco industry. The buying of foals to sell as yearlings became for some a very profitable venture, but during 1987 and 1988 the bloodstock industry was settling down and taking a more realistic attitude, much to the detriment of speculative foal buyers and stallion syndicators.

Epsom Derby winner Mill Reef, with Geoff Lewis aboard, was syndicated for £2 million in 1973.

Trainers and Training

A yacht, a car, and a big cigar – to say nothing of the champagne and caviar. That is often the public's mistaken image of the hard-working trainer, who in reality knows more about the dew at sunrise than he does about a starry night out.

The alarm rings for California's D. Wayne Lukas, the most successful American trainer of all time, at 3.30 a.m., and he never sleeps through it. The trainers of Newmarket, England and Chantilly, France, will not be lying abed either, as the racing world wakes to another day devoted to the fitness and care of thoroughbred horseflesh worth millions. Derby winner or selling race failure, all will be treated alike in the relentless quest for winners. The daily stable routine of brushing coats until they shine still goes on in places, but not at the Australian establishment of Colin Hayes, who believes grooming horses causes problems. D. Wayne Lukas may have made it to the top with almost indecent haste, but he would never have got there by cutting corners. He believes that as much effort should go into making a horse happy as is put into making him a highly-tuned athlete. Training horses is for people with a meticulous eye for detail, unflagging energy, and a firm belief that just around the corner is a Derby winner. And sometimes there is, as this chapter reveals.

Stable lads and girls play a vital part in getting horses fit to race. Here is part of a string on their way to exercise on the gallops at the Lambourn training centre, in Berkshire, one of the most famous of England's training areas.

A trainer is required to get a horse fit and then choose the race he is most likely to win. It sounds easy, but it is the most demanding job in racing. Whereas a jockey's work is finished the minute he dismounts from his last ride of the day, the trainer's worries go home with him.

A large stable of 200 horses may have a staff of over 100 on its books. Racing is big business and a trainer is often responsible for other people's property valued in the millions.

Where racing is centralized, horses are usually stabled on the racecourse. Their training ground will be an artificial surface within the main area. But elsewhere, in Britain especially, stables are privately owned or rented and are sometimes situated in splendid isolation, with grass training gallops of their own. Otherwise, towns like Chantilly and Newmarket are taken over almost exclusively for the training of horses and the extensive gallops are shared.

Climate plays a big part in the way horses are prepared. In Britain, where Flat racing is abandoned in the winter (although an all-weather track is planned for the winter of 1989), horses start to get on the move in late January, with perhaps three weeks of road work. This is followed by slow cantering for another three weeks and from there it is a steady progression to the first race, perhaps in April.

A horse will be exercised in the morning to suit his requirements, but is then shut up in his box, often for the rest of the day. He lives on a carefully controlled diet. Give him too little protein and he lacks energy; give him too much and it will have an adverse effect. Feeding, one of the most important aspects of training, can start with breakfast as early as 4.30 a.m. Between 10.00 and 12.00 he will be given another bowlful, but his main meal is in the early evening. In extreme cases, he may need a snack at around 10 p.m. In a day, he will consume 10–18 lb (4.5–8 kg) of hard feed (carrots, chopped hay, and bran and oats mixed, maybe, with molasses), plus a quantity of hay.

Australian Colin Hayes, who trains very successfully in the sunny area near Adelaide, brings his horses out twice a day. In the afternoon they will either have a swim in the equine pool or put in a 20-minute session on the treadmill. Hayes is dead set against having his horses brushed. He believes that too much fuss in the box can upset an animal and lead him into bad habits – like laying his ears back and taking a nip out of the stable lad. Swimming, which they also do after morning work, like sunshine, puts a gleam on their coats. The only brushing they get is at a racecourse before they run. Hayes does not train a horse hard, and he trains it, initially, for speed. When Bonhomie, winner of the mile-and-a-half (2.4 km) King Edward VII Stakes at Royal Ascot, arrived at his stable, Hayes sent him out first time for a 7–furlong (1.4 km) race — and he won.

In countries with tight little oval tracks, pace takes priority. Horses are trained for early speed to get a good position by the first bend. The runners settle once they have sorted themselves out, but they finish slower than they start. On galloping tracks, speed is reserved for the finish and a mile-and-a-half (2.4 km) event can often develop into a sprint over the last few furlongs.

American-born British champion, Steve Cauthen, maintains that when he was riding in America, he would cover the first furlong of a 6-furlong (1.2 km) race about four seconds faster than he would in England. Prominent and often controversial French owner, Daniel Wildenstein, protests that too many middle-distance races are run at a false pace and that reducing these to a short sprint does not produce a fair result. He advocates that prize-money should be withheld for winners who exceed a stipulated time, the state of the ground being taken into account.

It is quite usual for a trainer to run his horse in the no-dawdle Epsom Derby (1½ miles/2.4 km) without knowing for sure that his horse has the required stamina. It is doubtful that the horse will even have worked over more than 1¼ (2 km) miles in his preparation. The full-scale home trial, which was usually staged 10 days before Epsom and drew a crowd of interested on-lookers if it was on the Newmarket gallops, is a thing of the past. Breeding has always been considered the best guideline to stamina potential.

When the gallops at Lambourn become too firm, horses are exercised instead on a special all-weather strip.

The trainer is a highly respected specialist who is prepared to work long hours during a seven-day week. His standard of living is relative to the success of his horses, and many trainers who have failed to attract the high-spending owners are rewarded less well than their talent deserves. Part of the job is to advise owners, often in consultation with a bloodstock agent, of the best yearlings to buy within a set price range. On his judgement may depend the success, or otherwise, of his stable for the next year or two. How new trainers get owners in the first place is something of a mystery. They will usually have served as an assistant to an experienced trainer before they launch themselves. However, a bit of friendly 'poaching' does perhaps occur.

The principles of training have not changed over the years, although feed additives have helped, and a trainer's real skill is to pick the right horse for the right race on the right day. Horses peak in the same way as athletes and it is the timing of this peak for a big race that is a vital part of the trainer's art.

D. Wayne Lukas runs his horses more often than most, but they stand up to it well. He believes that a horse's mental fitness is as important as its physical well-being, and maybe it is because they are kept happy that they respond so well.

Discipline in stables has relaxed with the times. But even if a stable lad is seen smoking on horseback while riding to the training grounds, there is no evidence of animals having suffered from a more relaxed approach. Horses usually look magnificent in the paddock, while shattered racecourse records show that they are running better than ever. However, the cost of buying and setting up a stable of one's own is prohibitive for an aspiring young person and even successful retired jockeys find training a daunting prospect.

Ivan
ALLAN
b.1941

The owner of the 1984 English St Leger winner Commanche Run, Ivan Allan has been a successful trainer in Singapore and Malaysia since 1964. But his golden years were 1972–86. During that time he won nine Singapore Derbys and nine Perak Derbys, as well as taking the area's most valuable race, the Singapore Gold Cup, on seven occasions.

In the same period, Allan was successful in a total of 48 feature races in Singapore, Kuala Lumpur, Ipoh, and Penang. In 1987 he spent time in Europe and at Newmarket, where Chris Wall was his private trainer of some 18 horses, but he was back in Singapore with a licence in 1988.

Roger
ATTFIELD
b.1939

Canada's outstanding trainer of 1987, Roger Attfield was sixth in the North American money-won list with $3,626,475. No other Canadian-based trainer has ever matched that total. His 101 winners in North America put him behind only D. Wayne Lukas and

Jack Van Berg in the Top Ten. Eighty-eight of his victories were scored in Ontario.

Born in Newbury, England, Attfield went to Canada in 1970. He trained briefly for Roy Kennedy before joining Bud Baker at the Norcliffe Stable. After going public for two seasons, he began training exclusively for Kinghaven Farms in 1984.

Roger Attfield set a new record for a Canadian-based trainer with his 1987 prize-money earnings.

Lazaro
BARRERA
b.1924

Cuban-born Lazaro Barrera joined the short and exclusive list of trainers who have won the American Triple Crown when superhorse Affirmed landed the treble in 1978.

Barrera learned his trade at Oriental Park, Havana, before moving to Mexico City in 1945. Three years later, he went to the USA to work at small tracks, including Randall Park. It was not until 1971, when he brought Tinajero from Puerto Rico, that he began to attract national attention. In 1974, Lou Wolfson, owner of Harbor View Farm, wanted Barrera to train for him exclusively, but loyalty to old friends like Tinajero's owner, Rafael Escudero, made the offer

Jim Bentley left his native Ireland to become one of Canada's outstanding trainers. His vintage year of 1971 included Queen's Plate winner Kennedy Road.

unacceptable. Wolfson was so impressed by the trainer's character that he used him anyway.

National champions Bold Forbes (Kentucky Derby and Belmont Stakes, 1976), Lemhi Gold (Marlboro Cup and Jockey Club Cup, 1982) and Tiffany Lass (Kentucky Oaks, 1986) all came under his wing. Eclipse Award top trainer in 1976, 1977, 1978, and 1979, Barrera led the earnings list for three consecutive years, 1978–80, and won his 100th stakes race with American Standard, at Los Alamitos, in 1984.

Barrera's fondest memories are of Affirmed winning the Triple Crown and Bold Forbes taking the Kentucky Derby, but he will never forget the ten races between Affirmed and Alydar in 1977 and 1978. There was seldom more than a neck between them, but Affirmed came out the 7–3 winner.

Two open-heart operations have struck Barrera's favourite food, black beans, white rice, roasted pig, and fried bananas, off his menu, but his hunger for winners remains. He was elected to the Hall of Fame in 1979.

Jim
BENTLEY
b.1903

Born in County Limerick, Ireland, Jim Bentley, one of Canada's outstanding trainers, rode his father's Ballinode in the hunting field. The mare went on to win the Grand Sefton Chase, at Liverpool, and the 1925 Cheltenham Gold Cup.

Bentley arrived in Canada in 1928 and both rode and trained jumpers during the 1930s. His best year was probably 1971, when he saddled Kennedy Road to win Woodbine's Queen's Plate, and Laurie's Dancer to take the Canadian Oaks, the Alabama, and the Delaware Oaks.

Hein
BOLLOW
b.1920

Hein Bollow is one of the very few top jockeys to have made the transition to top trainer. As a jockey, he was the dominant figure in German racing in the immediate post-war period, being champion on 13 occasions and winning a total of 1,033 races, including numerous Classic and prestige races. No doubt, as he was born in Hamburg, his four wins in the German Derby there gave him the most satisfaction.

Retiring from the saddle in 1962, Bollow quickly established himself as one of the top trainers in Cologne, his main owners in the early days being Gestüt Asta and Countess Batthyany, and, later on, Gestüt Erlengrund. The best horses he has trained are Nebos (Grosser Preis von Baden, Preis von Europa) and Marduk (German Derby, Grosser Preis von Baden), while in 1987 he won four of the five German Classics and came close to winning the Derby as well. In 1988, he trained Alte Zeit to win the two fillies' Classics and to run a neck second in the German Derby. With over 1,600 winners to his credit, Bollow is one of a small number of jockey-trainers to have won more than 1,000 races in each category.

Adrian
von BORCKE
b.1904 d.1987

Born into a Prussian landed family, Adrian von Borcke began as an amateur rider over the sticks in Berlin. He was very tall, but still managed to be champion amateur three times, before turning to training at the age of 25 in 1929. By German standards he was exceptionally young, but soon established himself in the top rank of Berlin trainers. After World War II he fled to the west and trained principally for Gestüt Erlenhof and Gestüt Röttgen, before retiring in 1968 to Baden-Baden. He named his retirement house close to the Iffezheim racecourse 'Orsini', after Erlenhof's high-class colt, who was ridden by Lester Piggott to win the German Derby. In all, von Borcke won the Derby seven times, a record since equalled by Sven von Mitzlaff.

Sir Cecil
BOYD-ROCHFORT
b.1887 d.1983

Successful in 13 English Classics, including six St Legers, Cecil Boyd-Rochfort was leading trainer five times and won more than £1,150,000 in prize-money for owners who included the Royal Family. A tall and elegant Old Etonian with a good tailor, he took charge of the Royal horses on the death of Willie Jarvis in 1943. Three years later he won the 1,000 Guineas for King George VI with Hypericum, and between 1952 and 1960 saddled good horses for the Queen. They included the 2,000 Guineas hero Pall Mall (1958), as well as Almeria, Aureole, Above Suspicion, and Doutelle.

Proud of his profession since taking out a licence in 1923, Boyd-Rochfort said he felt like 'packing up training straight away' when fined £100 after Premonition (8–1 on) had beaten his pacemaker Osborne (25–1) by a short head in the 1954 Winston Churchill Stakes at Hurst Park. Both horses were in the same ownership. The stewards claimed that the trainer had neglected his responsibilities in not giving Osborne's jockey (Roy Burrows) precise orders in accordance with a rule which stated that 'every horse which runs in a race shall be run on its merits, whether the owner runs another horse in the race or not'. Premonition, who won eight races, including the 1953 St Leger, had been involved in another controversy when disqualified after finishing first in the Irish Derby.

With the failure, by a head, of Prince Simon to beat Galcador (1950), it was Parthia (1959) who provided Boyd-Rochfort with his only Derby success. His most successful runner in the Classics was that fine filly Meld, who in 1955 took the 1,000 Guineas, Oaks, and St Leger. His other Classic triumphs were: **1,000 Guineas**: Brown Betty (1933); **Oaks**: Hycilla (1944); **St Leger**: Boswell (1936), Sun Castle (1941), Black Tarquin (1948) and Alcide (1958).

Boyd-Rochfort was awarded the Croix de Guerre in World War I while serving in the Scots Guards with his elder brother, Arthur, who won the Victoria Cross. Even in the years leading up to his retirement in November 1968, when he was knighted, he was a commanding figure.

Richard
BRADFIELD
b.— d.—

Born in the Bendigo District of Victoria, Australia, Richard Bradfield first came to prominence when Patron won the 1894 Melbourne Cup. At 27, he was probably the

youngest trainer to win the race. The Victory (1902), Night Watch (1918) and Backwood (1924) continued his marvellous Melbourne Cup sequence. During World War II, Bradfield received horses including Magpie, King Offer, and Lucknow, from prominent English owners William Clark and Lionel Robinson.

Clive
BRITTAIN
b.1933

A stable lad with the legendary Noel Murless for 21 years, Clive Brittain had the support of Greek shipping magnate Captain Marcos Lemos when he started training in Newmarket in 1972. His first winner was Vedvyas, at Doncaster, in the second month of the season.

Brittain's first Classic winner, Julio Mariner, was a 28–1 outsider when he took the 1978 St Leger; and Pebbles was returned at 8–1 for her 1,000 Guineas triumph in 1984.

Brittain's big year was 1985, when Pebbles took the Eclipse Stakes and the Champion Stakes before crossing to the USA for a Breeders' Cup Turf triumph at Aqueduct, New York. In 1986, he was back in the States, with Bold Arrangement, who, after picking up third-place money in Keeneland went on to be second (for $100,000) to Ferdinand in the Kentucky Derby at Churchill Downs. Both races were run on dirt. At the end of that year, Brittain won Tokyo's Japan Cup with Jupiter Island.

Captain Sir Cecil Boyd-Rochfort was a trainer who demanded perfection. Here he is seen paying special attention to the Queen's Doutelle with Harry Carr aboard.

37

Elliott
BURCH
b.1924

Burch was assistant to his father before taking over as head trainer for Mrs Isabel Dodge Sloane in 1957. In 1959 he saddled Horse of the Year, Sword Dancer, who won the Belmont Stakes a fortnight after beating older horses in the Metropolitan Handicap (1 mile/1.6 km).

Burch achieved the same feat ten years later with another Horse of the Year, Arts and Letters. He won another Belmont with Quadrangle and another Metropolitan with State Dinner. He also trained three-times grass champion and Horse of the Year, Fort Marcy, grass champion Run the Gantlet, and champion three-year-old, Key to the Mint, who followed Sword Dancer, Quadrangle, and Arts and Letters as winner of the Travers Stakes.

Frank
BUTTERS
b.1878 d.1957

Born in Vienna, Frank Butters trained in Austria before he was interned during World War I. On his release, he ran a stable in Italy before going to England and taking over Lord Derby's horses in 1926. That association ended in 1930, but Butters was soon in harness again, this time as trainer to the Aga Khan. It was a partnership that flourished for almost 20 years.

Before his retirement in 1949 he trained 1,019 winners in Britain. His Classic successes were: **Derby**: Bahram (1935) and Mahmoud (1936); **2,000 Guineas**: Bahram (1935); **1,000 Guineas**: Fair Isle (1930); **Oaks**: Beam (1927), Toboggan (1928), Udaipur (1932), Light Brocade (1934), Steady Aim (1946) and Masaka (1948); **St Leger**: Fairway (1928), Firdaussi (1932), Bahram (1935), Turkhan (1940) and Tehran (1944). Butters was Britain's leading trainer eight times.

Peter
CAZALET
b.1907 d.1973

Remembered for his many successes as National Hunt trainer to Queen Elizabeth the Queen Mother, Peter Cazalet seemed fated never to win the Grand National. Davy Jones (1936), Cromwell (1948) and Devon Loch (1956) all had victory plucked from their grasp. Cazalet's close friend, the late Lord Mildmay, was in the saddle when Davy Jones ran off the course between the last two fences. Twelve years later, his lordship was crippled by a sudden attack of cramp and could finish only third on his favourite horse, Cromwell. Worse was to follow. Five years after the great amateur rider's tragic death by

Shopping for Christmas, trainers Frank Butters (right) and Tom Waugh discuss the bargains at the Newmarket December bloodstock sales of 1931.

drowning, the Queen Mother's Devon Loch collapsed beneath Dick Francis when less than 100 yards (91 m) away from a spectacular royal triumph.

It was through Anthony Mildmay that the then Queen and Princess Elizabeth went into racehorse ownership together with Monaveen, who was bought by Cazalet in 1949. The steeplechaser, who won at Fontwell Park in October of that year, was the first horse to run for a Queen of England since the reign of Queen Anne. Twenty-three years later, Cazalet went back to the pretty Sussex track to record the Queen Mother's 250th success. The Fairlawne stable that sent out 82 winners in 1964–5, produced such royal favourites as Double Star II, The Rip, Laffy, Makaldar, and Manicou. And there was Bill Whitbread's exciting Dunkirk.

Land and business interests in Russia which were at one time controlled by his family before the Revolution, were mentioned in Cazalet's £626,000 will. He claimed that a 'considerable sum of money' was owed to him by the government of the USSR.

Henry CECIL
b.1943

The family flag that is hoisted at Henry Cecil's Warren Place stables after every Group 1 triumph is flown not only to honour the winner, but to signal Cecil's pride in an establishment of more than 200 horses and over 100 staff.

After 20 years of training, Cecil has not left himself many more giants to kill. Since the end of World War II, he and his family have, between them, been champions 20 times. His step-father, Sir Cecil Boyd-Rochfort (three times) and father-in-law Sir Noel Murless (nine times) set the pattern for 'King Henry's' eight titles: in 1976, 1978, 1979, 1982, 1984, 1985, 1987, and 1988. Cecil himself plays skittles with records. He sets them up and knocks them down with regularity, but one that even he will find hard to beat is his own total of 180 winners in Britain in 1987. That year brought prize-money of £1,882,000.

Cecil took out his first licence in 1969, after being assistant to his stepfather at Newmarket and was quickly into his stride that year with Eclipse Stakes winner, Wolver Hollow. His sweep of the English Classics started in the 2,000 Guineas with Bolkonski (1975) and then Wollow (1976). One In A Million took the 1,000 Guineas in 1979, followed by Fairy Footsteps in 1981. In between, Light Cavalry won the 1980 St Leger, but 1985 was a big year, with Slip Anchor giving Cecil his first Derby and Oh So Sharp winning the 1,000 Guineas, Oaks, and St Leger.

The stable's hopes of the Triple Crown rested on Reference Point early in 1987, but a sinus operation prevented him running in the 2,000 Guineas. The colt was fit in time to win the Mecca-Dante Stakes and went on to take the Derby, King George VI and Queen Elizabeth Stakes, and the St Leger. He was found to have an abscessed foot after failing in the Arc de Triomphe. Le Moss brought off the Cup treble, at Ascot, Goodwood, and Doncaster in both 1979 and 1980. Cecil's fondness for having a good stayer in the yard was then met by Ardross, who won the Ascot Gold Cup (1981 and 1982), Goodwood Cup (1981) and Doncaster Cup (1982).

W. Burling COCKS
b.1915

One of America's leading trainers of steeplechasers, 'Burly' Cocks was a successful amateur rider in the mid-1930s before injury forced him out of the saddle. He took out a trainer's licence and then opened a public stable at the family's Hermitage Farm, in Unionville, Pennsylvania. It has remained his base throughout the years.

Elected to the Hall of Fame in 1985, Cocks has won almost every important steeplechase in the USA, where he is known as 'the trainer of trainers'. Among those he has educated in the art of training are Jonathan Sheppard, who has become a perennial No.1 in the jumping field, Mike Smithwick, Tom Skiffington, and Billy Turner.

Cocks winters in Camden, South Carolina, and runs his stable from the Springdale Training Center from March to May. His $3 million purse-money earnings make him the third most successful trainer of all time, and he was honoured in 1973 with the F. Ambrose Clark Award for contributions to steeplechase racing. He was the leader for races won in 1948, when he tied with A. Ridgely White and Sid Watters Jr, and then again in 1959, 1965, 1980, and 1986. Cocks trained Zaccio, whose successes included the Colonial Cup (1981, 1982) and the American Grand National (1981). Zaccio was voted the champion steeplechaser in 1980, 1981, and 1982.

Luca CUMANI
b.1949

It was no surprise when Milan-born Luca Cumani won the 1988 Epsom Derby. Ever since he took out a licence to train at Newmarket in 1976, his intention of being the best in Britain has become clearer by the

It's hats off for Britain's popular champion Henry Cecil on Epsom Derby day. He won the trainer's title for the eighth time in 1988.

year. The son of wealthy champion trainer Sergio Cumani, he led a gentleman's life in Italy. He was a university student and a leading amateur rider of 85 winners before he took his first real job as a pupil assistant to Henry Cecil at Newmarket in 1974.

After Italian-owned colts won England's 1975 2,000 Guineas and Derby, Cumani started out on his own at Newmarket with 35 horses. His second runner, Konafa, was runner-up to Flying Water in the 1,000 Guineas of 1976, and his first winner was Three Legs, at York, in May of that year. The following year, Freeze the Secret was second in both the 1,000 Guineas and Oaks. In the latter he also saddled the third horse, Vaguely Deb. But it was Tolomeo's 1983 triumph in Chicago's Arlington Million, after running second in the 2,000 Guineas, that started to attract better horses to the yard.

Cumani's first British Classic success was with Commanche Run, in the 1984 St Leger. Against the trainer's wishes, his stable jockey Darrell McHargue was replaced in the race by Lester Piggott and soon afterwards went home to the USA. Kahyasi's 1988 English-Irish Derby double was the climax for a stable whose successes have included the Italian Derby, Italian, and French St Legers (all with Old Country); two Cambridgeshires (Century City and Dallas); and three consecutive Extel Handicaps (Free Guest, Fish'N'Chips, and Chinoiserie). Cumani's highest number of winners for a season in his first 12 years was 83 in 1987.

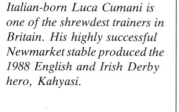

Italian-born Luca Cumani is one of the shrewdest trainers in Britain. His highly successful Newmarket stable produced the 1988 English and Irish Derby hero, Kahyasi.

Bart
CUMMINGS
b.1927

Trainer of the winners of a record seven Melbourne Cups, Bart Cummings is the son of Jim Cummings, who saddled Comic Court for a Melbourne Cup triumph in 1950. He was raised in Adelaide and, after trying a number of odd jobs, joined his father as an assistant. In 1953, Cummings started training in his own right and in 1958 paid his first visit to the New Zealand sales, from which he has since bought many top Australian performers.

Starting from his South Australia base, Cummings has won numerous trainers' championships for Victoria and South Australia. His first Melbourne Cup winner, Light Fingers (1965) was the start of a hat-trick of wins for the stable. Galilee took the prize the following year and Red Handed completed the sequence in 1967. In the 1970s, Cummings won five consecutive Adelaide and Melbourne Metropolitan trainer championships before moving to Sydney in 1977. He was the first trainer in the southern hemisphere to earn over A\$1 million in stakes money in a single season.

Cummings is responsible for a total of 21 cup wins. He also holds the record for the most wins in Australia's two-year-old championship event, the Golden Slipper, with four victories, and has trained other juvenile champions of 14 Group 1 races. Ex-Spendthrift Farm stallion, Taj Rossi, was also under the care of Cummings and provided him with his only win in the Cox Plate, Australia's premier weight-for-age contest.

Mathew
DAWSON
b.1820 d.1898

Trainer of 28 Classic winners, Mathew Dawson reached the peak of his profession. He was a no-nonsense Scot who spared no expense in the running of his stables. In his book *The Derby Stakes*, Roger Mortimer describes Dawson as a widely respected man and much loved by those who knew him best. Mortimer writes: 'He had no patience with weak men or bad horses, and heavy betting he abhorred. In fact, he had a certain contempt for money, unlike Fred Archer with whom he was so closely associated and whom he summarised as "that damned, long-legged, tin-scraping young devil". He was as good a gardener as he was a trainer and used to appear on the gallops in a tall hat, varnished boots and with a wonderful flower in his buttonhole. He spoke with a pronounced Scottish accent, which made even his strongest language sound like a benediction . . .'

Dawson was still saddling Classic winners in his seventies and had not retired by the time of his death. He scored Derby successes with Thormanby (1860), Kingcraft (1870), Silvio (1877), Melton (1885), Ladas (1894) and Sir Visto (1895).

Dawson died during a summer heatwave. As he lay dying he was told that his secretary, of whom he was very fond, had just departed on his honeymoon. 'Poor fellow, how damned hot he will be,' he murmured, and those were the last words he spoke.

John
DAY
b.1819 d.1883

Interest in nineteenth-century trainer John Day was stimulated in 1987 when his British record of 146 winners in a season (1867) was eclipsed by Henry Cecil's total of 180. Day trained at Danebury, Hampshire, for a largely crooked collection of owners, such as bookmakers who specialized in laying non-triers and, in some cases, non-runners.

Twelve of the trainer's record total of wins were contributed by the two-year-old filly, Lady Elizabeth. She started favourite for the 1868 Derby, but finished down the field at ruinous cost to her gambling owner, the Marquis of Hastings. Day, who rode the 2,000 Guineas winner of 1844, The Ugly Buck, also trained Derby heroes Cossack (1847) and Andover (1854).

Michael
DICKINSON
b.1950

In only four years as a National Hunt trainer, Michael Dickinson was champion three times. In one season as a Flat trainer he had four winners — and was sacked.

No young trainer has matched Dickinson's jumps records. After retiring from the saddle, Dickinson took over the Yorkshire stables from his father, Tony, in 1980. Four years later, at the age of 34, he had won two Cheltenham Gold Cups, three King George VI Chases, three Queen Mother Champion Chases, and a Hennessy Cognac Gold Cup. In addition, he sent out a record 120 winners in the 1982–3 season, when Bregawn, Captain John, Wayward Lad, Silver Buck, and Ashley House gave the stable an incredible 1–2–3–4–5 placing in the Cheltenham Gold Cup, which is unlikely ever to be matched. His 12 winners on Boxing Day 1982 will also take some beating.

Then, when his top horses were probably past their best, Dickinson handed over the Harewood yard to his mother, Monica, and

left the jumping scene to join wealthy owner Robert Sangster as his private trainer on the Flat. The Manton estate, Wiltshire, was eventually chosen for the project. It is reputed to have cost Sangster about £14 million by the time perfectionist Dickinson, who took 18 months to make his transition, had turned it into the most modern training establishment in the country. Late-maturing two-year-olds dominated the stable, and as the months of the 1986 season went by without a winner, rumours of a split were published and strongly denied. It was not until Veryan Bay scored at Lingfield on 16 September that Manton raised a cheer. Three more successes followed that season, for a total of £14,000 prize money.

Sangster announced the split in November, 1986. The owner said: 'Michael has done a wonderful job in creating such a magnificent training establishment as Manton. This has been almost entirely due to his dedication and hard work. But we do have fundamental differences of opinion which have made things very hard for both of us.' Sangster confirmed that what remained of Dickinson's five-year contract would be paid in full, but there was acrimony.

Dickinson left England to train in

Michael Dickinson, who trained the first five horses home in the 1983 Cheltenham Gold Cup, was Britain's champion jumps trainer three times in four years. But when he switched to the flat he was sacked.

the USA. Barry Hills took over at Manton for the 1987 season and produced 96 winners in Britain, with prize money of £509,881. But, whereas Dickinson had relied heavily on some 40 two-year-olds, Hills had a balanced yard of 150.

Dickinson's big winners were: **Cheltenham Gold Cup**: Silver Buck (1982), Bregawn (1983); **King George VI Chase**: Silver Buck (1980), Wayward Lad (1982 and 1983); **Queen Mother Champion Chase**: Rathgorman (1982), Badsworth Boy (1983 and 1984); **Hennessy Cognac Gold Cup**: Bregawn (1982).

And from 1942 to 1966 he won the Irish Grand National ten times. His big race victories include: **Cheltenham Gold Cup**: Prince Regent (1946), Arkle (1964, 1965, 1966), Fort Leney (1968); **Irish Grand National**: Prince Regent (1942), Shagreen (1949), Royal Approach (1954), Olympia (1960), Fortria (1961), Kerforo (1962), Last Link (1963), Arkle (1964), Splash (1965), and Flyingbolt (1966). Arkle also won the King George VI Chase (1965), the Hennessy Cognac Gold Cup (1964, 1965) and the Whitbread Gold Cup (1965).

Tom DREAPER
b.1898 d.1975

Give them plenty of jumping practice, but don't overwork them at home. With this rule in mind, great Irish trainer Tom Dreaper never had his string out for more than half an hour, although he schooled them twice a week. And results speak for themselves: his Greenogue, Kilsallaghan, stable produced wonderful chasers Arkle, Prince Regent, Royal Approach, and Flyingbolt, as well as Fort Leney, Fortria, and Leap Frog.

Cheltenham's Festival meeting saw plenty of Dreaper's brilliant chasers, but nowadays it is Arkle, snorting great white plumes of triumph into the cold March air, who is best remembered. This trainer started to win the Cheltenham Gold Cup in 1946 and went on until 1968, three years before his retirement.

John DUNLOP
b.1939

The first trainer in England to entrust himself with 200 horses, John Dunlop believes in percentages. The more animals you have, the more winners you should get. He took over the Duke of Norfolk's Arundel, Sussex stable from Gordon Smyth in 1966 and had his first Classic success with Black Satin in the 1970 Irish 1,000 Guineas. Shirley Heights won the Epsom Derby for him in 1978 and in 1980 Quick As Lightning took the 1,000 Guineas.

Dunlop won the 1986 St Leger with Moon Madness, who went on to triumph in the 1987 Grand Prix de Saint-Cloud. However, his biggest disappointment was Snaafi Dancer, who joined his stable as the world's most expensive yearling at $10.2 million. The colt was in training for two years, but never raced.

Peter EASTERBY
b.1929

Miles Henry Easterby, always known as Peter, is an exceptional trainer of a mixed string of jumpers and Flat horses. He certainly dominated the British hurdling scene between 1976 and 1981 with those immensely popular jumpers, Night Nurse and Sea Pigeon. They won four Champion Hurdles between them — Night Nurse in 1976 and 1977, Sea Pigeon in 1980 and 1981. Little Owl gave Easterby the big Cheltenham double by taking the 1981 Gold Cup. The stable won the Gold Cup in 1979 with Alverton, who later that same month tragically broke his neck.

Licenced since 1950, Easterby scored his first big wins on the Flat in 1965, with Old Tom (Lincoln Handicap) and Goldhill (King's Stand Stakes). Sea Pigeon, winner of £122,642 on the Flat and £154,402 over jumps for a total of £277,044, was a brilliant dual-purpose gelding. Two Chester Cups (1977 and 1978) and an Ebor (1979) were among his 16 successes in 45 outings on the Flat.

Tom Dreaper lights his pipe and reflects on some of his great steeplechasers. There were many of them, but none could match the peerless Arkle.

David Elsworth, Britain's champion National Hunt trainer in 1988, was fined a record £17,500 after Cavvies Clown failed dope tests.

Easterby was champion National Hunt trainer in 1978–9, 1979–80, and 1980–1. His other major winners include Saucy Kit (Champion Hurdle, 1967); Night Nurse (Irish Sweeps Hurdle, 1975); Bronze Hill (Lincoln Handicap, 1973); Within The Law (Schweppes Gold Trophy, 1979) and Sonnen Gold (Gimcrack Stakes, 1979).

David ELSWORTH
b.1939

Ten years after setting up stall as a market trader, David Elsworth became Britain's champion National Hunt trainer in the 1987–8 season. His winners included Grand National hero Rhyme 'N' Reason. He served his apprenticeship with Alec Kilpatrick from 1955 to 1958 and rode as a professional jump jockey from 1957 to 1972. He then became assistant trainer to Ricky Vallance and it was between leaving that job and taking out a licence for a mixed stable near Salisbury in 1978 that he was briefly a market trader.

Although much better known for his jumping triumphs, Elsworth has had many notable successes on the Flat since Raffia Set started the ball rolling at Salisbury in April 1979. They include Heighlin (Goodwood Cup, 1982), Mighty Fly (Lincoln Handicap and Royal Hunt Cup, 1983), Melindra (Wokingham Handicap, 1983), Naheez (Horris Hill Stakes, 1986), and Princess Athena (Queen Mary Stakes, 1987).

The versatile Heighlin (Triumph Hurdle, 1980) and Lesley Ann (Sun Alliance Chase, 1981) were Elsworth's big winners over jumps before he moved to Whitsbury in 1982. Many big winners followed, including Floyd (Imperial Cup, 1985), Desert Orchid (King George VI Chase, 1986 and 1988), Barnbrook Again (Ladbroke Hurdle, 1987) and Rhyme 'N' Reason (Grand National, 1988). Combs Ditch had two narrow defeats in the 'King George' — by a short head in 1984 and by a neck in 1985. Cavvies Clown was disqualified from three races he won in the 1987–8 season. Dope tests proved positive to the steroid 19–Nortestosterone, and Elsworth was fined a record £17,500.

Jim FITZSIMMONS
b.1874 d.1966

Born in Brooklyn, on land where the Sheepshead Bay track was built, 'Sunny Jim' Fitzsimmons began, at 15, as a jockey, mostly at bush tracks. After five years he combined riding with training. He saddled Bartender to win his first stakes race in the early 1890s and rode the same horse to score in the Brewers' Handicap at Pimlico. His first big break as a trainer came in 1923, when he took over the stable of William Woodward's Belair Stud, and later in the 1920s there began an association with the Phipps family that ended only on his retirement in 1963.

For Belair, he trained Triple Crown heroes

Gallant Fox (1930) and his son Omaha (1935). Granville (1936) and Nashua (1955) were both Horse of the Year. He was also in charge of champions Vagrancy, Faireno, and Happy Gal. For Mrs H. C. Phipps, Fitzsimmons trained the 1957 Horse of the Year, Bold Ruler, and champions High Voltage, Misty Morn, Castle Forbes, Diavolo, and Dice. His major successes include the Kentucky Derby (three times), the Belmont (six times) and the Preakness (four times). When he retired, he had been training for 70 years.

Josh
GIFFORD
b.1941

Winner of 51 Flat races as an apprentice, farmer's son Josh Gifford became Britain's champion National Hunt jockey in 1962–3, 1963–4, 1966–7, and 1967–8. His 122 winners in 1967 just beat Fred Winter's record 121, set in 1953. He rode for Ryan Price, whose Findon yard he took over with a trainer's licence in 1970. Price and Gifford made a good team. Together they won four of the first five runnings of the Schweppes Gold Trophy, with Rosyth (1963 and 1964), Le Vermontois (1966) and Hill House (1967).

Gifford's greatest training success was the 1981 Grand National triumph of Aldaniti, ridden by recovered cancer victim Bob Champion. Understandably, Gifford's skill in getting Aldaniti back on the track after breaking down at Sandown in November 1979 was underplayed in the wave of emotion that swept over Aintree that day. Other big winners from the stable include Approaching (Hennessy Cognac Gold Cup, 1978) and Shady Deal (Whitbread Gold Cup, 1982). Gifford had tried in vain to train a winner at the Cheltenham Festival meeting for 17 years before his luck turned in 1988 with Golden Minstrel (Kim Muir Challenge Cup), Vodkatini (Grand Annual Challenge Cup) and Pragada (Coral Golden Hurdle).

Theo
GRIEPER
b.1929

Although Theo Grieper has been established as a leading trainer in Germany for almost 20 years, he is known internationally as the trainer of Star Appeal, who won the 1975 Prix de l'Arc de Triomphe in sensational fashion. Although Star Appeal paid 119–1, making him easily the longest-priced winner of the Paris race, it was not really such a surprise, as he had earlier won the Eclipse Stakes with equal ease, to become the first German-trained winner in Britain for half a century. Grieper has never been afraid to send his horses on long trips and has had several notable successes in Italy and Belgium. He sent Daun to Tokyo, to be the best-placed European horse in the 1985 Japan Cup.

The German Derby has so far been Grieper's unlucky race, but he has a good record in the other German Classics and has won the Group 1 Aral-Pokal four times. Since 1969, he has trained in the grounds of Gestüt Röttgen, to the east of Cologne, and is one of the few German trainers with his own private gallops. For most of this period he has been private trainer for Röttgen, the breeders of Star Appeal, and although there are now other owners in the yard, Röttgen remains by far the most important.

Guy
HARWOOD
b.1939

Although he had saddled only one English Classic winner from his ultra-modern Sussex yard, it was always on the cards that one day Guy Harwood would produce a horse to excite the racing world. He did just that with Dancing Brave in 1986. The rider of 14 winners over jumps as an amateur while working in a family garage business, which he still runs, Harwood took out a training licence in 1966. In 1982, he sent out 120 winners, more than any other trainer, but can recall bleaker days when he had only 13 successes in one season on the Flat — nine of them in sellers.

Before the arrival of Dancing Brave, Harwood trained several good horses. Among them were To-Agori-Mou, winner of the 2,000 Guineas in 1981, Ela-Mana-Mou, who took the Royal Lodge Stakes (1978) and King Edward VII Stakes in 1979 before being sold into Dick Hern's stable, and Kalaglow (King George VI and Queen Elizabeth Stakes and Eclipse Stakes, both in 1982).

Dancing Brave was something else. He

Guy Harwood has trained many good horses. Most brilliant of them was Dancing Brave, whose amazing Arc de Triomphe victory followed a shock Epsom Derby defeat.

could be compared with the best of any era, and his narrow defeat in the 1986 Derby was controversial to say the least. Victories in the 2,000 Guineas, Eclipse Stakes, and King George VI and Queen Elizabeth Stakes were but preludes to a breathtaking European finale in the Prix de l'Arc de Triomphe. Sadly, he did not produce anything like his true form when he was a well-beaten fourth in the Breeders' Cup Turf race, at Santa Anita Park, California.

Colin HAYES
b.1924

Australia's principal trainer-breeder, Colin Hayes started with only a handful of horses he owned himself. He is now established as one of the country's leading thoroughbred players. Hayes took out a licence in 1950 and has since accumulated 26 Adelaide trainer championships to go with ten Melbourne Metropolitan titles. He passed A$1 million in prize money in the 1979–80 season and set a new Commonwealth record of 241 winners in 1981–2. Magnets was his 3,000th winner, scored at Flemington on 5 July 1980.

From his Adelaide base, Hayes has trained the winners of two Melbourne Cups, but had to wait until 1980 to break the ice with the Robert Sangster-owned Beldale Ball. His second success came six years later, with Hamdan Al Maktoum's At Talaq, who was previously trained in England by Harry Thomson Jones. Hayes also trained Dulcify and So Called to win Australia's main weight-for-age race, the Cox Plate. He set a new record in 1982 when he trained seven winners at Victoria Park and three winners at Caulfield, all on the same day.

Since 1965, Hayes has trained from his Lindsay Park Stud. The facilities available have helped him to set a world record for the number of Metropolitan winners in a day (ten) and, in 1986–7, to raise the record for total prize-money earnings in one season to A$5.2 million. Lindsay Park Stud, which Hayes owns and manages, is one of the most successful breeding establishments in the southern hemisphere. It has bred over 1,700 winners of more than 6,000 races, for prize money in excess of A$27 million. Its 4,940 acres (2,000 hectares) provide a home for up to 200 brood mares, of whom 120 are boarders. Hayes's second Melbourne Cup winner, At Talaq, stands at the farm.

Alec HEAD
b.1924

Jacques-Alexandre Head, always known as Alec, was the third son of English-born William 'Grand Bill' Head, rider and trainer extraordinary. His career was quite excep-

Colin Hayes runs one of the world's finest training and breeding establishments, near Adelaide, in Australia.

*Alec Head (**above**) is one of the greatest racing personalities France has ever produced. A formidable jumps jockey before turning to training, he is seen here riding his granddaughter's New Forest pony.*

*Nicky Henderson (**right**) produced See You Then to win three Champion Hurdles, and was twice top jumps trainer in Britain.*

tional and, even after his official retirement from training, he is still considered to be one of the most influential men of his time in the world of international bloodstock.

Head first rode as an apprentice on the Flat in 1940, and in 1945 turned his talent to jumping, with much success. Subsequently, he was associated with that great horse, Vatelys, on whom he won all the top hurdle races at Auteuil, including the French Champion Hurdle. Head took out a trainer's licence in 1947 and the following year saddled 29 jumping winners and another 27 on the Flat. He was leading trainer for the first time in 1952, at the age of 28, and maintained his supremacy for the next four years. His win with Kathleen in a jump race in 1958 was the 1,000th of his career. And yet the trainer was still only 34.

In 1955, Head moved from Maisons-Laffitte to Chantilly to train exclusively for the old Aga Khan, Prince Aly Khan, and Pierre Wertheimer. During his first 13 years of training, Head saddled two winners of the Prix de l'Arc de Triomphe (Nuccio and Saint Crespin), a French Derby and Grand Prix de Paris (Charlottesville) and two Grands Prix de Saint-Cloud (Chingacgook and Sheshoon). In Britain, he won the Epsom Derby with Lavandin, the 2,000 Guineas with Taboun, and the 1,000 Guineas with Rose Royale. Sheshoon took the Ascot Gold Cup, Nuccio won the Coronation Cup, and Rose Royale II the Champion Stakes. And Head had no fewer than three triumphs in the Irish 1,000 Guineas, with Pederoba, Butiaba, and Fiorentina.

After the death of the old Aga Khan and

Prince Aly's sad demise, Karim Aga Khan IV, owner notably of Charlottesville, stayed with Head for a while before they separated. The trainer held on to all the Wertheimer horses while Karim moved his string to rival François Mathet. Head's success story continued with the major victories of Ivanjica and Gold River in the Arc de Triomphe, Val de l'Orne and Roi Lear in the French Derby, and Pistol Packer in the French Oaks. He won three French 2,000 Guineas (Riverman, Green Dancer, and Red Lord), five French 1,000 Guineas (Yla, Toro, Ginetta, Ivanjica, and Dancing Maid) and the French Oaks (Reine de Saba).

By the time Head handed over the reins of his Chantilly yards to his eldest daughter, Christiane, on his 60th birthday in 1984, he had become a legend in his lifetime.

Nicky
HENDERSON
b.1950

Assistant trainer to Fred Winter from 1975 to 1978, Nicky Henderson rode 69 winners as an amateur. His biggest successes came in 1977, when he won the Imperial Cup on Acquaint and, despite a slipping saddle, took the Liverpool Foxhunters' Chase on Happy Warrior.

Henderson was granted a trainer's licence in 1978 and became champion in 1985–6 and 1986–7. He did very well to get three Champion Hurdle victories (1985, 1986, and 1987) out of the brilliant See You Then, whose leg problems restricted his racing. As Henderson put it: 'The horse does not have the best of wheels. There is only a limited mileage in them.' Among other big race wins were the Triumph Hurdle with First Bout (1985) and Alone Success (1987).

Dick
HERN
b.1921

Royal trainer Dick Hern, successful in over 40 Group 1 races, showed perfect timing when he produced Dunfermline to win both the Oaks and St Leger for Queen Elizabeth II in her Silver Jubilee year of 1977.

Hern was assistant to Michael Pope from 1952 to 1957 and then became private trainer to the abrasive Lionel Holliday. He may have been unlucky not to win the 1962 Derby for the owner with the favourite, Hethersett, who was brought down in a tangle of seven horses on Tattenham Hill, but the colt went on to gain compensation in the St Leger. Hern was leading trainer that year for the first time, an honour he celebrated by taking over from Jack Colling at West Ilsley, Berkshire. He saddled Provoke to be a shock 28–1 winner of the 1965 St Leger, but it was the arrival on the scene of Brigadier Gerard five years later that was to excite most public interest. The colt won his four races as a two-year-old in 1970 before taking the 2,000 Guineas in 1971. He was beaten only once in his 18 races.

Top trainer in 1972 and again in 1980 and 1983, Hern produced another Classic double for the Queen in 1974 with Highclere (1,000 Guineas and French Oaks), and in the same season took his third St Leger with Bustino. Willie Carson had replaced the stable's loyal jockey Joe Mercer by the time Hern won consecutive Derbys with Troy (1979) and Henbit (1980). Bireme (Oaks, 1980), Cut Above (St Leger, 1981, ridden by Mercer) and Sun Princess (Oaks and St Leger, 1983) provided more success in the Classics before Hern was seriously disabled in a hunting accident in December 1984. Paralysis did not stop him supervising his horses with a keen eye, but another blow struck in the summer of 1988 when he underwent major heart surgery. Neil Graham, who had been assistant to John Gosden in America, was put in charge of the West Ilsley yard during Hern's convalescence and recovery, but Hern took control again after a two-month break.

Sam
HILDRETH
b.1866 d.1929

Sacked from W. C. Whitney's New York stable in 1900, after winning the first of seven Belmont Stakes the previous year with Jean Bereaud, brilliant Sam Hildreth is said to have earned more than $250,000 in bets and purses during the next six months with his own stable of selling horses. His reputation as a horseman, rivalled only by that of James Rowe Sr during the first 30 years of this

century, was well earned, and he could be guaranteed to get the best out of moderate horses.

When anti-betting laws curtailed racing in the USA, the big stables looked to Europe, but Hildreth stayed on and from 1909 to 1911 became America's leading owner and trainer, with champions Fitz Herbet, King James, Novelty, Dalmation, and 1909 Belmont Stakes winner, Joe Madden, running in his colours. He saddled another five Belmont winners — Friar Rock and Hourless for owner August Belmont II; and, in partnership with Harry Sinclair, he produced Grey Lag, Zev, and Mad Play.

Barry
HILLS
b.1937

Two bets on a horse called Frankincense won Barry Hills the £15,000 he needed to take over Keith Piggott's Berkshire yard in 1969. He arrived there via an apprenticeship that brought nine winners and jobs with George Colling, as travelling head lad, and John Oxley, as head lad.

Left with £600 to put the show on the road, Hills quickly found owners and his string increased from 22 horses at the start to over 100 by 1973. This was the year Rheingold made up for his narrow defeat in the 1972 Epsom Derby by winning both the Arc de Triomphe and a second Grand Prix de Saint-Cloud. Always immaculate in his dress and

Major Dick Hern, one of Britain's most eminent trainers, showed great courage in his fight against paralysis, and later came back after heart surgery to supervise his powerful stable.

often smoking a large cigar, Hills had arrived in the big-time and was unlucky not to win the 1974 Oaks with Dibidale. Her saddle slipped, leaving Willie Carson to ride bareback. The filly, having lost her weight-cloth, was disqualified from third place, but her Irish Oaks win came as some consolation. English Classic triumphs followed for Hills, with Enstone Spark (1,000 Guineas, 1978) and Tap On Wood (2,000 Guineas, 1979).

Hills, who relishes a gamble if the odds are right, did not shy away from the challenge offered by a move to Robert Sangster's Manton Stables in 1987 after the controversial departure of Michael Dickinson. Hills handed over his Lambourn yard to his son, John, and in his first season at Manton trained 96 winners in Britain and won the Irish Derby with Sir Harry Lewis.

Heinz Jentzsch, who saddled his 3,000th winner in 1988, failed to win the German trainer's title only once in 28 years.

Max HIRSCH
b.1880 d.1969

Although Max Hirsch trained 100 stakes winners over 69 years, his last 12 months were, statistically, the best of his career. He was top New York trainer in 1968, with earnings of more than $900,000, and his last

runner, Heartland, won hours before his death. Born in Texas, Hirsch was only 12 when he hopped on a train to Maryland and headed for the races. He became a jockey and rode 60 winners in four years. He saddled his first major stakes winner, Norse King, in the 1915 Dwyer. Four years later he bought Grey Lag as a yearling for $10,000 and sold him on for $60,000.

Hirsch's first champion was Sarazen (1924), who was followed by Assault, Bridal Flower, But Why Not, High Gun, and Gallant Bloom. From the 1930s to the end of his life, he trained for Robert Kleberg Jr at the powerful King Ranch stables, where he turned Assault from an insignificant little colt into the 1946 Triple Crown winner. He took the Kentucky Derby and Belmont Stakes of 1950 with sore-legged Middleground and showed he had an eye for a young horse when be bought High Gun as a yearling for $10,200. He went on to win the Belmont, Dwyer, Manhattan Handicap, and Jockey Club Gold Cup. Hirsch was inducted into the Hall of Fame in 1959.

Heinz JENTZSCH
b.1920

In the world of thoroughbred racing, Heinz Jentzsch is a phenomenon. He has dominated his profession to a degree rarely equalled in any branch of professional sport. He has been champion trainer in Germany 27 times in the past 28 years, and 1966 was the only season since 1960 when he failed to top the list. During that period, he saddled five per cent of all winners trained in Germany and has won every German Group 1 race, most of them several times over. In June, 1988, he sent out his 3,000th winner, a figure no other German trainer has approached and few others in the world have bettered.

Jentzsch grew up in Berlin, where his father was a small trainer, moved west after the war and, following a spell in Munich with only modest success at training, settled in Cologne in 1959. In 1961 he trained Gestüt Schlenderhahn's Pantheon to finish third in the German Derby, the beginning of a long and highly profitable partnership with Germany's longest-established owner-breeder. One of their best seasons came in 1970, when Alpenkönig won the German Derby and three more Group 1 races; Lombard the 2,000 Guineas and St Leger; and Priamos (Pantheon's half-brother) the Prix Jacques le Marois.

Jentzsch regarded this last success as the high point of his career until two marvellous seasons (1985 and 1986) for Lirung and Acatenango, both owned by Gestüt Fährhof. Between them, they won just about every German race open to them, and both crowned

their career with a Group 1 success in France, Lirung making all to win the Prix Jacques le Marois and Acatenango taking the Grand Prix de Saint-Cloud.

Harry 'Allen' JERKENS
b.1929

Son of an Austrian cavalry captain who emigrated to the United States, Allen Jerkens was brought up among horses at his father's riding academy on Long Island. His ambition was to be a steeplechase jockey, but nine losing rides at the age of 17 convinced him that there must be better ways of making a living. He took out his first licence in 1950 and in that year celebrated the Fourth of July with his first winner, Populace. In the spring of 1962, he began a long association with Wall Street investor Jack Dreyfus Jr. He saddled such outstanding horses as Beau Purple, Prove Out, Duck Dance, and Handsome Boy for the Hobcau Farm.

Eclipse Award winner as the nation's leading trainer in 1973, Jerkens, at the age of 45, was the youngest in his profession ever to be elected to the Hall of Fame (1975). His runners have a reputation for upsetting top horses. He beat Kelso three times with Beau Purple, in 1962 and 1963; upset three-time champion filly, Cicada, with Pocosaba (1963); beat Buckpasser with Handsome Boy in 1967; and in 1973 accounted for Secretariat twice, with Onion and Prove Out.

of horses and politics. At the entrance to Oaklands there was a sign which read: 'There is nothing so good for the inside of a man as the outside of a horse.'

Leroy Jolley was helped to his first $1 million season, in 1975, by the Kentucky Derby triumph of Foolish Pleasure.

William JOHNSON
b.1782 d.1849

America's first great racing man, Colonel William R. Johnson, was born into a prominent land-holding family in the Halifax region of North Carolina. He raced his father's horses both there and in Virginia before he was 21. In 1806 and 1807, he started horses for 63 races and won 61 of them. He became known as 'Napoleon of the Turf', a title he kept even after the defeat of Henry by American Eclipse (1823) and Boston by Fashion (1842), in two great North v. South matches. Johnson trained more than 20 champions, among them Boston, the winner of 40 races, and Sir Archy, America's foundation native sire.

A member of the state legislature for 28 years, Johnson entertained such friends as Andrew Jackson, John Randolph, Henry Clay, and Richard Ten Broeck at his riverside Oaklands Plantation in Virginia. The talk on the front porch, overlooking a two-mile (3.2 km) training track, was mostly

Leroy JOLLEY
b.1938

A student for one year at the University of Miami, Leroy Jolley gave up studying to work in the barn for his father, trainer Moody Jolley. He served a two-year apprenticeship there before taking out a licence in 1958. Jolley's first winner, Somnus, was bred by his father and owned by his mother. He was only 24 when he saddled Ridan to finish third in the 1962 Kentucky Derby. In 1975, his earnings topped $1 million for the first time, after a Kentucky Derby triumph with Foolish Pleasure. Jolley won the 'Run for the Roses' with Genuine Risk in 1980 and she went on to be second in both the Preakness and Belmont Stakes. She was the first filly to compete in all three Triple Crown races.

Elected to the Hall of Fame in 1987, Jolley won Eclipse Awards with Foolish Pleasure (1974), Honest Pleasure (1975), What A Summer (1977), Genuine Risk (1980) and Manila (1986). Manila was successful in 12 out of 18 races, including the 1986 Breeders'

Cup Turf, to bring in more than $2.6 million. Jolley's son, Lee, is his assistant as well as the trainer of his own horses. Another son, Timothy, also works in the stable.

Benjamin
JONES
b.1882 d.1961

Born the son of a banker and large landowner, Ben Jones is spoken of in the same breath as the great trainers James Rowe Sr and Sam Hildreth. He trained six Kentucky Derby winners — Lawrin (1938), Whirlaway (1941), Pensive (1944), Citation (1948), Ponder (1949) and Hill Gail (1952). Whirlaway and Citation both went on to take the Triple Crown.

Ranked among America's leading owners and breeders during the 1920s, Jones did much of his racing at the bush tracks, running his own horses in the West and in Mexico. He earned a reputation for scoring with two-year-olds. Jones became private trainer to Herbert Woolf in 1931 and in 1939 took over Calumet Farm. After 1946, his son Jimmy was credited with Calumet earnings, but, in 1952, it was Ben who topped the trainers' list for the fourth time, with a division of the stable's horses. In 1953 he turned over all the Calumet horses to Jimmy. Jones was inducted into the Hall of Fame in 1958.

Syd
LAIRD
b.— d.1988

The death of Syd Laird in 1988 robbed South African racing of one of its best and most colourful trainers. He was a giant of the turf who saddled a record seven winners of the country's most famous race, the Rothmans July Handicap, in a star-studded career that spanned nearly 30 years. He won the trainers' championship eight times and only twice failed to finish in the Top Ten in 28 years. Laird began his career in racing as a jockey but had no sooner qualified than he was forced to retire because of weight problems.

After seeing action in Egypt and Italy during World War II, Laird returned to South Africa and later became assistant to another great trainer, his uncle, Syd Garrett. Laird was granted a trainer's licence in 1959 and his first July Handicap winner came two years later with the outsider Kerason. He went on to saddle scores of feature race winners and became a legend in his own lifetime. An expert judge of a yearling, he trained a string of champions, including Colorado King, Politician, and Sea Cottage, who many rate as the greatest horse to have raced in South Africa.

Lucien
LAURIN
b.1913

When he stopped riding the old Montreal circuit in 1942, Lucien Laurin had met with only modest success. He turned to training and went from 16 successes in his first year to 42 winners in 1946. Laurin produced Riva Ridge to be a champion two-year-old (1971), a double Classic winner at three, and a champion handicapper at four. He gave racing its first Triple Crown winner for 25 years when Secretariat took the honours in 1973.

D. Wayne
LUKAS
b.1935

Darrell Wayne Lukas spent nine years coaching high-school basketball and two years as assistant coach at the University of Wisconsin before going into racing in 1966 with a mixture of throughbreds and quarter-horses. In 1972, he settled in California, where quarter-horses were his speciality until 1978. He trained 23 world champions.

After a Preakness Stakes success with Codex in 1980, Lukas surged to the top, reaching the climax of his career among thoroughbreds with the 1988 Kentucky Derby triumph of Winning Colors. She was only the third filly to win in 114 runnings of the race. Eclipse Award winner as America's outstanding trainer in 1985, 1986, and 1987, Lukas became the USA's leading money earner regularly from 1983, shattering Charlie Whittingham's record with $5.8 million in 1984. He almost doubled that figure the following year and in 1987, brought in $17.5 million. In 1986, he became the first trainer to earn more prize-money ($12.3 million) than the nation's leading jockey (José Santos).

Apart from Winning Colors, Lukas has had an abundance of star fillies, including ill-fated Landaluce (1982), Althea (1983), Life's Magic (1984, 1985), Family Style (1985), Lady's Secret (1986), North Sider (1987) and Sacahuista (1987). Tejano's Hollywood Futurity success in 1987 made the colt the first juvenile 'millionaire'. That year Lukas became the only man other than Lazaro Barrera (four times) to win the outstanding trainer Eclipse Award more than twice. He took three Breeders' Cup events at Churchill Downs in 1988, following doubles in 1985, 1986, and 1987.

Lukas's son, Jeffrey, has looked after the New York division of the California-based stable since 1983.

Donald 'Ginger' McCain is seldom short of words – or a smile. Legendary Grand National hero Red Rum put the trainer's small seaside stables on top of the world.

Donald
McCAIN
b.1930

Red-haired 'Ginger' McCain will go down in history as the used-car dealer who trained Red Rum to win a record three Grand Nationals on the broad sands of Southport, Lancashire. Stabled behind the showrooms in a suburban setting, Red Rum thrived in his environment and the trainer always had him bouncing with enthusiasm on Aintree's big day.

McCain resents being regarded as a one-horse trainer. A permit holder at first, he took out a full licence in 1967 and met with a measure of success, especially on northern tracks. Glenkiln won ten races for him and Honeygrove Banker looked like making a useful hurdler before suffering a set-back. A tall man with a wide smile, McCain's sense of humour kept him riding high when things got tough.

François
MATHET
b.1908 d.1983

François Mathet's nickname was Napoleon and he had several traits in common with that brilliant, irascible, little Corsican megalomaniac. He was, for example, extremely difficult to get on with and detested being beaten. A product of the Saint-Cyr Military Academy, Mathet was a bruising amateur rider who set an incredible record of 51 successes in one season (1936) and who reigned supreme over his peers for five years. At a period when patrol films and photo-finishes were a luxury of the future, 'gentleman-rider' Mathet was a formidable opponent. One leading professional jump jockey of the day went on record as threatening to 'gallop all over the so-and-so if he ever falls in my way!'

After serving as a cavalry officer (he was decorated with the Croix de Guerre), Mathet took out a trainer's licence in 1944, with a few of his own horses to run under both rules. He kept a few jumpers right up to 1957, by which time he had saddled 97 winners of National Hunt races. They went when he became champion Flat trainer for the first time, the first of 20 such titles.

François Dupré was Mathet's first major patron and this big owner-breeder had a huge string. Among the Dupré horses was future double Arc de Triomphe winner Tantième (1950 and 1951). Soon his jockeys – and he 'trained' some of the best including Jean Deforge and Yves Saint-Martin – were winning in the famous colours of such owners as Volterra, de Atucha, Plesch, the Aga

François Mathet was an abrasive character, a bruising amateur rider and a brilliant trainer. The Frenchman won the 1963 Epsom Derby with Relko and trained for many famous owners.

Khan, Rothschild, Hunt, and Niarchos.

At his death, Mathet was responsible for over 150 horses and had saddled some 4,000 winners, including the greatest Classics as well as scores of smaller races throughout the country. A very private man, his love of his job amounted almost to fanaticism. A hard task-master, Mathet was equally demanding of himself and, in parallel with his training stables, he built up a highly successful stud, giving the prefix 'Dom' to all his colts and 'Marie' to his fillies.

Stan
MELLOR
b.1937

Although a successful trainer since 1972, Stan Mellor is still remembered for his record 1,034 National Hunt winners in a riding career in which he started as an amateur in 1952. He retired from the saddle in 1972 after being champion jockey three times, in 1959–60, 1960–61 (when he had 118 winners) and 1961–2. His major successes included the Whitbread Gold Cup on Frenchman's Cove (1962); the King George VI Chase on Frenchman's Cove (1964) and Titus Oates (1969); and the Hennessy Cognac Gold Cup on Stalbridge Colonist (1966).

A jockey with a very individual riding style, and now a trainer with an eye for the Flat prizes as well as the jumps, Mellor won the 1985 Stewards' Cup with Al Trui. Under National Hunt Rules, he saddled Pollardstown (1979) and Saxon Farm (1983) to take the Triumph Hurdle and won two Whitbread Gold Cups, with Royal Mail (1980) and Lean Ar Aghaidh (1987).

Stan Mellor was a record-breaking jump jockey before he switched to training both National Hunt horses and Flat racers.

Frank
MERRILL
b.1919

Hall of Fame member Frank Merrill has been Canada's leading trainer 22 times and led the North American standings in 1955, 1958, and 1960. His best season was 1958, when he saddled 191 winners and received a Sovereign Award in 1978. He trained the 1977 three-year-old champion, Dance In Time, and his other outstanding horses include Puss 'N Boots, Aim 'N' Fire, Lord Vancouver, Hoso, and Greek Answer.

Terrance
MILLARD
b.— d.—

Terrance Millard's domination of feature races in recent years is unparalleled in South African Turf history. His training establishment is at Bloubergstrand, in the Cape, on the shores of the Atlantic Ocean, and he attributes much of his success to being able to have his horses swim in the sea.

A keen horseman who worked as a film stuntman in Britain before turning to training, Millard rose to prominence when he won the South African trainers' championship in 1969. His domination really began in 1982, when he took the championship for the second time, and he has since won the title four times in six years. Dedicated and eager to apply the most modern training methods, he has added a new dimension to training in South Africa.

Millard has saddled the winner in every major feature race and has won South Africa's biggest race, the Rothmans July Handicap, four times in the last six years. The Game Gold Cup, one of the top staying races, has gone to his runners five times in the same period. Not only do his runners win most of the major features, but they often finish 1–2 or 1–2–3, as in the 1986 July Handicap. Thoroughly professional, Millard has captured many of his feature race wins with horses bought in Argentina or the USA. During 1988 he took the trainers' title for the sixth time, with earnings of R3.1 million — a South African record.

Sven
von MITZLAFF
b.1915

Descended from a long line of Prussian cavalry officers, Sven von Mitzlaff, despite his height of well over six feet (1.8 m), was an excellent rider over jumps and three times leading amateur in Germany. After World War II, he went to the west with one thorough-bred, which he owned, trained, and rode to success in a valuable chase at Baden-Baden. This success put him on the map, and he moved to Cologne where he soon became established as one of the top trainers in the country.

Although never champion, von Mitzlaff invariably filled the runner-up spot behind his neighbour Heinz Jentzsch, and his record in the Classics was even better than that of Jentzsch. Altogether he won the German Derby seven times, including four times for his principal owner, Gestüt Zoppenbroich. He was particularly successful with three-year-old fillies, and trained both Kandia and Las Vegas, the only fillies to have beaten the colts in a German Group 1 race in the past 30 years. He retired at the beginning of the 1987 season because of ill health, having saddled a total of 1,764 winners.

Sir Noel
MURLESS
b.1910 d.1987

Noel Murless was one of the world's greatest trainers. Nine times Britain's top trainer, he won 19 English Classics and two in Ireland. In 1967, he became the first in his own country to pass £200,000 in prize money in a season — the third time he had broken the record.

Murless learned under the Irish Hartigan brothers, Frank and Hubert, before setting up on his own at Hambleton Lodge, Yorkshire, in 1935. He followed Fred Darling at Beck-hampton in 1947, but although leading trainer for the first time in 1948, when he took the 1,000 Guineas with Queenpot, he never settled in Wiltshire. So, in 1952, he switched to Warren Place, Newmarket, from where he sent out a stream of winners.

The son of a Cheshire farmer, Murless won the Derby with Crepello (1957), St Paddy (1960) and Royal Palace (1967). His first Oaks triumph, by Carozza in 1957, was followed by Petite Etoile (1959), Lupe (1970), Altesse Royale (1971) and Mysterious (1973). St Leger honours went to Ridge Wood (1949), St Paddy (1960) and Aurelius (1961). Crepello (1957) and Royal Palace (1967) took the 2,000 Guineas and Petite Etoile (1959), Fleet (1967), Caergwrle (1968), Altesse Royale (1971) and Mysterious (1973) followed Queenpot to 1,000 Guineas glory.

At the end of a brilliant career, Murless commented: 'I have known four greats in my time — Abernant, Petite Etoile, Crepello and Gordon Richards.' Abernant was one of the fastest horses in living memory. On the retirement of Sir Gordon in 1954, Murless overlooked the misdemeanours of young Lester Piggott and in their opening season together the jockey topped 100 winners for

the first time. Murless retired in 1976, when Warren Place was bought by his son-in-law, Henry Cecil. He was knighted in the 1977 Jubilee honours.

Vincent
O'BRIEN
b.1917

If there is an Everest in racing, it has been climbed by Vincent O'Brien. The breadth of his success in both the Flat and National Hunt fields puts him among the greatest. O'Brien's record in the Classics, which includes the 1970 Triple Crown with Nijinsky, would be enough to satisfy the most demanding of trainers, but add to that his dominance in earlier years of the big jumping prizes and he presents all the credentials of a master craftsman.

O'Brien made his approach to six victorious Derby days at Epsom via the battlefields of Aintree and Cheltenham. Especially Cheltenham, where four Gold Cups, three Champion Hurdles, and Festival feasts of smaller fry (ten Gloucester Hurdles!) made him a March hare hard to catch. Cottage Rake pulled off a hat-trick in Cheltenham's chasing Classic in 1948, 1949, and 1950. Hatton's Grace completed the big hurdle

Sir Noel Murless was Britain's leading trainer nine times, and sent out 19 Classic winners between 1948 and 1973.

treble in 1949, 1950, and 1951.

There was stern stuff behind the twinkling eye and the soft brogue of this man from Tipperary and in 1953 he achieved the Gold Cup-Grand National double with Knock Hard and Early Mist. It seemed that Early Mist gave him a taste for Aintree. He was back in 1954 (Royal Tan) and 1955 (Quare Times) for another remarkable hat-trick. And then, in 1959, he finally put his jumpers in the out-tray to concentrate on the Flat.

The mixed stable had already produced Irish Derby winner Chamier (1953), but it was Ballymoss, in 1957, who gave the first hint of what was to come, when he took the 1957 English St Leger. He was back the following year to win the Eclipse, King George VI and Queen Elizabeth Stakes, and the Arc de Triomphe, which the stable went on to win twice more with Alleged (1977 and 1978). O'Brien became only the fifth man to train a winner of the Derby and Grand National when Larkspur scored at Epsom in 1962. And when Prince of Birds took the 1988 Irish 2,000 Guineas it was the Cashel stable's 43rd Classic winner in Europe.

The success of the 1970s could not be matched in the next decade and with a change in fortunes came a change in the trainer's set-up. After Stavros Niarchos pulled out of the stable's big-spending syndicate, O'Brien went public. A Dublin firm of brokers put together a package worth IR£10 million and investors bought into the company, Classic Thoroughbreds, at 30p per share. Thirty-eight yearlings were bought for IR£7.5 million. The company's colours were successfully carried for the first time in 1988.

Ireland's Vincent O'Brien is always the centre of attention. He listens more than he talks and his achievements are other men's dreams. Epsom Derbys, Aintree Grand Nationals, Cheltenham Gold Cups, Arc de Triomphes – he has won them all in his long career.

O'Brien's classic winners were: **Derby**: Larkspur (1962), Sir Ivor (1968), Nijinsky (1970), Roberto (1972), The Minstrel (1977), Golden Fleece (1982); **Oaks**: Long Look (1965), Valoris (1966); **St Leger**: Ballymoss (1957), Nijinsky (1970), Boucher (1972); **2,000 Guineas**: Sir Ivor (1968), Nijinsky (1970), Lomond (1983), El Gran Señor (1984); **1,000 Guineas**: Glad Rags (1966); **Irish Derby**: Chamier (1953), Ballymoss (1957), Nijinsky (1970), The Minstrel (1977), El Gran Señor (1984), Law Society (1985); **Irish 1,000 Guineas**: Valoris (1966), Lady Capulet (1977), Godetia (1979); **Irish 2,000 Guineas**: El Toro (1959), Jaazeiro (1978), Kings Lake (1981), Sadler's Wells (1984), Prince of Birds (1988); **Irish Oaks**: Ancasta (1964), Aurabella (1965), Gala (1969), Godetia (1979); **Irish St Leger**: Barclay (1959), White Gloves (1966), Reindeer (1969), Caucasus (1975), Meneval (1976), Transworld (1977), Gonzales (1980), Leading Counsel (1985); **French Derby**: Caerleon (1983).

Tom PAYTEN
b.1855 d.1920

One of 12 children, Tom Payten began training in Sydney in 1886 at the age of 31. In four years, he saddled 77 winners of feature races for the Hon James White, including four Derbys, three Oaks, seven St Legers, and six Sires' Produce Stakes. One of Payten's most notable achievements was to fill the first four places from his five runners in a two-year-old race in 1891. His other horse was last.

All told, Payten won the AJC Derby five times; the Victoria Derby four times; the Sydney Cup three times; the AJC Metropolitan three times; the AJC Epsom twice; the Australian Cup six times; the Ascot Vale Stakes three times; and the Champion Stakes once. His best horse was Abercorn, who beat Carbine on several occasions.

Angel PENNA
b.1923

A confirmed admirer of Napoleon, Buenos Aires-born Angel Penna has been a conqueror in three continents of the world. The leading trainer in Argentina (1952) and France (1974), he has won many great races.

After working for his trainer father in Argentina, he moved to Venezuela in 1954, but left his Caracas stables for the USA in 1961 to team up with such owners as Gustave Ring and William Levin. Penna's first winner in the USA was Ben Cover (1953), who had

travelled to Laurel with Washington DC International challenger, Mr Black. He went to France in 1972 to train for Countess Margit Batthyany and quickly gave her an Arc de Triomphe victory with San San (1972). Later, he joined Paris art dealer Daniel Wildenstein, who owned most of Penna's big winners in Europe. Among them was the exceptional filly Allez France, who won the Arc de Triomphe in 1974. She was the first of her sex to earn more than $1 million.

Penna's greatest year was 1976, when his French stables won three English Classics, with Flying Water (1,000 Guineas), Pawneese (Epsom Oaks) and Crow (St Leger). Pawneese returned to Britain that season to take the King George VI and Queen Elizabeth Stakes. The trainer's winnings were £240,000, only £21,000 short of Britain's champion trainer, Henry Cecil. In 1978, Penna returned to the USA to train for Ogden Phipps, and eight years later opened his own public stables. His biggest disappointment was the defeat of Bold Reason in the 1971 Kentucky Derby.

Martin PIPE
b.1945

Somerset trainer Martin Pipe has developed one of the most comprehensive training establishments in Britain since he was granted a licence in 1977. It includes an equine swimming pool, an indoor lunging ring, and its own all-weather gallop.

Pipe won the 1981 Triumph Hurdle with Baron Blakeney and on the Flat was successful in the 1983 Ascot Stakes (Right Regent) and the 1985 Windsor Castle Stakes (Atall Atall). He broke Michael Dickinson's National Hunt training record by saddling 129 winners in the 1987–8 season. They included Beau Ranger (Mackeson Gold Cup). Pipe's previous best total was 106 in 1986–7. On 29 December 1988 he reached a record-breaking fastest 100 winners for a season.

Jenny PITMAN
b.1946

Granted a licence in 1975, Jenny Pitman, formerly the wife of Fred Winter's ex-jockey, Richard Pitman, is the most successful woman trainer in National Hunt racing. She has won many of Britain's major steeplechases, including the 1983 Grand National (Corbière), the 1984 Gold Cup (Burrough Hill Lad) and 3 Welsh Nationals (Corbière, 1982, Burrough Hill Lad, 1983, and Stearsby, 1986).

Etienne POLLET
b.1912

French trainer Etienne Pollet learned his trade under the tuition of Jack Cunnington. He became leading trainer of the area bounded by Bordeaux, Pau, and Toulouse, but he was ambitious and in 1944 moved north to set up in Chantilly. The first few years in the Paris area were a struggle (1945 produced only nine winners), but Pollet persevered and by 1957 was a force to be reckoned with. He did not believe in 100-horse yards. Instead he had the quality of horse it took to win Classics. Top owner-breeders, like Mme Couturié, kept him supplied with potentially high-class youngsters.

Sea Bird II (1965 Epsom Derby and Arc de Triomphe) is still considered by many to have been the greatest horse of the century. But Pollet trained many other good animals, including Pan, Prudent, Right Royal V (French Derby), Thunderhead (English 2,000 Guineas), La Sorellina (French Oaks and Arc de Triomphe), Tahiti (French Oaks), Altipan (Grand Prix de Paris), Tyrone (French 2,000 Guineas), and Vaguely Noble (Arc de Triomphe). A brilliant handler of two-year-olds, Pollet also saddled no fewer than seven winners of the Prix de la Salamandre. A lifetime bachelor, he hung up his trainer's boots in 1970 on the last day's racing of the year at Longchamp.

Jenny Pitman, Britain's most successful woman trainer, seen here with her great Cheltenham Gold Cup champion, Burrough Hill Lad. She broke down in tears in 1988 when she lost her 1983 Grand National hero, Corbière.

Paddy
PRENDERGAST
b.1909 d.1980

One of Ireland's greatest trainers, Paddy Prendergast enjoyed nothing better than to raid British meetings, especially Royal Ascot, York, Goodwood, and Chester. Known as 'P.J.', or sometimes as 'Darkie', he was a jump jockey of little renown before starting his training career in 1940 with just two horses, Spratstown and Rare Rajah. But the horse who really sent him on his way was Pelorus, a three-year-old he bought for £150. Pelorus won 17 races for him, including six 'off the reel', and ran with much success both over jumps and on the Flat.

In 1945, Prendergast bought a yearling filly for 420 guineas. Called Port Blanc, she came to Goodwood to win the Harvest Stakes and provided the trainer with his first success in England. She was the forerunner of many good two-year-olds, owned mostly by Americans who wanted a quick return for their money. And this they got. Prendergast made his mark in Britain again in 1951 with Windy City's triumph in the Gimcrack Stakes. The horse was also the second of seven successive Phoenix Plate winners for the stable, which took the Gimcrack four times in 15 years.

The Pie King came to Royal Ascot in 1953 and became the first of Prendergast's six

Paddy 'P.J.' Prendergast launched many successful raids on Britain from his base in Ireland. He was one of Europe's greatest trainers.

winners of the Coventry Stakes in 17 years. Another of the trainer's favourite races was the Champagne Stakes, which he won five times between 1959 and 1966. Daemon (1955) was the first of his five triumphs in the Chester Vase, but he had to wait until Martial's 2,000 Guineas victory in 1960 to open his account in the English Classics, having already won the Irish Derby twice, with Dark Warrior (1950) and Thirteen of Diamonds (1952).

The golden year was 1963. In all, he won six Classics in the season, including the Epsom Oaks with Noblesse and the Doncaster St Leger with Ragusa. The stable took the Eclipse Stakes with Khalkis and, to top it all, Prendergast was leading trainer in both England and Ireland. In 1964, when he was British champion again, he won the 1,000 Guineas with Pourparler and the Eclipse with Ragusa. But he did not need Classic triumphs to take the title for a third time, in 1965. His main successes that year were with Meadow Court (King George VI and Queen Elizabeth Stakes) and Carlemont (Sussex Stakes). Between 1950 and 1965 he trained 12 of Ireland's top 16 two-year-olds.

Apart from crossing swords with the Jockey Club in 1953 over the running of Blue Sail, Prendergast had a mostly smooth and profitable passage in England.

Prendergast had 17 Classic triumphs in Ireland. They were: **Irish Derby**: Dark Warrior (1950), Thirteen of Diamonds (1952), Ragusa (1963) and Meadow Court (1965); **2,000 Guineas**: Kythnos (1960), Linacre (1963), Ballymore (1972) and Nikoli (1980); **1,000 Guineas**: Princess Trudy (1950), Gazpacho (1963), Wenduyne (1969), Sarah Siddons (1976) and More So (1978); **Oaks**: Five Spots (1952); **Irish St Leger**: Arctic Vale (1962), Christmas Island (1963) and Mistigri (1974).

Ryan
PRICE
b.1912 d.1986

Talk to Ryan Price about gamblers in his stable and he would put on the look of a man affronted. 'Never bet more than a tenner in my life,' became a stock phrase. But there is no doubt that some of his owners pulled off big coups, especially over the jumps. A fearless and accomplished point-to-point rider, Price took out a trainer's licence in 1937 and, after serving as a Commando, saddled his first post-war winner, Broken Tackle, in a selling handicap chase at Plumpton on 18 May 1946. Sussex was always his favourite county and it was after training at Wisborough Green and Lavant that he settled at Findon in 1951. In the 1952–3 season, he saddled 78 winners and his £15,358 prize money came second by only £157 to Vincent O'Brien's total.

Top trainer in 1954–5, 1958–9, 1961–2, 1965–6, and 1966–7, Price won the Champion Hurdle with Clair Soleil (1955), Fare Time (1959) and Eborneezer (1961). His biggest triumph followed with the 1962 Grand National success of Kilmore, and in 1969 he took the Cheltenham Gold Cup with What A Myth. One of his greatest, and most controversial, achievements was to win the Schweppes Gold Trophy hurdle race four times out of its first five runnings. Rosyth's second Schweppes success, in February 1964, brought about Price's disqualification from training. Although his stable was completely disbanded, he was back again with a licence at the start of the next season.

Le Vermontois won the race in 1966, but it was the victory of Hill House a year later that had Price in trouble again. The Newbury stewards did not accept his explanation over the improvement in form and, after Hill House failed a dope test, it took six months of intensive investigation to discover that the horse manufactured his own cortisone. Price was exonerated.

Price, who had trained his first Flat winner, Fala, way back in 1953, created a shock in 1970 when he decided to hand over his National Hunt horses to Josh Gifford. In 1971, Price turned all his attention to the Flat, winning the 1972 Oaks with Ginevra and the 1975 St Leger with Bruni. He retired in 1982 and died four years later.

Fred
RIMELL
b.1913 d.1981

Fred Rimell was a British National Hunt champion jockey and leading trainer. Apprenticed to his father, Tom, at Kinnersley, he rode successfully on the Flat before switching in 1932 to jumping. He was champion jockey in 1938–9, 1939–40, 1944–5, and 1945–6. When injury forced him to retire from the saddle in 1947, he had already held a trainer's licence for two years. One of racing's most popular and respected characters, he had a magnificent record at Aintree, winning four Grand Nationals, with E.S.B. (1956), Nicolaus Silver (1961), Gay Trip (1970) and Rag Trade (1976). In 1976, he completed the Cheltenham Gold Cup-Grand National double.

Champion trainer in 1960–1, 1968–9, 1969–70, and 1975–6, Rimell always claimed that it did not take an out-and-out stayer to win the National. He proved it with handsome little Gay Trip, who had never won beyond 2½ miles (4 km) before his Aintree triumph. Other big winners included; **Cheltenham Gold Cup**: Woodland Venture (1967), Royal Frolic (1976); **Champion Hurdle**: Comedy of Errors (1973 and 1975); **Whitbread Gold Cup**: Andy Pandy (1977);

*Fred Rimell (**left**) was one of Britain's most popular and successful National Hunt trainers. Four Grand National winners gave him a sparkling record at Aintree.*

Irish Sweeps Hurdle: Normandy (1969), Comedy of Errors (1973 and 1974).

Rimell's wife, Mercy, who had been his assistant trainer, carried on with a licence at Kinnersley on the death of her husband. She won the 1983 Champion Hurdle with Gaye Brief.

Robert
ROBSON
b.1765 d.1838

Trainer of 34 Classic winners, Robert Robson shares with John Porter and Fred Darling the distinction of saddling seven Epsom Derby heroes. They were: Waxy (1793), Tyrant (1802), Pope (1809), Whalebone (1810), Whisker (1815), Azor (1817) and Emilius (1823). This total still stands as a record and the only trainer to have approached it in modern times is Vincent O'Brien, with six.

James
ROWE Sr
b.1857 d.1929

Later to become America's greatest trainer, James Rowe was introduced to racing at the age of ten by Colonel David McDaniel, on whose horses he became leading jockey three times (1871–3). He took the Belmont Stakes twice as a jockey, on Joe Daniels and Springbok, and eight times as a trainer.

While training for Mike and Phil Dwyer (1879–85) Rowe was in charge of Miss Woodford, America's first $100,000 winner. Other champions were Hindoo, Luke Blackburn, Bramble, Onondaga, George Kinney, and Runnymede. That job led to his becoming a starter in New York and a steward in California. August Belmont I

Another winner for Australia's record breaker, Tommy Smith. His magnificent achievements include two triumphs in the coveted Melbourne Cup.

then took him (1888–90) to train champions Raceland, Fides, Potomac, and La Tosca. For L. S. and W. P. Thompson, Rowe produced 1897 champion L'Alouette and for James R. Keene, between 1900 and 1912, he trained champions Commando, Sysonby, unbeaten Colin, Peter Pan, Delhi, Court Dress, Ballot, Maskette, and Sweep. Between 1913 and 1929, his champions for H. P. Whitney were Regret, Whisk Broom II, Borrow, Dominant, Rosie O'Grady, Johren, Vexatious, Tryster, Prudery, Mother Goose, Maud Muller, Whiskery, and Whichone.

There is no doubt which horse Rowe thought was the greatest. He wanted his epitaph to read simply: 'He trained Colin.' The trainer was inducted into the Hall of Fame in 1955.

James
SCOBIE
b.1860 d.1940

A trainer until the age of 70, James Scobie had his first winner in 1880, at Flemington, when Zephyr scored over hurdles. He went on to take four Melbourne Cups, with Clean Sweep (1900), King Ingoda (1922), Bitalli (1923), and Trivalve (1927). He also saddled five consecutive winners of the Victoria Derby, which he won seven times in all. Other successes included the VRC Sires' Produce (six times), VRC Ascot Vale Stakes (12 times), Australian Cup (four times), Champion Stakes (three times), and the VRC Oaks (four times). Scobie had the nickname of 'Handsome Jim'.

Jonathan
SHEPPARD
b.1940

An Englishman born near Newmarket, Jonathan Sheppard has been a workaholic since he started to train steeplechasers in the USA in 1966. He is now out on his own with a record $4 million in prize money. Sheppard was educated at Eton and worked on the Stock Exchange before landing in the USA in 1961. He joined the legendary Burly Cocks at his Unionville, Pennsylvania, farm for nine months and, after a brief return to England, rode the trainer's horses to some 25 victories.

Sheppard earned Eclipse Awards with Athenian Idol (1973), Café Prince (1977 and 1978), Martie's Anger (1979), and Flatterer (1983–6). Flatterer, who was second to See You Then in Cheltenham's 1987 Champion Hurdle, ran up a record four consecutive victories in the Colonial Cup (1983–6) and in 1983 became the first horse to win American Steeplechasing's Triple Crown. Although completely dominant in the jumping game, Sheppard saddled Storm Cat to win the prestigious Young America Flat race and the same horse was beaten by only a nose in the 1985 Breeders' Cup Juvenile. Sheppard, who claims not to have switched on a television set for 25 years, spends much of his time travelling from his Unionville farm to supervise 100 horses stabled at various tracks.

Tommy
SMITH
b.1918

A horse called Bragger put Tommy Smith on the road to stardom when he won at Rosehill on 14 March 1942. Smith went on to win a record 33 straight Sydney premierships and, in doing so, broke every training record on the Australian calendar. His feats include training of horses in a Trifecta (horses placed first, second, and third) on seven occasions; training a record 43 two-year-old winners in one season (1984–5); and winning six races on one card at Randwick in 1972 while scoring another success at Eagle Farm on the same day.

Smith has trained a record 32 Derby winners and won more than 5,000 races, including 4,000 in the Sydney Metropolitan area. His record season was 186 winners and his big race successes include: Melbourne Cup (twice); Caulfield Cup (four times); AJC Derby (nine times); Victoria Derby (five times); W. S. Cox Plate (seven times); Australian Cup (three times); AJC Metropolitan (seven times); Epsom Handicap (seven times); Doncaster Handicap (six times);

Sydney Cup (three times); Rosehill Guineas (nine times); Rothmans Hundred Thousand (five times), and the Golden Slipper (five times). Smith turned himself into a public company in 1986, naming it 'Tulloch Lodge' after his greatest ever performer, Tulloch. He was associated with Australia's first $1 million winner, Kingston Town, as well as Bounding Away, Australia's highest two-year-old-stakes winner.

Joseph 'Yonnie' STARR
b.1905

A member of the Canadian Hall of Fame, Yonnie Starr had his initial success training for Conn Smythe, before reaching his peak with Jean-Louis Lévesque. Russian-born Starr trained North American champion two-year-old filly, La Prévoyante, who was also Canada's 1972 Horse of the Year. Other champions he saddled were Ace Marine (1955), Wonder Where (1959), Fanfreluche (1970), L'Enjoleur (1974 and 1975), and L'Alézane (1977).

Starr, who was at first a jockey's agent to such outstanding riders as Par Remillard, George Seabo, Red Pollard, Frankie Mann and Eddie Litzenberger, has to his credit as a trainer success in the Queen's Plate with Ace Marine (1955), Caledon Beau (1958), Jammed Lovely (1967), and L'Enjoleur (1975).

Woodward STEPHENS
b.1913

'Woody' Stephens saddled his first winner, Bronze Bugle, at Keeneland in 1940, but three years later moved to New York and has been there ever since. The title of his auto-biography, *Guess I'm Lucky*, does not reflect the talent of the man. He began his career, at the age of 13, by breaking yearlings for a banker in Midway, Kentucky, Stephens's home state. He went on to become a jockey, winning his first race on Directly, in 1931. Eventually, he became too heavy to ride, and joined trainer John S. Ward as assistant.

Top US trainer in 1983, Stephens won a record five consecutive Belmont Stakes with Conquistador Cielo (1982), Caveat, Swale, Crème Fraîche, and Danzig Connection. Of the fifth triumph he said: 'I knew when my horse crossed the finish line I had set a record that would never be broken.' The hero of the 100th Kentucky Derby with Cannonade (1974), he was presented with the trophy by Princess Margaret. He won the Derby again with Swale (1984) and a street in Midway is named in his honour.

Stephens, elected to racing's Hall of Fame in 1976, trained champions including Bald Eagle (1960), Never Bend (1962), Sensational (1976), Smart Angle (1979), Heavenly Cause (1980), Conquistador Cielo (1982), Devil's Bag (1983), Swale (1984), and Forty Niner (1987). Bald Eagle took the Washington DC International in consecutive years (1959 and 1960).

Michael STOUTE
b.1945

Barbados-born Michael Stoute has made a significant impact on British racing since he took out a licence to train at Newmarket in 1972. Pat Rohan, Doug Smith, and Tom Jones, who all taught him the business, must have done their job well. He was still only 27 when Alphadamus gave him his first good prize, in the 1973 Stewards' Cup, and in 1978 Oaks heroine Fair Salinia started him off on the Classic trail.

Ill-fated superhorse Shergar brought off the English–Irish Derby double in 1981, when Stoute was top trainer for the first time. Shareef Dancer (Irish Derby, 1983) and Shadeed (2,000 Guineas, 1985) preceded another title in 1986. Stoute became the second trainer, after Henry Cecil, to pass the

Michael Stoute was Britain's champion in 1981 and 1986. He became only the second trainer to win more than £1 million in prize money.

£1 million prize-money mark, and his total set a new record. That was the year when Shahrastani completed the English–Irish Derby double, with other major successes coming from Colorspin (Irish Oaks), Sonic Lady (Irish 1,000 Guineas, Sussex Stakes, and Coronation Stakes), Shardari (Matchmaker International), and Ajdal (Dewhurst Stakes).

Stoute rectified his original assessment of Ajdal in 1987. Fourth in the 2,000 Guineas and ninth in the Epsom Derby, the colt was then put to sprinting and took both the July Cup and the William Hill Sprint. That same year, Unite won the English and Irish Oaks, while Milligram scored in both the Coronation Stakes and Queen Elizabeth II Stakes. The stable had 105 winners and again passed £1 million, but it was good enough for only second place behind Henry Cecil, who was on his most devastating form. Doyoun's triumph in the 2,000 Guineas of 1988 had a mixed reception and he was third in the Derby.

Fulke Walwyn extended his hospitality across the world when he met Japan's 1966 Aintree Grand National entry, Fujino-O, at London Airport. He stabled the jumper at his Berkshire yard.

Alec
TAYLOR
b.1862 d.1943

The leading trainer in Britain 12 times, Alec Taylor took over the Manton stables from his father in 1902. He was top of the list in 1907, 1909, 1910, 1914, 1917–23, and again in 1925, two years before he retired.

Taylor won 21 Classics, including the Triple Crown twice — in 1917 with Gay Crusader and 1918 with Gainsborough. His Classic winners were: **Derby**: Lemberg (1910), Gay Crusader (1917), and Gainsborough (1918); **Oaks**: Rosedrop (1910), Sunny Jane (1917), My Dear (1918), Bayuda (1919), Love In Idleness (1921), Pogrom (1922), Saucy Sue (1925), and Short Story (1926); **1,000 Guineas**: Saucy Sue (1925); **2,000 Guineas**: Kennymore (1914), Gay Crusader (1917), Gainsborough (1918), and Craig an Eran (1921); **St Leger**: Challacombe (1905), Bayardo (1909), Gay Crusader (1917), Gainsborough (1918), and Book Law (1927).

Federico
TESIO
b.1869 d.1954

Turin-born Federico Tesio dominated training and breeding in Italy as owner and manager of the Dormello Stud and racing stable. He bred and/or trained the winners of the Gran Premio di Milano (23 times), the Derby Italiano (22 times), the Premio d'Italia (21 times), and the Criterium Nazionale (21 times), a record that cannot be matched anywhere in the world.

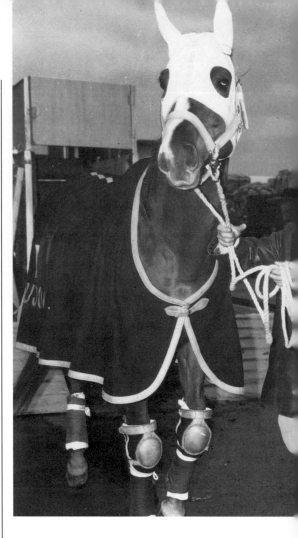

Tesio went to school at Barnabite College, in Moncalieri, and grew up in the Piedmont area. An orphan soon after birth, he first appeared on a racecourse as an amateur rider, aged 22, and became stable jockey to ex-royal jockey Tom Rook. The partnership helped Tesio to become champion amateur in Italy. Planning for his future, Tesio began to import mares in 1893 which would form the base of the Dormello Stud. He bought in his own country, as well as in France and Britain.

Tesio began training and racing his home-bred horses before the turn of the century, but his first Dormello crop of importance arrived in 1901. The batch of two-year-olds that raced in 1903 included Workington's daughter, Verrocchia, who was top-rated juvenile of her year. She became Tesio's first runner in the Derby Italiano (1904) and finished a creditable fourth.

But it was not until 1909 that Tesio's stable dominated a season. That year saw the start of a supremacy in domestic racing that was to last until 1923. At the end of 1909, he had trained the leading colt (Fidia) and filly (Angelica Kauffman) as well as the top-rated two-year-old Tanagra. The floodgates opened. Tesio trained the winners of four of the next five Italian Derbys (1911, 1912, 1914, and 1915) and won the race again in 1917 with Giampietrina. From 1919, he had five consecutive successes in the race.

Tesio began to challenge abroad in the 1920s. Scopas scored the trainer's first foreign victory, in the Coupe d'Or de Maisons-Laffitte, and Apelle won the Critérium de

Maisons-Laffitte in 1925. In 1932, Tesio and the Incisa families merged and the trainer worked under the Tesio-Incisa name. The combination had an immediate reward when Jacopa del Sellaio took the Derby Italiano.

The end of 1936 saw the start of Tesio's greatest period as a trainer, thanks to Donatello, El Greco, and Nearco. Donatello retired in June 1937, by which time Nearco was unbeaten in seven races, Donatello was undefeated in four starts, and El Greco lost only to Donatello. Nearco followed his Derby Italiano victory with Tesio's biggest foreign win to date in the Grand Prix de Paris of 1938, when his filly Bistolfi took the Prix d'Ispahan.

Tesio died in May 1954 — sadly before the success of Botticelli in the Ascot Gold Cup (1955) and the victories of his most famous home-bred, Ribot, in two Prix de l'Arc de Triomphe (1955 and 1956) and the King George VI and Queen Elizabeth Stakes (1956).

Jack
VAN BERG
b.1936

Nebraska-born Jack Van Berg has saddled more winners than any other trainer in the world. He began working with horses at the age of 13 and was still a teenager when he had his first success. He took over the entire stables of his famous father, Marion, in 1971.

Van Berg won a record 496 races in 1976,

when he also led the country for both winners and prize-money earnings. He was the first trainer to bring off that double. Eclipse outstanding trainer of 1984, he was introduced into racing's Hall of Fame in 1985, and in 1987 became the first to train 5,000 winners. He was in line for a $5 million bonus and a place in history as trainer of a Triple Crown winner when his 1987 Kentucky Derby and Preakness Stakes hero, Alysheba, went to Belmont Park for the clincher, but could finish only fourth. Van Berg and Alysheba also missed the winner's share of a $3 million purse five months later when the colt was beaten a nose by Horse of the Year, Ferdinand, in the Breeders' Cup Classic.

Van Berg, who led the nation in winners for eight years, supervises more than 150 horses, and there are divisions of his stables in California, Arkansas, Louisiana, Nebraska, Kentucky, and Illinois. Communications cost him $50,000 per year in airline expenses and $3,000 a month in telephone charges. Bill Mott and Frank Brothers are among his former assistants who have gone on to national recognition.

Fulke
WALWYN
b.1910

One of only three men to ride and saddle a Grand National winner, royal trainer Fulke Walwyn has been charming the National Hunt scene with his warm personality and dazzling it with his skills for more than 50 years. Throughout his military career at Sandhurst, and with the 9th Lancers, he was a leading amateur rider. In 1936 his friend, Major Noel Furlong, gave him the Grand National mount on Reynoldstown, who had won the race the previous year. Reynoldstown obliged again and the following season Walwyn turned professional, only to be told his riding days were over after he fractured his skull in a fall at Ludlow in 1938. Walwyn responded to the bad news by taking out a trainer's licence at Lambourn and, when he went to war in 1939, had saddled 18 winners. It speaks volumes for his courage that, in 1946, he took on that heavyweight millionairess and ferocious gambler, Miss Dorothy Paget, as an owner. When she died, in 1960, he had saddled 365 winners in her colours.

Walwyn won the 1964 Grand National with little Team Spirit and was leading trainer five times. He started to train for Queen Elizabeth the Queen Mother in 1973. His other major successes include: **Cheltenham Gold Cup**: Mont Tremblant (1952), Mandarin (1962), Mill House (1963), The Dikler (1973); **Champion Hurdle**: Anzio (1962), Kirriemuir (1965); **King George VI Chase**: Rowland Roy (1947), Mandarin (1957 and 1959), Mill House (1963), The Dikler (1971); **Whitbread Gold Cup**: Taxidermist (1958), Mill House

Jack Van Berg outstrips the world for the number of winners he has saddled. He was the first trainer to reach the 5,000 mark, and won a record 496 races in 1976.

61

(1967), Charlie Potheen (1973), The Dikler (1974), Diamond Edge (1979 and 1981), Special Cargo (1984); **Hennessy Cognac Gold Cup**: Mandarin (1957), Taxidermist (1958), Mandarin (1961), Mill House (1963), Man of the West (1968), Charlie Potheen (1972), Diamond Edge (1981).

of Equipalazone were found in his system. First again in 1972, Rock Roi lost the race for interference to Erimo Hawk. Of all the trainer's triumphs, none was more memorable than Grundy's narrow defeat of Bustino in the 1975 King George VI and Queen Elizabeth Stakes.

Peter WALWYN
b.1933

Peter Walwyn was educated into racing by Geoffrey Brooke after formal schooling at Charterhouse, and was not above putting his hand to anything, including mowing the lawn. He went to Brooke in 1953, helped to supervise such good horses as Our Babu, Rustam, and Idle Rocks, and was eventually promoted to acting head lad. After three years there, he held the licence for his cousin, Helen Johnson Houghton.

Walwyn set up on his own at Lambourn in 1960. The first horse offered to him was that great campaigner Be Hopeful, who went on to win 27 races. In 1965, he moved to Lambourn's Seven Barrows stable and in 1970 won his first Classic with Humble Duty (1,000 Guineas). Walwyn was champion trainer in the years that Polygamy won the Oaks (1974) and Grundy won the Derby (1975). He has done well with many good horses, but had cruel luck with Rock Roi, who was twice disqualified from first place in the Ascot Gold Cup. After the 1971 race, 6 g

Dermot WELD
b.1948

No wonder Dublin's Phoenix Park is Dermot Weld's favourite racecourse. At the early July meeting there, in 1985 and 1986, he trained five winners on the two six-race cards. A qualified vet, he learned the training business under his father, Charles, and spent about a year in Australia with Tommy Smith. Weld was a top-class amateur rider. Champion in 1969, 1971, and 1972, he had winners abroad, in the USA, France, South Africa, and England. They included the Moët and Chandon Silver Magnum at Epsom.

Ireland's champion trainer in 1984, 1985, and 1986, Weld led the field 12 times for the number of races won and, in 1985, his 136 victories were, at that time, a record for this century in both Britain and Ireland. Weld has won seven Classics, including the 1981 Epsom and Irish Oaks with Blue Wind. His other successes were in the Irish 1,000 Guineas (twice), the Irish 2,000 Guineas, and the Italian 2,000 Guineas (twice). The stable sometimes has the occasional good jumper to

Dermot Weld has good reason to smile. He has claimed Classics in his native Ireland, as well as England and Italy, and his stable repeatedly tops the table for races won.

keep its interest going through the winter, but Weld's greatest National Hunt victory was in the 1988 Irish Grand National, with Perris Valley. He was the only chaser then in training at the yard which, in the past, housed Aintree Grand National specialist Greasepaint.

Charles
WHITTINGHAM
b.1913

The top stakes winner of all time, Charlie Whittingham began his outstanding career in 1934 after being a part-time trainer. After World War II service with the Marines in the Pacific, he worked for Horatio Luro in New York before signing on for Liz Tippett's Llangollen Farm.

Winner of more $100,000 races than any other trainer, Whittingham saddled three horses in the Hollywood Gold Cup for three different owners and finished 1–2–3 with Kennedy Road, Quack, and Cougar II. Nicknamed 'Bald Eagle', he was Eclipse outstanding trainer in 1971 and again in 1982. Voted into racing's Hall of Fame in 1974, he has trained for an assortment of famous people, including Greer Garson, Judy Garland, Burt Bacharach, Nelson Bunker Hunt, George Steinbrenner, and Robert Sangster.

Whittingham was the first trainer ever to top earnings of $4 million for one year (1982) and then made it a habit. He won national titles with Porterhouse (top two-year-old 1953); Ack Ack (Horse of the Year, sprinter, and top older horse 1971); Turkish Trousers (three-year-old filly 1971); Cougar II (grass horse 1972); Perrault (grass horse 1982); Estrapade (female grass horse 1986); and Ferdinand (Horse of the Year 1987). He became the oldest trainer, at 73, to win a Kentucky Derby when Ferdinand, only his third runner in the race, scored in 1986. The horse went on to take the Breeders' Cup Classic and the Hollywood Gold Cup the following year. When applying for his credentials in New York, 'Bald Eagle' listed his hair colour as brown. 'That's the way I remember it,' he explained.

Fred
WINTER
b.1926

Fred Winter shares with the late Fred Rimell the distinction of having been both National Hunt champion jockey and top trainer. He served his apprenticeship with both his father, Fred, and H. Jelliss. He rode his first winner, Tam O'Shanter, at Salisbury on 14 May 1940, at the age of 13, and worked in a

factory in World War II before being commissioned as a paratrooper. When he was demobbed, Winter was too heavy to ride on the Flat again and his first success over fences came on Carton, at Windsor on 27 December 1947. Soon afterwards, he broke three vertebrae in his back and was off the track for a year.

Before his retirement from the saddle in April 1964, Winter won two Grand Nationals (Sundew, 1957, and Kilmore, 1962); two Cheltenham Gold Cups (Saffron Tartan, 1961 and Mandarin, 1962); three Champion Hurdles (Clair Soleil, 1955, Fare Time, 1959 and Eborneezer, 1961) plus three King George VI Chases, and the Grand Steeplechase de Paris. In addition, he won four jockeys' championships, in 1952–3, 1955–6, 1956–7, and 1957–8, while his 121 winners in the 1952–3 season set a record. From a total of 4,298 rides in Britain and abroad, Winter had 929 successes. One of his most remarkable rides was on Mandarin in the 1959 Grand Steeplechase de Paris. The bit broke at the fourth fence and Winter was left to win the marathon with the help of only strong legs and superb balance.

Turned down for the job of racecourse starter, Winter began training in 1964. In his first season he won the Grand National with American challenger, Jay Trump (1965), and 12 months later repeated the feat with Anglo. Bula (1971 and 1972), Lanzarote (1974) and Celtic Shot (1988) all triumphed in the Champion Hurdle, while Midnight Court took the 1978 Cheltenham Gold Cup. Winter was leading trainer in 1970–1, 1971–2, 1972–3, 1973–4, 1974–5, 1976–7, 1977–8, and yet again in 1984–5.

Fred Winter in happier times with his horses. A great jump jockey before becoming a trainer, he fractured his skull in a fall at home in 1987 and handed over the reins to assistant, Charlie Brooks.

Racing Around the World

There are very few countries which do not hold race meetings in one form or another but, for reasons of space, this chapter must confine itself to the major racegoing nations. Britain, France, and North America lead the world in racing, not only providing extensive sport but being the most influential forces in the breeding industry.
Australia and South Africa also offer high-quality racing supported by a well-organized breeding industry.
South America provides enthusiastic racing, rather than quality sport. However, Argentina is the exception. It has a highly organized racing programme centred around the Buenos Aires tracks and a breeding region around Capitan Sarmiento, an hour's drive from the capital.
Racing in the Far East, notably in Japan and Hong Kong, is geared almost exclusively to the benefit of the punter, with a large number of horses with proven careers being imported from both Europe and Australia.

Jockeys look tense as they get on with the job at Goodwood's popular summer meeting.

Racing as we know it today can be traced back to the early 1600s, when King James I took a house just outside Newmarket and became a regular visitor to the area. His son Charles I continued to visit the area, but it was Charles II who spent a large amount of his time in the Suffolk town. This royal interest in horse racing makes Britain the oldest of the leading racing countries.

The 1700s provided the foundation for many of the races still run today. The Royal Meeting at Ascot was started by Queen Anne in 1711, the St Leger in 1776, and the Derby in 1780. Racing administration began to take shape with the establishment of the Jockey Club in 1752 and was followed later that century by the publication of the Racing Calendar and the General Stud Book. Both of these works were by James Weatherby, the founder of the firm responsible to this day for the Jockey Club's administration.

But it was not until about a hundred years later that one of racing's clearest thinkers, Admiral Henry Rous, put into operation his ideas. The Admiral attended to various minor problems in racing, but he will always be best remembered for his thoughts on handicapping. He introduced logic and consistency where there had previously prevailed a rather extraordinary process of assessing horses' weight by their size. And his observations formed the basis for handicapping horses throughout the world.

Horses here, there and everywhere, at Newmarket in 1790. Royalty spent a lot of time in the Suffolk town, which is still regarded as the headquarters of British racing.

The role of the bookmaker

Britain differs from the rest of the racing world for two reasons — the enormous involvement of bookmakers as opposed to a centralized betting system, and the diversity of the racecourses, which do not act as training centres. Betting on horses is as old as racing itself. Initially it was match betting, normally between the owners of the two competing horses, but as racing developed so did a new breed, the bookmaker. 'Bookies' have always had to carry a tag of unrespectability. This slur is wholly unwarranted today but was not without foundation in the 1800s when they employed any method to produce the desired result.

Skulduggery by the bookmakers led to the adoption of a veil of secrecy by owners and trainers in an attempt to forestall any dishonest activity before a race meeting. Anybody not connected with the yard was considered a threat, and even the stable staff were not to be trusted. To avoid the 'touts' or work-watchers, especially at Newmarket, trainers would 'pull-out' before dawn. The weights carried by horses in their work were carefully maintained and known only by a select few, in order to confuse not only the work-watchers but also the riders.

But this secrecy was not only intended to foil any mischievous behaviour by the bookmakers, for many of the owners and trainers themselves pulled all manner of strokes to 'land a substantial gamble'. Even so, the bookmakers' net allowed few fish to escape, although one of their greatest losses came in the 1836 St Leger, when Ellis, owned by Lord Bentinck, was reported to be in Sussex a few days before the race. The bookmakers' reaction was to lay the horse at long odds on account of this information, only to see the horse at Doncaster on the day of the race. It was a closely guarded secret — he had been brought north by the first horse-drawn horse-box.

Legal on-course betting

It was not until 1928 that the House of Commons passed a Bill legalizing Tote betting on racecourses. At the time many considered it the end of bookmakers, but it was most certainly not. The fact is, the British punter enjoys betting against the bookmaker — a truth which the purist or the clerical assessor fails to grasp. Today, racing in Britain suffers from one major problem, lack of prize money, and yet this is a problem which other countries, primarily France, have shown would not exist if a 'tote-monopoly' existed.

The year 1962 saw the introduction of the high-street betting shop, which revolutionized betting in Britain, for it enabled the ordinary man to bet daily without having to go racing. Previously it was either a case of having an account with a bookmaker or going 'to the sports'. Visitors to Britain still find it extraordinary that betting, especially on a credit account, is simply a matter of

picking up a telephone, giving a name and number, and then placing a bet. However, with the advent of betting shops the whole emphasis of betting changed. More and more multiple and accumulator bets were introduced to entice the small punter with the prospect of a large return.

A choice of betting

Betting on the racecourse has not altered dramatically. A punter has the choice of a bookmaker or the Tote. The latter generally caters for the smaller punter or the punter keen on forecast betting or trying to win a jackpot (selecting six consecutive winners). Bookmakers can be broken down into two basic categories — 'rails bookmakers' and 'board bookmakers', who operate in the Tattersalls enclosure. The latter tend to be market farmers and while a few take big bets, the majority bet with the ordinary racegoer. On the other hand, the rails bookmakers take nearly all the big bets. They are so called as they sit 'on the rails' separating the members' enclosure and the Tattersalls enclosure, thereby allowing members to bet without leaving their enclosure.

The most noticeable difference between the two types of bookmaker is in the prices they offer. The board bookmakers in Tattersalls advertise their prices on boards (hence their name) so that a punter can wait around for the best available price. Rails bookmakers do not have boards and the punter has to go up and ask what price 'the layer' is offering about any one horse. This is nothing more than 'head-to-head' negotiating and if the punter is a well-known backer the bookmaker might knock half a point off to safeguard his book.

Rails bookmakers may be divided into the large firms of bookmakers who have off-course betting shops and the individual layers. Of the big-firm bookmakers, Ladbrokes, William Hill, and Corals, through the old established firm of Heathorns, are represented on the 'rails'. If any horse is being well backed off the course the information is relayed back to the course and the big firms back the horse heavily on the course, thereby reducing its price and ultimately their liability. It is when a major gamble is afoot that the 'tic-tac' men really come into operation. Tic-tacs are strategically placed around the betting-ring, sending to their bookmakers through a code of hand signals any substantial market moves or large bets.

The strength of the bookmaker

Surprisingly, the largest layers on the rails are not the big firms but individual rails bookmakers who make a true book. They are in a position to accept a large bet, whereas the representative of a big firm is answerable to head office and therefore might have to refer the matter before betting with the big punter. This is not wholly acceptable to the professional punter as his

cover is blown and the information will be quickly transmitted throughout the market, necessitating a reduction in the price. Among the many attractions of racing in Britain is the betting-ring and the ability to hunt and negotiate for the best price.

There are 35 Flat courses in Britain, with very little similarity between any of them. They are left- and right-handed and the majority are a complete circuit, although there are some horseshoe-shaped courses. While they all vary in stiffness, some are flat and some are hilly.

Trainers send their horses all over the country to win races, providing competitive racing everywhere, from Catterick, in Yorkshire, where in 1987 the richest race was worth £2,798 to Ascot, in Berkshire, where the richest race was worth over £135,000. However, there is a definite North-South divide, with a preponderance of top trainers in the South. Furthermore, the majority of top race meetings take place in the South, with only York really holding its own against its southern counterparts, although Doncaster (home of the St Leger), Haydock and Chester all put on very good racing.

North-South divide

This divide naturally causes some resentment in the North of England, for although racing is well supported by northern race-

Fortunes are won and lost in betting on the Epsom Derby. On-course bookmakers chalk up the odds and it is up to the punter to hunt around for the best prices.

goers, the prize money in the North is substantially lower, which prompts owners to have horses in training in the South. Consequently, northern trainers tend to have smaller strings and lower training fees. Northern trainers are a tough breed who would be prepared to accept the situation if it were not for the fact that their southern counterparts go north to win races with racehorses which are bred to compete, in theory at least, at Royal Ascot.

While top-class northern racing might not match up to that of the South, it does have some of the most competitive handicaps, setting the season off in March with the Lincoln and ending it with the November Handicap, both at Doncaster. After the initial excitement of the Lincoln there is a lull before Flat racing starts in earnest in mid-April with the Guineas Trials, the forerunner of the Guineas meeting at Newmarket at the beginning of May.

Following Newmarket, the Derby and Oaks trials take place at York, Goodwood and Chester (the smallest course in Britain, — 1 mile/1.6 km) with the Derby and Oaks being held at Epsom at the beginning of June. Mid-June sees one of the highlights of the year, Royal Ascot. The meeting lasts for four days, with a fifth day known as Ascot Heath. The five days provide a feast of good racing, although throughout the world Royal Ascot conjures up before all else the idea of England's High Society, with ladies in large hats wearing the very best the fashion houses can offer and men in morning coats and top hats. It is a truly unique occasion, with a Royal Procession over the course on each of the four Royal days. Yet for all the pomp and circumstance, its tally of 14 Group races in four days is unequalled anywhere in the world.

Racing at Newmarket

At Newmarket, the July Course, as opposed to the Rowley Mile course, is the scene of the next major meeting, with the feature event being the sprint, the July Cup. At the end of the month the King George VI and Queen Elizabeth Stakes (considered by many to be the foremost middle-distance race in Europe) is run at Ascot, after which the only other five-day meeting, 'Glorious Goodwood', takes place.

Goodwood, set in the middle of the South Downs in Sussex, is indeed worthy of its nickname. It offers fantastic views and on a lovely summer's day in July it is difficult to imagine a more perfect place to spend a day racing. The course formerly held a very prominent position in the year's social diary but, unfortunately, in recent years it has lost some of its appeal as a Society event. Nevertheless, the racing is still of great interest to the keen follower of the sport, with the Sussex Stakes over 1 mile (1.6 km) bringing together many of Europe's best 'milers'.

The North of England then plays host to the country's top racing with the Gimcrack meeting at York in the middle of August and the St Leger meeting at Doncaster at the beginning of September. It is then back to Newmarket at the end of the month for two of the major two-year-old races, the Cheveley Park for fillies and the Middle Park for colts, both over ¾ mile (1.2 km), and the first leg of the Autumn Double, the Cambridgeshire Handicap. Then, to Newmarket again in the middle of October for the Champion Stakes and the second leg of the Autumn Double, the Cesarewitch Handicap.

The above is only a brief outline of the Flat season, and it must not be forgotten that from April through to November there is at least one meeting a day, six days a week (Sunday racing has yet to be introduced). During the summer, meetings are also held in the evening, contributing to a total of over 3,000 races in any season.

Training in Britain

There are over 7,000 horses in training in Britain, distributed between nearly 400 trainers. In Britain, as in other countries, with the possible exception of France, trainers do not train on the racecourse and so can be found in Scotland, in Wales, and indeed throughout the British Isles. Nevertheless, Newmarket is the focal point of the whole racing industry. More than just a centre, it is racing's headquarters. With its Jockey Club rooms, the horseracing museum, two race-courses, over 50 stables with enormous train-

Whips are out at the business end of a Royal Ascot race. Betting is heavy at this four-day June meeting.

ing facilities, the senior sales company Tattersalls with its huge sales complex, many of the country's leading studs in the surrounding countryside and offices throughout the town of all the leading bloodstock agents, Newmarket is the home of every aspect of racing.

The two racecourses, the Rowley Mile Course and the July Course, held 29 days' racing in 1987, including seven Group 1 races. Over 2,500 horses are kept in the 50 yards, including the strings of such famous names as Henry Cecil, Michael Stoute, and Luca Cumani, each trainer having well over 100 individuals under his care.

Newmarket offers the trainer every facility to bring the best out of his horses. Helped by substantial Arab backing, the Newmarket gallops, always providing plenty of variety, have improved greatly during the 1980s, the latest and best all-weather gallops having been built there.

Although Newmarket is racing's headquarters there is fierce rivalry with the country's second biggest racing centre, Lambourn in Berkshire. Lambourn is the collective name for a large area of Berkshire and Wiltshire, although the village itself houses a number of yards, with a general emphasis on National Hunt racing. Such famous trainers as Fred Winter and Fulke Walwyn have sent out a host of good jumpers, but Flat trainers have also held their own. Peter Walwyn at Seven Barrows was responsible for the 1975 Derby winner Grundy, while his immediate neighbour Henry Candy, with some of the finest gallops in England trained the brilliant filly Time Charter, winner of the 1982 Oaks and the King George VI and Queen Elizabeth Stakes of the following year.

To the west of Lambourn, Jeremy Tree trains at Beckhampton's famous yard. One of the most respected men in racing, Tree has an admirable record with such horses as Known Fact and Rainbow Quest. Just down the road from Beckhampton is Manton, with one of the most modern, not to mention impressive training establishments in Europe. Owned by Robert Sangster, the whole place was modernized under the careful eye of Michael Dickinson but has since been taken over by the very successful Barry Hills.

To the east of Newmarket lies West Ilsley and the base of the Royal trainer Major Dick Hern, one of the country's most successful trainers over the past 20 years. With gallops spreading the length and breadth of the village, horses have little opportunity to complain of boredom. The stables' record testifies to their success: two Derbys, three Oaks, and six St Legers, as well as one of the most famous horses to be trained this century: Brigadier Gerard, winner of 21 of his 22 races.

South of Newbury, in Berkshire, Ian Balding trains at the village of Kingsclere, made famous by the brilliant Mill Reef and the novel *Watership Down*. Again, the superb gallops offer all a trainer needs if he is to get the very best out of his charges, while the views are a marvel for the riders.

John Dunlop, probably Britain's largest trainer with well over 200 horses under his care, trains close to England's south coast at Arundel, in Sussex.

Home of the Derby

Working back towards London, the next venue is Epsom, the home of the most famous race in the world, the Derby. Situated on the southernmost edge of the capital's suburbs, Epsom used to be a major training centre but has recently lost some of its importance, not only in the number of horses trained but also in terms of quality. However, it retains some of racing's characters, such as Ron Smyth, champion National Hunt jockey in 1942 and one of the cleverest trainers in the game.

Next, north to Yorkshire, where both Malton and Middleham can boast many a fruitful venture south to take on their southern counterparts. Malton, not far from York, the northern Ascot, is, like Lambourn, the collective name for the surrounding area. The family name closely associated with Malton is Easterby. The two brothers M. H. (Peter) and M. W. (Mick) have never been afraid to 'put their money where their mouth is' and over the years have proved highly successful both on the Flat and over the jumps.

But, colourful as the Easterby brothers are, the name Elsey should not be left out when mentioning Malton. Bill Elsey has, in the last 20 years done what no other northern trainer has done — sent out two Classic winners. In 1967 he won the Oaks with Pia and in 1972 took the St Leger with Peleid, an impressive feat when one considers that only one other Classic winner has come out of the North — Waterloo, winner of the 1972 1,000 Guineas and trained at Richmond, in Yorkshire, by Bill Watts.

Richmond is the nearest town to Middleham, described by many as the coldest place on earth. As someone with first-hand experience of the place, I have little cause to disagree with the description on a cold winter's day, but my memories will always be of summer, when you could not find a more beautiful place. The Moor, the name given to the gallops, is not extensive but has two major assets in its favour — it is stiff and the northern grass is tough. The common land is grazed by both cattle and sheep in summer, which is occasionally a nuisance and something the purists in the South would find difficult to comprehend. But it seems to have litle effect on the horses, for Captain Neville Crump has trained three Grand National winners there and, at the other end of the racing spectrum, Dick Peacock won the Kings Stand, over ⅝ mile (1,000 m), with Fearless Lad in 1982.

The Irish racing scene

Throughout the world the word 'thoroughbred' is synonymous with Ireland. The notion

Middleham Moor, Yorkshire, provides stiff gallops in beautiful surroundings. Neville Crump has trained three Grand National winners there.

One of the world's greatest trainers, Vincent O'Brien, talks horses during a break on his famous Ballydoyle House gallops, in Co. Tipperary.

of rich, green paddocks filled with mares and foals might be an oversimplification, but there can be no denying the fact that the country lives and breathes racing. Ireland's racing scene is very similar to that of Britain — bookmakers, very big bookmakers and decentralized racing ranging from the glamour of Phoenix Park to the beeches of Laytown. Training facilities are equally varied, from the multi-million-pound establishment at Ballydoyle, County Tipperary, of Vincent O'Brien to 'the field behind the house'.

Vincent O'Brien, a legendary figure the world over, has a record that is unparalleled — six Derbys, two Oaks, three St Legers, and four 2,000 Guineas, as well as the host of other top-class races which put him in a league of his own. Ballydoyle has, over the years, developed into the most complete and elaborate training unit in the world. The one-time jump trainer O'Brien, through his expertise and business acumen — well illustrated by the formation of the most powerful racing partnership in the world with Robert Sangster and his son-in-law John Magnier — has every type of gallop, every modern gadget, and, most importantly, 50 of the world's best-bred horses. But O'Brien's domain does not end at Ballydoyle, for down the road is Coolmore, the leading stud in Europe, with many of the most sought-after stallions available today.

But racing in Ireland would be very dull if dominated by O'Brien. The names Dermot Weld, Liame Browne, Jim Bolger and O'Brien's son David all play their part. Weld, who trains at The Curragh (Ireland's Newmarket and home of all the country's Classics) is the largest Irish trainer and in 1985 produced a record 135 winners. Those successes were spread over some 20 different courses. The showpiece course is Phoenix Park — 'The Park' — recently revamped and the venue for Ireland's richest races. One of the most popular courses is Galway, with its festival in late July which combines flat and jump racing.

Racing in France

Go into any French café on a Sunday morning and you will be confronted by studious punters trying to work out the afternoon's Tiercé, an institution in France. Only on a Sunday do the French as a whole take an interest in horse racing, for all the Sunday newspapers carry a Tiercé supplement giving a detailed insight into the form of all the runners. The Tiercé plays a major part in France's total betting turnover of over FF20,000 million, of which FF1,000 million goes back into the industry. A money-spinner it may be, but the Tiercé is generally a handicap and can give a false picture of French racing. It must be remembered that at the top level racing in France is of the very highest quality.

Ask the ordinary racing enthusiast about the sport in France and he is likely to mention Longchamp, the Prix de l'Arc de Triomphe, Yves Saint-Martin, and perhaps Deauville. Tell him there are over 250 courses and he will look at you aghast, but it is hardly surprising as the top racing is wholly concentrated on the Paris tracks and Deauville in August, giving a distorted picture.

Chantilly (with its neighbour Lamorlaye) situated 25 miles (40 km) north of Paris, is the home of French racing. It is an extraordinary place, hidden in the beech forest of the Condés with a château built in a similar mould to Versailles overshadowing the racecourse. The track itself is the venue for both the French Derby (Prix du Jockey Club) and Oaks (Prix Diane). Hidden around the town and in the forest are some 80 yards with over 3,000 horses, which use the miles of woodland tracks to get to the beautifully maintained gallops. There are grass gallops on the great expanse of Les Aigles and a mass of sand gallops in the forest.

Home of the great French trainers

All the greatest French trainers have trained at Chantilly, many in charge of more than one yard. The French were the exponents of the 'large string', François Mathet having at one stage of his career 250 horses in his care, scattered over six different yards. The inevitable question is asked: how did he know what was going on? The answer: a touch of genius with more than a sprinkling of organization, shown to maximum effect every morning on the gallops. Mathet would stand in the centre of the 'training ground' in the forest and from all the different tracks each string from each yard would arrive at exactly the arranged time. Faultless military precision formed the bedrock and then genius took over. Mathet could name every animal as it passed and remember how it worked, later placing it to good effect.

Mathet's string might have been the largest, but many other trainers had or have equally impressive strings. Alec Head, the son of Willie, is a racing 'all-rounder' — he was not only a brilliant trainer, but is the father of both Freddie, one of France's leading jockeys, and Criquette. Criquette quickly showed all her father's flair for training and established herself as one of the country's leading trainers, sending out Ma Biche to win the 1,000 Guineas in 1983. François Boutin, first trainer for the Niarchos family, started in 1964 and since then has won nearly every major race in Britain and France.

Another great trainer is the colourful Maurice Zilber, who went through a golden period when associated with Nelson Bunker Hunt, training so many good winners in the distinctive green-and-white colours. These include Dahlia, winner of the King George VI and Queen Elizabeth Stakes in 1973 and 1974, and Empery, winner of the Derby in 1976 and Youth winner of the Prix du Jockey Club (French Derby) in the same year. A more recent success story is that of Patrick Biancone, who trained horses such as Sagace, winner of the Prix Ganay and Prix de l'Arc de Triomphe, for the Paris art dealer Daniel Wildenstein.

At Newmarket many of the yards are owned by the trainers. By contrast, many of the large French owners — the Aga Khan, Mahmoud Fustok, and the Rothschilds, for example — have their own yards. To drive past these establishments provides clear enough evidence that when they were built there was little concern for expense.

Maisons-Laffitte and, on a lesser scale, the area surrounding Deauville, are the only other sizeable training centres. Away from Paris, in the provinces, the emphasis changes to centralized training on the racecourses.

The primacy of Paris

Racing in the French provinces is a world apart from that of Paris. It is undeniably very competitive, but for provincial trainers there is none of the intimidation of hundred-plus strings. The racing is far more localized, although the Chantilly trainers do raid the lesser tracks with their inferior horses. But, for the Chantilly trainers, the racing scene is really centred on Paris. With Longchamp, Evry, Saint-Cloud, and Maisons-Laffitte, as well as the 'home course', Chantilly, the Paris area gives them all the challenge they demand and meets all the needs of the Parisian racegoers too. Unfortunately, the latter is a fairly rare breed and the mighty stands of Longchamp and Evry, offering some of the finest facilities in the world, are never filled.

From March to November, except for the break in August, there is the opportunity every weekend to watch Group racing at one of the courses. Longchamp, with 48 Group races, has every reason to be nominated Europe's premiere racecourse. Included in the total are 18 Group 1 races and, at the beginning of October, racing fans' eyes throughout the world are focused on the Parisian course as it plays host to what is probably the finest day's racing anywhere.

'Arc Day' is unique, for an atmosphere is generated which could never be repeated anywhere else in the world. The English consider they make the day, rather like the Irish at Cheltenham in March, and statistical evidence shows there is some truth in such an arrogant suggestion. For English racegoers, Longchamp during the first weekend in October is something of an institution and they swarm over in their thousands.

What the French describe as 'the greatest race in Europe' draws a truly international crowd. The Prix de l'Arc de Triomphe is similar in nature to its counterpart of two months earlier, England's King George VI and Queen Elizabeth Stakes. It is a 2,400-metre (1½ mile) race for three-year-olds and upwards, attracting the very best from three or more crops. Whereas the Ascot race is run in the middle of the season, when horses are more likely to show their true form on good or fast ground, the 'Arc' has for the purist a number of drawbacks. Notable among these is its lateness in the season, when the ground tends to be soft because of the French enthusiasm for watering their courses.

A true challenge

Nevertheless, every owner of a horse with the remotest chance in the race cannot resist the challenge of the 'Arc' — one which requires the full use of every attribute associated with the thoroughbred if the horse is to prove successful. The field is never small and so the race tends to be fairly rough, with 'hard luck' and 'has been' stories reverberating for weeks afterwards. But, for all the stories, the fact remains that the winner of the 'Arc' is always a proven champion. Champions make their own luck, and losers, in the cold light of day, rarely have a case when laying the blame on the way the race was run. European horses running in America on dirt tracks might have an excuse, but racing on grass is alike in France and Britain, although each course has its idiosyncracies. It is this similarity that attracts such international competition, commencing in

February with the meeting at Cagnes-Sur-Mer.

Cagnes might be described as a festival, but it is no match for its northern equivalent Deauville, in August. Deauville is very much part of the social calendar, with a feast of top-class racing to match the cachet of the event. In days gone by, racing would move as a whole to Deauville — horses, trainers and stable-lads would stay in the area for the whole month. With racing shared between the huge, well-equipped course and its smaller neighbour, Clairefontaine, there was no need to return to Chantilly. In recent years Clairefontaine has grown with the development of the training centre.

Nowadays there is far more commuting to races. The reason is twofold — first, transport has improved considerably, and secondly, there used to be a theory, now less influential, suggesting that horses stabled at Deauville for the whole month might have initially appreciated the sea and beaches but soon became lazy and soporific, doing little to improve their chances of winning.

Racing at Deauville

The feature races at Deauville are the Prix Jacques Le Marois and the Prix Morny. The former is among Europe's top mile (1600 m) races for three-year-olds and upwards. The premier French yearling sales take place during the same month, putting the racing spotlight on Deauville. Unfortunately, however, the yearling sales do not hold the position they should. France could have been Europe's leading racing country, but its breeding industry has declined since its high-point during the war years, when the Boussac empire produced a host of international winners.

The stud farms of Normandy are similar to their training counterparts in Chantilly — built with the emphasis on splendour. Again, they are owned by France's famous owner-breeders, who have international bloodstock interests in Britain and the USA but no interest in producing commercial yearlings. The French blame taxation for the decline of their breeding industry. But while government policies have in fact greatly benefited the racing industry, little has been done to help the breeder, so that a glut of France's top horses have gone to the USA. In an attempt to counteract this decline the Société d'Encouragement (the French administrative equivalent of the Jockey Club) introduced a number of incentive schemes for the breeder, but the sad truth is that few of France's top horses originate in that country.

German and Italian racing

To take the cynical viewpoint, West Germany and Italy provide the 'pot-hunting' owner and trainer with a golden opportunity for rich pickings, for the horses there have difficulty in winning equivalent races in France and Britain. Some might consider this an unfair comment, but it is true that clever trainers

Chantilly racecourse, in France, may not have the modern amenities of 'big sister' Longchamp, but it certainly has an historic background.

wishing to improve a family, constantly visit both countries. That is not to say, though, that domestic racing in both countries is incapable of producing champions.

Star Appeal's victories in the Prix de l'Arc de Triomphe and the Eclipse in 1975 made those who might have temporarily forgotten, remember that West Germany, with its highly organized and determined breeding industry, is more than capable of producing a champion. But German breeding policy has had its drawbacks, with fierce German protectionism inhibiting the use of international bloodlines.

Since many of the top races, including the Classics, are confined to German-bred horses, there is a danger that they could be left lagging behind in relation to the international competition. Following World War II there were only 250 thoroughbreds left in the country and the National Stud was on the wrong side of the Iron Curtain. That the West Germans have managed to regain a position of some importance is a tribute to their breeding industry.

In a modern age so dominated by Nearco bloodlines top breeders in Europe have gone to Germany looking for good families to act as a complete outcross. Encouraged by increasingly successful results, commercial breeders have brought the old German families more and more into their plans.

German supremacy

The greatest stud in West Germany is Schlenderhahn, which dates back to 1869 and is owned by the Oppenheim family. It has been a source of constant winners and remains unrivalled. Similarly the great Heinz Jentzsch cannot be matched when it comes to the German trainers who have dominated the sport over the last 25 years. Sadly, his name would mean little to the average German, for media coverage of racing is minimal and the crowds on the racecourse could never be compared for size with those of France or Britain.

Baden-Baden is undoubtedly the country's most famous racecourse. As picturesque as the town itself, its importance can be attributed to 'the waters', the casino, and the social cachet it has acquired over the centuries. The August festival, combining both Flat and jump racing attracts plenty of foreign runners and, while it is no Deauville, it is of a far higher standard than anything else seen in Germany.

The race-courses of the Ruhr — Gelsenkirchen-Hurst, Cologne and Krefeld, and Düsseldorf — cannot be said to have picturesque surroundings, unless coalmines and factory chimney upon factory chimney are considered appealing to the eye. But the courses themselves cannot be faulted. They are very flat, with a figure-of-eight inside the

Longchamp, Europe's premier racecourse, attracts about 10,000 racegoers from England for the Arc de Triomphe, in October.

Flying hooves kick up the dirt at Florida's Gulfstream track. The course will stage the 1989 Breeders' Cup.

normal course to accommodate jump races, and are all well maintained, with privet hedges and a mass of flower beds. Three hours' hard driving north brings you to Hamburg, home of the German Derby. However, the racing, except for the Derby and the Group 3 Sprinter in July, does not compare well with that of, for example, Baden-Baden.

Italian racing is far more commercial and, because of the genius of the great trainer Federico Tesio, has stamped itself forever in the history books. Much of Italy's racing is moderate, but since the 'Wizard of Dormello' bred both Nearco and Ribot, the Italians had every reason to say the greatest-ever thoroughbred breeder was their countryman. Unlike the sport in Germany, Italian racing is far more international — there are none of the restrictions seen in Germany and there is never a shortage of Italian voices at the yearling sales. There is also far more racing; in fact, there are a similar number of races to those run in Britain, although there are only some 50 Group races, with the majority of Group 1 races being divided between Rome and Milan.

The death of Tesio in 1954 and an unhealthy economic climate in Italy brought about a sharp decline in the racing industry. The breeding industry suffered and with many of the leading prize winners going abroad, Italian racing at the end of the 1970s looked distinctly unhealthy. But the 1980s

have seen a turn-around, with a determined effort to produce a real champion. Italy was finally rewarded when Tony Bin, trained by Luigi Camici, won the 1988 Prix de l'Arc de Triomphe as a five-year-old from another five-year old, the outstanding Mtoto.

Racing in the USA

In common with most American sporting activities, horse racing in the USA is difficult to compare with that of other parts of the world. But one thing is definite — try and draw any parallels with Europe and you will come unstuck at once. The courses are different, the structure of racing is totally dissimilar, training methods bear no resemblance to those of Europe, and races are run with a different emphasis on tactics.

Show an American jockey Epsom and he will laugh, but ask him to ride around the course and he might cry, for the concept of hills is beyond his racing experience. In fact, there is one similarity between racing in Europe and the USA — the course is left-handed! In the USA, uniformity is the name of the game, for every course is left-handed, flat, oval-shaped, just over a mile (1.6 km) in length and with a surface unflatteringly called 'dirt'. That is not to say that there is no racing on grass — many of the courses have a 'turf' track inside the 'dirt', but races on grass are rare and to consider racing in the USA as on anything but dirt is wrong.

A 'dirt' track comprises a predominantly sandy loam built on a hard-core base, with a collection of additives, including oil, to make the surface more durable and resistant to changing weather. It produces very firm running conditions when dry, but it is very hard on horses' legs when there is a change in the weather. While Britain struggles to find a surface which strives to be truly 'all-weather', the American dirt seems to do a pretty good job. A visit to Aqueduct, only a stone's throw from New York's Kennedy Airport, at the end of December, is testimony to the fact. With temperatures well below freezing point, there might seem to be little chance of racing — certainly in Britain the course would not have passed the previous day's inspection. But this is not the case in New York, for racing can take place without any difficulties. Constant maintenance by the ground staff with a fleet of tractors and harrows, combined with the dirt's 'freeze-resistant' properties, provides a surface more than adequate to race on, if slightly fast.

Adverse weather for fast times

Ironically, the fastest dirt surface follows tumultuous rain, when the course takes on the look of a large growing tray. The dirt can only absorb a certain amount of water, and with the hard base limiting drainage the water sits on the course, producing what the 'going' reports describe as a 'sloppy' surface.

Indeed, the dirt is so wet that the horses gallop straight through it onto the hard base, which explains the fast times. When a course is 'sloppy', the harrows are exchanged for sponges in an attempt to squeeze the water off the course, which is known as 'flunking out'.

Such conditions might produce fast times but they also make life very uncomfortable for the horse and the jockey. Race commentaries also take on a different character as the horses turn into the straight, since it is very difficult to differentiate between runners when the field looks identical in that every competitor is covered from head to toe in dirt. With so much dirt flying around, the US jockey has to perfect a skill unique to this style of racing — changing goggles.

Naturally, a single pair of goggles would quickly result in a 'blind' jockey and so up to six pairs are stacked together. As one pair gets too dirty to see through, it is whipped down only for the next to temporarily fulfil its role. Unfortunately, the horses cannot be equipped with goggles and have to manage as best they can. But it is something they soon learn to accept.

While the structure of racing in Britain and, to a lesser extent, France, appears to be geared to the big owner and trainer, the reverse can be said of America, where there is a race for nearly every horse. Some would argue that to race bad horses and allow them to win is bad for the breed as a whole. But such an argument is very short-sighted. It is true that it is wrong to breed from bad horses, thereby saturating the market with poor runners, but if an owner has bought a horse he should be given every opportunity to win a race.

Increased opportunities

The American outlook offers the small trainer a chance to 'make the game pay' — something his British counterpart is hard-pressed to do. Training is conducted almost exclusively on the course, with trainers renting barns or just boxes from the racecourse. This system accommodates trainers of every size, from the man who wishes to train only a handful of horses to the large established trainers with great strings. It also takes many of the financial pressures off the trainer, for a trainer who is forced to buy or rent a yard is faced with a huge financial commitment which is made worse if he cannot fill every box.

Transport costs in the USA are minimal compared to those in Europe (unless the horse is top-class). Dirt does not suffer from wear and tear in the same way that grass does, so that racecourses can hold meetings over lengthy periods. For example, California's Hollywood Park and Arlington Park, on the edge of Chicago, both hold meetings with well over 100 days of continuous racing. The whole operation is centralized, minimizing unnecessary expenditure.

They're off! Breeders' Cup day at the USA's Hollywood Park attracted the stars of stage and screen, as well as the best horses.

body is happy? The racecourse is happy because it has the runners, the punter is happy, the trainer is happy, and the owner has probably had a winner that would have been doubtful had the claiming system not been in existence. With over 100 racecourses in North America, there is scope for nearly every horse to win a race of some kind.

Massive popularity

Racing is America's leading spectator sport, with attendance figures exceeding 50 million. With such a welter of interest, racing at the very top level generates a mass of interest and produces horses who rank alongside such national football heroes as Dan Mareno and Joe Mantana. Such names as Secretariat, Spectacular Bid, Affirmed, and John Henry have all in recent years been regarded as wonder horses.

But what does it take to be regarded as a wonder horse in America? To win the American Triple Crown is not a bad shot. This means taking the Kentucky Derby at Churchill Downs over 2,000 m (1¼ miles), the Preakness Stakes a fortnight later at Pimlico, and ending with victory in the Belmont Stakes at Belmont Park, New York, over 2,400 m (1½ miles). That is a fairly good way of becoming a hero, as proved by both Secretariat and Affirmed, but what the American racegoer really wants to see is the horse running; not locked away in some distant part of the country, subject to constant rumours and making rare, winning appearances. In the USA, Shareef Dancer, winner of an Irish Derby on only his second appearance and then retired to stud, would have little hope of being remembered.

After the Triple Crown there are a multitude of races with a greater international flavour about them. These are contests such as the Washington DC International at Laurel Park, the Arlington Million at Arlington Park, and the recently introduced Breeders' Cup Series, which moves each year and in 1988 was at the home of the Derby, Churchill Downs.

The Breeders' Cup day should, by definition, be the best day's racing in the world. Every race is a Grade 1 contest designed to attract the very best in the world, with races run on both dirt and turf. While the ingredients suggest it has achieved its goal with international fields for all the races, its timing, November, makes it seem an after-thought. But while it might appear as such to someone used to seeing the season draw to a close at the beginning of November, in the USA there is no 'season', for racing is staged from 1 January to 31 December. Somewhere there will be horse racing on any given day.

A horse's life

The life of an American racehorse is far from easy. Once he arrives at his trainer's barn, broken and ready to go (they get all their initial preparation away from the racecourses)

American races are framed in the interests of the owner and trainer, and the racecourse managers realize the need to attract runners to promote the betting turnover. The term 'stakes race' is frequently not understood outside America. You might hear a good horse described as 'a stakes winner'. While it is true that the best horses are stakes winners, the term simply refers to a race in which the owner has to pay to run. This might seem strange to Europeans, for in Europe every owner pays to enter and run in a race. By contrast, in America the average owner might never have to pay an entry fee. In 'maiden', 'allowance' and 'claiming' races, for example, the racecourse puts up the prize money out of its betting returns and there is no entry charge.

A maiden race is for maidens at starting, while allowance races are for winners of maidens and claiming races. But it is the latter that is most important for the small trainer, for it allows him to handicap his own horse. There are 'claimers' worth over $100,000 down to $5,000. Of course, the only cause for concern for connections is that their horse might be claimed by someone else.

Some trainers depend totally on claimers, but what does that matter, as long as every-

he will be subjected to a regime for which his frail legs were not wholly designed. The single word 'speed' encapsulates US horse-racing. It is not a quaint idea nor a coincidence that runners go to post led by a pony, for the truth is, once they are on the track they are used to running, and running pretty fast most of the time. Everything is regulated by the clock. Jockeys and work riders are brilliant 'clockers' and will tell you exactly how long they took to cover a distance. Trainers clock every piece of work and this dependence on speed on a dirt surface round left-hand bends eventually brings about more than a little wear and tear.

Without the horses you have no racing, a point not lost on most of the states who allow the administration of 'bute' (butazolidin) and lasix. 'Bute' acts as a very strong aspirin-cum-painkiller, allowing the horse to work when it would otherwise be confined to its box. Lasix deals with the 'bleeder', a horse that breaks blood vessels. This slight waiving of the rules to protect state racing is not seen to be acceptable by some of the eastern states which, like Britain and France, feel there is no room for any medication on the racecourse.

Medication or no medication — the very word is emotive in American racing circles — go around the barns of Woody Stevens, Charlie Whittingham, or Wayne Lukas (whose horses win more than $6 million each year) and stable routine takes on a whole new meaning. Stable staff are not in short supply — two, possibly three, people will be involved with any one horse on any one day. There is the lad, who cares and tends to the beast, a work rider, and perhaps a hot-walker to lead the horse around after exercise. While American training methods might seem rather aggressive, every horse is treated as if he is the ante-post Derby favourite, with temperatures constantly charted, muscle lotions rubbed into aching muscles, and expert attention paid to the legs.

Although US racing is never closely associated with the activities of American Society, Saratoga, north of New York, becomes a social playground during August. Fresh from the world's most dynamic yearling sales in Lexington, the circus moves to Saratoga. Lexington means real horse business, being the capital of the richest bloodstock region in the world and the home of all the leading stallions in America and most of the leading performers for both France and Britain. But the climate in Lexington in July is not relaxing and, with so many dollars travelling to and fro, a move to Saratoga is welcomed by one and all. The place has style — and plenty of it. And that is true of the racecourse, the stands, the sales, and the people. If you want a US summer holiday, try Saratoga in August.

A gambler's paradise

Go racing in the Far East and you will witness a sport totally orientated towards gambling.

Horsemanship does not come naturally to the Japanese and Chinese and the racegoer in the Far East thinks wholly in terms of form-guides and 'betting-windows'.

Japan has, since the last war, tried to build up a racing industry with a similar structure to that of most European countries, where breeding augments the racing. Unfortunately, it has not proved very successful so far, and while Japan has imported a number of stallions from both Britain and America and bought plenty of brood-mares, it has yet to breed a champion of note.

It is not that the quality of horse bought to improve the breed is poor — such stallions as Yellow God, Sun Prince, and My Swallow have all found their way to Japan, as has Grundy, still best remembered for his epic duel with Bustino in the King George VI and Queen Elizabeth Stakes. The sad truth is that Japan lacks a number of the basic requirements to produce good horses.

The Japanese only race at the weekends, but during any weekend you are likely to get more punters at Tokyo racecourse than at all the days combined of the Royal meeting at Ascot. Furthermore, in one month the Japanese will have easily surpassed Britain's annual betting total.

Riders work up an appetite for breakfast in early morning exercise on Keeneland racecourse, at Lexington.

Tokyo racecourse is rather spectacular — a dirt track, a grass track, and a stand more than 400 yards (366 m) long meet all the needs of the racegoer. Rather like Japanese meals, the day's racing is a drawn-out affair, and with over 2,000 betting-windows there is plenty of opportunity to have a bet.

Go to any British racecourse and you will find a crowd at the 'pre-paddock', looking for the numbers for the next race or even the one after that, and walking around. In Japan and Hong Kong there are pre-race formalities but they are designed more to demonstrate efficiency than allow the punter a look at the field. But then he does not really want to look at the horses, his sole concerns being the race-card, his tipping sheets, and the latest odds. The race is nearly academic — it is only the result he is interested in. With such a commitment to gambling, the money authorities in Japan have imposed security restrictions beyond westerners' wildest dreams.

Centralized training

Unlike anywhere else training in Japan is centralized, while racing is de-centralized. There are 11 racecourses, but to ensure all is correct training centres have been built such as MIHO, 100 miles (160 km) from Tokyo and home for half the racecourse population in Japan. The place is a hive of activity well

The Chinese moved a mountain to make room for their modern Sha Tin racecourse in Hong Kong.

before dawn, with a floodlit training track and a fully appointed stand from which the horses are watched and clocked US-style.

Only qualified personnel (jockeys and work riders) are allowed on the track, while all other workers in the centre have to be registered. This might not seem out of character with any racing country but try looking up Pat Eddery or Willie Shoemaker before racing and see what happens. To avoid any corruption jockeys report to the racecourse the day before racing and are then locked up in a hostel with no communication from the outside world until racing begins.

Unfortunately, Hong Kong suffered in 1987 a major scandal involving 'race-rigging' and corruption among jockeys and trainers, although it seems inevitable that such practices should take place in such a lucrative business. On the positive side, great credit must be given to the Hong Kong Jockey Club and Police for weeding out the offenders, from the grass-roots right to the top.

Racing in Hong Kong has grown out of all recognition since its early days, when it was a way of amusing British soldiers stationed there. How such a small place with so many people all living on top of one another can have one, let alone two, racecourses is one of the unnumbered wonders of the world.

Originally there was only Happy Valley,

perfectly adequate for the racegoer, although a nightmare for a horse and rider. The whole course takes up 45 acres (18 hectares) of precious Hong Kong land and the 1,500-metre (9⁄10 mile) track makes many a track look like a galloping course. But that was of no concern to the Chinese punter and in 1971, once the whole business was being run by an efficient administration, enough money was generated in the following years to build a new racecourse. But the problem was, where?

In 1979 Sha Tin was opened, a racecourse far in advance of anything else in the world. Had you been an observant visitor to Hong Kong a few years before you would have felt sure there had been a mountain instead of the racecourse, and you would have been right. The Chinese proved they were robust and determined workers when they built the Great Wall and, similarly, after five years' toil they had replaced a mountain with a racecourse 2,000 m (1¼ miles) round with a 1,000-metre (5⁄8 mile) straight and every electrical aid for the punter.

Unlike Japan, Hong Kong relies totally on the importation of horses, generally from Britain and Australia. With fewer than 1,000 horses, the punter has a fair — or so one would think — chance of coming out on top but, like anywhere else in the world, the system is the winner. It generates enough money to attract top jockeys from Britain in the winter months and trainers who have found it increasingly difficult to come out in front at home.

However, it is a cultural shock for both horse and trainer — there is no Newmarket Heath in Hong Kong and horses, like trainers, find themselves living in high-rise accommodation around the racecourses. Training facilities consist of the track and the roof-top — gallop on the track, walk on the roof — quite simple when you get used to it.

Racing in South America

Nearly every South American country races but only one, Argentina, can claim to have played an important role in world racing. As with Italy and Federico Tesio, Argentina's fame rests fairly heavily on the shoulders of the great Forli, probably the greatest horse to have been bred and raced in the South American country and subsequently sire of Thatch, Home Guard, and Forego following his exportation to America in 1966 to stand at stud in Kentucky. In fact, he was sent to America on a temporary visit but for various reasons never returned to Argentina, a destiny probably responsible for his name appearing in so many pedigrees throughout the world.

But Forli was no fluke, for racing in Argentina is of the highest standard. The question one is forced to ask, is: how many of their other champions might have been proven as sires throughout the world if they had been given the chance? In such a commercial and international racing climate it is surprising that so little attention has been paid to

Argentinian racing. Maybe it is the country's remoteness that accounts for this neglect.

In general, South Americans can be described as natural horsemen and it is this close affinity with the animal that brings about a very easy and 'laid back' attitude to the racehorse.

Racing in Argentina is centred around two racecourses in Buenos Aires, Palermo and San Isidro. They are totally different and yet both are designed to bring out the very best in the horse. Palermo has a dirt surface, San Isidro grass, and with both courses each running two of the races that make up the Argentinian Quadruple Crown the true champion is forced to show himself capable of acting on both surfaces.

Palermo is an amazing racecourse, situated in the centre of the capital. In fact, it is a wonder that the oldest racecourse in Argentina is still in existence, considering its locality, but it seems in no danger of disappearing along with its neighbours across the road, the polo grounds that lost the Argentinian Open, the most exciting polo tournament in the world.

Home of the Argentinian Derby

The racecourse holds two meetings a week and is the home of the Polla de Potullos and the Gran Premio Nacional (the Derby run over 2,500 m/1½ miles). San Isidro might not be the country's premier course but it certainly holds the most important race of the Quadruple Crown, the Gran Premio Internacional Carlos Pellegrini for three-year-olds and upwards, run over 2,400 m (1½ miles).

San Isidro stages two races of Argentina's Quadruple Crown on grass. The other two events are run on dirt at Palermo.

The Argentinian economy could never be called stable. It is a country with a wealth of resources but crippled by inflation. Go to San Isidro and hear how the whole course, which was closed in the early 1970s by the central authorities for some irregularities, was refurbished in the latter part of the decade and you will then appreciate the national passion for racing. The work that was put into the whole place prior to its re-opening in 1979 has made it one of the foremost racecourses in the world. The course is 3,000 m (1⁹⁄₁₀ miles) round, putting it on a par with the big tracks in Europe and the mass of stands up the straight (over 600 m/640 yards) allows 100,000 racegoers to enjoy the excitements of a very extended day's racing. The cards are substantial. Forget the six races, with perhaps a seventh or eighth if the maiden is split, that are usual in Britain — in Argentina you expect to see at least 10 races.

The Argentinian style of race riding is similar to the North American technique — very low and close to the horse. However, the same cannot be said about the lads riding out in the morning. Throughout South America the lads ride bare-back, or, to be strictly accurate, they have either a pad or an exercise sheet under them, but there is no hint of a saddle and not a stirrup in sight. An Argentinian gaucho is as much at home on a horse as a monkey is in a tree, and as he sets off he brings his knees up onto the withers and looks as relaxed and stylish as his American or European counterparts.

It is an eye-opener to watch gaucho lads dealing with horses. They are firm and sometimes nearly cruel, but underneath they are very close to the horse and terribly sensitive.

San Isidro on a busy morning makes Piccadilly Circus or Times Square look like a village high street, but everybody is in total control.

The teaser's work

A teaser's life is not a happy one, for his job is to indicate to the stud groom if a mare is in season and ready to be covered. I once saw an old teaser lose his temper and go for our 'cow-ponies'. Equipped with only the briefest of bridles and a length of raw-hide rein, the gaucho in no time at all had calmed his charge down, jumped on his back and hack-cantered him back to the stud on a loose rein.

San Isidro, Capitan Sarmiento, and a crowd at the races with a basic knowledge of horses was proof enough that another Forli is not far away; nor is another Angel Penna, a trainer of immense charm presently in the USA, who has achieved more throughout the world than any other of his profession.

Racing in Australia

It is best to avoid Australia on the first Tuesday in November if you suffer a nervous reaction when the words 'horse racing' are mentioned, for it is the country's biggest sporting day — Melbourne Cup Day. It is Australia's answer to Derby Day at Epsom, except that the race has little long-term significance, even if the heads of those connected with the winner suffer from long-term throbbing! Like all the Australia Cup races, the Melbourne Cup is a staying handicap run over 3,200 m (2 miles). The prestige of winning the race has more to do with it being a national institution than the fact that it is a horse race.

Melbourne Cup day brings to a close the three weeks of the Melbourne Festival. Those three weeks prove rather wearing on even the most ardent party-goer as everything builds to a crescendo for the great race itself. Over 100,000 enthusiastic racegoers aim for Flemington Park on the Tuesday, but the enthusiasm for racing tends to wilt as the day wears on, with many of the so-called 'racegoers' showing a greater preference for lunch and being seen with the right people than for the racing. Be that as it may, when an Australian has a bet he likes to do the job properly and Melbourne Cup day will see the equivalent of £3 million sterling bet on the course, and a further £5 million off the course. If the 'morning suits' are not a reminder of Britain, the bookmakers will certainly be.

Australia runs a system unique to itself — on-course bookmakers competing with the Tote (TAB) and the Tote running a monopoly off the course catering for betting on nearly everything. It is a system that benefits everyone — the industry through the Tote monopoly off the course, the racecourse with an incentive for the punter to go racing, and finally the punter who has a choice — bookmaker or Tote.

Australia has some 400 racecourses, but the only place to be on the first Tuesday in November is Flemington, the attractive home of the famous Melbourne Cup.

That is not the only similarity with Britain for, unlike much of the world, which has a preference for racing on dirt, in Australia it is on grass. But most significant is the attraction of Australia for the large owners. It is a mark of the buoyant state of racing that an owner such as Robert Sangster, whose famous emerald-green and blue sleeves have been carried to so many notable victories throughout the world, is a great supporter of Australian racing. More recently, the powerful Maktoum family have expanded their enormous empire to Australia.

A wealth of racing venues

With some 400 racecourses, there is no shortage of racing and, as in America, the country's size calls for administration on a state-by-state basis, each running its own programme of races around a national framework. Local racing happens all the year round, but at the top end of the scale there is a circuit of state festivals. Each state holds a Cup race as a grand finale — Perth at Christmas, Sydney at Easter, and Brisbane in July, with about three weeks of racing at the surrounding courses. Horses can follow the festivals but with the majority of Australia's best horses based in Sydney, Adelaide, and Melbourne, there is little need to go to Perth or Brisbane.

For the racing enthusiast Sydney is the place to live. The home of Tommy Smith and Bart Cummings, two of Australia's legendary trainers, the city offers racing of the highest quality at Rosehill and Randwick, while there are good supporting cards at both Warwick Farm and Canterbury. With such an emphasis on Cup races, Australia has, over the years, drifted away from speed towards stamina. Consequently, the breeding industry had suffered and it was decided at the end of the 1970s to promote the Golden Slipper at Rosehill, which until the advent of the first Goff's Cartier Million at Phoenix Park, Dublin, in 1988, was the richest two-year-old race in the world.

The Melbourne festival is the highlight of the Australian racing year. The Cup itself has already been discussed, but the three weeks leading up to the Cup provide racing to match anywhere in the world, with the Caulfield, Guinness, Oaks, and Cup.

A great Australian trainer

If Australia can name only Phar Lap as a great Australian horse, it soon makes up for it with jockeys and, above all, one trainer, Colin Hayes. It was no coincidence that Robert Sangster, with such a wealth of knowledge, chose Hayes as his trainer.

Unlike other Australian trainers, Colin Hayes decided to 'go it alone'. Lindsay Park is a self-contained unit designed by Hayes solely for the production of winning racehorses. Situated in South Australia, 100 miles (160 km) north of Adelaide, it has everything except a racecourse in its immedi-

ate vicinity. Ideas put forward by the great Australian maestro have been put into practice throughout the world. Not least of these is the building of stables rather like dog kennels, with a caged area of sand behind the box, allowing the horses to sun themselves and relax with a roll.

But the Hayes empire stretches much further than just a training establishment, for it is surrounded by one of Australia's leading studs, which allows individuals to be closely monitored from the very earliest stages. Such achievements have made Colin Hayes the doyen of Australian trainers — a thinking man constantly searching for new ideas and further improvements.

Australians around the world

Australian horsemanship has been put to good effect throughout the world with Hutchinson, Moore, Pyers, and Thompson becoming household names in both France and Britain. Ron Hutchinson, with his famous 'head-nod', formed a great partnership with John Dunlop during the 1970s, while Brent Thompson was persuaded by Robert Sangster to leave Australia where he was Colin Hayes's first jockey and ride for him in Britain. Thompson is, in fact, a New Zealander, but it was in Australia that his early reputation was built.

Gary Moore followed the example set by Bill Pyers and has become one of France's leading jockeys, holding one of the most sought after jobs — first jockey to Criquette Head, and brought off a unique family double when partnering Ravinella to victory in the 1988 1,000 Guineas, a race his father Gary had won 21 years earlier on Fleet.

Horses take to the pool at Lindsay Park, Australia, where Colin Hayes has a magnificent stud and stables.

Famous Racecourses

The American world of racing is not round at all, but oval. The USA has settled for the almost standard oval-shaped racecourse with an artificial surface on the left-handed, flat main track. It will do nothing for the horse that prefers to run right-handed and hock-deep in mud, but it serves the purpose for centralized racing, which may be staged almost continuously on an American course for months. What these tracks lack in variety, they make up for by providing the racegoer with modern amenities that stretch beyond the imagination of the spectator at, say, the English Derby. And yet no country in the world has such a wide choice of recognized racecourses as Britain, where artificial surfaces have been a long time in coming. Everything stops for frost in Britain, but at least a horse can run left-handed-right-handed, uphill, downhill, and cover 1½ miles (2.4 km) without passing the winning post twice.

This chapter goes from New York's Aqueduct to a deeply contrasting galloping track at York, England. On the way it takes in a whole variety of courses from Aintree to Woodbine. But there is one thing they all have in common — they are a stage on which the finest thoroughbreds of the world can play their parts for the enjoyment of us all.

Runners in the long-distance Ascot Stakes head away from the packed stands at the Royal Meeting.

ARGENTINA

Argentina has two major racecourses, Palermo (dirt) and San Isidro (turf). They share the 'Quadruple Crown' races. Palermo stages the Polla de Potrillos, over 1,600 m (1,749 yards) and the Gran Premio Nacional over 2,500 m (2,733 yards). San Isidro is the home of the Jockey Club Stakes (2,000 m/2,187 yards) and the biggest race of the year, the weight-for-age Carlos Pellegrini. Run in December, the latter was shortened in the 1970s from 3,100 m to 2,400 m (3,389 yards to 2,624 yards).

Palermo, situated close to the centre of Buenos Aires, and opened in 1876, is the older of the two courses. It is right-handed with a straight of 1,000 m (1,093 yards). The racing surface is a mixture of clay and silt from the bed of the River La Plata.

San Isidro is Palermo's junior by 59 years. Situated a few miles outside the capital, it was opened in 1935, but was closed from the mid-1970s until 1979, when, in contrast to the government-run Palermo, it was put under the control of the Argentine Jockey Club. It boasts two grandstands and has a capacity of over 100,000. This sort of attendance is usually achieved for the running of the Carlos Pellegrini. The two turf tracks take up an area of 32,000 square metres (345,000 sq ft).

The main one can cater for straight-run 1,000 m (1,093 yards) races and events of up to 2,700 m (2,952 yards). A training centre nearby consists of five oval-shaped courses inside each other. The two innermost circuits have a river-sand surface and the outer track is turf. The two remaining strips are a mixture of dirt and sand. Over 1,000 horses are stabled at the training centre, which offers some of the best facilities in the world.

AUSTRALIA

The Australian racing programme is finely balanced. Although the publicity revolves around features such as the Melbourne Cup and the Golden Slipper Stakes, there are ample set-weight, weight-for-age, and Classic events to provide the ultimate test for all types of horse over a variety of distances. One anomaly is that some handicaps, including the Melbourne Cup, are classed as Group 1, which proves a little confusing to some outsiders when studying yearling catalogues.

Racing thrives in all parts of Australia on a variety of courses — the manicured lawns of Flemington and Randwick contrasting with the outback tracks such as Birdsville, where racegoers will fly in by private plane.

Tension mounts as horses parade before the Melbourne Cup, at Flemington, Australia. Although the race is a handicap over the unfashionable distance of two miles (3,200 m) it is the country's most coveted prize.

ADELAIDE

Racing in Adelaide has benefited from the presence near by of trainer Colin Hayes's magnificent stables and stud. Bart Cummings started his training days there before switching to Sydney for greater prize-money rewards. The Adelaide Cup carnival is run at about the same time as the Brisbane winter carnival and loses some of the better horses to Queensland. An innovation in the last decade was the running of the Australasian Oaks in March to coincide with the Yearling Sales.

Balaclava, Gawler, Murray Bridge, Strathalbyn, and Oakbank are Adelaide's provincial racecourses, but there are three metropolitan tracks. Victoria Park, only 1½ miles (2.4 km) from Adelaide, dates back to 1879. Its main races are the Adelaide Guineas and the Escott Cup, both over 1 mile (1.6 km). It is a left-handed track with a circumference of 2,610 yards (2,387 m). There is a straight of 696 yards (637 m).

Morphettville started up in 1860 with the first running of the South Australian Derby. Fire destroyed the grandstand in 1976 and the track was closed for almost a year. The left-handed course of 2,565 yards (2,346 m) has a straight of 385 yards (352 m). Feature races staged by the South Australian Jockey Club are the Adelaide Cup, the South Australian Derby and Oaks, and the Marlboro Plate (formerly the Goodwood Handicap).

Cheltenham, which dates back to 1890, is left-handed, with a circumference of 2,244 yards (2,052 m) and a straight of 320 yards (293 m). The course hosts the Port Adelaide Guineas and the Port Adelaide Cup.

BRISBANE

Brisbane's two metropolitan tracks are situated close to each other, near the airport. The provincial racecourses are Bundamba, Southport, Caloundra, Esk, and Gatton.

Brisbane racing takes the spotlight in May, June, and July, when it provides excellent prize money and facilities. Many trainers take advantage of the facilities available at Eagle Farm and Doomben and, more recently, at Southport on the Queensland Gold Coast 50 miles (80 km) away. Horses sent to these centres during the winter come back to racing in the spring much stronger than those who stay in the colder areas.

Eagle Farm dates back to 1866, when the first Queensland Derby was run. The Brisbane Cup was inaugurated in the same year. This is the city's major track and it attracts trainers from all the other states, as well as from New Zealand. It is a right-handed track of 2,215 yards (2,026 m). Feature races conducted by the Queensland Turf Club are the Elders Handicap, the Brisbane Cup, the Queensland Derby, the Queensland Oaks, the Ansett Cup, the Castlemaine Stakes, and the Grand Prix. Apart from the Ansett Cup and the Grand Prix, the races have Group 1 status.

Doomben goes back to 1933 and was, until 1988, the major carnival venue following the Eagle Farm carnival. It staged the Doomben Ten Thousand (now the Rothmans Hundred Thousand) and the Doomben Cup (now the Fourex Cup). Both are Group 1 races. The Queensland Turf Club and the Brisbane Amateur Turf Club, which controls Doomben, switched the carnival to a date before the Eagle Farm carnival, and it proved a great success. Doomben is a tight right-handed track of 1,877 yards (1,717 m).

MELBOURNE

The citizens of Melbourne, and migrants who landed there on their way to the goldfields, got wind of Archer's prospects in the first Melbourne Cup, at Flemington, in 1861. Their anticipation of filling their pockets with winning bets on Archer might have lost its edge if they had known that the horse had walked 550 miles (880 km) to run in the race. The journey from New South Wales a month before the event was taken in daily stages, the horse being alternately ridden and led by his groom.

Blissfully unaware of Archer's marathon, backers made him the second favourite in a field of 17 runners, and without giving them a moment's anxiety he tore away to win easily.

Champagne corks start popping at breakfast time on Melbourne Cup day, but these racegoers in the Members' Stand at Flemington have left the bars to bet on Australia's greatest gambling race.

It was a crippling result for the bookmakers. A report to the Victoria Turf Club read: 'Altogether the betting world just now is in a fog. The solvent members of the room will meet on Monday next to see what can be done.' Archer, trained by Etienne Livingstone de Mestre, raced for £710 prize-money in front of a hugely delighted crowd.

Flemington, situated in beautiful surroundings, opened for the first time on 3 March 1840, for a three-day meeting. In 1859 the Victoria Jockey Club staged a race for the championship of the Australian colonies which, despite runners from Adelaide being lost at sea in a shipwreck, was well acclaimed. The rival body, the Victoria Turf Club, had to come up with a counter-attack, and so the idea of the Melbourne Cup was hatched. In 1864, the opposing factions came together to form the Victoria Racing Club, which has run the sport ever since.

Flemington, which got its name from Fleming's butchers shop in a road nearby, is now, like several other Australian racecourses, a mixture of the best in European design and American sophistication. Australian courses tend to have more individual characteristics than those in the USA. Generally, the situation is a little like that of Paris, France. With a system of centralized racing, each Australian state capital has its own tracks — usually three or four — within easy travelling distance of its busy centre. They are well appointed Flat courses with none of the gradients to be found in England.

Flemington conforms to this pattern. A racegoer with intent to bet can mail an apologetic letter to his bank manager from Melbourne's General Post Office and be on the course 20 minutes later. It would take a lot longer on Melbourne Cup day, which for many years has been one of Australia's greatest events.

Flemington is a big course by Australian standards. It is a left-handed track of just under 1½ miles (2.4 km) in circumference. One of the special features is its straight six-furlong (1.2 km) course, on which such major sprints as the Newmarket Handicap are run.

The Melbourne Cup is run on the first Tuesday of November every year and is naturally the centrepiece of the four-day Melbourne Cup carnival. The race, open to geldings, is a 2-mile (3.2 km) handicap on the Flat, but it would be a serious mistake to believe that the distance, or the fact that it is a handicap, devalues it in any way. It can be described as a handicap for Group-class horses over a distance which, for most of the runners, is a little farther than they would prefer. The carnival is spread over four days. It starts with the Victoria Derby as the feature race on the Saturday before the Cup, with other races, such as the LKS Mackinnon Stakes and the Dalgety, providing many of the Cup contenders with one last chance to add the finishing touch to their preparation for the big race. The URC Oaks is run on the Thursday, two days after the Cup, and the final fixture of the four-day festival is on the following Saturday.

During the week there are scores of parties and official functions all over the city. And the nation truly does stop for the three minutes plus it takes to run the Cup. The Prime Minister will have already given his tip for the race to the public and Parliament takes time off from its business to see if the PM's elected horse can beat the opposition.

Caulfield is another of Melbourne's tracks. Home of the Caulfield Cup, Caulfield Guineas, and 1,000 Guineas, it is over 1¼ miles (2 km) in circumference. The Moonee Valley course features the W. S. Cox Plate, a premier weight-for-age race. Sandown Park, opened in 1965 and tailor-made for the comforts of the racegoer, has a back straight higher than the home straight to make for easy viewing from the stands.

PERTH

Western Australian racing has made many inroads into the national calendar over the past 20 years, with significant increases in prize money attracting top trainers from the eastern states. There are several wealthy owners who race extensively in Perth, including Robert Holmes à Court, Laurie Connell, Bill Holmes, and John Roberts.

The main racing season is during December and January. A problem facing horses from other states is their acclimatization to the very hot conditions. Track surfaces are usually hard. Bunbury and Pinjarra provide the sport on provincial tracks, while Ascot and Belmont Park are the metropolitan courses.

Ascot, 5 miles (8 km) from Perth, is left-handed, with a circumference of 2,210 yards (2,022 m). There is a straight of 330 yards (302 m) and races are conducted over 11 different distances. The first Perth Cup was run in 1879 on a track set alongside the picturesque Swan River. The course was remodelled in 1982, but the lay-out has changed little. The main races are the Perth Cup, the Australian and West Australian Derbys, the Railway Stakes, and the WATC Sires' Produce Stakes.

Belmont Park is used extensively during the winter months. The West Australian Guineas and the Belmont Guineas take place during the summer carnival.

Situated 2½ miles (4 km) from the centre of Perth, Belmont Park is a left-handed track of 1,856 yards (1,699 m). There is a straight of 364 yards (333 m).

RANDWICK

First steps towards establishing Sydney's Randwick racecourse were taken in 1832, when the Hon Edward Deas Thomson (later Colonial Secretary) chose the site south of the city. Known as 'The Sandy Course on Old Botany Road', it was approved by Governor Bourke in January 1833. When the first race meeting was held there a few months later, several thousand people are said to have walked from Sydney along a bush track through swamps and hills. There was regular racing at 'The Sandy Course on Old Botany Road' until 1838, when the track deteriorated to the point where it came to be used only for training purposes. A new track, at Homebush, became Sydney's main centre of racing for the next two decades.

In 1860, the Australian Jockey Club transferred back to 'The Sandy Course on Old Botany Road', where a new grandstand designed for 1,500 spectators had been erected. The district where the 'new' track stood became known as Randwick, after Simeon Pearce's home village in England, and the course was renamed 'The Randwick Metropolitan Racecourse'. The opening day was 29 May 1860, and the attendance was estimated at 8,000.

This is the Randwick Racecourse we know today. The course stages many of Sydney's major races, including the Sydney Cup, the AJC Derby, the AJC Oaks, the Metropolitan Handicap, the Epsom Handicap, the Doncaster Handicap, and the AJC Sires' Produce Stakes. Although there is racing at least twice a week on one of Sydney's four metropolitan courses, the feature of the whole season is Randwick's

annual Easter Carnival, which features four top-class days of sport. It is at this meeting that races such as the Doncaster Handicap, Sydney Cup, Derby, and Oaks are run.

Sydney's three other courses are also within easy reach of the city centre. Warwick Farm is an Australian Jockey Club track, but Rosehill and Canterbury are the 'babies' of the progressive Sydney Turf Club. Rosehill's Golden Slipper Stakes, the country's richest two-year-old race, is the feature of the STC's year. The 1,200-metre (1,312 yards) dash carries prize money on a par with the Melbourne Cup. There is strong rivalry between the STC and the Victoria Racing Club over which race will emerge as Australia's richest event.

Although criticized by outsiders for encouraging two-year-olds to be 'pushed' early in their careers, the Golden Slipper has been won by juveniles who have gone on to become outstanding horses later, and frequently over much longer distances. Outstanding among the winners were Todman, Sky High, Pago Pago, Eskimo Prince, Storm Queen, Vain, Baguette, Luskin Star, champion Manikato, and Bounding Away.

The H. E. Tancred Stakes, the Group 1 middle-distance feature of the STC's calendar, was run along international lines in 1988. Highland Chieftain, from John Dunlop's Arundel base in England, spearheaded an overseas challenge for the first time. But the visitors were unable to counter the outstanding Bart Cummings-trained three-year-old Beau Zam, who won impressively.

The whips are out at Sydney's Randwick racecourse as runners thunder home against a suburban backdrop. All of Sydney's four courses are within easy reach of the city centre.

TASMANIA

Tasmania does provide runners at Melbourne meetings, but their standard of racing is generally lower than that of the bigger centres. Elwick racecourse is in Hobart, and Mowbray in Launceston. The former, sited alongside the River Derwent, dates back to 1875, with the first running of the Hobart Cup. Mowbray first staged the Launceston Cup in 1865. The courses usually present their carnivals during January and February.

CANADA
WOODBINE

Ontario's showcase track, Woodbine, stages both the Rothmans International and North America's oldest continuously running stakes race, the Queen's Plate. The Rothmans International has undergone many changes since it was first run over 1¹⁄₁₆ mile (1.7 km) as the Long Branch Championship, at Long Branch, in 1938. It was open only to Canadian-bred three-year-olds, but the following year was renamed the Canadian Champion Stakes and entries had to be Canadian-owned. In 1940, the race was open to horses of all ages, but owners had to be resident in Canada. In 1954 the Championship became a race for three-year-olds and upwards, without residence restrictions.

The distance was changed twice before it settled at 1⅝ miles (2.6 km) when the race moved to Woodbine from Long Branch in 1956 and was staged as the Canadian International Championship Stakes. Two years later it was contested on turf for the first time. In 1981 it became the Rothmans International and in 1987, when the distance was changed to 1½ miles (2.4 km), the purse was $750,000 guaranteed. It was the country's richest race.

The Queen's Plate (1¼ miles/2 km) has enjoyed the Royal Bounty and the Royal approval since its inception in 1860. On 1 April 1859, the Toronto Turf Club, petitioned Queen Victoria to grant a Plate for a race in Ontario. The event was inaugurated in June the following year at the Carleton track, situated in a rustic area of Toronto. Canadian racing had hit on bad times in 1881 when Joseph Duggan, owner of old Woodbine, went to Toronto's highly respected postmaster, T. C. Patteson, for help. Patteson, with the agreement of the Club's president, Sir Casimir Gzowski, decided that racing would establish itself for all time as a Canadian institution if a member of the Royal family could be persuaded to visit Woodbine.

And so a plot was hatched. The Governor-General of Canada was the Marquis of Lorne. The Marchioness of Lorne was Princess Louise, daughter of Queen Victoria. Sir Casimir, aide-de-camp to the Queen, invited the Lornes to be his house guests in Toronto at a time when the spring meeting at Woodbine was on. The visitors agreed to have an afternoon at the races with their host. Patteson leaked the news to the press and the Princess's presence at the track attracted what was said to be the largest sporting crowd in Canadian history. In 1939, King George VI and Queen Elizabeth saw the race, won by Archworth. Queen Elizabeth II and Prince Philip were there for the hundredth running in 1959 and Queen Elizabeth the Queen Mother made her sixth visit in 1985.

A boost to Woodbine's 1988 programme was the addition of the Arlington Million. The prestigious Chicago race had to find a temporary new home while construction work went on to complete the US $120 million 'new' Arlington Park.

CHILE

Chile can claim to have the oldest racecourse in South America — the Club Hípico de Santiago. Founded in 1869, the capital's principal track also predates all North American racecourses, with the exception of Saratoga, New York. The grandstand is similar in design to that at Longchamp, Paris.

The Club Hípico course runs clockwise and consists of two turf courses and an inner dirt track used for training horses stabled on the premises. Racing takes place all the year round, on Wednesdays and Sundays, with the meetings finishing under floodlights. Sixty per cent of races are handicaps, but the track stages one leg of the Triple Crown, the Polla de Potrillos, over 1,700 m (1,859 yards).

Santiago's other course, Hipodromo Chile, is the country's most important dirt track. Founded in 1904, it is, in contrast to Club Hípico, anti-clockwise. The main track has a straight of approximately 400 m (437 yards) and measures 2,000 m (2,187 yards) for a full circuit. Racing is staged throughout the year, on one mid-week day and on Saturday. The final leg of the Triple Crown, the St Leger, is run at Hipodromo Chile over 2,200 m (2,405 yards). The third leg, El Derby, is run at Valparaiso Sporting Club.

FRANCE
AUTEUIL

Auteuil, situated in Paris, is France's premier jumping course. It possesses everything Longchamp has, plus such a diversity of obstacles as to completely faze any National Hunt enthusiast accustomed to plain fences, the odd open ditch, and the occasional water-jump. The course boasts every hazard

encountered in early English chasing, as portrayed in eighteenth-century engravings. A bank, a stone wall, posts and rails sloping over water, two wide water-jumps, a bull-finch, and several open ditches including the Rail, Ditch, and Fence, which looms up on the back straight. Although this fence is slightly softer, it is also slightly higher and wider than Aintree's Chair!

Auteuil's biggest races are in June, when the Grand Steeple-Chase de Paris and the Grande Course de Haies (Champion Hurdle) are run. In the spring, the feature races are the Prix Murat (chase) and the Prix du Président de la République (handicap chase). The chases, Prix La Haye Jousselin and Montgomery, are among the star contests in the autumn.

The Grand Steeple-Chase de Paris has been run over various distances and, for a long time when over 6,400 m (4 miles), took in every single chase obstacle at Auteuil. But a few June heatwaves, which caused a number of horses to suffer, led the Société to shorten the race to its present distance of about 5,600 m (3½ miles).

CHANTILLY

France benefits, or otherwise, from central-ized racing, with the main national off-course betting (PMU) meeting being held daily, seven days a week, on one of the 'Parisian' tracks. These are (excluding the £22 million futuristic complex at Vincennes, which is now devoted to trotting): Longchamp, Saint-Cloud, Maisons-Laffitte, Chantilly, Evry, and Deauville for the Flat; Auteuil and Enghien for jumping. Flat racing has been held in France, on and off, for centuries, the earliest surviving account of a horse race being mentioned in a Breton poem dated A.D. 500, which relates how a race was held to determine on whom the local king would bestow his daughter's hand. The name of the winner has not survived.

In the eighteenth century, les Sablons, Vincennes, and Fontainebleau were the main courses, all within a short gallop of one of the royal châteaux. Racing conditions were atro-cious and when these courses were replaced in 1770 by the Champ de Mars, where the Eiffel Tower now stands, there was little improve-ment. But things looked up when Prince Lobanoff, together with some sporting cro-nies, went hunting one day in the Chantilly forest. There he discovered the vast, natural lawn fronting the abandoned Condé château and palatial stables. He immediately organized a friendly race along the lawn with his friends and returned to Paris with the news that he had found the perfect place for a new racecourse.

The racecourse at Chantilly was inaugu-rated on 15 May 1834, with three races watched by a crowd said to be in the region of 30,000, a number which is difficult to credit, considering that Chantilly was at that time a three-hour journey from Paris. That same year the Société d'Encouragement decided

The stands at Chantilly, near Paris, France, date from the belle époque. *They may be inadequate by modern standards, but their old world charm gives the course an atmosphere all its own.*

to form their own private social club, which they named le Jockey-Club. June of the following year saw these messieurs allocating the sum of 5,000 francs annually for a new race (unusually reserved for three-year-old colts and fillies, born and bred in France) to be named the Prix du Jockey-Club, or Derby Français. It was run for the first time in 1836 and entries had to be made before 1 November 1835.

The race was initially scheduled for 16 May, and the colts were to carry 100 lb (45.5 kg), the fillies 97 lb (44 kg). In the event, to avoid a clash with a Champ de Mars meeting, the inaugural running of the French Derby was held on a cold, damp 22 April. Seven animals were entered and five ran. The winner was Lord Seymour's Frank, the favourite, ridden by stable jockey Robinson. He easily beat the Duke of Orleans's Brougham, which was followed by M Lupin's Belida.

The first Prix de Diane (French Oaks) was held at Chantilly in 1843, to general indifference.

Today's Chantilly has changed a bit, but the present stands date from the *belle époque* and are woefully inadequate, though charming. Festive marquees deck the old Condé lawn and a superior picnic ambience reigns. There are now only seven days of racing a year at Chantilly, between the first and third Thursdays in June, surrounded by what is probably the best training centre in the world. The Prix du Jockey-Club and the Prix de Diane are on the first and second Sundays

Longchamp is the flagship of French racing and the home of the Prix de l'Arc de Triomphe. The charming tree-shaded paddock, which also serves as the winner's enclosure, has been walked by many of Europe's greatest horses.

after the opening meeting and other feature races are the Group 3 Prix de Sandringham (three-year-old fillies, 1,600 m/1 mile); Berteux (three-year-olds, 3,000 m/15 furlongs): Chemin du Fer du Nord (four-year-olds and over, 1,600 m/1 mile): Jonchère (three-year-old fillies, 1,600 m/1 mile): du Lys (three-year-old colts and geldings, 2,400 m/1½ miles) and the Group 2 Prix du Gros Chêne (1,000 m/5 furlongs).

DEAUVILLE

When the Duke Auguste de Morny, a fervent supporter of racing, discovered Deauville, this Norman fishing village boasted 100 inhabitants and vast stretches of sandy dunes. Morny turned it into a highly fashionable summer resort, with racing as its greatest attraction. The French aristocrats and rich bourgeois flocked to Deauville as their London counterparts once descended on Brighton.

The first Deauville races were held on the beach in 1863, but a year later the race course was inaugurated in fine style with a sensational budget. Indeed, the first Prix Morny, for two-year-olds, was held the following year with prize money of FF5,000.

There are several top-class races, the most sought-after being the Group 1 Prix Morny (1,200 m/6 furlongs) and the Group 1 mile (1,600 m) contest, the Prix Jacques le Marois.

EVRY

Evry was inaugurated in 1970, and today this attractive course near Evry new town, some 20 minutes from Paris, is just as floral as its predecessor, Le Tremblay. The most modern of the capital's courses, excluding Vincennes, it has taken some time to attract reasonable crowds, but Evry has judiciously enticed runners from among the better provincial horses with a very enlightened calendar. The stands are extremely attractive and the whole complex is surrounded by beautiful gardens. All in all, it is a fine racecourse, worthy of a Classic or two. In fact, the Sport de France is an innovative Société, full of bright ideas, such as the Evry Million (francs) offered to the three-year-old filly which wins the three Group 3 Prix Chloë, Daphnis, and Minerve.

LONGCHAMP

A *long champ*, a grassy clearing or field, near the banks of the Seine in the Bois de Boulogne was a favourite spot for assignations of all types, from duels to picnics. At one end was an abbey, with a windmill just outside the gates. Today, all that remains is the windmill, many times rebuilt, which now houses some of the Longchamp racecourse's elec-

trical equipment. The abbey is remembered in the Prix de l'Abbaye de Longchamp, arguably the greatest European championship sprint, while the windmill features in the Prix du Moulin de Longchamp, a prestigious Group 1 contest over 1,600 m (1 mile).

The racecourse on the *long champ* was built to replace the awful track at Champ de Mars, in Paris, and opened with the Emperor and Empress in attendance, on 26 April 1857. The Société d'Encouragement had been given permission to build a racecourse there in 1856, two years after the site, together with all of the Bois de Boulogne, was acquired by the City of Paris.

For years, the star event at Longchamp was the Grand Prix de Paris, run for the first time in May 1863, but in 1920 the Société, vexed perhaps at the trotting authorities for having just created the Prix d'Amérique in honour of the World War I allies, took the Prix de l'Arc de Triomphe and made it into a top-class race for three-year-olds and upwards. It took French racing a while to recover from World War II, but Longchamp was soon restored to its former splendour and, in 1965, rebuilt.

The entire course is 2.8 km (1 mile 6 furlongs) in circumference but a variety of loops at the top end, to the right of the stands, enables various courses and distances to come into play. It has a long, gruelling straight and a most effective, computerized watering system which defies the comprehension of all but the scientists. The majority of the most sought-after races, except for the main two Classics, are held here: the two Poules d'Essai (French Guineas); the Grand Prix de Paris (now run over 2,000 m/10 furlongs); the Prix Royal-Oak (French St Leger); the Abbaye, Forêt, and Moulin, over 1,000 m, 1,400 m, and 1,600 m/5, 7, and 8 furlongs, respectively, and the showpiece, the Prix de l'Arc de Triomphe, run on the first Sunday in October. This event (2,400 m/1½ miles) is open to three-year-olds and over, and is the richest and perhaps the most prestigious race in Europe.

Longchamp opens its gates annually at Easter for its spring meeting, closes during June for Chantilly, opens again just for the Grand Prix de Paris weekend and then is closed until September when the big autumn confrontations begin.

MAISONS-LAFFITTE

Maisons-sur-Seine, only 7½ miles (12 km) due west of the Arc de Triomphe, was at one time a small village on the banks of the Seine. In 1777, the Count d'Artois, Louis XVI's brother, bought the château there and took up racing very seriously. He housed up to 80 racehorses in his newly restored stables and

The windmill at Longchamp is a reminder of the old days, when duels were fought in its shadow.

organized Flat races along the wide banks of the river which fronted his home.

After the Restoration, a rich banker, Jacques Laffitte, moved in and the village acquired his name. Laffitte made it a point of honour to rival the English in all aspects of horse racing organization. He produced good racing on a good course and attracted the Parisian socialites to his village to watch and participate. Plots of land in the château's vast park and woods were among the prizes, and it was thus that several racing stables were built there, forming the embryo of the present, magnificent, Maisons-Laffitte training centre, which is administered by the Société des Steeple-Chases de France.

In 1878, the genial Spanish inventor of the PMU betting system, Joseph Oller, rented the Ferme de Maisons-Laffitte, a large tract of largely fallow agricultural land beside the château park, and threw himself into racing administration. He organized no fewer than 76 ëetings beside the Seine during the next four years. The present racecourse dates from 1886, but has been rebuilt several times.

'Maisons', as it is universally known, boasts the longest straight course in the world. It is a completely level 2 km (10 furlongs) with three possible winning posts, and plenty of length left for pulling up. Its big races are the Prix Robert Papin (1,100 m/5½ furlongs), the Critérium de Maisons-Laffitte (Group 2; 1,400 m/7 furlongs), the Group 3 Prix Messidor and La Coupe de Maisons-Laffitte (2,000 m/10 furlongs straight).

SAINT-CLOUD

Saint-Cloud is a sharpish, left-handed course which favours horses with a fast turn of foot and tactical riding. The star event is the sought-after Grand Prix de Saint-Cloud, a Group 1 contest for three-year-olds and upwards. It was run under the name of Prix du Président de la République until 1939, and at Maisons-Laffitte up to 1914. A host of famous horses have won it: brilliant individuals such as Corrida, Tanerko (twice), Exbury, Relko, Sea-Bird II, Hopeful Venture (for Queen Elizabeth II), Rheingold (twice), Dahlia, the two Mill Reef-Crown Treasure brothers — Glint of Gold and Diamond Shoal — and Teenoso, among others. The late François Mathet trained eight Grand Prix winners between 1957 and 1981. Yves Saint-Martin was the winning jockey seven times.

Other principal races spread throughout the year, but occurring particularly during July, include the Critérium de Saint-Cloud for two-year-olds, promoted to Group 1 status when the Prix Robert Papin was demoted, and run in the autumn. Also run at the course are the Prix Maurice de Nieuil, Edmond Blanc, Jean de Chaudenay, Exbury, Eugène Adam, Pénélope, Cléopâtre, and Eclipse.

WEST GERMANY

The Baden-Baden racecourse is actually situated in the village of Iffezheim, some 8 miles (13 km) north-west of the spa town, and close to the Rhine and the French border. Because of the proximity to France, there has always been a strong French influence, and the first meeting was organized by Eduard Bénazet, a Frenchman who held the casino licence. There are still close links with the casino, which sponsors several races. After the Franco-Prussian war of 1870–71, the French influence abated and the Internationaler Club was formed to stage the race meetings, as it does to this day. Most of the members of the Club are aristocratic Germans, or members of the leading breeding and racing families.

After World War I, Baden-Baden's importance was reduced as social patterns changed, but the racecourse has had a new lease of life since the end of World War II and the loss of Hoppegarten racecourse, which is now in the Soviet Zone. Under strong management, the summer meeting during the last week of August and the first week of September has steadily increased in prestige and is now by far the best racing in Germany. The meeting lasts for six days, including three days off, and reaches its culmination on the first Sunday in September when the Group 1 Grosser Preis von Baden is competed for.

Although primarily a Flat course, Baden-Baden also stages several hurdles races and steeplechases, which include 'The Hill', the ascent and descent of a sharp bank on the far side of the course. The course is left-handed, with fairly tight bends and a pronounced dog-leg about 1½ furlongs (0.3 km) from the line. In fine weather there is a pleasant view of the rolling foothills of the Black Forest.

Hamburg racecourse, situated in the suburb of Horn, about 3 miles (4.8 km) east of the city centre, is significant only because of the German Derby, which has been run there since 1869. The Derby meeting, which lasts for seven days at the beginning of July, is the only meeting held at Hamburg. The racecourse is used as a public park for 51 weeks of the year and, as a result, conditions are not always ideal. But the authorities are doing their best to improve both the facilities and the standard of racing. The Derby attracts a crowd of about 40,000 and a big sum is bet on the race through the course tote.

Cologne racecourse is situated in the suburb of Weidenpesch, about 2 miles (3.2 km) north of the city centre, and now offers a well-balanced programme throughout the season. It includes six Group races, the most important being the Mehl-Mülhens-Rennen (German 2,000 Guineas) in mid-May; the Union-Rennen in mid-June and the Elite-Preis and Preis von Europa in late September. The Europa is the most valuable race of the German season, attracting horses from all over Europe, and has been won four times by runners from the Soviet Union. Proposals in the early 1980s to sell the track to the city and build a new racecourse and training centre outside Cologne came to nothing. Since then considerable sums have been spent on improving facilities, which are now only second to those of Baden-Baden.

ENGLAND
AINTREE

With only one racing fixture, Aintree racecourse lies woefully dormant for 51 weeks of the year; a lush oasis of splendid under-used turf on the outskirts of Liverpool. But for three days, the eyes of the world are on these sprawling 300 or so acres (121.5 hectares) which go to make up the most demanding test of horse and rider ever devised.

The Grand National Steeplechase, now run over 4½ miles (7.2 km) and 30 unique fences, has enthralled and excited successive generations for 150 years. The brainchild of a Liverpool publican, William Lynn, the great 'chase across country' began at Aintree, in 1839, as the Grand Liverpool Steeplechase, but that historic occasion was preceded by ten years of hard, diligent work by Lynn to attract racegoers to the area. Having leased the racecourse from Lord Sefton in 1829, the genial hotelier at first sought only to offer an alternative Flat-racing venue to that at near by Maghull. But such was the encouraging response from the public to his first effort, in July 1829, that Lynn threw all his energies into developing his enterprise.

A Mr Francis became the first owner to lead in a winner at the new track, after his Mufti triumphed in the Croxteth Stakes (1½ miles/2 km), and a sign that Aintree was preferred to Maghull came in 1830, when the Summer Cup was transferred from the latter to the new course. The St Leger winner, Birmingham, thrilled the Aintree crowds by winning at the Autumn meeting in 1832, having carried off a prize at that year's Maghull spring fixture, but within two years the Maghull track had ceased to function, leaving Lynn the sole organizer of horse-racing in the Liverpool area. With the support of both Lords Derby and Sefton, he went from strength to strength in his determination to provide top-quality competition at Aintree, and, in 1834, the first running of the Knowsley Dinner Stakes fell to the Oaks and St Leger winner, Queen of Trumps.

It was about this time that hurdle racing was introduced into the autumn meeting, and with it arrived the outstanding cross-country rider of the period, Captain Martin Becher. Winning two hurdling events on the same day, astride Vivian, the bewhiskered captain proceeded to regale Lynn with tales of the Great St Albans Chase, and so it was that the idea of a similar contest at Liverpool was planted. After two experimental affairs at the old Maghull track, the first Grand Liverpool Steeplechase to be held at Aintree took place on 26 February 1839, before an estimated crowd of 40,000. At the end of a thrilling race of 4 miles (6.4 km) across country, Lottery and jockey Jem Mason captured their place in the record books.

Grand National runners take the water jump in front of the packed Aintree stands. From there, the horses swing left-handed to face another circuit of formidable fences in the world's greatest steeplechase.

EAST GERMANY

Hoppegarten racecourse is situated about 12 miles (19 km) east of Berlin, in the German Democratic Republic. The course was built in 1867 and for three-quarters of a century was dominant in German racing. For most of this period, the track and the training centre belonged to the Union-Klub. Training facilities were excellent and were the closest to Chantilly and Newmarket, with a huge area given over to shady walks, about 30 miles (48 km) of gallops on sand and grass, and woods.

Hoppegarten reached its zenith in the period between the Wars, when Berlin was not only the German capital, but also Europe's liveliest city. All the leading stables were established there and four of the five Classics (the German Derby has always been run at Hamburg), as well as most of the other top races, were staged there. Under the Nazis, the course reached a peak of popularity which no other racecourse in Germany has ever approached. All this came to a sudden halt with the German defeat and the fall of Berlin. Hoppegarten ended up in the Soviet Zone, and although the course and training centre still exist, racing in East Germany is of low standard and Hoppegarten is now a shadow of its former self.

Despite some fierce opposition from prominent members of the Jockey Club, the new Liverpool event was an overwhelming success with the general public, and in 1843 the race became a handicap, being won by Vanguard and another colourful character of the age, Tom Olliver. The first Irish success was registered by Matthew in 1847, the year in which the event was given the title the Grand National. Twelve months later, the Liverpool Spring Cup came into being. Another landmark in the history of Aintree was reached at this juncture when Edward William Topham assumed overall command at the course. Previously clerk of the course at Chester, Topham introduced the Liverpool Oaks to Aintree in 1851.

In 1884, The Prince of Wales was represented in the Grand National by The Scot and although the royal competitor found Becher's Brook beyond his ability, the heir to the throne's interest in the event silenced all the critics of the race once and for all. Prince Edward's allegiance to it was finally rewarded in 1900, when Ambush II carried his colours to victory. In the meantime, Flat racing had continued to flourish, with the legendary Fred Archer appearing in the winner's enclosure many times.

The halcyon days of the National were undoubtedly the 1920s and 1930s, when the race captured the imagination of wealthy American owners, and when attendances on the big day exceeded 250,000.

In response to the announcement in 1964 that Mrs Mirabel Topham was to sell the racecourse she had purchased from Lord Sefton 15 years earlier, there came an anguished outcry from the media and the public that the fine traditions of Aintree should not be sacrificed to industrial development. Not even that greatest of all National horses, Red Rum, and his amazing achievements, could lift the question mark of uncertainty which hung over Aintree for almost 20 years, although a glimmer of hope did emerge when local property developer, Bill Davies, bought the course in November 1973 for £3 million. His Walton Group received the finest possible start to their administration when Red Rum won his second National. He was the first horse to complete the double since Reynoldstown, in 1935–6, but severely increased admission charges the following year made the 1975 event the worst attended in living memory.

Further difficulties arose when Mr Davies launched his plans to hold an Aintree Derby at the autumn meeting, for these included a demand that the Levy Board make a sizeable donation to the prize money for the race. Totally disenchanted with the Jockey Club, the volatile Davies declared that there would be no more racing at Aintree, but later, to his eternal credit, he handed over management of the racecourse to the bookmakers Ladbrokes. Their advanced marketing techniques and thorough understanding of

racing brought about over the next seven years a distinct improvement.

Inevitably, there were victims of the new regime, the most notable being Flat racing. This took place for the last time on the opening day of the 1976 meeting, when the Liverpool Spring Cup was won by Royal Match. Much of the glamour and dignity returned to the revamped Liverpool races, with increased prize money from a welter of sponsors enticing the finest hurdlers and chasers. The crowds began to flock back.

The incredible third National win of Red Rum, in 1977, and the fairytale success of Aldaniti and his jockey Bob Champion four years later, so entranced us all that the possibility of Aintree closing as a racecourse slipped from our minds. But Grittar's run to glory in 1982, under the able jockeyship of Jockey Club member Dick Saunders, appeared for many anxious months to be the final curtain on a glorious episode in Britain's sporting heritage. But, with mere minutes to spare, Canadian distillers Seagram came to the rescue of the ill-fated National appeal and, through the company's care and generosity, the Grand National has regained its rightful place in international racing.

Aintree has two left-handed courses: the main course, over which the Grand National is run, a triangular circuit of nearly 2¼ miles (3.6 km); and the Mildmay Course, which is approximately 1¼ miles (2 km) round, with conventional fences. The run-in for the National is 494 yards (452 m).

Even before racing begins at Royal Ascot, the huge crowd packs the stand to watch the arrival of the royal party, who are driven down the course from the new Golden Gates, at the start of the straight mile (1.6 km) course.

ASCOT

Royal Ascot is that rare thing — a world event. Like Wimbledon, it is known to millions not usually interested in sport. To the uninitiated, it is often better known for its fashion than for its racing. Yet the racing is superb. The four days of the Royal meeting are held from Tuesday to Friday of the second week of June. A suit replaces the top hat and morning coat for a less formal meeting on the Saturday. Each of the 24 races at the Royal meeting is famous in its own right. None of them is sponsored, and the added prize money in 1988 amounted to some £900,000.

Although Ascot is very traditional, it is constantly adapting to new conditions and opportunities. In 1988, the famous 5-furlong (1 km) sprint, the King's Stand Stakes, was controversially demoted from Group 1 to Group 2, although the winner's prize money was slightly increased, to £65,000. In the same year, the St James's Palace Stakes (won by more horses subsequently famous than any other Royal Ascot race) was upgraded to Group 1 and became the first race of the meeting to top the £100,000 mark for the winning horse. It thus overtook the traditional market leader, the Ascot Gold Cup (2½ miles/ 4 km) which is nevertheless promoted in value to £85,000 added. The fillies' Coronation Stakes, which commemorates the coronation of Queen Victoria, was lifted to Group 1, and in 1988 doubled its value.

The Berkshire course, which covers a magnificent 200 acres (81 hectares), lies 6 miles (10 km) from Windsor Castle and 30 miles (48 km) from London. It is Crown property and non-profitmaking. The track resembles a capital 'P' lying on its side. The round course, running right-handed, measures 14 furlongs (2.8 km), with a straight of only 3 furlongs (0.6 km). The straight mile (1.6 km), initially downhill, runs from the new Golden Gates, through which the royal party drives on each day of the Royal Meeting. A new straight, at a greater angle to the grandstand, was laid down when the present stands were built in the 1950s.

The cavalry charge for the Royal Hunt Cup, run over the full mile (1.6 km) on the Wednesday, is one of the most spectacular sights in racing and provides celebrated gambling. There are always plenty of runners, the post-war record being 39, in 1961, when King's Troop won. Equally spectacular is the Wokingham Stakes, in which the conditions have remained virtually unchanged since the 6-furlong (1.2 km) handicap was introduced in 1818. It is Ascot's oldest surviving handicap. The jockey with the most outstanding record at Ascot is Lester Piggott, who rode 307 winners, including 109 at the Royal meeting.

Ascot's link with royalty is very real. The racecourse came into being when Queen Anne, last of the Stuart Monarchs and a hunting fanatic like all her family, declared that a racecourse must be built on Ascot Heath. This involved little more than having

Cheltenham provides the perfect setting for National Hunt racing. Its March Festival, over three days, stages a superlative jumping programme.

the stones picked up and erecting a few posts and rails, and the Queen herself attended the first race meeting, on 11 August 1711. The Master of the Buckhounds was put in charge from the course's initiation until the death of Queen Victoria in 1901. Since that year, the Sovereign has appointed the Representative to run the racecourse on his/her behalf. The personal involvement in racing of the present Queen leads her to take a keen and informed interest in Royal Ascot.

The popularity of the racecourse increases every year. More people apply for first-time vouchers to the Royal Ascot Enclosure than can be accommodated, and a limit on tickets to the grandstand and paddock has also been introduced. That list, too, had to be closed in 1988 for the Wednesday (Hunt Cup) and Thursday (Gold Cup and 'Ladies' Day'). But space in the vast Silver Ring and on the course, which used to be a perquisite of the carriage trade, is virtually unlimited.

Entry into the Royal Ascot Enclosure is supervised by Her Majesty's Representative, from an office in St James's Palace, London. It used to be the case that no-one who had been divorced could enter the Royal Enclosure. The convention was that, whichever party was 'guilty', the man was considered to be divorced by the woman. Thus, divorced men, however 'innocent', were excluded. When the stands were rebuilt, the Royal Enclosure became the Royal Ascot Enclosure, without moral qualifications. Today the Royal Enclosure proper is confined to the strip of turf walled in before the royal box.

In total, there are at Ascot 13 days of Flat racing annually, while the jumping course, opened on 30 April 1985, stages nine days of National Hunt sport. There has long been a tradition of a day's racing in the autumn in aid of charity. In 1987 a Festival of British Racing was inaugurated to stage the country's most valuable programme. Its centrepiece is the Queen Elizabeth II Stakes, now a Group 1 race.

The Group 1 King George VI and Queen Elizabeth Diamond Stakes, run at the end of July, is acknowledged to be Ascot's premier event. Formed by the amalgamation of two good races, plus generous sponsorship from De Beers, it brings together three-year-olds and upwards over 1½ miles (2.4 km) for the first time in the season. It was introduced to mark the Festival of Britain in 1952 and has provided some memorable races, not least the epic battle between Grundy and Bustino, in 1975.

CHELTENHAM

There can be no steeplechasing course in the world to match Cheltenham for both the beauty of its surroundings and the quality of its racing at the three-day Festival meeting in March. Situated below the picturesque hills of the Cotswolds, Prestbury Park has for years been the testing arena in which the best of the Irish jumpers, with thousands of their followers, cross the sea to battle with the English. Just occasionally, America and France join in, but the Festival is essentially a show of strength between neighbours. Sadly, the days have gone when trainers like Vincent O'Brien and Tom Dreaper could be relied upon to send the Irish punter home with all expenses paid and a present for his wife. The creaming off by English buyers of horses bred in Ireland has taken its toll, but there will always be holes in the net.

Cheltenham comprises the Old and New courses. They are tough, but fair, undulating left-handed tracks, 1½ miles (2.4 km) round, with a gruelling uphill run-in of 237 yards (217 m). It is this final stretch which draws out all the deep reserves of courage possessed by only the most determined horses. Punters who count their winnings at the last obstacle often find that even an each-way ticket turns out to be a worthless piece of paper. Reputations are made and lost at Prestbury Park. It is a course for champions and the names of the greatest Gold Cup heroes reverberate down the years: Easter Hero, Golden Miller, Cottage Rake, and peerless Arkle; a heroine, too, that glorious but ill-fated mare Dawn Run, whose unique double in the Gold Cup (1986) and Champion Hurdle (1984) is unforgettable. Hatton's Grace, Sir Ken, Persian War, and See You Then all completed Champion Hurdle trebles and it is against them that talented horses of the future will be measured.

The first Cheltenham Gold Cup was a weight-for-age 3-mile (4.8 km) Flat race for three-year-olds and upwards, which was run on Cleeve Hill in August 1819. The Duke of Gloucester attended the three-day meeting. The county's first well-organized steeplechase, subsequently the Grand Annual, was staged at Andoversford in 1834. It was won in 1839 and 1840 by the legendary rider Gem Mason and his Grand National hero, Lottery. The present course was used for the first time in 1902. Messrs Pratt took over the management five years later and, in 1908, the Cheltenham Steeplechase Company was formed. By 1914, new stands were complete. The accommodation was used as a war hospital from 1915 and racing did not begin again until 1919.

The Festival became a three-day meeting in 1923, and in 1924 the Cheltenham Gold Cup, a weight-for-age steeplechase for five-year olds and upwards over 3 miles 2 furlongs (5.2 km) was run for the first time. It was followed in 1927 by the launch of the Champion Hurdle Challenge Cup, which was won in its second year by the legendary Brown Jack. A new Tattersalls stand was completed at Cheltenham in 1958. Since then, there has been a rolling programme of improvements to the main grandstand, with the first stage completed in 1979. The average total attendance for the Festival is 115,000. There are 16 days of racing through the season, with one of the main features being the Mackeson Gold Cup, a handicap chase over 2½ miles (4 km) in November.

EPSOM

Four hundred thousand people do not gather together in one place on a mid-week afternoon in high summer without good reason. And Derby Day, on Epsom Downs, is reason enough. It is not only the highlight of the world's racing calendar for the international connoisseur of thoroughbreds — for some it is a champagne social occasion. But for everyone, it is the excitement and fun of being part of the world's most widely shared sporting experience.

Epsom racecourse, which stages three meetings a year, *is* the Derby. Many will attend all four days of the June meeting, which includes the fillies' Classic — the Oaks — and the Coronation Cup, but the vast majority of the teeming thousands will just melt away through the Surrey lanes, not to be seen again on the Downs for another 12 months. There are now Derbys in many countries, although none pretends to compete. The Epsom winner guarantees wealth to the owner, the prize money being only a small fraction of the millions of pounds the horse will be worth at stud.

The horseshoe-shaped course of 1½ miles (2.4 km) on which the Derby and Oaks are run is unique. Just before the runners have reached half-way, they will have risen 134 ft

(41 m) from the start. Soon after passing this highest point of the track, they sweep left-handed down the steep Tattenham Hill to the sharp left-hander at Tattenham Corner. The 4-furlong (0.8 km) straight, which rises only at the last 100 yards (91 m), has a camber from the stands side towards the far rails which, at the winning post, measures about 6 ft (1.8 m). Epsom is a course only for the horse who will stay balanced both coming down the hill and in the straight, and who has both speed and stamina. In 1915, Tattenham Corner was made less severe, but that is the only change to the course since 1872.

The racecourse, only 14 miles (22 km) from Piccadilly Circus in the heart of London, is part of a Metropolitan Common and regulations applying to London Commons also apply to Epsom Downs. Problems that have arisen over the rights of the public to take exercise and air have been resolved over the years and the Epsom and Walton Downs Regulation Act of 1984 ensured that racing would continue. The crowd of 400,000 mentioned earlier is an estimate made by the police on Derby Day 1988. There is still no admission charge for spectators who spill off the trains and arrive on the Downs on foot to watch the races from outside the enclosures.

Racing has been staged at Epsom for well over 300 years. There is certainly evidence of it taking place in 1648, but there is no official record until 7 March 1661. The first Derby, won by Diomed, was run in 1780, the year after the inauguration of the 1½-mile (2.4 km) race for three-year-old fillies. This was called the Oaks, after a house of that name

Epsom's antiquated grandstand from the famous Tattenham Corner. Derby runners swing into the straight and, for one horse, fame and fortune is only four furlongs (800 m) away.

leased near the town by the Twelfth Earl of Derby. There were 17 subscribers at 50 guineas each for the 1779 launch, which was such a success that a similar race, this time for three-year-old colts and fillies over 1 mile (1.6 km), was planned for the following year. It was to be named either the Derby Stakes or the Bunbury Stakes, in honour of Sir Charles Bunbury, the leading figure of the Turf at that time. It is said that a toss of a coin during a house party at The Oaks decided the issue. The distance of the Derby was lengthened to 1½ miles (2.4 km) for its running in 1784 and has not changed since.

Derby Day became so popular in Victorian times that businessmen in London were obliged to regard it as an unpaid holiday for the work force. Even Parliament took the day off. There was a massive exodus from the city, especially from the East End. But even if many of the day trippers straggled home without knowing, or caring, which horse had won the Derby, it was at least the one day in the year when the highest and the lowest shared the same grand and happy occasion.

GOODWOOD

Towards the end of July, on a fine raceday, Goodwood is indeed, as it is commonly described, 'glorious'. The bright green of the curving, right-handed course ribbons between white rails against fields of ripening crops and a background of Prussian-blue woods. To the south a summer haze dims the English Channel. It is England at its best.

The racecourse lies on the crest of the South Downs in Sussex, 65 miles (104 km) from London and 5 miles (8 km) from Chichester, and the nearest railway station. Goodwood's setting is unique, as is its link with an historic ducal house. The present impressive, late-Georgian mansion was built to the design of Sir William Chambers (1720–96) and greatly enlarged and altered by James Wyatt (1746–1813).

The Goodwood estate was bought in 1694 by the First Duke of Richmond, the son of Charles II and his French mistress, Louise de Kerouelle. Charles Lennox had, in 1675, been made First Duke of Richmond in the English peerage and Duke of Lennox in the Scottish peerage. (It was the Fifth Duke, so closely linked with the development of the racecourse, who was created Duke of Gordon in 1876.) Today, the Earl of March, the heir to the Ninth Duke, is very much the man behind the racecourse. He has a practical and pragmatic approach to the problems of controlling a huge family business which includes farming, forestry, property,

Goodwood's stands have been criticized since they were built in 1980. But the view they offer over the Sussex Downs makes the course one of the world's most attractive.

leisure industries, the racecourse and even an airfield. His maxim is: 'If it's there, make it work — and pay.'

Goodwood became a racecourse almost by accident. When the nineteenth century opened, England was braced to meet invasion by Napoleon and troops were 'stood-to' along the south coast. In 1800, the Third Duke of Richmond put on a scratch race meeting for the entertainment of the officers. It was a great success and, in 1801, a public, but still modest race meeting was arranged. That fixture could well have been snuffed out at once, like so many English racecourses of the time. But its popularity kept it alive and it became the hobby of the Fifth Duke.

The Duke had been badly wounded in the Battle of Orhez (1814), in which Wellington defeated the French. His doctors insisted that he must give up hunting, so he devoted his organizational ability towards making Goodwood 'the finest racecourse in the land'. He was inspired and guided in this by Lord George Bentinck, the arrogant, far-seeing reformer of nineteenth-century racing, who had such an influence on the power of the Jockey Club and the general standing of the sport in Britain. The Duke's innovations were numerous and beneficial.

Goodwood marked the end of the London season. No wonder a foreign visitor wrote, 'with magnificent scenery, first class racing and the cream of England's society to inspire and gratify him, a stranger would indeed be fastidious who did not consider Goodwood the perfection and paradise of racecourses'. Goodwood retains its style. There are always many more would-be occupants of its members' stand than will be admitted. The new members' grandstand was built in 1980, at the same time as 30 luxurious private boxes. The cost was over £3.5 million, but the stand still has many critics. Goodwood week is popular with jockeys, many of whom bring their families for the nearby seaside as well as the racing. But it is not an easy course to ride, partly because of its undulations. It is not a particularly severe track and suits an active, happy horse more than a dour stayer.

Goodwood is continually changing and improving its shape. In 1988, no fewer than 54 of the 112 scheduled races had found sponsors, and prize money had risen to a record £1.25 million. In 1987 attendance figures rose by 13 per cent. The Stewards' Cup, now sponsored by the bookmakers William Hill, is one of the biggest gambles of the year, the runners spreading right across the course for this 6-furlong (1.2 km) dash. The Predominate Stakes, Goodwood's Derby trial, over the full distance, had not perhaps gained as much popularity as the trials at York and Lingfield, so, in 1988, it was cut from 12 to 10 furlongs (2.4 km to 2 km).

Goodwood's Group 1 Swettenham Stud Sussex Stakes, run in 1988 with £200,000 added, is the most valuable all-ages 1 mile (1.6 km) race in Europe. The Schweppes Golden Mile (1.6 km), on the following day, is the richest mile handicap in Europe, with £75,000 added. Another valuable race over the distance is the Waterford Crystal Mile (1.6 km), at the late August meeting, when the Skol Spring Classic Final (£60,000 added) was 1988's most valuable 5-furlong (1 km) handicap in Europe.

NEWMARKET
Rowley Mile and July Course

Racing has taken place at Newmarket since King Charles II rode against his courtiers on the broad stretch of heathland to the west of the town, following his restoration to the throne in 1660. Whereas in those days there was one course, the Beacon course, with a circumference of 4 miles (6.4 km), this prestigious venue nowadays has two separate courses. On the side of the heath farthest from Newmarket is the July Course and nearer the town is the Rowley Mile, which in fact extends to 2½ miles (4 km), with just the one right-hand turn 1¼ miles (2 km) from home. The latter course owes its name to Charles's nickname 'Old Rowley', which, in turn, derived from the name of his favourite hack, Rowley.

The monarch founded the Spring and Autumn Meetings at Newmarket, which remain two of the focal points of the racing calendar. These are run on the Rowley Mile. The Craven Meeting in early April is followed by the Spring Meeting at the end of the month, both being of three days' duration. At the other end of the season, the four-day Autumn Meeting, opening in late September, precedes by a fortnight the three-day Houghton meeting, so-called because leading members of the Jockey Club used to stay with Lord Orford at Houghton Hall for the racing.

The two greatest races run at Newmarket are its Classics, championship races for three-year-olds over the straight mile (1.6 km), at the Spring Meeting. These are the 1,000 Guineas, for fillies only, run on the last Thursday in April and the 2,000 Guineas for colts and fillies, though rarely contested by the latter, run the following Saturday. Back in 1809, the first 2,000 Guineas was won by Wizard owned by the Yorkshire sportsman Christopher Wilson and ridden by Billy Clift. The same owner and jockey were associated with Charlotte, successful in the first running of the 1,000 Guineas in 1814.

Famous winners of the 2,000 Guineas include Lord Exeter's Stockwell (1852), so successful at stud that he went on to be dubbed 'The Emperor of Stallions'; West Australian (1853), who became the first horse to complete the Triple Crown in the Derby and the St Leger; Prince Charlie (1872), never beaten in 11 races at Newmarket; and the Duke of Westminster's magnificent, unbeaten Ormonde, another Triple Crown winner. In 1902, Sceptre became the last of the four fillies to have won both the 2,000 Guineas and 1,000 Guineas.

The features of the Craven meeting are the Classic trials, the Craven Stakes, over a mile (1.6 km) and the 7-furlong (1.4 km) Nell Gwyn Stakes (named after Charles II's most famous mistress), which have often served as informative rehearsals for the 2,000 Guineas and 1,000 Guineas respectively.

A pair of valuable handicaps, the Cambridgeshire and the Cesarewitch, two prestigious races for two-year-olds, the Middle Park Stakes and the Dewhurst Stakes, and the Champion Stakes (1¼ miles/2 km), which lives up to its name most years, are the main attractions of the principal Newmarket meetings in the second half of the season. The Cambridgeshire, run over the straight mile and a furlong (1.8 km) and the 6-furlong (1.2 km) Middle Park Stakes are staged at the Autumn Meeting and the Cesarewitch, the Champion Stakes, and the Dewhurst Stakes at the Houghton meeting.

The Dewhurst Stakes often provides a valuable clue as to the outcome of the Classics of the following year. Nijinsky (1969), Mill Reef (1970), Grundy (1974), and The Minstrel (1976) all completed the double in the Dewhurst Stakes and the Derby, while Wollow (1975) and El Gran Señor (1983)

went on to win the 2,000 Guineas over another furlong (0.2 km) on the course the following spring. As the Cesarewitch is run over a gruelling 2¼ miles (3.6 km), with just the one turn, an out-and-out stayer is needed to win it. The Champion Stakes provides the final clash between top-class three-year-olds and their elders. Mares and fillies, who are at their best in the autumn, have an excellent record in the race and during the 16 years from 1973 to 1988, have won it no fewer than 11 times.

A major modernization programme was complete by the time of the opening for the 1987-8 season of the Rowley Mile course.

Attending a meeting on Newmarket's July Course, amid the wonderful display of flowers on a shimmering summer's day, is one of the greatest pleasures afforded by the English Turf. The loveliness of the setting, though, does no more than complement the standard of the racing, especially at the three-day July meeting, generally held in the first full week of the month.

The principal events of the fixture are the Group 1 July Cup, the Princess of Wales's Stakes, and the Child Stakes. In addition, there are two good races for two-year-olds: the July Stakes, the oldest juvenile race in the world, founded in 1786, and the Cherry Hinton Stakes for fillies. And there is always a strong field for the Bunbury Cup, a 7-furlong (1.4 km) handicap, named after Sir Charles Bunbury, who was a founding father of racing and the owner of the first Derby winner.

The valuable July Cup is a championship race for sprinters. Recent winners include that very imposing horse, Chief Singer, who beat Never So Bold in 1984. Older horses, who are in the top class over middle distances, clash in the 1½ mile (2.4 km) Princess of Wales's Stakes, which has fallen to Classic winners like Light Cavalry and Lupe. The Child Stakes, run over a mile (1.6 km), brings into contention fillies of the very highest class. As well as at the big meeting, there is racing on the July course on intermittent weekends throughout the summer.

SANDOWN PARK

Voted Britain's Racecourse of the Year in 1988, Sandown Park stages both top-quality Flat and jumping races. Situated about 14 miles (22 km) south-west of London, it is one of the country's best-placed and popular tracks. The modern grandstand is on a small hillside above the testing right-handed course. There is a clear view of almost the entire arena, even from ground level. Sandown is a young course, having been opened in 1875, and was the first in Britain to be completely enclosed by fencing.

Hwfa Williams, his brother, General Owen Williams, and Sir Wilfred Brett were the men who started racing at Sandown, which is an oval of 1 mile 5 furlongs (2.6 km) with a testing uphill run-in of 4 furlongs (0.8 km). There are no 6-furlong (1.2 km) races. The main Flat race staged there is the long-established Eclipse Stakes, which has to compete for runners with the highly prestigious King George VI and Queen Elizabeth Diamond Stakes at Ascot's later July meeting. Sandown is very popular in the winter too. The Imperial Cup still has a high standing among the country's top hurdle races and was the most valuable until overtaken by the Schweppes Gold Trophy, inaugurated in 1963.

One of Sandown's most popular meetings of the year is Whitbread Gold Cup day, in April. It is a steeplechase of 3 miles 5 furlongs (5.8 km) and is the only National Hunt event on an otherwise Flat-racing programme. It attracts top-class horses and has produced many memorable battles. The most testing part of the steeplechase course is the back straight, where fences come close together: a mistake at the first of them can have a disastrous knock-on effect.

YORK

York is one of the best racecourses in Europe. It is often called the 'Ascot of the North', but in reality it has an air of history, quality, and friendliness all of its own. Situated about a mile (1.6 km) outside the city and its famous Minster, the Knavesmire course stages 15 days of Flat racing every year. The Mecca-Dante Stakes, in May, is a Classic trial won by subsequent Epsom Derby heroes, Shirley Heights (1978), Shahrastani (1986), and Reference Point (1987). The Ebor meeting, in August, features three Group 1 races and is the highlight of the York season.

More than 200,000 racegoers a year enjoy the Knavesmire, where racing has been presented since 1731. But there has been racing at York since Roman times, when horses were matched against each other on Rawcliffe and Clifton Ings, a stretch of land to the north of the city and then part of the Forest of Galtres. The first detailed record of a race meeting dates back to 1709, but it is known that other contests took place in 1607 on the frozen River Ouse between Micklegate Tower and Skeldergate Postern. In 1633, King Charles I watched a race on Acomb Moor.

Flooding caused frequent problems on the Clifton Ings course; in 1730 a move was made to the Knavesmire, itself a boggy stretch of dead-flat, undrained, common land. Much had to be done before the track was fit for racing in 1731. The famous Gimcrack Stakes was named after a small grey who

The paddock at Sandown Park is well placed beneath the modern stands. The course, which is close to London, was voted Britain's top track.

High-rise buildings tower over floodlit runners at Hong Kong's Happy Valley track.

1846. From the early days, racing took place in January, February, and March, to coincide with the Lunar New Year. A tight, right-handed grass course, Happy Valley introduced an inner sand track in 1973 and racing on it was originally held under lights. It was never as popular as the racing on grass, which attracts capacity crowds of 42,000.

Sha Tin racecourse opened in Hong Kong's New Territories on 7 October 1978. It was built on 250 acres reclaimed from the sea and features a right-handed grass track.

INDIA

Within walking distance of the busy city centre, Calcutta racecourse started out in 1769 in the leafy suburbs at Akara. This was in the area where the King of Oudh and some of his descendants, deposed by the British, lived in their palatial garden houses. At that time, the track was marked out for the day over rough round and was so narrow that races were restricted to four horses. The course was moved to its present site, at the Maidan, in 1809. In the days of the Bengal Jockey Club, race meetings were held in the mornings and were followed by lavish breakfasts.

Racing was dominated by Arab-bred horses until about 1855, when the English and Australian breeds came on the scene. By then, the Calcutta Turf Club had been operating for eight years, a committee of five managing the affairs of the Club and five stewards supervising the racing. Calcutta was the first centre in the Indian subcontinent to stage a Derby. It was inaugurated in 1842 and confined to maiden Arabs over a distance of 2 miles (3.2 km). The Calcutta Derby Stakes carried for the winner a fabulous prize of 5,000 rupees, which, in today's terms, would be a colossal sum. The race was replaced in 1856 by the Viceroy's Cup, over the St Leger distance, and by the time an Indian filly, Hovercraft, won in 1964, it had become the Queen Elizabeth II Cup.

Lord Ulrich Browne dominated the Indian racing scene for 25 years from 1860. His two major reforms were redrafting the Rules of Racing and the revision of the Weight-for-Age Scale. The Calcutta Derby Sweep, introduced in 1867, grew to the huge sum of 12½ million rupees at its peak. It produced a high level of stake money and huge grants were given to local charities, but it was killed off by the Irish Sweep. Steeplechasing was popular in Calcutta in the 1870s and the first Grand National was run in 1895. The last one, in 1929, was won by Kilbuck, who ran and fell in the 1931 Aintree Grand National. Calcutta has a good galloping grass track and stages its own 1,000 Guineas, 2,000 Guineas, Oaks, Classic Derby, and St Leger.

India's racing is concentrated in several

won 26 races in his career but was unsuccessful in his only two runs at York, in 1768 and 1769. The York Race Committee, founded in 1842, is still the body responsible for running the Knavesmire. The latest project is a £2.5 million grandstand adjacent to the parade ring.

York's fair and testing course is left-handed and flat, with a circumference of 2 miles (3.2 km) and a straight run-in of 5 furlongs (1 km). Major races at the three-day August meeting include the Group 1 International (1¼ miles/2 km, for three-year-olds and upwards); the Group 1 Yorkshire Oaks (1½ miles/2.4 km, for three-year-old fillies); the Tote Ebor Handicap (1¾ miles/2.8 km); the Gimcrack Stakes (6 furlongs/1.2 km, for two-year-olds); and the Group 1 William Hill Spring Championship (5 furlongs/1 km, for three-year-olds and upwards).

HONG KONG

Racing is thought to have taken place in Hong Kong within four or five years of the settlement of the Colony, probably in 1845 or 1846. Happy Valley racecourse was established on a flat marsh known as Wong Nei Chung (Valley of Yellow Mud), which had been drained in the 1840s. The first meeting was probably held on 17 and 18 December

centres, with Bombay (which has a summer course at Pune), Bangalore, Hyderabad, and Madras all fiercely proud of their independence. Each centre runs its own racing and stages its own series of Classics. One of the highlights of the season is an invitation race, hosted by the major courses on a rota basis, in which the country's top horses compete.

IRELAND
THE CURRAGH

The Irish Racing Calendar, first published in 1790, included details of 22 race meetings, among them The Curragh, Roscommon, Downpatrick, Tralee, and Sligo. They exist today, but not in all cases on the original site. Ireland now takes in 27 grass tracks, with a unique one-day meeting held annually on the beach at Laytown, County Meath, the tide permitting. But the headquarters of Irish racing is The Curragh, where the Turf Club administration centre is to be found.

The location of the racecourse, where all five Irish Classics are run, is on a vast heath in Kildare and was part of the lands of the Hill of Allen, one of the palaces of the Kings of Leinster. 'Curragh' is an old Irish name for a racecourse, and King James II attended his first meeting there in 1686. But we have to move on over half a century, to 1741, for the first officially recorded winner at The Curragh — Lord Bessborough's bay mare, Dairy Maid, winner of two heats of an annual prize of £60.

Long before another century had passed, Flat racing in Ireland suffered a decline. It was time for a boost, so Lord Howth, The Marquis of Drogheda, and the Earl of Charlemont inaugurated the Irish Derby in 1866. Its first winner was Selim, owned by an Englishman. In contrast to the first Derby, which drew an entry of 38, the revamped Irish Sweeps Derby, set up under the aegis of Joe McGrath in 1962, attracted an entry of 627 horses — a world record for a Classic. And when the event had only one entry stage for the first time, in 1974, the total soared to 744. The popularity of the race has continued, with many owners of Epsom Derby winners keen to challenge at The Curragh for the Derby double. The most recent of eight colts to win both Classics was the Aga Khan's Kahyasi, in June 1988. The same owner had achieved the feat earlier with Shergar (1981) and Shahrastani (1986).

Through most of the 1980s, attendances dropped at several Curragh fixtures. In response, the Curragh Committee was formed, with Michael Osborne, Sheikh Mohammed Al Maktoum's Irish manager at nearby Kildangan Stud and Woodpark Stud, as its chairman. There followed a modernization of the racecourse's facilities, great improvements to the course itself and several plans for the future.

LEOPARDSTOWN

Leopardstown is a splendid, rectangular galloping track which provides Dublin, and the country as a whole, with attractive Flat and National Hunt racing in modern surroundings. It was built on the site of a model farm founded in 1860 by Benedictine monks, who deserted it in 1882 for England.

Leopardstown Club opened up a new era of racing in Ireland, setting an infinitely higher standard of stakes. A group of Dublin businessmen had bought the land and appointed a Captain George Quinn to oversee its development. The design of the course was based on that of Sandown Park, near London, and the first meeting was held on 27 August 1888, when a massive crowd turned out. Leopardstown soon received the all-important royal patronage when the Duke and Duchess of York (later King George V and Queen Mary) attended in the summer of 1897.

Captain Quinn managed the course until 1912, when he was succeeded by F. Harold Clarke who, together with his son Fred, was to shape the future of the course. In 1969, Fred Clarke was responsible for the sale of Leopardstown to the Irish Racing Board, thus ensuring that it would never be sold for development. The Board immediately set about the task of making it Ireland's premier racetrack. This involved the construction of new stands, enclosed betting halls, and dining

Ireland's premier track, The Curragh, puts on a good show – including flowers – for its five Classic races.

and bar facilities, as well as new stables, offices and service areas. The track was relaid and extensive drainage and watering systems were installed, so all was ready for a grand reopening, to a capacity crowd, in January 1971. In December 1987 a new seated stand and 16 private suites, in addition to those built the previous year, were opened.

Ireland's first Epsom Derby winner, Orby, made his debut at Leopardstown. In 1892, that great Aintree performer, Manifesto, won the Irish Champion Chase there, all his other racing having been in England, while the early 1940s saw Prince Regent winning on the course. But an even greater steeplechaser, Arkle, arrived two decades later. He won three times over the Dublin track before the first of his three Cheltenham Gold Cup victories. In fact, Arkle prefaced each of his Gold Cup triumphs with a visit to Leopardstown, where his only failure was in an amateur Flat race on his second start.

The Leopardstown course has always been innovative. In January 1898, the executive sanctioned the then new starting machine, and both the film patrol and the photo-finish were pioneered there. When it came to sponsorship, the course was again in the vanguard, and it staged Ireland's first Sunday meeting on 21 July 1985. Leopardstown also introduced Computote, which is based on the pari-mutuel betting system.

PHOENIX PARK

Phoenix Park's 100-acre (40.5 hectares) racecourse, located in the north-west corner of Dublin, is one of the most famous, and certainly the most fashionable, in Ireland. It was only the second Irish racecourse, Leopardstown being the first, to be started on club lines. Phoenix Park's foundation was due to the energies of the clever Corkman, J. H. H. Peard, and his friends, among whom Sir John Arnott, the first baronet and father of the notable Irish trainer, Maxwell Arnott, stood out prominently. Peard had managed the long-defunct Cork Park for many years before he felt there was need for another high-class track near Dublin. The £75,000 capital was acquired and they modelled the grounds and stands to a great extent on England's old Hurst Park track.

Racing at Phoenix Park dates from 1902, meetings extending from late March or early April until October, with the August Horse Show meeting and the sprint for the Phoenix Stakes being the season's highlights. This race is now the Heinz '57' Phoenix Stakes and is run over 6 furlongs (1.2 km) instead of the original five (1 km). The Park was managed by J. H. H. Peard's son, Harry, from 1939 to 1950, when his widow Fanny took the job. She became only the second woman in Europe to hold such an appointment, Mirabel Topham of Aintree fame being the first. Mrs Peard was politely forced

to retire in March 1969, when rumours had it that there was about to be a take-over. This did take place, but much later, and was due to a sharp recession that brought Phoenix Park close to bankruptcy. And so the Irish trainer Vincent O'Brien and football-pools magnate, Robert Sangster, came to the rescue by buying and refurbishing the complex.

The new owners embarked on an extensive and successful sponsorship, which had a very strong American connection, and founded the Phoenix Champion Stakes, with a guaranteed value of not less than £400,000. Run for the first time in September 1984, it was won, appropriately, by Sangster's Sadler's Wells. But matters did not carry on smoothly for long and there were hints of possible closure when the Racing Board could not see their way clear to take over the course. Profits had fallen alarmingly by 1987 and, in November, the club stand was destroyed by fire.

A rebuilding programme was started under the new management of CSI Ltd, a British sports-promotion company with Vincent O'Brien as chairman and Jonathan Irwin, of Goff's, as managing director. John Sanderson, the ex-manager of York racecourse, and the widely experienced Mike Watt, are board directors. The total prize money for 1987 was over £1.7 million and over £2.5 million in 1988.

In 1988 Phoenix Park was the venue for the first running of the prestigious Cartier Million.

Phoenix Park, close to Dublin city centre, has been through troubled times, but prize money in 1988 amounted to over £2.5 million.

PUNCHESTOWN

The great Punchestown Spring Meeting was established in a minor way in 1847, but filling, as it did, a distinct place in the Irish racing year, it was reconstructed in 1861. The seal was set on its fame when the Prince of Wales, later King Edward VII, paid his first visit to the home of steeplechasing in 1868. The present location was set up in 1850, with Lord Drogheda, Lord Mayo, and Lord Waterford immediately taking an active interest. The meeting became known as 'Peerless Punchestown', although it was anything but peerless, according to one historian.

Lord Drogheda was most instrumental in establishing the Kildare Hunt meeting. Known as the 'Admiral Rous of the Irish Turf', he died suddenly in London on Irish Derby Day, 1892. It was under Percy La Touche, who had taken over control in 1886, that the meeting grew in festival spirit and in importance. The hunt chase of 4 miles (6.4 km), which continues to this day, is named in his honour.

Towards the end of the last century, Punchestown was symbolized by the famous Beasley brothers, Harry, Tommy, Willie, and John, who emerged from the amateur ranks. In fact, the greatest participating figure in the entire history of the course was Harry Beasley, who won every notable jump race at Punchestown, Fairyhouse, Liverpool, and even at Auteuil. He was 85 when he had his last ride, at Baldoyle, in June 1935. His death four years later signified that an epoch-making era in steeplechasing had ended.

Punchestown's banks, stone walls, brooks, 'doubles', drop fences, in fact every variety of obstacle, were unique until the introduction of bush fences in 1960. A hurdle course was opened in 1963 and the Kildare Hunt meeting was increased from two days to three. Lord Drogheda had aimed to keep the meeting distinct from all the others, but the need for change had to be faced and today Punchestown has both Flat and National Hunt fixtures. It is much less conservative now, with sponsorship playing a vital role, and modern amenities to suit all needs.

ITALY

The first recorded meeting in Italy was staged in Florence in 1837, an event followed by a meeting at Naples later that year. Racing was a low-key affair throughout the nineteenth century, although racecourses at Capannelle (Rome) and San Siro (Milan) had both been inaugurated during the 1840s. The first boost to the sport was the formation of the Jockey Club Italiano in 1881. But it was not until Federico Tesio founded in 1898 the influential stud, the Razza Dormello-Ogliata, that horses of quality started to appear.

Capannelle, situated in a suburb of Rome, stages three of the five Italian Classics, the Premio Regina Elena and Premio Parioli (1,000 and 2,000 Guineas) and the Derby Italiano, which was first run as the Derby Reale over this course and distance (2,400 m/ 1½ miles) in 1884. The season starts in February and continues through to June, when it halts for the traditional midsummer break. Although meetings begin again in September, Capannelle stages only one more big race, the all-aged Premio Roma over 2,000 m (10 furlongs) in November. This is the last Group 1 race of the European calendar.

San Siro racecourse, tucked away in an exclusive suburb of Milan, is the busiest of the Italian tracks, with over 80 racing days a year. The season runs on similar lines to those of Rome — March through to July — and then there is an autumn meeting which continues until mid-November. Milan stages the two big all-aged, middle-distance races of the Italian calendar, the Gran Premio di Milano in June, and the Gran Premio del Jockey Club e Coppa d'Oro in mid-October. As well as those championship events, the course hosts the Oaks d'Italia in May and the premier two-year-old race, the Gran Criterium, in October. A Group race is staged most Sundays and a handful of hurdle and steeplechase races are run as an adjunct to a day's Flat racing programme.

The racecourse at Turin was granted the honour of staging an Italian Classic for the first time in 1988, when the St Leger Italiano was moved there from Milan.

Kuala Lumpur plays a major role in the Singapore and Malaysia racing programme.

NEW ZEALAND

A great country for breeding, New Zealand has provided Australia with many of its best Flat horses and its jumpers have been popular imports to English stables.

Ellerslie, home of the New Zealand Derby, is the country's premier racecourse and one of two in Auckland. The course has racing on two tracks for more than 40 days throughout the year. Hurdles and steeplechase races are also staged. The steeplechase course features Ellerslie's famous 'Hill', which has two fences on top, and one at the bottom, on the exit side.

Trentham is the oldest course in New Zealand. Both the Oaks and St Leger are run there. Flat and left-handed, it is banked on all turns. A big, galloping track, Trentham is conducive to fast times and a number of Australasian records have been set there. They include the world electronic record for 2 miles (3.2 km) (3 minutes 16¾ seconds) set by Il Tempo in 1970.

Riccarton, on the South Island, is New Zealand's largest course and stages the 1,000 and 2,000 Guineas. It is a left-handed circuit, 2,400 m (2,624 yards) in circumference, with a straight of 500 m (547 yards). Jump racing, very strong on the South Island, dominates during the winter, with the New Zealand Grand National and Grand National Hurdles being the big attractions in August.

JAPAN

Tokyo racecourse boasts a grandstand more than 400 yards (366 m) long, crowds of 100,000 at meetings held only at weekends, and a betting figure of around £8 million on a single afternoon. The track can hold 180,000 spectators and the grandstand alone can accommodate 89,900. The record attendance is 169,174. Amenities are constantly being improved, from the exclusive Guest Room, where the whole course can be seen at a glance, to the advanced betting and pay-out facilities.

Japan started western-style racing, which was staged by resident foreigners of Yokohama, in 1861, and the following year

the Yokohama Race Club was organized, with events held on an oval track. In 1870, there was Festival racing for the first time, at a shrine in Kudan dedicated to the spirits of the war dead. In 1878 the Nippon Race Club was founded as an amalgamation of the Yokohama Race Club and the Yokohama Racing Association, with General Saigo as one of its founders. Meetings were held regularly in spring and autumn. Between 1878 and 1887, there was racing at several centres, including Tokyo, and co-operative racing societies were formed. Tokyo is now the main track of ten run by the Japan Racing Association. Nakayama, Kyoto, and Hanshim lead the others.

Tokyo started to host international racing with the introduction of the Japan Cup in 1981. In the first seven years, winners came from the United States (Mairzy Doates and Half Iced), Ireland (Stanerra), Japan (Katsuragi Ace and Symboli Rudolph), the UK (Jupiter Island), and France (Le Glorieux). It is run over 2,400 m (1½ miles) on the left-handed oval turf course. There are also a dirt course and a steeplechase course.

SINGAPORE AND MALAYSIA

The Malaysian racing scene moves between Singapore, Kuala Lumpur, Ipoh, and Penang. Each course stages Saturday and Sunday meetings for two weeks before moving on to the next centre on a rota basis. They are all good left-handed grass tracks, with Kuala Lumpur being the tightest.

Singapore's Bukit Timah course presents the most valuable races, the most important being the Singapore Gold Cup (2,200 m/2,405 yards), the Singapore Derby (2,400 m/2,624 yards), and the Lion City Cup (1,200 m/1,312 yards). Kuala Lumpur puts on the Selangor Tunku Gold Cup (2,000 m/2,187 yards), the Piala Emas Sultan Selangor (1,600 m/1,749 yards), and the Selangor Agong Gold Cup (1,200 m/1,312 yards). The Perak Derby, Perak Sultan's Gold Vase, and the Coronation Cup are run at Ipoh, while Penang stages the Yang Di Pertuan Negri Gold Cup and the Penang Sprint Trophy as its main events.

SOUTH AFRICA

Gosforth Park is one of two major racecourses in the Transvaal, the leading racing province in South Africa. All Saturday race meetings in the Transvaal are held at Gosforth Park and the other principal track, Turffontein. Racing started at Gosforth Park, situated to the east of Johannesburg and about ten minutes' drive from the city centre, at the turn of the century. One of the founder members, John Wilson, who was secretary and clerk of the course, was born at Gosforth, in Cumbria, in the north of England, and the course was named after his hometown.

Gosforth Park is widely considered to be the most innovative track in South Africa. It was the first in the world to hold an international jockeys' race and the first in South Africa to broadcast an on-course commentary and to screen a race live from overseas. The course is right-handed, triangular in shape, and has a circumference of 2,300 m (2,515 yards). The straight (1,000 m/1,093 yards) joins the cambered far bend at the 700 m (765 yards) mark and the near bend at the 500 m (547 yards) mark. Major races at Gosforth Park include the R300,000 Administrator's Classic, the richest event in the country for three-year-olds, the R150,000 Computaform Sprint over 1,000 m (1,093 yards), one of the most valuable sprints in the country, and the R150,000 Lancôme Handicap, the richest handicap for fillies and mares.

Greyville racecourse, situated in the heart

of Durban, in the province of Natal, is host each year to South Africa's most famous race, the Rothmans July Handicap, which is run on the first Saturday in July over 2,200 m (2,405 yards) of the pear-shaped track. Greyville is home of the Durban Turf Club, which struggled in its early days against its rival the Durban Sporting Club. The latter was absorbed by the Durban Turf Club.

In addition to the July Handicap, Greyville's major races include the Daily News 2,000, which forms the last leg of the South African Triple Crown for three-year-olds, and the Administrator's Champion Futurity Stakes, the country's most important test for two-year-olds.

USA
AQUEDUCT

Racing every day of the year (except Tuesdays and some bank holidays) on New York Racing Association courses attracts more than four million customers to Aqueduct, Belmont Park, and Saratoga. The industry provides about 40,000 jobs in New York City and, with 300 off-track betting shops, the average amount of money handled daily on NYRA races totals some $7.7 million. Jamaica racecourse was under the same non-profit, non-dividend-paying ownership until it was closed down in 1959 and the track was sold for housing development.

When the original Aqueduct, with Thomas

New York's famous Aqueduct track was given a facelift for the 1985 Breeders' Cup, which was broadcast to 25 countries.

Reilly as president, opened in Queens on 27 September 1894, fewer than 700 racegoers and only eight bookmakers turned up for the six races at the 6-furlong (1.2 km) course. It was not sanctioned by the Jockey Club until the autumn of the following year. In 1905, Phillip J. Dwyer, one of the Jockey Club founders, took over. He leased more land, which was subsequently purchased, rebuilt the stands, and enlarged the track. Thirty-five years later, the circumference of the course was reduced from 1¼ miles to a mile (2 km to 1.6 km).

The four-track package cost the newly-formed New York Racing Association $20 million in 1955. Between 1956 and 1959, Aqueduct, situated on the shores of Jamaica Bay, was again torn down. Six days before it reopened, the doors on Jamaica were closed for good. While Belmont Park was being re-built (1963–7), most of its racing was switched to Aqueduct, where attendances soared to more than six million each year.

An inner track for winter use was constructed in 1975 and the following year Sunday racing was introduced to 'Big A'. But it was Steve Cauthen who made the course's biggest headlines in the 1970s by astounding the nation with a sequence of successes in January and February of 1977. Included in the spree were 23 winners in one week.

On 14 October 1980, pre-race testing began of all horses racing at Aqueduct and the other NYRA tracks. Blood samples were taken from all the afternoon's runners. On 11 October 1981, Equestris, the $7 million track-side dining room, was opened. The restaurant, 300 ft (91 m) long, with seven terraced levels, can seat 1,400 people. In addition, there are plush lounge areas with built-in television monitors, two viewing areas, and numerous bars. Its success was reflected in the betting, which soon topped $400 per head. Aqueduct invested in a $3 million facelift for the 1985 Breeders' Cup, which was broadcast to 25 countries. That day, $28,722,573 was wagered by 36 tracks and numerous 'simulcast' outlets across the USA.

Aqueduct covers an area of 203 acres (82 hectares). There is a main course of 1⅛ miles (2.2 km) and a turf course of ⅞ mile (1.4 km). The track has some 100 days' racing at its winter/spring meeting and about 60 days at its autumn meeting. The Wood Memorial Stakes is one of the track's highlights.

BELMONT

Home of the Belmont Stakes, the last of the three races that make up the famous Triple Crown series, New York's Belmont Park began as a right-handed course in May 1905. It did not adopt anti-clockwise racing until 1921. The biggest attraction in the early years concerned aviation rather than horses. In 1910, Orville and Wilbur Wright supervised an air display that drew 150,000 spectators to

Belmont Park, 35,000 of them riding the Long Island Railroad to get there. Eight years later, Belmont made history as the terminal of the first American air-mail service between New York and Washington DC. But there was soon significant activity on the ground at Belmont, too. In 1923 a crowd of 45,000, the largest for a match race in 100 years, turned out to see Kentucky Derby winner Zev challenge English Derby hero Papyrus. The purse was $110,500. Zev, the 4–5 favourite, won by five lengths and Wall Street betting was estimated at $3 million.

In 1963, engineers found faults, caused by old age, in the grandstand. It had to come down and racing in New York was restricted to Aqueduct and Saratoga until 1968. The new Belmont, rebuilt at a cost of $30.7 million, was open in time for the hundredth running of the Belmont Stakes, won by Stage Door Johnny. There had been no Triple Crown hero since Citation in 1948. It was being claimed that, with a large increase in foals and the expansion of racing across the USA, the treble was becoming increasingly difficult to achieve. But the 25-year famine was ended in no uncertain terms by the great Secretariat. After setting a new fastest time in the 1973 Kentucky Derby, he shattered the world record by clocking 2 minutes 24 seconds in a 31-length Belmont Stakes triumph. Woodford 'Woody' Stephens lit up the 1980s by training five consecutive Belmont Stakes winners. Conquistador Cielo (1982) was followed by Caveat, Swale, Crème Fraîche, and Danzig Connection.

Belmont is situated on a site of 430 acres (174 hectares). There is a main course of 1½ miles (2.4 km), the Widener turf course 1⁵⁄₁₆ miles (2.1 km), and an inner turf course of 1³⁄₁₆ miles (1.9 km). The course hosts many Grade 1 races. Apart from the Belmont, the biggest attractions are the Woodward Stakes, the Champagne Stakes, and the Turf Classic. Racing is staged from the middle of May to the end of July and from the end of August to mid-October.

CHURCHILL DOWNS

Three miles (5 km) from downtown Louisville, Churchill Downs has been the home of the Kentucky Derby since 1875. Sir Barton won it in 1919 and went on to become the first of a select band of Triple Crown heroes. The Derby (1¼ miles/2 km), which has been run every day of the week except Sunday, is traditionally a May race. It is the first leg of the Triple Crown, which is a three-race series completed in five weeks by the Preakness Stakes (1³⁄₁₆ miles/1.9 km) at Pimlico and the Belmont Stakes (1½ miles/2.4 km) at Belmont Park. No other course in America can hope to break the attendance record of 163,628 set on the Churchill Downs for the 1974 Derby. Ninety-nine years earlier, 10,000 turned up for the inaugural running.

The 1930s, 1940s, and 1970s were golden decades in Triple Crown history. Each produced at least three winners but, after Citation took the honours in 1948, there was a gap of 25 years before Secretariat (1973) closed the breach. And he did so in style, shattering the Derby track record along the way. The Crown has been won only once in consecutive years — in 1977–8, when Affirmed followed hard on the heels of Seattle Slew, who was the first unbeaten colt to pull off the treble. The following chart shows the winners of the Triple Crown since 1919:

The distinctive towers are a landmark of Churchill Downs, scene of the famous Kentucky Derby. Only 11 winners of the great race have gone on to complete the Triple Crown.

TRIPLE CROWN WINNERS

Year	Horse	Jockey	Owner	Trainer
1919	Sir Barton	John Loftus	J. K. L. Ross	H. G. Bedwell
1930	Gallant Fox	Earl Sande	Belair Stud	James Fitzsimmons
1935	Omaha	William Saunders	Belair Stud	James Fitzsimmons
1937	War Admiral	Charley Kurtsinger	Samuel D. Riddle	George Conway
1941	Whirlaway	Eddie Arcaro	Calumet Farm	Ben A. Jones
1943	Count Fleet	John Longden	Mrs J. D. Hertz	Don Cameron
1946	Assault	Warren Mehrtens	King Ranch	Max Hirsch
1948	Citation	Eddie Arcaro	Calumet Farm	Ben A. Jones
1973	Secretariat	Ron Turcotte	Estate of C. T. Chenery	Lucien Laurin
1977	Seattle Slew	Jean Cruguet	Karen L. Taylor	William Turner Jr
1978	Affirmed	Steve Cauthen	Harbor View Farm	Lazaro S. Barrera

Florida's Gulfstream Park was once abandoned. Hard work by the Donn family has built up the course so successfully that it was chosen to host the 1989 Breeders' Cup Day.

The track, original grandstand, and clubhouse at Churchill Downs were built in 1874–5. The man behind the work was Colonel M. Lewis Clark, the grandson of the explorer William Clark. He had spent two years in Europe to study racing with the idea of starting a great series in Louisville to attract attention to the Kentucky breeding industry. Clark, who was to shoot himself 12 days before the 1899 Derby, was supported by local businessmen, who were thriving after the Civil War. He estimated that the $32,000 raised by the incorporation of the Louisville Jockey Club (320 original members each subscribed $100) would be enough to fund the project, and 80 acres (32.5 hectares) were leased from his uncles, John and Henry Churchill. After the oval of 1 mile (1.6 km) was built, Clark needed a further loan to complete the 2,000-seat grandstand, stabling for 400 horses, and a small clubhouse.

In 1886, the Louisville journalist Ben Ridgley was the first writer to refer to the Louisville Jockey Club as Churchill Downs. The Derby distance was 1½ miles (2.4 km) until 1896, when it was shortened to 1¼ miles (2 km) by the secretary, Charlie Price. He reasoned that the original distance was too long for the three-year-olds in the springtime. In 1894 a group headed by W. F. Schulte bought Churchill Downs from Clark. They pooled $100,000 and replaced the original grandstand and clubhouse with barns and a 285-foot (87 m) grandstand was built for $40,000.

Financial problems remained, however, and in 1902 a Louisville tailor, Matt J. Winn, was persuaded to get together a band of local investors to buy the Downs for $40,000. They rebuilt the clubhouse, which still stands, for $20,000, and it was ready in time for the 1903 Derby. That year, the spring meeting showed its first profit ever. Winn and his partners sold the course in 1918 for $650,000. It went to a syndicate headed by the multi-millionaire banker James Brown, but Winn, who, when he died at the age of 88 in 1949, had seen all the 75 Derbys run up to that year, remained as vice-president and general manager.

Fifteen of the first 28 Kentucky Derby winners were ridden by black jockeys, who played a vital part in shaping early American racing history. Isaac Murphy is featured in this book, but several others are worthy of note.

Oliver Lewis, for example, won the first running of the Derby (1875), on Aristides. He was one of the fourteen black riders in a field of fifteen. James Winkfield, in each of his four years of riding in America, was never worse than third in the Derby. He is among the very few jockeys who rode consecutive winners of the race, namely His Eminence (1901) and Alan-A-Dale (1902). His explosive career began with a year's suspension for causing a four-horse pile-up on his first-ever mount. In 1901, his third full year back on the track, Winkfield rode 161 winners and in 1903 went to Russia, where, it is said, he rode for the Czar. He rode throughout Europe and became fluent in several languages. It is estimated that he had about 2,300 winners before his retirement at the age of 48. William Walker was a successful jockey for 20 years — he rode the 1877 Kentucky Derby winner Baden-Baden — before taking up training and becoming an expert on breeding.

It was in 1925 that the New York sports columnist Bill Corum first referred to the Kentucky Derby as the 'Run For the Roses', a tag which it has kept to this day. It is said that the rose became the race's official flower in 1884, which was the year after the New York socialite E. Berry Wall presented a bloom to every lady who attended a Derby party in Louisville. The first account of roses decorating a winning horse was in 1896, when Ben Brush was presented with a collar of white and pink roses.

In 1931, at the track's request, the florist Mrs Kingsley Walker designed and produced the winner's garland. Her intricate pattern, using 500 of the darkest-red roses and greenery stitched on a cloth-backed blanket, was first modelled by the 1932 hero, Burgoo King. Only three fillies, Regret (1915), Genuine Risk (1980) and Winning Colors (1988) were successful in the 114 Derbys run up to 1988. The role of honour is completed by 104 colts and seven geldings. The last gelding to score was Clyde Van Dusen (1929). Fillies have their own Classic, the Kentucky Oaks, inaugurated in the same year as the Derby.

Churchill Downs has meetings in the spring and autumn totalling some 80 days of racing. The main track is an oval with a chute of 1 mile (1.6 km). On its inside is a turf course of ⅞ mile (1.4 km).

GULFSTREAM PARK

Florida's main track, Gulfstream Park, first opened in 1939, to survive only four disastrous days' racing. The owners were forced to close the doors when money ran out, and the course was abandoned to weeds. For five years the enormous grandstand stood empty at the crossroads of Hallendale Beach Boulevard and Route 1, mid-way between Fort Lauderdale and Miami. It was bought by the Scottish-born landscape gardener James Donn Sr, who built up the track until his death in 1972, when his son, James Donn Jr, took over.

The Donn family's hard work was rewarded when Gulfstream Park was chosen to stage Breeders' Cup Day in 1989. Their big annual race, the Florida Derby, has been successfully used as a stepping-stone for horses who go on to contest the Triple Crown events.

HOLLYWOOD PARK

A short drive from downtown Los Angeles, Hollywood, Beverly Hills, and the Californian beach cities, Inglewood's Hollywood Turf Club was formed under Jack L. Warner, of the Warner Brothers film corporation. When Hollywod Park opened in 1938, the 600 original shareholders included many stars, directors, and producers of the film world. Among these were Al Jolson, Walt Disney, Bing Crosby, Sam Goldwyn, Darryl Zanuck, Wallace Beery, Irene Dunne — the list reads like a show business Who's Who.

For most of the 1950s, more racegoers flocked to Hollywood Park than to any other track in the country. The boom was welcomed, for it followed the gutting by fire in 1949 of the grandstand-clubhouse building, which had been recently enlarged at a cost of $1 million. The spring/summer meeting of that year was held on schedule by Californian neighbour Santa Anita Park. One of the 'firsts' claimed by Hollywood Park was the introduction of the film patrol. In 1941, the year before World War II suspended racing, eight patrol judges were each equipped with a lightweight movie camera attached to binoculars. Each judge recorded one section of a race and when the film had been spliced together, it was viewed by the stewards the following morning. The system was refined and perfected in 1945, when cameras were installed in towers.

The Lakeside Turf Course (9/10 mile/1.4 km), featuring four chutes and six infield lakes, was opened in 1967, and five years later $3 million was spent on general improvements. The Hollywood Gold Cup, over 1¼ miles (2 km), was first run on the track's opening day in 1938, when it was won by the legendary Seabiscuit, and the race is still a major attraction. The Hollywood Invitational, won by John Henry in 1980, 1981, and 1984, is one of the other big events of the year. It is run over 1¼ miles (2 km) on turf. The Grade 1 Sunset Handicap (1½ miles/2.4 km), on turf, is another big draw, and the Hollywood Futurity, an autumn race for two-year-olds, carries $1 million guaranteed.

Host to the first Breeders' Cup Day in 1984, Hollywood Park staged it again in 1987. Thanks to unprecedented participation throughout the country, a national single-day wagering record was set up with $36,398,366 going through the pools. Dates of fixtures are variable, but the track operates a five-day week, providing about 100 days of racing a year. Meetings are held between late April and late July and between the first week in November and Christmas Eve.

LAUREL

Situated between Washington DC and Baltimore, Laurel got under way in 1911, under the direction of the Laurel Four County Fair. Three years later, New York City grocery magnate, James Butler, bought the track and appointed as general manager the promotions expert Colonel Matt Winn, who had put the Kentucky Derby on the map.

Laurel staged three memorable match races. The first of these, over 1¼ miles (2 km) in 1917, was Belmont Stakes hero Hourless *v.* Omar Khayyam, winner of the Kentucky Derby. Hourless had come out second best when the pair met in the Brooklyn Derby, but took his revenge at Laurel by a length. A year later, top two-year-olds Billy Kelly and

Hollywood Park attracts stars both on and off the track. Original shareholders included Walt Disney and Bing Crosby.

The impressive entrance of Santa Anita welcomes racegoers on about 120 days every year.

coveted Triple Crown. First run in 1873, the race was originated two years before the Kentucky Derby and six years after the Belmont Stakes, the other two Triple Crown races. A record crowd of 87,652 marked the 111th running of the Preakness in 1986. Situated within the city limits of Baltimore, the Pimlico track is an oval of 1 mile (1.6 km) with chutes of 6 furlongs (1.2 km) and 1¼ miles (2 km). The grass course was installed in 1954.

The main grandstand and entire clubhouse are glass-enclosed and air-conditioned for all-weather racing. Among other attractions on the track are the Dixie Handicap, the Black-Eyed Susan Stakes, and the John B. Campbell Handicap.

SANTA ANITA PARK

Fourteen miles (22 km) from Los Angeles, in the suburb of Arcadia, Santa Anita Park offers punters more than 120 days of sport a year.

There has been thoroughbred racing in California for more than a century. Soon after Elias Jackson 'Lucky' Baldwin acquired the Old Rancho Santa Anita in 1875, there were competitive events on the training course off what is now Colorado Boulevard. Baldwin built the first public course on Santa Anita land and opened it on Thanksgiving Day 1907. The oval track of 1 mile (1.6 km), grandstand, and stables were situated where Arcadia County Park now stands. This original Santa Anita Park operated for two years. Baldwin owned a 40-horse stable on site. He

Eternal clashed for a $20,000 prize over 6 furlongs (1.2 km). Eternal scored by a head and owner J. W. McClelland gave his purse money to the Red Cross. A match over the same distance in 1923 again involved the best two-year-olds, Sarazen showing his superiority over Happy Thoughts.

After Baltimore industrialist Morris Schapiro bought the track in 1947, and appointed his son, John D. Schapiro, president, new life was breathed into Laurel. A major new race, the Washington DC International, which brought together some of the world's top horses at 1½ miles (2.4 km) on grass, was introduced. England's Wilwyn (1952) was its first winner. Outstanding colt Sir Ivor, hero of the 1968 English Derby, is also on the track's roll of honour.

In 1986, after a decline in interest in the International, nominations for the race were allowed for the first time, a change from the previous invitation-only system. And in 1988, Frank J. De Francis, who in 1984 had bought Laurel with partners Robert and John 'Tommy' Manufso, introduced a $1.9 million two-day Turf festival to attract the Europeans.

PIMLICO

Opened in October 1870, Baltimore's Pimlico track is the second oldest, after Saratoga, in the USA. The Maryland Jockey Club, which operates the course, is the nation's longest-established sporting association. It was formed in Annapolis in 1743 and granted a charter by Congress in 1840. General George Washington was a frequent visitor to Annapolis races and President Andrew Jackson was a club member when the track and headquarters were moved to Baltimore in 1830.

Pimlico is best known as the home of the Preakness Stakes, the middle leg of the

had four winners of the American Derby at Chicago's Washington Park, when it was much more famous than the Kentucky Derby.

After Baldwin's death, in 1909, there were barren years. It was not until pari-mutuel betting was legalized in California, in 1933, that new tracks could be constructed on solid economic foundations. The Los Angeles Turf Club Inc. was set up. It bought part of Baldwin's Rancho Santa Anita estate to build a new Santa Anita Park close to the old course. The venture got under way on Christmas Day 1934. Dr Charles H. Strub was the driving force then and until 1958.

The average daily attendance in 1934–35 was 9,926, whereas in the late 1980s it is more than 30,000. The average pari-mutuel handle in those exciting first 65 days was $244,579, compared with upwards of $6 million in the 1980s. World War II closed Santa Anita from 1942 to 1944, so 1986–7 became its golden anniversary of racing on the rebuilt track. And Laffit Pincay, who has the highest prize-money earnings of all time, celebrated by becoming the first jockey ever to ride seven winners there in one day. Pincay had already twice scored six successes on a Santa Anita card, but 14 March 1987 was to be his day for the Magnificent Seven. Without a ride in the first event, he achieved 1-1-1-1-1-1-3-1 on a nine-race card. He won with his last mount on 13 March and his first two rides on 15 March, to score ten out of 11 races, including seven wins in consecutive races.

The Oak Tree Racing Association, hosts of the 1986 Breeders' Cup, takes over at Santa Anita for about 30 days of racing every autumn. Profits go to thoroughbred enterprises, mainly in California. Breeders' Cup Day brought in an Oak Tree record of 69,155 spectators. It also broke the existing pari-mutuel record with an incredible handle for a single day of $15,410,409.

The main sandy loam track is an oval of 1 mile (1.6 km), with a distance of 330 yards (302 m) from the last bend to the finish line. There is also a turf course, which stretches for approximately 1¾ miles (2.8 km).

SARATOGA

New York's Saratoga racecourse is the oldest in the USA. On the opening day in 1863, the first winner was a filly named Lizzie W. The track has earned the title 'Graveyard of Favorites' since the aptly named Upset beat Man O' War in the 1919 Sanford Memorial Stakes. It was Man O' War's only defeat in a career spanning 21 races. Then, in 1930, Triple Crown champion, Gallant Fox, was beaten by a 100–1 rank outsider, Jim Dandy, for the coveted Travers prize. The shocks continued in 1973, when Secretariat, the first Triple Crown winner for 25 years, started at odds of 1–10 for the Whitney Handicap and went under to Onion.

Saratoga was crammed with 50,359 expectant spectators for the rematch between Triple Crown champion Affirmed and old rival Alydar in the 1978 Travers Stakes. The largest crowd ever saw Alydar placed first after the disqualification of Affirmed.

There is racing at Saratoga during August. The main track is 1⅛ miles (1.8 km) in circumference and there is a turf course of 1 mile (1.6 km) with an inner turf course for steeplechasing of ⅞ mile (1.4 km).

VENEZUELA

Venezuela's principal racecourse, La Rinconada, is situated on the outskirts of the capital city, Caracas. Built in 1939 to the design of Arthur Froelich, who created New York's Aqueduct and Belmont Park, La Rinconada stages all Venezuela's Group 1 races, including its principal weight-for-age contest, the Clásico Simón Bolívar (2,400 m/ 2,624 yards). It is also the venue for the country's Triple Crown series of the José Antonia Paez (1,600 m/1,749 yards), the Ministerio de Agricultura y Cria (2,000 m/ 2,187 yards) and the República de Venezuela (2,400 m/2,624 yards).

Racing at La Rinconada is anti-clockwise. The 1.6 km (1 mile) dirt track has floodlight facilities for night racing and there is a turf course for training purposes. Racing is staged every Saturday and Sunday throughout the year. A three-tier grandstand can accommodate over 50,000 people, with more than 10,000 of them seated.

*Situated below the San Gabriel Mountains, Santa Anita Park (**left**) is a great place to race. With the benefit of California sunshine, it draws an average daily attendance of more than 30,000.*

Famous Owners

In recent years horse racing has become more competitive on the international level, even though Europe and the USA continue to dominate the sport. With improvements in communications and, in particular, in the transportation of horses, events like Chicago's Arlington Million, Tokyo's Japan Cup, California's Breeders' Cup, and the recently instigated Goff's Cartier Million, staged at Dublin's Phoenix Park, have all advanced the cause of internationalism in racing.

Other aspects of this trend include the importation by the Japanese of an increasing number of stallions from Britain, the predominance of European horses in Hong Kong's training stables, the international investment by wealthy owner-breeders such as the Maktoum family, or the simple fact of the popularity of New Zealand-bred steeplechasers in Britain's West Country.

A predominant position in the horse-breeding industry is held by a number of owners based variously in the USA, the Middle East, France, Britain, and Ireland. This chapter reflects this ascendancy but, for reasons of space, it is not possible to include all those owners who merit inclusion. Indeed, it is far from easy to list in sufficient detail the achievements of those who are included. It should be added that every effort has been made to avoid personal preferences in compiling this brief catalogue of truly international owners.

A tense moment at Newmarket bloodstock sales as the auctioneer puts another thoroughbred under the hammer.

Prince Khalid
BIN ABDULLAH

Prince Khalid Bin Abdullah is a leading member of the Saudi Arabian royal family. Based in Riyadh, he set a precedent for his Arab relatives and neighbours by investing widely in Western bloodstock and establishing a string of racehorses in training throughout the UK.

The Prince's team is now divided between several top-class trainers, notably Guy Harwood, Jeremy Tree, and Barry Hills, although his horses have also been trained with success by Bill Elsey, Henry Cecil, Ron Smyth, and Maureen Piggott. The Abdullah pink-and-green strip has now become one of racing's most familiar sights, and the fact that champion jockey Pat Eddery is retained to ride all the Prince's horses.

A quiet, unassuming personality, Khalid Abdullah commands the respect and loyalty of the entire racing community. His ambition to win the Epsom Derby has yet to be realized, although Dancing Brave, last rounding Tattenham Corner yet beaten only by half a length by Shahrastani in 1986, must rank as one of the unluckiest losers of all time. Dancing Brave must be the most brilliant performer to represent the Abdullah string. Winner of the 2,000 Guineas, the Coral-Eclipse, and the King George VI and Queen Elizabeth Diamond Stakes, the Lyphard colt crowned his three-year-old career with a clear-cut success in the prestigious Prix de

Khalid Abdullah has been a popular owner since he started to invest in British racing in 1978. He won the Prix de l'Arc de Triomphe twice – with unlucky Epsom Derby loser, Dancing Brave, and Rainbow Quest.

l'Arc de Triomphe at Longchamp, Paris.

Among the other outstanding racehorses to carry the Abdullah silks are the 'Arc' winner Rainbow Quest, the talented Rousillon, who landed the Waterford Crystal Mile in 1986, and the successful stallion Known Fact, a game if fortuitous winner of the 1980 2,000 Guineas.

Hopes rose in autumn 1987 that Warning would maintain the Prince's run of victories in the Guineas, but sadly the Guy Harwood-trained colt was below par in the spring and was forced to miss the race. The decisive style with which Warning disposed of older rivals in Goodwood's Sussex Stakes confirmed his position at the top of the 1988 Free Handicap.

Khalid Abdullah holds a majority interest in Juddmonte Farms, a limited company which controls studs in Berkshire, Kentucky, and County Meath, and owns the Bury Road stables in Newmarket. His influential position as a leading owner-breeder and generous benefactor of British racing has led to his election as an honorary member of the Jockey Club, an extremely rare accolade for someone born outside the United Kingdom.

In the autumn of 1988, the Prince extended his breeding interests in England with the purchase of the Dullingham Stud in Newmarket. This has been renamed The Eagle Lane Farm. Among the stallions on duty here are Paul Mellon's international winner Glint of Gold.

H.H. Prince Karim
AGA KHAN

The fourth Aga Khan, educated in Switzerland and Harvard, is the grandson of the illustrious Aga Khan III, Sir Sultan Muhammed Shah. The latter's world-famous green and brown hooped colours were well-nigh invincible in the years preceding World War II, and maintained their success rate during the immediate post-war seasons. The current Aga's grandfather won the Derby no less than five times.

H.H. Prince Karim, known as 'K' to his closest friends, had been entrusted with the succession to the Imamate while his grandfather was still alive. At university he obtained an honours degree in Middle Eastern studies which fitted him to this role, but he was also an accomplished sportsman and an outstanding skier. His father, Prince Aly Khan, had assumed control of the family's racing empire on the death of the Aga Khan III in 1957. Two years later Prince Aly established new prize money records in both England and France. Sadly, he was killed in a car crash on the outskirts of Paris in 1960.

At the age of 24, Prince Karim suddenly found himself heir to a huge string of thoroughbreds and ten studs — the Ballymany, Gilltown, Ongar, Sallymount, Sheshoon, and Williamstown in Ireland, plus four more in France. Though previously the least

interested of his 'racing mad' family, Prince Karim followed his father's example by buying out the shares of his brother and half-sister before making up his own mind about future plans. Perhaps encouraged by the timely victories of horses like Charlottesville, Sheshoon, and Petite Etoile, he opted to retain his racing inheritance.

During the past decade the Aga Khan has immersed himself in the worldwide development of his stock, achieving such success that his record is now on a par with that of his grandfather. In 1977 he purchased the entire stock of 80 horses from the Dupré family and two years later was rewarded by the victory of Top Ville in the Prix du Jockey Club. A further £5 million bought the Boussac stable and neighbouring stud, including the 1978 Prix du Jockey Club winner Acamas. To house this new influx of horses, the Aga Khan built a luxurious new complex near Gouvieux.

The Aga's horses now race worldwide. His string was trained by François Mathet until the latter's death. The bulk of his team are now under the charge of Alain de Royer-Dupré. In England his trainers are headed by Michael Stoute, although Fulke Johnson-Houghton and Luca Cumani are also involved.

Shergar and Lashkari are regarded by the Aga as the finest horses to have been bred at his studs. Lashkari won the Breeders' Cup Turf Stakes. Shergar triumphed in the Derby. He also won the 'King George', but was beaten in the St Leger. His kidnapping and disappearance proved an incalculable loss to the Aga's breeding interests.

Shahrastani and Kahyasi are the Aga's two most recent Derby winners. Both also carried off the Irish equivalent, in which Kahyasi proved his courage by rallying to beat Insan, despite cutting into himself earlier in the race. So keen has the Aga now become on the progress of his horses that he rarely misses the opportunity to watch them race.

Countess Margit
BATTHYANY

A resident of Monaco, the Countess was born in 1911. She is the owner of the Haras Du Bois-Roussel stud, managed so capably by Louis Champion. There are 50 resident brood-mares and the stallions include Nikos, Noblequest, and Noir et Or. The Countess now races exclusively in France and Germany. Her colours are: blue, with orange sleeves and checked cap. Her horses are trained by Jacques Cunnington at Chantilly.

Among the leading horses that the Countess has bred are Pia, Samos, Caro, Night Music, Nebos, and Princess Eboli. Of these only Pia enjoyed notable success in England. Trained by Bill Elsey at Malton, the filly won the Oaks, the Lowther, and the Park Hill Stakes. Countess Batthyany's

major victories have been predominantly in France, where San San took the 'double' in the Prix de l'Arc de Triomphe and the Prix Vermeille. Caro won the French equivalent of the 2,000 Guineas, as well as the Prix d'Harcourt and the Prix Ganay. Marduk and Nebos have been important winners in Germany. The former carried off the Deutsches Derby, the Grosser Preis von Baden and the German St Leger. Nebos won the Preis von Europa and the Preis von Berlin twice. He also landed the Grosser Preis von Baden.

In 1988 the Batthyany silks were seen in a very favourable light on the French circuit. Gabina started her campaign winning both the Prix d'Astarte and the Prix de la Seine at Longchamp. Later she finished an honourable third to Soviet Star and Miesque in the Prix du Moulin. The colts Philippi and Rampoldi also performed impressively that year. Philippi won the Prix Robert Papin and Rampoldi proved too smart for All Along as well as running fourth to Tagel in the Prix Saint-Romain. Countess Batthyany also provided the Prix Morny runner-up, Ecossais. With such striking individuals currently in training, her fortunes look assured for many seasons to come.

The Dowager Lady
BEAVERBROOK

The Dowager burst onto the racing scene in the mid-1960s. Her husband, who died in 1964, had owned horses in the 1920s but his enthusiasm waned. Lady Beaverbrook decided to revive the famous chocolate brown and green crossbelts. She spent large sums at the yearling sales, and sent her horses to be trained by Walter Nightingall and Sir Gordon Richards.

Lady Beaverbrook's early efforts were

The fourth Aga Khan is carrying on the racing traditions of his family with great success. He won the Epsom Derby with Shergar, Shahrastani and most recently, Kahyasi.

Lady Beaverbrook has been a wonderful supporter of British racing for more than 20 years. Her popular racing colours of beaver brown, maple-leaf green cross-belts and cap have been carried by many good horses, including Bustino and Minster Son.

Not one to pull his punches, Phil Bull leads racing's most ardent campaigners. His head for figures led to the creation of the famous Timeform publication.

doomed to dismal disappointment, and she had to wait until 1974 before she found a colt of both courage and ability. This was Bustino, who finished first in the Lingfield Derby trial, fourth at Epsom, and second to Grundy in the 'King George' at Ascot. The last-named race has gone down in history as one of the most exciting contests of this century. It matched two magnificent thoroughbreds trained by masters of their profession, Peter Walwyn and Dick Hern, and ridden by two of the finest jockeys of modern times, Pat Eddery and Joe Mercer.

Compensation for Bustino and Lady Beaverbrook came in the St Leger, a race that the owner was to win again in 1988 with Minster Son, bred by the victorious jockey Willie Carson. Lady Beaverbrook's racing fortunes took a turn for the better in the 1970s, by which time the majority of her horses were trained by Major Dick Hern.

Boldboy won numerous big sprint handicaps, including the Vernons Sprint Trophy, which now boasts Group 1 status. Richboy was another popular winner, and Relkino took the Benson and Hedges Cup at York. Totowah, trained by Michael Jarvis, was one of Lady Beaverbrook's particular favourites. He gained victories in the 1978 Ebor Handicap and the 1979 Northumberland Plate. In more recent years her colours have been carried prominently by Petoski, who won the 'King George' in 1985, and top-class colts like Charmer and Minster Son. The latter will be back in training in 1989 as a four-year-old.

Lady Beaverbrook was born in 1910. Few owners of her seniority can approach her sprightly enthusiasm for the game and her bubbling delight in the winner's circle after the 1988 St Leger was a joy to behold.

Phil BULL

Few owners can have contributed more to the development of racing than Phil Bull. Born in 1910, the stocky, white-bearded Bull is naturally pugnacious, and his controversial views have ruffled more establishment feathers in his lifetime than generations of owners have managed in a couple of centuries. His determination to reform Rule No. 153 has yet to bear fruit, but it can only be a matter of time before his view prevails and a horse is not automatically disqualified because its jockey has contravened the code. Bull's colours are cerise with a white circle.

After attending Hemsworth Grammar School, Bull graduated from Leeds University and his mathematical genius, allied to his fascination with time, led eventually to the creation of his own brain-child, Timeform. The influence of this system worldwide has become greater than any single publication could ever possibly hope to achieve.

Timeform's ratings, speed figures, erudite comments, and superb sequence of racehorse annuals have become indispensable to the whole racing industry. The creator of Portway Press Limited, Bull remains the figurehead behind it. He pioneered the idea that racehorses should be tested over a mile (1.6 km) before the end of their two-year-old careers, and also established the Timeform Gold Cup at Doncaster, the forerunner of today's Futurity Stakes.

In 1947, Bull bought the Hollins Stud at Warley, near Halifax, and during the postwar years he was a leading patron of Captain Charles Elsey's Malton stable. Eudaemon, who won the Gimcrack and the Champagne Stakes, the Ebor winner Sostenuto, and Romulus, who finished runner-up in the 2,000 Guineas and later won the Prix du Moulin, were just three of a long line of famous horses to be bred at the Bull stud.

In recent years the owner's best-known winner has been Philoctetes, who brought off the double in the Vaux Gold Tankard and the Northumberland Plate. Although his string has been drastically reduced since the mid-1970s, Bull still has the occasional horse in training with Peter Easterby.

Nelson BUNKER HUNT

Nelson Bunker Hunt has dispersed his stock twice in ten years. In 1979 he sold his entire crop of yearlings at Lexington for a total of $12,305,000. In the late 1980s serious financial problems caused him to sell his entire racing empire for a total of $46,911,800. Five hundred and eighty horses went under the hammer in a two-day sale at Keeneland. The top price paid was $2,500,000 for the brood-mare Sangue, while Allen Paulson handed over $1.1 million for Dahlia.

Ironically, Mr Bunker Hunt won his third Eclipse award three months later as America's champion breeder of 1987. The sale brought to a halt one of the world's leading blood-stock operations and put an end, albeit temporary, to an international racing career. In America alone, horses owned by Nelson Bunker Hunt had won 42 Group or Grade 1 races over three decades, and their victories in Europe have included such world re-nowned events as the Epsom Derby and the Prix de l'Arc de Triomphe.

By the mid-1950s Nelson was investing widely in bloodstock, purchasing brood mares and establishing studs in Lexington, Virginia, and outside Deauville, in France. Soon he had his own string with John Cunningham in France and his racing interests in the USA were in their infancy.

The Bunker Hunt name will always be associated with two world-famous horses, the stallion Vaguely Noble and the filly Dahlia. Nelson had tried to buy Vaguely Noble straight out as a yearling but was outbid. Later he succeeded in buying a half share in the colt and was part-owner when Vaguely Noble won the 'Arc'. Eventually he was able to purchase a controlling interest in the horse, and Vaguely Noble sired him a series of outstanding performers, the pick of whom were Dahlia, Nobiliary, Exceller, the Derby winner Empery, Mississippian, and Ace of Aces. Bunker Hunt also bred the international star Youth, who won the French Derby, the Canadian International champion-ship, and the Washington DC International.

Though Nelson's colours—light and dark-green check, light-green sleeves, white cap—were carried successfully by horses prepared at Arundel by John Dunlop, his European reputation was made by Maurice Zilber, who saddled Empery to win the Derby and also trained Dahlia. This superb filly won the King George VI and Queen Elizabeth II Diamond Stakes in 1973 and repeated the victory the following season. She also won York's Benson and Hedges Cup in 1974 and 1975, an unparalleled record for a filly in post-war times. Nelson was consequently leading owner in England for the seasons 1973 and 1974.

The Bunker Hunt horses were also winners in Ireland, where Decies landed the Irish 2,000 Guineas. In recent seasons his team in France has been trained by François Mathet's former assistant Jonathan Pease at Gouvieux. Swink won the 1986 Grand Prix de Paris for the Hunt-Pease duo.

In the USA, Nelson has retained his famous Bluegrass Farm Stud in Kentucky and in 1987 won the Hollywood Invitational Turf Handicap with the Charles Whittingham-trained Rivlia. In September 1988 Nelson disposed of his racing stable to the Canadian horseman John Sikura. The sale left him without any thoroughbreds in training.

Kenneth Fabian COX

Kenneth Cox is a leading industrialist in Australia, where his companies produce a major share of the steel required for the building trade. As befits a business tycoon, he is a most successful administrator, serving on the committee of the Victoria Racing Club and for many years in the forefront of those organizing the many and varied events which promote Melbourne Cup Week.

One of the most respected voices in Australian racing, Cox is also the Governing Director of the Stockwell Stud at Digger's Rest, in Victoria. In this position he has organized business with such streamlined efficiency that the stud is the envy of the continent. The reputation of Stockwell, founded 28 years ago, was made by the amazing success story of the British-based stallion Showdown, who came to Digger's Rest at the end of the 1960s. In ten years his progeny totalled A$3,236,232 in prize money.

Other popular stallions at Stockwell are Arctic Explorer, Landau (whom Cox bought from Queen Elizabeth II), Water Mill, another expatriate from Great Britain, the French-bred Comeram, and the New Zealand stallion Vite Cheval. In recent times the directors have turned Stockwell into a stallion facility, offering owners the chance of sending their stallion there, retaining their ownership of the horse but paying a set fee for the privilege of having it stand there. The scheme has become very popular because facilities at Stockwell are second to none, with permanent staff supervision on a 24-hour basis, resident vets, computerized re-

Nelson Bunker Hunt had wide interests in racing and breeding. Financial problems broke up his empire, and by September 1988 he did not have any thoroughbreds in training.

Louis Freedman's greatest achievement was to breed the Derby and St Leger winner, Reference Point. His biggest disappointment was to miss taking a shot at the Triple Crown with his champion, who was unfit to run in the 2,000 Guineas.

cords, and expert equine dieticians. The fertility record remains steady at 84 per cent.

Among the top-class racehorses bred by the Stockwell Stud are Tontonan, who won ten listed and Group races from a total of sixteen starts, including the Doncaster Handicap and the Golden Slipper; Toyshow, who was unbeaten as a two-year-old; Love a Show, winner of the Blue Diamond; Show Ego, successful in the Queensland and Victoria Oaks in addition to winning the Australian Derby; and Allez Show, the record-time holder for 900 metres (984 yards) at Randwick.

Cox loves to see his horses in the winner's circle, but his maximum bet is five dollars. In addition to his administrative duties, he is President of the Australian Equine Research Foundation.

Bertram and Diana FIRESTONE

Joint proprietors of the Gilltown Stud in County Kildare, the Firestones have raced with conspicuous success on both sides of the Atlantic. Bertram Firestone is chairman of the Firestone Corporation and a director of Fasig-Tipton bloodstock sales in the USA and Goff's sales in Ireland. Diana Firestone was a successful showjumper in the USA.

Bertram Firestone's colours are green, with a white diamond back and front, green-and-white diamonds on sleeves, and green-and-white quartered cap. Diana's colours

are the same but with a green cap. Both Firestones employ an international squad of trainers: Messrs Mott and Sheppard in America, Dermot Weld in Ireland, and Messrs Hollinshead, O'Gorman, and Piggott in England. Their French trainers are André Fabre and François Boutin.

Bertram Firestone trained his own horses in Maryland, Florida, and Kentucky during the 1981 and 1982 seasons. Between their two studs, the Catoctin in Virginia and the Gilltown in Ireland, the Firestones have bred a long line of outstanding winners headed by General Assembly, Theatrical, Musical Lark, and Spark of Life.

Both husband and wife have owned many equally famous stars. Bertram was fortunate enough to have General Assembly running in his own colours. He won the Travers Stakes and was second in the Kentucky Derby. Theatrical won the Derrinstown Stud Stakes before being sold to Allen Paulson. Red Alert took Goodwood's Stewards' Cup and Kings Company the Irish 2,000 Guineas.

No mean rider himself, Bertram Firestone showjumped at the major events in the USA while still at school. He won the International Mad Hatter's Race in Ireland in 1974. As an owner, he received in 1982 the New York Turf Writers' Association award for outstanding breeders. In 1987 he still figured prominently on the winning owners' list.

Diana Firestone's horses have a tremendous record in the USA. Genuine Risk was champion three-year-old filly of 1980, winning, among other big events, the Kentucky Derby. April Run won the 1982

Washington DC International and Optimistic Gal headed the two-year-old Free Handicap in 1975. In Europe Mrs Firestone saw her colours carried to victory in both the English and Irish Oaks by Blue Wind.

Louis FREEDMAN C.B.E.

Louis Freedman was born in 1917. A leading financier in the City of London, he is a senior director of Land Securities Investment Trust Ltd and holds directorships in other similar organizations. He was educated at University College School, London, and from 1938 to 1946 served with the Royal Artillery. Freedman is a long-established member of the Jockey Club and a former President of the Racehorse Owners' Association. His colours are yellow with black spots and yellow sleeves and cap.

The owner's first major winner was I Say, whom Walter Nightingall trained to finish third in the 1965 Epsom Derby. The following year I Say won the Coronation Cup and Freedman bought the famous Cliveden Stud from the Astor family. The purchase proved invaluable, for the new owner's three top-class fillies have been outstandingly successful in the paddocks. Lucyrowe, originally trained by Walter Nightingall's widow before moving to Peter Walwyn, won the Nassau Stakes and the Coronation Stakes. Attica Meli took the Yorkshire Oaks and Polygamy was saddled by Peter Walwyn to finish runner-up in the 1974 1,000 Guineas before going on to triumph in the Oaks.

The Freedman colours have been carried by a continuous sequence of outstanding fillies with Mil's Bomb, One Over Parr, and Royal Hive each winning Group races during the 1970s, and Ever Genial and One Way Street maintaining the habit in the 1980s. Freedman bought Beech House Stud from Lady Sassoon but resold it in 1975.

He keeps 17 mares permanently at Cliveden and in 1987 achieved a lifelong ambition by breeding Reference Point to win the Epsom Derby. By Mill Reef out of Freedman's 1981 Sun Chariot winner Home on the Range, Reference Point won Doncaster's Futurity Stakes as a juvenile but had to be nursed through painful sinus trouble before opening his account as a three-year-old in the Mecca Dante Stakes. A relentless front-running galloper, he became a supremely popular winner of the Epsom Derby.

Reference Point now stands at Sheikh Mohammed's Dalham Hall stud. His Derby winning time was only fractionally slower than that of the Aga Khan's Mahmoud in 1936 and faster than that of Golden Fleece, who triumphed in 1982. Freedman's horses are now divided between the stables of Henry Cecil, Alec Stewart, and Peter Walwyn.

Raymond R. GUEST O.B.E.

Raymond Guest was born in New York in November 1907 of an English father. Guest Senior stood as a Member of Parliament, became a junior minister in the government of Lloyd George.

During the 1930s Guest bred and raised his own horses at Plowhatan Plantation in Virginia. During World War II he served as a Commander in the US Navy, before spending six years as a member of the Senate, representing Virginia and finally being sent to Ireland as US ambassador in 1965. Although Guest was interested in horses all his life, it was not until the 1960s that his own made their mark on the international scene, with Larkspur carrying his colours to victory in the 1962 Epsom Derby. The Guest colours are chocolate, with pale blue hoops and cap.

Larkspur cost 12,000 guineas at the Ballsbridge yearling sales. He was a chestnut son of Never Say Die, out of a dam called Skylarking, who had won three races for Lord Derby over distances of up to 1¾ miles (2.8 km). Sent to Vincent O'Brien, Larkspur showed promise as a two-year-old but made no impression on the more fancied runners in Doncaster's Timeform Gold Cup. Success in the 1½-mile (2.4-km) Wills Gold Flake Stakes at Leopardstown persuaded O'Brien to let him go to Epsom, where he was partnered by Neville Sellwood and started the outsider of the O'Brien pair at 22–1. Luckily for Larkspur, he escaped the carnage on the run downhill to Tattenham Corner, and once in the straight was always travelling like a winner. He held on gamely to account for the two French horses Arcor and Le Cantilien.

Guest's finest horse was Sir Ivor, a perfectly proportioned bay by Sir Gaylord out of Attica. He cost $42,000 at Keeneland, USA. His only defeat as a two-year-old came on his debut and he crowned his juvenile days with a handsome victory in the Grand Critérium at Longchamp. Sir Ivor's hallmark was his brilliant turn of foot. He won the 1968 2,000 Guineas and displayed decisive acceleration in the Derby, to beat Connaught and Mount Athos. Victory in the Washington DC International ensured a landslide majority in the election for the 1968 Horse of the Year. After standing as a stallion in Ireland, he returned to America.

The most successful of Guest's American-based horses was the Preakness Stakes winner Tom Rolfe, who was voted top US three-year-old for 1965. His most expensive purchase was Hula Dancer, bought for NF1,020,000. The filly won the 1,000 Guineas and the Prix du Moulin but did not stay the trip in the French Oaks.

Guest also owned the dual Cheltenham Gold Cup winner L'Escargot. Trained by Dan Moore, L'Escargot ran twice in the

Owner Raymond Guest congratulates Sir Ivor and Lester Piggott after their triumph in America's 1968 Washington International, at Laurel.

Robert Holmes a'Court achieved his great ambition when he won the 1984 Melbourne Cup. Three years later the Stock Market crash struck him a bitter blow.

Grand National before winning in 1975. The gelding then travelled to the USA, where he added the Meadowbrook Chase to his winning tally. L'Escargot's international feats won him the Jumper of the Year award and the Goff's Golden Horseshoe.

In recent years the Guest horses have been trained by Angel Penna in France and Jonathan Sheppard in the USA.

R.D. HOLLINGSWORTH

Richard Hollingsworth, who was born in 1918, went to Eton before joining Lloyds as a stockbroker. He was commissioned in the Royal Berkshire Regiment and served throughout World War II. A member of the Jockey Club, he inherited the Arches Hall Stud when his father died in 1945 and has bred a long line of top-class winners.

Felucca, the daughter of Hollingsworth's father's first buy, Felsetta, has proved an outstanding brood-mare. Three of her produce went on to win Doncaster's important fillies' race, the Park Hill Stakes. The first of these was Ark Royal, who finished second to Meld in the Oaks and bred big-race winners in Ocean and Hermes. Kyak, successful at Doncaster in 1956, produced Mariner's Raft, while Cutter, who went on to take the John Porter Stakes and run third in the Oaks, was the dam of Sloop and the grandam of Sharp Edge.

More recent winners to be bred at the Hollingsworth stud include Bireme, who achieved the Musidora–Epsom Oaks double in 1980; the 1986 Goodwood–Doncaster Cup hero Longboat; Buoy, who carried off the

Coronation Cup and the Great Voltigeur in consecutive seasons; and Band, runner-up in both the Irish and French St Legers.

Yearlings from Arches Hall Stud regularly command good prices at the Newmarket October sales.

Hollingsworth's horses were originally trained by George Colling. They then passed to his successor John Oxley and are now in the care of Major Dick Hern. Hollingsworth's colours are crimson with silver braid.

Robert HOLMES A' COURT

The repercussions that followed the international Stock Market's 'Black Monday' in October 1987 severely affected Robert Holmes a'Court's racing empire in Australia. The investments of the businessman and banker of international repute took a hammering, but until then his string had been on the ascendant and his great ambition to land the Melbourne Cup had been achieved in 1984 with Black Knight.

Black Knight's sire was, at the time of his purchase, the most expensive stallion ever to have stood in Western Australia. He was also the first stallion to be bought by Robert Holmes a'Court for his Heytesbury stud, near Perth. Silver Knight cost A$65,000. He had himself won the Melbourne Cup in 1971 and also carried off the New Zealand St Leger. Black Knight's dam, Brenta, was contrastingly cheap. A modest performer on the track, she too was the original brood-mare bought for the Heytesbury stud and Holmes a'Court paid only A$600. One of Brenta's earlier foals, White Label, a full sister to Black Knight, had been trained with conspicuous success by George Hanlon at Melbourne and when Black Knight showed traces of ability as a juvenile he was sent east to join the Hanlon stable.

In the early days the gelding proved difficult to handle and on a visit to the yard, Holmes a'Court, an accomplished horseman himself, showed his stable-lad just how things should be done by removing his suit jacket, tucking his trousers into his socks, and riding Black Knight round the Epsom training complex on a long rein.

Plans to run Black Knight in the 1983 Melbourne Cup had to be shelved when he wrenched a fetlock in his preparatory race, the Geelong Cup. Recuperation was spent on Holmes a'Court's estate in Victoria, where the gelding was worked quietly round the surrounding hills by Sue Farmer, the wife of the owner's racing manager.

Ironically, the 1984 Geelong Cup again proved a bogey race. After finishing an unlucky second to Chagemar, Black Knight returned to the unsaddling enclosure with blood pouring from a gash on one of his hind legs. Miraculous efforts by George Hanlon with poultices, ice packs, and salt water paid off. Black Knight was able to reappear in the Dalgety three days before the Cup, and this outing put him in 100 per cent condition for the big occasion. Fifth turning into the straight, Black Knight responded the moment Peter Cook asked him to quicken. He won by two and a half lengths at odds of 10–1.

Holmes a'Court's colours are maroon with a white Maltese cross and a white cap.

Mrs Vera HUE-WILLIAMS

The widow of the late Roger Hue-Williams, who died in 1987, Vera Hue-Williams was brought up in Russia and, together with her husband, was associated with many business and financial ventures. Her residences in this country are St James's Place, London, and Woolton House at Newbury, in Berkshire. The family formerly owned the Rathasker stud in County Kildare but sold the property to the Burns family, retaining control of the Woolton House stud.

Nearly all the major Hue-Williams winners have begun their lives at the Woolton House stud. Among them are famous names like Supreme Court, winner of the King George VI and Queen Elizabeth Diamond Stakes, Aurelius who triumphed in the St Leger in 1961, and Altesse Royale, that brilliant filly who completed the English–Irish Oaks double after beginning her three-year-old campaign with a brave win in the 1,000 Guineas.

Mrs Hue-Williams's colours are scarlet with a white 'V' and cap. The scarlet jacket has seen many other triumphs. Bally-Russe took the Queen's Vase in record time. Favorita showed tremendous pace to win races of the calibre of the Cornwallis Stakes and the Jersey Stakes. I Titan doubled up with the Ascot Stakes and the Vaux Gold Tankard. Seraphima won the 'Nell Gwyn' and was placed in the 1,000 Guineas and the Oaks.

On one never-to-be-forgotten occasion Mrs Hue-Williams's English Prince crossed to Ireland to take on her husband's Imperial Prince in the Irish Sweeps Derby. Amid intense family rivalry, it was English Prince who prevailed. He has since made a name for himself as a leading stallion in Australia. In England Mrs Hue-Williams's team is divided between the stables of Peter Walwyn, Ian Balding, and Henry Cecil. In France her trainer is J. Cunningham, Junior.

Perhaps the greatest disappointment suffered by the Hue-Williams family was the dual Ascot Gold Cup disqualification of Rock Roi, one of the greatest stayers of the early 1970s and winner of the Prix du Cadran, the Goodwood Cup, the Doncaster Cup, and the Gordon Stakes.

H.J. (Jim) JOEL

The only son of the late Jack Joel, Jim Joel was born in 1894 and educated at Malvern, serving with the 15th Hussars during World War I. Jack Joel was responsible for registering the famous black colours with the red cap. The family fortune was made in South Africa at the turn of the century and the Joels have raced horses in Britain since 1900.

Jack Joel won eleven Classics and was leading owner three times. Sunstar secured the Derby in 1911 and Humourist obliged ten years later. Jack's brother Solly won the Triple Crown with Pommern in 1915 and Solly's son Stanhope Joel owned Chamossaire, who triumphed in the St Leger in 1945.

Jim inherited £5,000,000 on the death of his father in 1940, taking over both the control of his string and the Childwick Bury Stud near St Albans, in Hertfordshire. Jim Joel revitalized the stud and within four years had inspired it to win a Classic, Picture Play taking the 1944 1,000 Guineas in the hands of Charlie Elliott. Picture Play was the grandam of Royal Palace, who delighted his owner by completing the 2,000 Guineas–Epsom Derby double in 1967.

During the intervening 23 years, Jim Joel had celebrated many big successes with horses in training with Ted Leader, Jack Watts, and Sir Noel Murless, yet further Classic success had remained elusive. Since Royal Palace broke the ice again in 1967, Jim Joel has frequently owned Classic contenders. Connaught was runner-up in the Derby in 1968, Light Cavalry, trained by Henry Cecil, took the St Leger in 1980, and Fairy Footsteps

Jim Joel, the grand old man of British racing, still enjoys a day out at tracks near his London home. His current ambition is to win the Epsom Oaks.

won the 1,000 Guineas in 1981. Other notable victories have come from Henry the Seventh, whom Bill Elsey saddled to win the Eclipse, Procne, whom Bill's father Charles trained to victory in both the Park Hill Stakes and the Ebor, and Major Portion, who was runner-up in the 1958 2,000 Guineas.

In his time Jim Joel has spread his net around many different stables including those of Derek Candy, Tom Jones, George Todd, and Staff Ingham. Today the bulk of his horses are trained by Henry Cecil. Despite his age of 93, Jim Joel is still keen to go racing, and was in the paddock at Sandown during the summer of 1988 to watch the progress of his top-class colt High Estate. Sadly, he was abroad when Maori Venture won the 1987 Grand National at 40–1. He has had horses in training during the winter for many seasons, mainly with the Turnells, but more recently with Josh Gifford at Findon, in Sussex.

Jim Joel is a senior member of the Jockey Club but has never sought office.

Eugene KLEIN

Eugene Klein did not come into racehorse ownership until 1982, when he bought his first thoroughbreds at the Keeneland Select yearling sales. Six years later he and his wife owned some 200 horses and the family's big-race successes in this comparatively short period have outstripped the achievements of many long-established stables.

Klein was President of National General Corporation, an enormous transglobal conglomerate. He has also been President and owner of the San Diego Chargers football team. Today he concentrates entirely on building up his racing and breeding interests, which are centred on his Del Reyo farms at Rancho Santa Fe in California. His colours are: yellow jacket, blue collar and sleeves with yellow rings and inverted chevron, yellow cap with blue segment and peak. The trainer for the Kleins is the charismatic D. Wayne Lukas who is in charge of advising his client on the purchase of yearlings and breeding investments.

Success came overnight to Eugene Klein. Life's Magic crowned what was only the owner's second season by winning prize money of nearly $900,000 as well as earning an Eclipse. Other major stakes winners have included Miss Huntingdon, Saratoga Six, Fiesta Lady, and Lady's Secret. The last-named became only the fourth female competitor to be honoured as Horse of the Year. By July 1987 Lady's Secret had pushed her career earnings to $3,021,425. As a three-year-old, she won a trio of Grade I stakes. She surpassed in her four-year-old season, gaining ten Grades stakes triumphs.

These triumphs have recently been matched by the remarkable displays of the Kentucky Derby winner Winning Colours, a roan filly by Caro. Not only did the three-year-old become the third filly to land the Kentucky Derby this century, she also won the Santa Anita Derby and narrowly failed to make it three straight victories when she finished third in the Pimlico Derby. Klein was leading American owner in 1988.

The Family AL MAKTOUM

In recent years no family has made a more lasting or generous contribution to the welfare of British racing than the Maktoums. Their influence, although enormous in the UK, is international.

The Maktoums dominate Dubai, where they combine the roles of royalty and political leadership. Immensely rich from the revenues of their oil industry, their ever-growing number of horses in training put them on a par with the most famous owners of the twentieth century. Their near monopoly of the top stallions in the UK does not please all sections of the racing community, but they are universally respected for their sportsmanship and regard for the traditional virtues of the Turf. Maktoum money is also behind the emergence of *The Racing Post*.

Every year the family spends a small fortune at the big yearling sales. At Keeneland in 1986 they purchased 40 per cent of the yearlings on offer.

The Queen, an enthusiastic supporter of racing, presents the trophy to winning owner, Sheik Ahmed Al Maktoum, after Mtoto's triumph in the 1988 King George VI and Queen Elizabeth Stakes, at Ascot.

Ahmed Al Maktoum

Like his relations, Sheikh Ahmed lists his UK address as c/o The Dalham Hall Stud, Newmarket, Suffolk. He is perhaps the least widely known of the Maktoums but, thanks particularly to the efforts of his magnificent horse Mtoto, his colours (yellow with black epaulettes) are becoming increasingly familiar.

Mtoto will soon be standing as a stallion at Dalham Hall. He was raced lightly as a youngster because of his thin-soled feet. The problem eased with age, however, and helped by the expert guidance of trainer Alec Stewart and his South African jockey Michael Roberts, Mtoto has established himself as an outstanding racehorse. Winner of the Coral-Eclipse Stakes in consecutive seasons, Mtoto further enhanced his reputation with a splendid win at Ascot in the 1988 'King George'.

Sheikh Ahmed's other favourite horse has been Wassl, who took the Irish 2,000 Guineas in 1983. His team is divided between a wide range of well-known trainers, notably John Dunlop, Alec Stewart, Luca Cumani, and Major Dick Hern.

Hamdan Al Maktoum

Second eldest of the Maktoum brothers, Hamdan has an enormous number of horses in training and owns two important studs, the Derrinstown Stud in Ireland and the Shadwell Stud at Newmarket. Sheikh Ahmed's Irish 2,000 Guineas winner Wassl stands at the Derrinstown, while Green Desert is the resident stallion at Newmarket. The Sheikh's colours are royal blue with white epaulettes and striped cap.

Al Bahathri, after whom Hamdan named his fine all-weather gallop at Newmarket, became the champion Irish-trained three-year-old in 1985, and At Talaq gained him international honours with his Melbourne Cup success.

Top handicappers to run in Hamdan's blue-and-white-striped cap include the first winner of Goodwood's Schweppes Golden Mile, Waajib. Two of his best Group race winners are Al-Sylah and Doulab.

Maktoum Al Maktoum

Crown Prince and the eldest of the brothers, and Deputy Prime Minister to the United Arab Emirates, Maktoum was the first of the family to secure a Classic victory and has a string of big-race winners to his name.

Maktoum's colours differ only slightly from those of his brother Hamdan. His jockeys wear a light blue cap and his jacket is embossed with a white chevron. The Crown Prince has enjoyed wide success with horses trained by Harry Thomson-Jones and Michael Stoute. Touching Wood was prepared by the former trainer to land the St Leger in 1983, while Michael Stoute saddled Shareef Dancer and Shadeed, who gained later Classic success in the Irish Sweeps Derby and the English 2,000 Guineas.

The Maktoum colours are also popular in France, where the majority are under the care of Mme Criquette Head. Ma Biche came over to Newmarket from this stable to win the 1,000 Guineas in 1983.

The Sheikh is a member of the Jockey Club and owns two studs, both under the name of the Gainsborough stud management. Stallions at the Newbury venue include the Classic winner Touching Wood.

Mohammed Bin Rashid Al Maktoum

Popularly known as Sheikh Mohammed, this brother is the youngest and most internationally successful of the family. He is Defence Minister of Dubai and a prolific accumulator of top-class bloodstock. His colours are maroon and white.

The Sheikh's colours were first seen in Britain in the late 1970s and he was top prize money winner in 1985, when his home-bred filly Oh So Sharp won the 1,000 Guineas, the Oaks, and the St Leger. His list of big race winners includes such household names as Indian Skimmer, Jalmood, High Hawk, Bairn, Pebbles, Sonic Lady, and El Cuite.

Sheikh Mohammed employs an enormous list of trainers. In Britain he has enjoyed a fabulous sequence of victories with Henry Cecil. Abroad, his trainers include André Fabre in France and Charles Whittingham in the United States. His racing manager is Anthony Stroud and, under the umbrella of the Dalham Hall Stud, he owns a further half dozen top studs. Reference Point is the latest of a long line of outstanding stallions to stand at Dalham Hall, which will also enjoy the services of Mtoto from the start of the 1989 season.

The all-conquering Maktoum family assembles at Royal Ascot to greet yet another of their many winners.

Paul MELLON K.B.E.

Paul Mellon's colours continue to grace race tracks on both sides of the Atlantic. Commentators in the UK are delighted to see one of his horses taking part, and the black jacket with the gold cross are easy to identify. His US colours may not stand out so clearly yet they have been carried with such distinction that they are familiar to racegoers right across the continent. The Mellon colours in Europe are black with gold cross back and front, and black cap with gold cross. In America they are grey with primrose-yellow sleeves and cap.

Mellon was born in 1907. His home, Rokeby Farms in Upperville, Virginia, remains a leading American stud, with 35 brood-mares on site.

A dedicated Anglophile from an early age, Mellon studied history at Cambridge, where the desire to collect *objets d'art* took root. Art became his consuming passion and his collection is now numbered among the finest in the world. He is also an honorary member of the Jockey Club.

The Mellon horses came to the fore in America as recently as 1964. Quadrangle caused a stir when he got up to beat the famous Northern Dancer in the Belmont Stakes. Arts And Letters was Mellon's initial champion, achieving a 'four-timer': the Belmont, the Travers, the Woodward, and the Jockey Club Gold Cup all came his way in 1969. Arts And Letters was nominated Horse of the Year, an honour that Mellon was to receive in successive years with Fort Marcy, who went on to land the Hollywood Park Invitation Turf Stakes and to take the Washington DC International twice.

Mellon's list of American Group race wins is impressive and includes household names like Key To The Mint, Run The Gantlet, Fit To Fight, and Hero's Honour. His horses race under the name of the Rokeby Farms and are currently trained for him by Mackenzie Miller.

Mellon's European success began with the great Mill Reef, trained by Ian Balding and ridden by Geoff Lewis. Although he was beaten by Brigadier Gerard in the 2,000 Guineas, Mill Reef's three-year-old career encompassed the Greenham, the Epsom Derby, the Eclipse, the King George VI and Queen Elizabeth Diamond Stakes at Ascot, and finally the Prix de l'Arc de Triomphe. As a juvenile he had won the Coventry Stakes, the Gimcrack, and the Dewhurst.

Kept in training at four, Mill Reef justified his owner's decision by winning both the Coronation Cup and the Prix Ganay. Tragically, a broken bone curtailed his racing career but he proved an outstanding stallion at the National Stud. Other popular Mellon winners in Europe include Glint Of Gold,

An enthusiastic supporter of racing on both sides of the Atlantic, Paul Mellon has an impressive list of American Group Race winners. Mill Reef was his outstanding horse in England.

whose triumphs gained him major honours in France, Italy, and Germany.

Mellon retains eleven brood-mares at Kingsclere, in England, and had several promising juveniles running in his colours during the 1988 season.

James David MITCHELL T.D.

The Mitchell family, of which James David is the senior member, own the Yarraman Park stud at Scone, in New South Wales. With 2,000 acres, there is plenty of room for their normal quota of 45 mares. The Mitchells are regular vendors at the Sydney yearling sales, where the best price paid for one of their yearlings has been $80,000. The stud was started by the former top Australian jockey George Moore and sold to the Mitchells in 1968. Stallions currently on duty include Rutland, County, and Memento.

The Mitchells are farmers on a grand scale and breeding racehorses is a commercial part of the business. The best horses owned by the Mitchells have been Nobbidge, who won the Group III Princess Handicap, Top Of The Pops, Robber Baron, and Dial A Disc. Their horses are now trained by F. W. Mitchell but James himself once held a trainer's licence. James Mitchell's colours are black, gold striped sleeves, and black-and-gold quartered cap.

Eric MOLLER

Eric Moller died in London in 1988, at the age of 81. He and his brother Ralph were joint partners in the White Lodge Stud at Cheveley, near Newmarket, until the latter's death in 1980. It is understood that the future of the stud has been assured and that the horses will continue to carry the popular colours, which are chocolate, gold braid and sleeves, and quartered cap.

The White Lodge was bought by the Mollers in April 1944 and the foundation mare was Horama, whom they had acquired for 2,100 guineas on the recommendation of Nicky Morriss, a boyhood friend and owner of the nearby Banstead Manor Stud. Harry Wragg, who trained for the Mollers, had ridden Horama to her initial victory and all the horses subsequently carrying the Moller colours are from the Horama line.

Eric and Ralph Moller were brought up in Shanghai and were destined to take over the family shipping line. During the 1930s the Moller brothers were well known amateur riders in China, where Eric rode the winner of the Shanghai National.

Until his death, Ralph, nicknamed Budgie,

was the guiding hand behind the fortunes of the White Lodge Stud, assisted by trainer Harry Wragg. For many years the stud produced a line of brilliant fillies, including Sovereign, Full Dress II, who won the 1,000 Guineas, Topsy, Amaranda, Favoridge, and Favoletta. Moulton, winner of the Benson and Hedges Gold Cup, was their most successful colt.

The 1980s saw a change in policy. The stud began to send out a succession of top-class colts, coinciding with the death of Budgie and the retirement of Harry Wragg. Teenoso won the 1983 Derby for Eric Moller, and the decision to keep him in training as a four-year-old was justified when Teenoso carried off the King George VI and Queen Elizabeth Diamond Stakes. Most Welcome finished runner-up to Reference Point in the 1987 Derby and Red Glow started favourite in 1988, finishing fourth to Kahyasi. Teenoso, representing the fourth generation of the Horama family, now stands as a stallion at Lord Caernarvon's Highclere stud. He remains in the ownership of the Mollers, and his first crop of runners are now in action.

Eric Moller leaves a widow, Norma, but no children. It seems likely that the horses will continue to be trained by Geoffrey Wragg and run in the name of the White Lodge Stud, which still has around 30 mares in residence. Percy's Lass, Eric's Group-class filly, recently won the valuable Bonusprint Stakes at Kempton under the banner of the family stud.

Mr and Mrs J.R. MULLION

The Mullions entered racehorse ownership after World War II. John Mullion's colours are white with a Robertson tartan sash and cap. Mrs Mullion's colours are white, red collar and cuffs, and tartan cap.

The couple bought the Ardenode Stud, in County Kildare, in 1956 and at the same time asked Paddy Prendergast to train their horses. The horses were owned separately and ran in different colours. At first Mrs Mullion was the more successful: Floribunda won the King George VI and Queen Elizabeth Diamond Stakes and the Nunthorpe, while Gazpacho took the Irish 2,000 Guineas, as did Ballymore. John Mullion's only significant winner at this stage was Floresence, who won the Portland Handicap.

Mrs Mullion also owned the flying filly Paddy's Sister, a great success in 1959.

John Mullion came into his own in 1963. Ragusa won the Irish Sweeps Derby and if Nijinsky, whose starting price was 7–2-on, is discounted, the Paddy Prendergast-trained colt was the shortest-priced winner of the English St Leger since 1946, when he romped home at odds of 5–2-on.

Ragusa had also justified odds of 4–6 in the King George VI and Queen Elizabeth Diamond Stakes. The following season he added the Eclipse to his name. The Mullions extended Ardenode Stud to accommodate

John Mullion, with his wife, Meg, welcome Ragusa after his victory, at odds of 2–5, in the 1963 English St Leger.

FAMOUS OWNERS' RACING COLOURS

Prince Khalid Bin Abdullah

H.H. Prince Karim Aga Khan

Countess Margit Batthyany

Kenneth Fabian Cox

Bertram and Diana Firestone

Louis Freedman C.B.E.

Mrs Vera Hue-Williams

H.J. (Jim) Joel

Eugene Klein

Mohammed Bin Rashid Al Maktoum

Paul Mellon K.B.E. (UK)

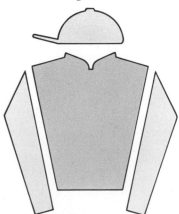

Paul Mellon K.B.E. (USA)

The Dowager Lady Beaverbrook

Phil Bull

Nelson Bunker Hunt

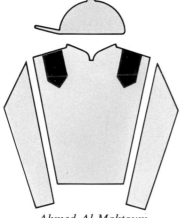

Raymond R. Guest O.B.E.

R.D. Hollingsworth

Robert Holmes a'Court

Ahmed Al Maktoum

Hamdan Al Maktoum

Maktoum Al Maktoum

James David Mitchell T.D.

Eric Moller

S.R. Mullion

FAMOUS OWNERS' RACING COLOURS

Mrs J.R. Mullion

Stavros Niarchos

G.A. Oldham

Allen Paulson

H.M. Queen Elizabeth II

H.M. The Queen Mother

Baron Guy de Rothschild (USA)

Robert Sangster

E.P. Taylor

Jacques Wertheimer

Lord Howard de Walden

Daniel Wildenstein

Baroness von Oppenheim

Baron Guy de Rothschild (UK)

Dr Carlo Vittadini

Zenya Yoshida

their new stallion. In the 1970s, the home-bred Sarah Siddons won the Irish 1,000 Guineas for Mrs Mullion and the pendulum continued to swing her way during the following decade. Roget Collet saddled Ukraine Girl to win her the French 1,000 Guineas in 1981. Three years later Princess Patti won the Pretty Polly Stakes and the Gilltown Stud Irish Oaks, while in 1986 Con Collins prepared Welsh Fantasy to win the Windfields Farm Gallinule Stakes.

The Mullions have also been interested followers of racing in Hong Kong.

Mr J.L. Mullion died in 1988; his colours pass to his son S.R. Mullion.

Stavros NIARCHOS LL.D.

A millionaire Greek shipowner, Stavros Niarchos has been much decorated by his homeland. His honours include the Grand Cross of the Order of the Phoenix and he is a Commander of the Order of St George and St Constantine. He lives in St Moritz.

Niarchos entered the racing scene in the late 1950s and his Pipe of Peace finished third in the 1957 Epsom Derby, which was won by Crepello. His colours are dark blue, light-blue cross belts, striped sleeves, and white cap.

After a brief flirtation with the Turf, Niarchos gave up ownership for twenty years, before re-emerging to compete with Robert Sangster in the sales battle to secure the most sought-after yearlings. Frustrated at paying over the odds because of Sangster's equally determined opposition, Stavros joined forces with the Vernons' tycoon. He basked in the reflected glory of the major successes enjoyed by the Sangster–O'Brien team until the emergence of the Maktoums.

Niarchos pulled out of the syndicate during the 1980s but his racing interests have continued to flourish and he has a longer list of trainers than any major owner in the racing industry. Messrs Boutin, Bary, Sepulchre, and Madamet guard the Niarchos interests in France. His English-trained horses come under the control of Henry Cecil, Jeremy Tree, Guy Harwood, and Oliver Douieb. In the USA he has employed Robert Frankel and Charles Whittingham, while his Irish-based horses come under the care of Vincent and David O'Brien. Niarchos's studs are Haras de Fresnay-le-Buffard, in France, and Spring Oak Farm, in Lexington, Kentucky.

Greinton, winner of the 1985 Hollywood Gold Cup, and Gallanta, who finished second in the Prix Morny and landed the Prix Cabourg, are the two best-known progeny from Stavros Niarchos's French stud, where Persepolis is the most popular of his five stallions.

The Niarchos colours have been carried to victory worldwide. Notable winners include Northern Trick, who won both the Prix de Diane and the Vermeille; Seattle Song, victor of the Washington DC International; Nureyev, so unlucky to be disqualified from the 1980 2,000 Guineas; Law Society, who carried off the 1985 Irish Sweeps Derby; and the marvellous filly Miesque, Nureyev's most illustrious daughter. She won six of her eight races in 1987, the pick of which were the 1,000 Guineas, the French equivalent at Longchamp, the Prix du Moulin, and the Breeders' Cup Mile at Hollywood Park.

Miesque has proved equally outstanding as a four-year-old, winning the Prix d'Ispahan first time out, defeating Khalid Abdullah's top colt Warning in the Prix du Haras de Fresnay-le-Buffard.

The Niarchos knack with fillies continues in England. At Royal Ascot in 1988 his Magic of Life, Seattle Slew's eleventh Group 1 winner, won the Coronation Stakes.

G.A. OLDHAM

Gerald Oldham was born in 1925. A successful businessman with multiple interests in the financial world, he is now based in Geneva and races extensively in France and Italy. Educated at Eton and Trinity College, Cambridge, Oldham spent four years with the Coldstream Guards.

The Oldham colours are chocolate with white hoops and a white cap. The Oldham string was trained by Harry Wragg at Newmarket until the end of the 1960s. In recent years François Boutin has been in charge.

Early winners for Oldham included Lucero in the Irish 2,000 Guineas, Talgo, who took the Irish Derby before finishing runner-up in

Gerald Oldham has a smile for his 1975 Ascot Gold Cup hero, Sagaro. The stayer put up repeat performances in 1976 and 1977 for a unique hat-trick.

the St Leger, and the consistent but unlucky Fidalgo. Harry Wragg prepared the colt to run second in both the Epsom Derby and the St Leger, but at least he had the consolation of gaining outright success in the Irish Derby.

From his base in Geneva, Oldham twice dispatched Expresso to land the Grosser Preis von Baden, while the same horse raced prominently in England, where the Vaux Gold Tankard was his most valuable victory. Expresso sired Oldham's greatest horse, Sagaro, but before the latter's all-conquering form in the mid-1970s, the owner had seen his colours successful in the 1969 St Leger with Intermezzo. The colt was trained at Newmarket by Harry Wragg and partnered by Ray Hutchinson.

Sagaro is the only horse to have won the Ascot Gold Cup three times 'off the reel'. His consecutive triumphs covered the period 1975–7, when he was trained by François Boutin. In 1974 Sagaro gained the distinction of beating Bustino in the Grand Prix de Paris, then run over 3,000 metres (approximately 1$\frac{9}{10}$ miles) at Longchamp. Sagaro was purchased by the Horserace Betting Levy Board for the modest sum of £175,000. Despite the fact that he had an acknowledged turn of foot, he was not popular with current breeders, who disdain 'staying' blood in favour of speed and the proven ability to win over middle distances.

Sagaro stood at the Lockinge Stud, in Berkshire, at a fee of 1,400 guineas but after a spell in Lincolnshire at the Limestone Stud he was transferred to the Emral Stud as a potential National Hunt stallion at a fee of only £400 on the basis of 'no foal, no fee'. For a magnificent racehorse who won every season from two- to six-years-old, this was adding insult to injury and Sagaro died of a heart attack early in 1986. Ironically his successor at the Emral Stud is his half-brother Scorpio. Both horses had originally been bred at Oldham's County Dublin property, the Citadel Stud Establishment.

Sagaro's best progeny have been the Chester Vase winner Super Sunrise and the Cambridgeshire victor Sagamore, both of whom subsequently raced with success in the USA.

Baroness von OPPENHEIM

The Baroness inherited the world-famous stud, Gestüt Schlenderhahn, in 1952 on the death of her husband, Baron Waldemar. The stud had been founded by an earlier Baron von Oppenheim in 1869 and has remained in the control of the Cologne banking family ever since. It is situated between Cologne and Aachen and has an unparalleled record in German racing. Eighty-four Classic winners have been bred at the Schlenderhahn stud, including the winners of

16 German Derbys, 14 German Oaks, 25 St Legers, ten Grosser Preis von Baden-Baden, two Preis von Europa, and 28 German Guineas.

Since the end of World War II, the stud has sent out 150 Pattern race winners. The Baroness has headed the breeders' list 35 times and has been leading owner no fewer than 30 times, gaining her most recent award in 1982. Sayonara, the dam of Slip Anchor (the 1985 Derby winner) was bred at the stud, which is also responsible for the grandam of Sagace and Simply Great. Baroness von Oppenheim's colours are: red with blue sleeves and black cap with red diamond and gold tassel.

The most famous stallions based at Schlenderhahn are Lombard, Priamos, and Solo Dancer. There are some 35 broodmares permanently residing at the stud, which is administered by the very able manager Meyer-Zu-Dute. He has regularly introduced new blood into the stud by purchasing mares from Newmarket and America. The most famous of these was Promised Lady. Bought for 3,700 guineas at Newmarket in 1964, she foaled Lombard, a prolific winner in Germany and France.

Lombard himself would have raced in England, had he not contracted a virus. He stood for a while at Newmarket's Banstead Manor Stud before returning to Germany. Lombard proved a fruitful stallion, and his progeny have been victorious in France and Germany. His daughter Sharifa won at Newmarket in 1978, the first time the Oppenheim colours had triumphed in England since Weissdom in the 1920s.

Among other top-class racehorses bred at Schlenderhahn are Artaxerxes and Alpenkönig. The Oppenheim string is trained by Heinz Jentzsch.

Allen PAULSON

Allen Paulson believes in perfection. Once he decides to get into a project, nothing short of the very best will satisfy him. 'Make it as perfect as you can' is the motto of Gulfstream Aerospace Corporation, of which Paulson is president and chief executive. The exhortation could also apply to his current priority – the non-stop drive to create the 'ultimate' in the bloodstock industry which he has based on his luxurious main breeding centre at Brookside North, in mid-Kentucky.

Paulson is a self-made multi-millionaire. Born on a Midwest farm in Iowa, he was working on a cattle ranch near San Francisco by the time he was 15 years old. He joined TWA as an apprentice mechanic in 1941 before serving with the Army Air Corps. By dint of hard work he became a flight engineer with TWA, and in that capacity invented a valve that enabled airplane engines to obtain equal lubrication both in the top and bottom cylinders. He sold the idea worldwide and patented four similar ideas.

Paulson founded California Airmotive Company in 1961 and fourteen years later became the first distributor of Learjet. Success followed success. For his achievements in the aviation industry Paulson became the fortieth recipient of the Wright Brothers Memorial Trophy in 1987. Two years previously he had sold his remaining interest in Gulfstream Aerospace to Chrysler Corporation, making a net profit of over $550 million. He remains President of the new company until he is 70.

Paulson entered racehorse ownership in the 1960s with a modest string but opted out until his resources were such that he could 'do it right'. In 1983 Paulson judged that that moment had come. He bought freely at Keeneland's select summer yearling sales, spending $5,438 million on ten yearlings. This was only the start, for he paid handsomely to secure stock at the Fasiq-Tipton summer sale, the Saratoga sales, and later at the Keeneland Fall sales. To house his new purchases Paulson bought Brookside West, in southern California, as a training centre, and his Kentucky base, Brookside North.

By 1985 Paulson was the tenth leading owner in America. The following year he had risen to third on the list. Paulson has continued to invest in new bloodstock but mainly in the form of purchasing of world-class stallions and brood-mares to further the cause of his breeding empire. Stallions of the quality of Theatrical, Dahar, Palace Music, and Mistral Dancer combined with broodmares of the calibre of Dahlia, Committed, and My Charmer are the raw material of future champions.

Paulson now races on an international stage. His stallions also travel the world, with Dahar and Strawberry Road carrying out

Aviation engineer Allen Paulson is flying high as an owner. His racehorses and stallions travel the world.

stud duties in Australia as well as in Kentucky. Paulson has begun to enter the European scene on an ambitious scale. In addition to his American trainer, John Gosden, soon to be training at Newmarket, he has horses with François Boutin and Dermot Weld.

Recent Group 1 successes in America for Paulson include the 1986 victories of Estrapade in the Oak Tree Invitational Stakes and the Budweiser-Arlington Million. During 1988 his Blushing John landed the Prix de Fontainebleau and the Dubai Poule d'Essai des Pouliches, the equivalent of the English 1,000 Guineas. François Boutin has also saddled Tersa to win Paulson the Prix de Morny at Deauville.

H.M. Queen ELIZABETH II

Since her accession in 1952, Her Majesty the Queen has won some 400 races on the flat. She is an acknowledged expert on breeding matters, is a most proficient rider herself, and, like her mother and daughter, thoroughly enjoys her connection with 'the Sport of Kings'. Her colours are: purple, gold braid, scarlet sleeves, and black velvet cap with gold fringe.

English reigning monarchs have won thirteen Classics since the death of Queen Victoria. Minoru won the Derby for Edward VII in 1909. George V, who was probably the least interested in racing matters, gained a single Classic success, George VI picked up four wartime victories, and to date the present Queen has won five. Her Majesty's

Classic victories have been with Carozza, who landed the Oaks in 1957 under Lester Piggott; Pall Mall, who took the 2,000 Guineas the following year; Highclere, the winner of the 1974 Oaks and, most recently, Dunfermline, whom Willie Carson partnered to victory in both the 1977 Oaks and St Leger.

The Queen's enthusiasm for racing is said to stretch as far back as the day in 1942 when her father, George VI, took her to Beckhampton to watch Big Game and Sun Chariot go through their paces under the watchful eye of Fred Darling. Both went on to win wartime Classics in the Royal colours. The Queen likes to keep in close touch with news about her horses both at the Royal studs and in training. She is a frequent caller at West Ilsley, Kingsclere, and the Newmarket stables of William Hastings Bass, who is her newest and youngest trainer. Her Majesty owns the first-named stable, where Major Dick Hern controls her interests.

The Royal studs were founded during the mid-sixteenth century, when Henry VIII set up his own establishment at Hampton Court. King Edward VII, whose passion for the thoroughbred was insatiable, founded both the Sandringham and Wolverton Studs in Norfolk, while the Queen herself is the inspiration behind the smaller Polhampton Stud at Kingsclere, where the top-class stallions Bustino and Shirley Heights are in residence. Over the years, many of racing's most famous names have been bred under the banner of the Royal studs. Eclipse, Persimmon, and Aureole are well-known examples and the Queen's two Oaks winners, Highclere and Dunfermline, were both home-bred fillies. Lord Porchester, now the Seventh

No ruler could have greater enthusiasm for racing than Queen Elizabeth II. Here she is seen being driven down the course at Royal Ascot, with Prince Philip at her side.

Earl of Caernarvon, is the Queen's Racing Manager.

In addition to the Classic wins already mentioned, Her Majesty has had numerous other successes. Aureole, second to Pinza in the 1953 Derby, went on to win the Coronation Cup, the Hardwicke Stakes, and the King George VI and Queen Elizabeth Diamond Stakes at Ascot. Agreement took seven races between 1957 and 1961. Almeria was an outstanding filly, landing the Ribblesdale Stakes, the Yorkshire Oaks, the Park Hill Stakes, and finishing runner-up in the 'King George'. Above Suspicion came home first in the 1959 St James's Palace Stakes and Canisbay won the Eclipse Stakes at Sandown in 1965. Height of Fashion scored five times in the early 1980s, and popular recent winners include Versatile, Insular – leased to her trainer Ian Balding – and the two-year-old filly Watersplash.

H.M. Queen Elizabeth
THE QUEEN MOTHER

The Queen Mother personifies all that is most cherished by followers of National Hunt racing. Even in her eighties she braves rain, wind, and cold to watch her horses run. Win or lose, her sportsmanship never falters and she always has a kind word for her trainers and stable staff. Her reaction after Devon Loch had unaccountably slipped up on the flat when assured of victory in the 1956 Grand National was typical. Her first thought was for the welfare of the horse, her second for jockey Dick Francis, and her last for her own disappointment. 'Well, that's racing, I suppose,' she remarked.

The Queen Mother's first horse was Monaveen, trained, as were so many of her early winners, by the late Peter Cazalet at Fairlawne near Tonbridge, in Kent. Monaveen triumphed in the royal colours but, sadly, broke a leg and had to be destroyed while racing at Hurst Park. Her horses specialize in the winter game. The majority are chasers, although she has had the good fortune to win several top hurdle races. In recent years she has added to her string by leasing a handful of horses from the Queen. Rhyme Royal and Insular are two such examples.

That highly respected trainer Fulke Walwyn, who rode Reynoldstown to win the Grand National in 1936, prepares the Queen Mother's jumpers at Lambourn. He is a holder of the C.V.O. and is one of her closest confidants on all matters concerning the sport.

The past thirty winters have witnessed a long line of popular winners in the famous colours of the Queen Mother, which are: blue, buff stripes, blue sleeves, and black cap with gold tassel. Headed by Monaveen and Devon Loch, her winners include such past heroes as Manicou, the winner of Kempton's King George VI Chase, Makaldar and Tammuz, top handicap hurdlers of their time, The Rip, who has a race at Ascot run in his memory, and Game Spirit, a winner of 21 races and almost invincible at Newbury.

Other notable winners owned by the Queen Mother are Isle Of Man, Double Star, Inch Arran, and Special Cargo, the latter winning a Whitbread Gold Cup and three Grand Military Gold Cups.

Baron Guy
DE ROTHSCHILD

The senior member of the world-famous banking family, Baron Guy was born in 1909. He has raced extensively both in the UK and France. In the UK his colours are blue with yellow hoops and yellow cap and in France blue with yellow cap, the latter being his best-known silks.

The Baron's horses have had difficulty in the English Classics, but have gained outright success in other big races. Exbury won the Coronation Cup, as did Tropique, who added an Eclipse to his tally. Guersant carried off the Hardwicke Stakes at Royal Ascot. At that time the Rothschild horses were trained by Geoff Watson at Chantilly. François Mathet took over the string for a while but today the horses are with young Jean-Marie Beguigne.

The Rothschild family has raced on both sides of the channel for around 120 years. Baron Guy's grandfather won four English Classics in 1871. Favonius won the Derby and his full sister Hannah obliged in the 1,000 Guineas, the Oaks, and the St Leger. Hannah gains her name from her owner's daughter, who married the Fifth Earl of Rosebery.

The Queen Mother is an ardent supporter of National Hunt racing. Here she presents the Whitbread Gold Cup to Mr R. Burridge, owner of popular 1988 winner, Desert Orchid.

Guy de Rothschild owns the Haras de Meautry, in Deauville, where the resident stallions are Kenmare and Crystal Glitters. Among the big races won by the Baron are the Prix Royal-Oak with Lady Berry, the French 1,000 Guineas with Timandra, the Prix de l'Arc de Triomphe with Exbury, and the Washington DC International with Diatome. In 1988 the Baron emerged from the doldrums to welcome home both Indian Rose and Reine du Ciel. Indian Rose won the Prix Vermeille but was not 100 per cent fit for the 'Arc', in which she was ridden by Pat Eddery. She started slowly and never threatened to take a hand in the finish. Indian Rose's dam Lady Berry won the 'Royal Oak' in the Rothschild colours and remains one of the Baron's favourite characters. Indian Rose was unsettled by the Epsom undulations and finished a well-beaten fourth to Diminuendo. In the 'Arc' the chestnut was below par and reportedly ran a temperature. Reine du Ciel proved one of France's top two-year-old fillies during 1988 and could have good prospects for the Classics.

Robert SANGSTER

Born in 1936, Robert Sangster is the son of the founder of Vernons Football Pools. He lives at The Nunnery, outside Douglas on the Isle of Man, but is an international personality, with a foot in most important doors and with

Robert Sangster owns horses all over the world. He claims that Melbourne Cup day is the most enjoyable meeting of the year.

world-class horses racing for him in all parts of the globe. It did not start that way and there have been problems en route, but Sangster's racing empire and bloodstock syndicates compete on level terms with Paulson and the Maktoums.

Sangster bought his first racehorse in the early 1960s for a mere £500. Chalk Stream was a modest gelding trained by Eric Cousins and he was never going to set the world alight. It was Cousins, though, who provided Sangster with his first major success. Brief Star won the Ayr Gold Cup at 10–1 carrying only seven stone (44.5 kg). Northern lightweight Cliff Parkes was in the saddle.

A year earlier Sangster had founded the Swettenham Stud in Cheshire. From humble beginnings it has flourished into one of the most successful in England. Horses of the calibre of Authaal, Chapel Cottage, Committed, Magic Flute, and Solinus, and many more, have been bred at the Swettenham. Foals are traditionally sold at the Newmarket December sales and the stud won both the Goff's T.B.A. and the English 'Leading Breeder' awards in 1985.

Sangster was elected to the Jockey Club in 1972 but spent much of the next three years out of the country. When he returned in 1975 it was with the specific intention of taking up racing on a major scale and he had as his ultimate goal the building up of an international bloodstock empire. He aimed to enter the US market buying well-bred yearlings, sending them to Europe to race, and then selling them back to the States by syndication. In particular he planned to win Group races and major Classics with the object of gaining the maximum value from the winner's future stud career.

To be successful, the Sangster scheme required money, the professional expertise of a top trainer, and a lot of luck. The first and second conditions were met instantly. The financial resources were available and Vincent O'Brien's skills could not be faulted. At the outset Sangster was short of luck and it was not until the arrival of The Minstrel that his fortunes took an upward swing. The Minstrel won both the English and the Irish Derby and the 'King George' at Ascot. In the autumn Alleged landed the Prix de l'Arc de Triomphe, a race he was to win again as a four-year-old.

The Minstrel is a perfect example of how the Sangster scheme could succeed. The colt cost $200,000 as a yearling and was syndicated at the end of his three-year-old campaign for £9 million. Sangster was leading owner five times between 1977 and 1984. His colours – green, royal-blue sleeves, and white cap with green spots – took major honours in Europe, America and Australasia.

There have been major disappointments. The Derby winner Golden Fleece died prematurely. El Gran Señor ought to have won at Epsom but was touched off by Secreto. The expensive Manton experiment was initially a serious drain on the finances. Sangster has ridden the setbacks and, under Barry Hill's experienced handling, his Manton dream is now bearing fruit.

Around 400 horses carry the famous Sangster colours every year. His massive breeding operation, centred on the Coolmore Stud in Ireland and his own Swettenham Stud, produces around 200 foals a year. His interests in Australia, where Tommy Smith is responsible for training the majority of his team, are growing steadily.

E. P. TAYLOR

Edward Taylor has provided the inspiration for the growth in this century of Canada's racing industry. A native of Ottawa, he was born in 1901. Educated at McGill University, he was in charge of Canada's munitions' production during World War II.

An ardent supporter of Winston Churchill, Taylor became President of War Supplies Ltd, and after the war built up a personal fortune from investment in oil and precious metals. Having been interested in racing since childhood, Taylor now used his resources to revive the reputation of Canada's ailing race-tracks. His policy was centralized racing.

As Chairman of the Ontario Jockey Club, Taylor presided over the closure of many poorly supported minor tracks and provided the initial finance to modernize the more successful major venues. Fort Erie and the original Woodbine were retained, the latter being renamed Greenwood.

A small fortune was then spent on building a luxurious new Woodbine, near Toronto – the venue for the 1988 Arlington Million and the home of the Canadian International Championship. The latter event has been won by some of the world's finest thoroughbreds, including such names as Secretariat, Dahlia, Snow Knight, Admetus, and Youth. The highlight of Canada's domestic programme is the Queen's Plate, also transferred to the new Woodbine.

Taylor has dominated the Queen's Plate, breeding 18 winners and owning ten. Among his winners have been Northern Dancer, who brought off the Kentucky-Preakness Stakes double, the most influential sire of modern times, and Flaming Page. Together, these two produced the English Triple Crown winner Nijinsky.

Taylor founded Windfields Farm Limited, whose record of winners bred reads like an international role of honour – Northern Dancer, Nijinsky, The Minstrel, Victoria Park, El Gran Señor, Secreto, Storm Bird, and many others. Since its inception in 1949, Windfields has bred over 300 stakes winners. Taylor's colours are turquoise with gold cap and gold spots on sleeves.

Dr Carlo VITTADINI

Dr Carlo Vittadini owned Grundy, whose titanic struggle with Bustino in the 1975 King George VI and Queen Elizabeth Stakes is still rated the most thrilling contest of the past 20 years. Grundy immortalized the Vittadini colours by winning the Irish 2,000 Guineas and the English and Irish Derbys, as well as the 'King George'. These colours are: dark blue, yellow hoop and armlets, and dark blue cap with yellow spots.

Grundy has been only one of a long line of top-class racehorses to carry the Vittadini silks. Noel Murless trained Exar to win both the Doncaster and Goodwood Cups in 1960. Exar proved a marvellous bargain — costing less than 2,000 guineas as a yearling, he won over £25,000 in prize money. Palatch achieved victory for the owner in the Musidora stakes and the Yorkshire Oaks. In the same year that Grundy won the Epsom Derby — 1975 — Palatch was only narrowly beaten by Val de l'Orne in the Prix du Jockey Club.

Dr Vittadini is not a medical man, but a millionaire Milanese banker, the chairman of Banca Agricola Milanese. His trainers are Peter Walwyn and Henry Cecil in Britain and M. Benetti in Italy, where his horses have won several Italian Derbys. Exar was victorious in both the Gran Premio d'Italia and the Gran Premio di Milano, and Accrale achieved the same feat. They are the only two imported horses ever to complete this double.

The Beech House stud at Newmarket is owned by Dr Vittadini and managed by his daughter Franca, widely recognized as the finest lady jockey of the past decade.

Jacques WERTHEIMER

The Wertheimer family established the Chanel cosmetic empire. Pierre Wertheimer, Jacques's father, won the 1923 Stewards' Cup with Epinard and 33 years later carried off the Epsom Derby with Lavadi, his very first runner in the race.

On her husband's death in 1965 Madame Wertheimer took over the control of the family's racing interests. She won the French Derby in 1973 with Roi Lear, but two years later passed her control to her son Jacques. The Wertheimer colours are: royal blue, two white seams on the reverse side of the silks and a single central stripe down the front, white sleeves and cap.

In his first year Jacques won the French Derby with Val de l'Orne. In 1976 his Ivanjica triumphed in the Prix de L'Arc de Triomphe under a brilliant ride from Freddie

Edward Taylor, of Northern Dancer fame, has dominated Canada's famous Queen's Plate. He has bred eighteen winners of the race, and owned ten of them.

Head, who secured a clear passage on the far rail and persuaded his mount to swoop on the leaders inside the final furlong. In 1978 Jacques Wertheimer became the leading French owner and breeder, when his brilliant fillies Dancing Maid and Reine de Saba carried off both of the fillies' Classics. Dancing Maid was also narrowly beaten by Fair Salinia in the Epsom Oaks.

At his stud in Normandy Jacques has some 50 brood-mares. For many years his string was trained for him by Alec Head at Chantilly. Alec's daughter, Criquette, now has that responsibility. The Heads regard the Wertheimers as perfect owners. They do not bet, and leave the training entirely to their trainers. The Wertheimer colours have been to the fore recently. They have carried off the Prix de l'Opéra in 1987 and 1988 with Monastella and Athyka, the latter springing a surprise under the powerful driving of Guy Guignard.

Further wins have come from Animatrice, who followed her brave third in the Epsom Oaks with a sparkling performance which landed the Prix de la Nonette. Most important of all was the success of Rivière d'Or in the Prix Saint-Alary at Longchamp in 1988.

Lord Howard de Walden receives the trophy after his 1985 Epsom Derby triumph with Slip Anchor.

Lord Howard
DE WALDEN

Born in 1912, the Ninth Baron de Walden was educated at Eton and Cambridge, where he gained an M.A. in 1934. Lord Howard de Walden, whose family title was created in 1597, served with the Westminster Dragoons during World War II. He is Chairman of the de Walden Estates Ltd, which own substantial property in the West End of London. The family seat is Avington Manor, Hungerford, Berkshire, and Lord Howard de Walden also owns two studs: the Plantation Stud at Newmarket, Suffolk, and the Thornton Stud outside Thirsk, in Yorkshire.

Racing has been his Lordship's consuming interest. His horses were originally trained by Jack Waugh and Sir Noel Murless at Newmarket, with a smaller number being sent to George Todd at Manton. His Flat-race string is now divided between Peter Walwyn, Henry Cecil, and, in the north, Ernie Weymes.

Lord Howard de Walden's horses have carried off many of the racing calendar's most prestigious events. The home-bred Slip Anchor, trained by Henry Cecil, was a pillar-to-post winner of the 1985 Epsom Derby, the colt having previously taken the Lingfield Derby Trial. Kris was an invincible miler, being successful in the Lockinge, the St James's Palace Stakes, the Sussex Stakes, and the Waterford Crystal Mile, before bringing his career to a climax in the Queen Elizabeth II Stakes at Ascot.

Diesis gave the de Waldens victory in the Middle Park and the Dewhurst, while in earlier generations the apricot colours were successful with household names like Almiranta, Oncidium, and Magic Flute.

Unlike many establishment figures, Lord Howard de Walden takes great pleasure in watching his horses perform under rules. Lanzarote, who carried Richard Pitman to victory in the Champion Hurdle, won a further 17 hurdle races. The gelding had begun his career with Ernie Weymes in Yorkshire before joining the Lambourn trainer Fred Winter, who looked after all his Lordship's National Hunt performers. Lord Howard de Walden maintains 22 mares at his Newmarket stud, where his Derby winner Slip Anchor is the stallion. At Thirsk, the resident stallion is Kris.

Lord Howard de Walden is one of the Turf's most distinguished administrators. A member of the Jockey Club, he has been senior steward three times, taking up his duties in 1957, 1964, and 1976.

Daniel
WILDENSTEIN

Daniel Wildenstein lives close to the Champs Elysées, in the centre of Paris. His grandfather had shares in several horses during the latter part of the nineteenth century but they always ran in the name of his business partner and it was Daniel's father who first registered the now-famous Wildenstein colours: royal blue with light-blue epaulettes and cap.

During the 1920s Wildenstein's father had between 80 and 100 horses in training, many of them leased from the Rothschild family. The string failed to win any of the French Classics but won a fair share of important races including the Prix de

Deauville three times. The Wildensteins survived the Depression of 1931 but during World War II their entire stock was confiscated by the Germans.

In 1954 Wildenstein set about restoring the family's racing fortunes. He paid a sizeable sum for the winning two-year-old Beau Prince. The decision proved justified when the colt won the Grand Critérium. Daniel was now in charge of organizing the Wildenstein racing interests. He introduced American blood into the family's breeding stock and became the first European to buy on a large scale at Keeneland. By 1970 he owned some 70 mares and had around 100 horses in training with Maurice Zilber at Chantilly.

In the same year he paid $285,000 for Allez France and also bought Flying Water, who went on to win the English 1,000 Guineas and the Champion Stakes.

Early in the 1970s he moved his horses from Zilber to Angel Penna, forging a combination that was soon to become irresistible. Their first winner in England did not come until Lianga landed the July Cup, but by that time the partnership had already cleaned up in France with Wildenstein's favourite filly, Allez France. In 1973 she had won the Prix Vermeille and the French 1,000 Guineas.

The following season Allez France gained the first of her owner's three triumphs in the 'Arc' and in 1975 she might well have added to her reputation with a popular success in the 'King George' at Ascot, had Wildenstein not decided to withdraw her at a late stage. He was leading owner in Great Britain the next season. Pawneese won both the Oaks and the 'King George'. Flying Water ran home a comfortable winner of the 1,000 Guineas, going on to take the Champion Stakes in 1977, after which Angel Penna took control of the Wildenstein interests in America and Peter Walwyn became his trainer in Britain.

The new arrangement did not stand the test of time. Walwyn saddled Crow to win both the Ormonde Stakes and the Coronation Cup in 1978. He was also in charge when that grand stayer Buckskin carried off the Prix du Cadran. But when Mr Wildenstein openly criticized his jockey, Pat Eddery, for failing to win the Ascot Gold Cup, the trainer told his patron to remove his horses. Henry Cecil then assumed care of the owner's British interests but the Newmarket maestro also had his differences with the Parisian art millionaire and since 1982 Patrick Biancone has enjoyed the Wildenstein patronage.

The duo have enjoyed some tremendous victories, particularly with All Along and Sagace. In addition to her 'Arc' win, the versatile All Along took the Prix Vermeille, the Turf Classic at Belmont Park, the Washington DC International, and the Rothmans Canadian International. Other household names to pass through Biancone's hands have been Metal Précieux, Vacarme, and Strawberry Road.

Zenya YOSHIDA

Zenya Yoshida owns the highly successful Shadai studs in Japan. His breeding interests in Britain are carried out on his behalf by the British Bloodstock Association at Newmarket and he also keeps a team of broodmares on the Fontainebleau farm in Kentucky.

Yoshida has been the leading ownerbreeder in Japan for many years, training a regular flow of Classic winners in his home country as well as running horses in Europe, where his trainers are Richard Carver and John Cunnington. The Yoshida colours are: black and yellow stripes, red sleeves.

In addition to his many Classic winners in Japan, the Tokyo-based businessman has been represented by several top performers in the USA and Europe. Wajima, who raced under the banner of the East-West stable, numbered Saratoga's Travers Stakes among his victories, which also included the Marlboro Cup.

Probably the best horse to have carried the Yoshida silks was the Richard Carver-trained Lassalle, whose major wins were crowned by success in the 1972 Prix de l'Espérance and the 1973 Ascot Gold Cup.

Cunnington's major scorer for Yoshida was the 1974 Prix de la Forêt winner, Northern Taste. The Japanese owner also had a controlling interest in the King's Stand winner, Flirting Around, who won the Prix de Meautry and triumphed at Ascot in the colours of Mme Haussmann.

Controversial French owner Daniel Wildenstein leads in Sagace after the 1985 Prix de l'Arc de Triomphe. Sagace was disqualified and the race awarded to Rainbow Quest.

The Great Jockeys

Any competent jockey should win with a horse who, on the day, is the best in the race. The great jockey is the man who wins when other riders would have lost. Success has to do with judgement and tactics, of course, but what makes a champion is the ability to inspire a horse to surpass his normal limits of speed, stamina and courage. It is this quality which has, through the years, separated riders such as Lester Piggott, Bill Shoemaker, and Yves Saint-Martin from the rest. Nobody knows exactly what is transmitted from these riders during a race, but there is no doubt that the horse gets the message.

For those at the top of the profession, the rewards are high. But for those nearer the bottom of a steep ladder, the self-deprivation of food and drink brings only modest recompense. The school-leaver who enters an apprenticeship in racing with dreams of glamour and riches has a long, hard road to travel and thousands throughout the world never make it to the end. This chapter, by contrast, is all about the success achieved by talent, the utmost dedication to the job, and an unquenchable thirst for winning.

Tension mounts, and the world's greatest Classic is only minutes away as jockeys weigh out for the 1893 Epsom Derby.

Peter ALAFI
b.1936

At the time of the Hungarian uprising in 1956, Peter Alafi was a promising apprentice in his native Budapest, while his elder brother Lajos was already a successful jockey. Alafi fled Hungary and ended up in Krefeld, to the west of Düsseldorf, and quickly established himself in the top flight of West German jockeys. He enjoyed a long and successful partnership with the Cologne trainer Sven von Mitzlaff, for whom he won numerous big races, including four German Derbys. In June 1986, he rode his 2,000th winner, to come within striking distance of Otto Schmidt's all-time German record of 2,216 wins.

Eddie ARCARO
b.1916

Amazingly, Eddie Arcaro never headed the list for races won, although by the time of his retirement in 1961 his 4,799 successes ranked second only to Johnny Longden's total. Six times the USA's leading money winner, Arcaro's total purse earnings of $30,039,543 put him millions ahead of what any jockey had ever achieved. That figure would have been even greater if he had not tried to unseat another rider in September 1942. The stewards banned him for a full year, but on his return he had learned his lesson and became the very best. He had great hands and there were none better in switching the whip.

Fred Archer was a winner all the way, until he lost the will to live. His suicide, at the age of 29, put a nation into mourning and ended a short, but spectacular career. He was among the greatest jockeys of all time.

Elected to the Hall of Fame in 1958, Arcaro was an excellent judge of pace and for 20 years collected the big prizes. He is the only jockey ever to win the Triple Crown twice, on Whirlaway (1941) and Citation (1948). His big prizes included five Kentucky Derbys, six Preakness Stakes, six Belmonts, eight Suburbans and 10 Jockey Club Gold Cups. Arcaro's superb talent was in demand for all the good horses. He rated Citation the greatest of them, but there was competition from Kelso, Nashua, Native Dancer, Bold Ruler, Assault, High Gun, Hill Prince, Sword Dancer, Jaipur, Whirlaway, Real Delight, First Flight, and Nellie Flag.

Fred ARCHER
b.1857 d.1886

A bullet ended the life of Fred Archer on the afternoon of 8 November 1886. One of the greatest jockeys of all time, and a national hero, had committed suicide at the age of 29. Distraught at the death of his wife, Nellie, soon after the birth of their daughter two years earlier, Archer's health was heavily taxed both by depression and a diet that fringed on starvation. Taken ill while riding a few days before his death, he was helped back to his Newmarket home, where he was found to have typhoid fever.

Archer's physical condition quickly improved, but he had lost the will to live and the pistol he kept in his bedroom was at hand. He was deeply mourned by an admiring nation, who only a year before had seen him ride a record 246 winners for his twelfth consecutive jockeys' championship. It was a seasonal target for all to beat, until Gordon Richards scored 259 in 1933. And it was Richards who was the first to pass Archer's career total of 2,748 winners collected since the latter opened the account in 1870.

Archer took off in 1874 and 1875 with wins in the 2,000 Guineas, 1,000 Guineas and the Oaks, which formed the foundation for 21 Classic triumphs in the last 13 years of his life. They were arduous years. The demands of the body to be properly nurtured fought against the demands of the saddle, which dictated that he should ride at weights dangerously low for a man 5 ft 10 in (1.8 m) tall. His temper often frayed under the strain of severe self-deprivation, but he was much admired and many in high places sought the company of racing's biggest hero yet.

A hard man to ride against, with not much quarter given, Archer's record of Classic winners alone is a reflection of the glory he attained: **2,000 Guineas**: Atlantic (1874), Charibert (1879), Galliard (1883), Paradox (1885); **1,000 Guineas**: Spinaway (1875), Wheel of Fortune (1879); **Derby**: Silvio (1877), Bend Or (1880), Iroquois

(1881), Melton (1885), Ormonde (1886); **Oaks**: Spinaway (1875), Jannette (1878), Wheel of Fortune (1879), Lonely (1885); **St Leger**: Silvio (1877), Jannette (1878), Iroquois (1881), Dutch Oven (1882), Melton (1885), Ormonde (1886).

Cash
ASMUSSEN
b.1962

Handsome, intelligent, articulate, shrewd — that sums up the American Cash Asmussen, whose acknowledged riding talent was appreciated less in Ireland than anywhere else in the world. Based in the winter in Laredo, Texas, Asmussen flew from America to Paris in 1982 to reject an offer to ride all of Stavros Niarchos's horses in Europe. But when he saw the quality of François Boutin's string he changed his mind.

Asmussen was French champion jockey in 1985 and, after switching to Mahmoud Fustok, took the title again in 1986. With the departure of Pat Eddery, Vincent O'Brien signed up the American, who moved to Ireland for the 1987 season. It was here that the rider, with some 1,000 winners behind him and a tall reputation in France, met with public hostility for the first time. When he lost races the Irish punters thought he should have won, they jeered him openly. They were used to all-action jockeys, but Asmussen's style does not allow for a lot of movement in the saddle.

There were rumours of a split with the stable in the autumn of 1987. These were denied until a parting of the ways early in 1988. Part of Asmussen's package deal with O'Brien had been that he should ride, when available, for Robert Sangster's Manton stable, but he did not take all the opportunities offered at the smaller English meetings. After the rift with O'Brien, Sangster claimed that the American had made a verbal agreement to ride as Manton's Number 1 jockey in 1988, but after protracted negotiations, Asmussen returned to France to join champion trainer, André Fabre, with a one-year agreement. He had no reason to regret the decision. From the very start of the 1988 season, Fabre's stable was in great form and, in July, Asmussen rode his hundredth winner of the season, to record the fastest century in France. He went on to beat Yves Saint-Martin's 1964 record of 184 winners aboard Vampirella, at Rouen, on 1 November 1988. In the same month he became the first jockey in France to reach 200 winners.

Asmussen's big-race successes include: Japan Cup: Mairzy Doates, (1981); Washington DC International: April Run (1982), Seattle Song (1984); French 2,000 Guineas: L'Emigrant (1983), Fast Topaze (1986); Irish St Leger: Eurobird (1987).

Braulio
BAEZA
b.1940

During the 1959 season, in his native Panama, Braulio Baeza rode 309 winners. This represented success in a quarter of all races run. The following year, he moved to the USA, where he led in purses won from 1965 to 1968, and again in 1975, his last full year in the saddle. A brilliant horseman, Baeza was aboard 24 different champions and won just about every major Stakes race in the country. He took the Champagne with two-year-old champions Bold Lad, Buckpasser, Successor, Vitriolic, and Honest Pleasure. His three-

*Cash Asmussen (**left**) was christened Brian, but changed his name even before the prize money started rolling in. An American in Paris, he has the rare distinction of having ridden 200 winners in one season in Europe.*

Braulio Baeza aboard victorious Roberto at York. They formed the only partnership ever to beat the great Brigadier Gerard.

Scobie Breasley (above) was among the most famous of the Australians who carved out a riding career in Britain. He was always looking for a place on the rails and, when possible, preferred to ride a waiting race.

year-old champions in the Travers Stakes were Buckpasser, Arts and Letters, Key to the Mint, and Wajima.

Baeza broke the mile (1.6 km) record with Buckpasser in 1966, and lowered it to 1 minute 32 ⅖ seconds with Dr Fager in 1968. Baeza's skill was shown off in front of the British public when, in 1972, the Irish trainer Vincent O'Brien flew him across the Atlantic to partner Roberto in the Benson and Hedges Gold Cup at York. Baeza's brilliant front-running ride ended with the stunning first (and only) defeat of Brigadier Gerard. The jockey's other champions included Damascus, Susan's Girl, Ack Ack, Chateaugay, Foolish Pleasure, and Affectionately. He retired from the saddle with 3,140 winners and was elected to the Hall of Fame in 1976. After assisting Sam Cardile, he took up training in 1978 and saddled his first horse on 13 January 1979, at Aqueduct.

Bobby BEASLEY
b.1936

An admitted alcoholic, Harry Beasley's grandson, Bobby, conquered his addiction to make a remarkable comeback to the jumping scene. The winner of the Cheltenham Gold Cup (Roddy Owen, 1959), Champion Hurdle (Another Flash, 1960), and the Grand National (Nicolaus Silver, 1961), Bobby's illness contributed to an early retirement. But he made a spectacular return to the saddle to win both the Irish Sweeps Hurdle (1972) and Cheltenham Gold Cup (1974) on Captain Christy.

Harry BEASLEY
b.1850 d.1939

The hero of the 1891 Grand National on Come Away, Ireland's Harry Beasley rode his last winner at the age of 85. Twice successful in the Grand Steeplechase de Paris, and in four Grand Seftons at Aintree, he retired from the jumping scene in 1918, but did not quit the saddle entirely until he had won a Flat race at the now defunct Irish course, Baldoyle.

Scobie BREASLEY
b.1914

An Australian from Wagga Wagga, Scobie Breasley rode 2,161 winners in Britain between 1950 and his retirement from the

saddle in 1968. Apprenticed to Pat Quinlan in 1928, Breasley had his first big race win at the age of 16 on Cragford in the 1930 Sydney Metropolitan. The horse was allowed to keep the race, but his young rider was suspended for two months for crossing over to the rails too sharply. He was not afraid to admit: 'I just loved those rails and would get against them no matter where my horse was drawn.'

Breasley's first two years with Noel Cannon's English stable brought 139 winners, including a Classic triumph on Ki Ming in the 2,000 Guineas (1951), but at the end of 1952 he packed up and returned to Australia. There he picked up the threads, but was back in England in 1953 after a renewed offer from Cannon. He won the 1,000 Guineas on Festoon (1954) and two Epsom Derbys within three years on Santa Claus (1964) and Charlottown (1966). In 1958 he won the Coronation Cup, Eclipse Stakes and the Arc de Triomphe on Ballymoss, but the colt's owner, John McShain, blamed him for defeat in the Washington DC International. He was never asked to ride for McShain again.

Breasley was champion jockey four times (1957, 1961, 1962, and 1963). His highest total was 179, in 1962. One of his major achievements in Australia was to win the Caulfield Cup five times. The exact total of winners he rode in his home country is not known, but it is estimated at 1,090. Breasley started training in 1969 and saddled Steel Pulse to win the 1972 Irish Derby. He left Epsom after six years for stables in France and then the USA, returning briefly to England in 1978 before settling in the West Indies in 1980.

Tommy BURNS
b.1899

Twice champion jockey in Ireland, Tommy Burns became known as 'The Flying Scotsman'. Very shrewd and dedicated, he served his apprenticeship under his father, James Burns, at Ayr, Scotland, and rode his first winner, in England, in 1913. He arrived at The Curragh, in Ireland, in June, 1915, while still an apprentice and rode principally for Maxwell Arnott, Jimmy Dunne, Philly Behan, and Sam Jeffrey.

Burns, whose son Thomas Pascal (T. P.) Burns became champion Irish jockey three times and had Classic wins on the great Ballymoss, rode with the top jockeys of this century — Steve Donoghue, Brownie Carslake, Frank Wootton, Danny Maher, Freddy Fox, Gordon Richards, and Fred Templeman. His last ride was in the Queen Anne Stakes at Royal Ascot in 1954, when, on Upadee, he beat Lester Piggott on Big Berry.

Burns was very strong, possessed great skill, and was greatly feared by the leading jockeys of his time. He captured 21 Irish Classics, but Raeburn (1936) provided his only Irish Derby triumph. A successful trainer in later life, he sent out Vimadee to win the 1961 Irish St Leger. Asked, at the age of 89, to name the best horse he ever rode, his answer was spontaneous: 'Without a doubt, it was the filly, Resplendent, later the dam of Windsor Lad. We won both fillies' Classics on The Curragh and beat all except Lord Astor's Short Story in the Epsom Oaks.'

Tom
CANNON
b.1846 d.1917

The leading British jockey in 1872, Tom Cannon later became a well-known trainer. He rode 13 Classic winners: **Derby**: Shotover (1882); **2,000 Guineas**: Pilgrimage (1878), Shotover (1882), Enterprise (1887), Enthusiast (1889); **1,000 Guineas**: Repulse (1866), Pilgrimage (1878), Busybody (1884); **Oaks:** Brigantine (1869), Marie Stuart (1873), Geheimniss (1882), Busybody (1884); **St Leger**: Robert the Devil (1880).

One of the jockey's sons, Mornington, won the 1899 Triple Crown with Flying Fox; another son, Kempton, scored his main Classic win in the 1904 Derby on St Amant.

Joe
CANTY
b.1896 d.1971

The most versatile of the great jockeys in a marvellous period of horsemanship in Ireland, Joe Canty's weight problems forced him to mix the Flat with jumps. He was brilliant at both. Queen of the Brush was his first winner, at The Curragh, in 1912.

Canty lost his claim in 1914, and, in 1919, won the first of seven Irish jockeys' championships, achieved under both Rules. He had a keen brain, and great hands and strength — and excelled at both snooker and poker.

Two of his four Irish Derbys were for Sir Harold Gray (Hocus Pocus and Sea Serpent). His third, Mondragon (1939), was trained by his brother James Canty, but the classiest of all was The Phoenix.

In 1925, Canty established a new jockeys' record by riding 117 winners for the high average of 34.51 per cent, and two years later he fell just one short of the century. By 1929, he had become the leading rider for the fourth time, with 91 wins. He was champion again in 1931 and made it seven championships by 1934. Hubert Hartigan provided him with six of his 17 Classic winners. Having invested his money wisely, Canty died a wealthy man.

Willie
CARSON
b.1942

Born in Stirling, Scotland, Willie Carson was three years into his apprenticeship before he rode his first winner, Pinker's Pond, on 19 July 1962. Ten years later he won his first Classic, with High Top in the 2,000 Guineas, and took the jockeys' title from Lester Piggott, with 132 winners. He started scoring centuries in 1971 and since then has been one of the most consistent jockeys of his time.

Carson joined Gerald Armstrong at Middleham, Yorkshire, in 1959 and, with just one winner on his slate was transferred in 1963 to Gerald's brother, Sam Armstrong at Newmarket. Two years after losing his apprentice claim in 1965, he joined Bernard van Cutsem to ride for Lord Derby. Champion jockey for a second time (164 winners) in 1973, he took the Irish Oaks and Yorkshire Oaks with Dibidale the following year. Dibidale might have won the Epsom Oaks, too, but her saddle slipped. Carson abandoned the saddle and after a rodeo performance finished third, only to be disqualified for losing the weightcloth.

The jockey claims his greatest moment

Willie Carson is one of Britain's most consistent riders. He both bred and rode the 1988 St Leger winner, Minster Son.

Steve CAUTHEN
b.1960

Soon after breaking a run of 110 consecutive losers, Kentucky-born Steve Cauthen signed up for owner Robert Sangster and in March 1979 left the USA to ride in Britain. After his first race, at Churchill Downs on 12 May 1976, he took America by storm. The first winner came five days after his debut, when Red Pipe scored at River Downs. During one week in January 1977, Cauthen won a record 23 races and by 10 February he had passed $1 million in earnings. On 10 December, he became the first jockey to win $6 million in one year.

Riding 487 winners in 1977, Cauthen earned three Eclipse Awards — top jockey, top apprentice jockey, and the Award of Merit. In 1978, he became the youngest rider to take the Triple Crown, with Affirmed, and it was towards the end of that year that he went to ride regularly in California, where he hit his losing run. Cauthen made his mark soon after joining trainer Barry Hills in England. His first winner there was Marquee Universal at Salisbury on 7 April 1979, and within weeks he won the 2,000 Guineas with Tap on Wood. His 52 successes of that season were surpassed by his 130 in 1984, when he became Britain's first American-born champion since Danny Maher in 1913.

Soon after taking over from Lester Piggott as Number 1 to Henry Cecil's Newmarket stable in 1985, Cauthen dominated the Classics with the Epsom Derby hero Slip Anchor and Oh So Sharp (1,000 Guineas, Oaks, and St Leger). Slip Anchor gave him cause for double celebration, for it made him the only jockey ever to win both the English and Kentucky Derbys. Champion in 1985 with 195 winners, Cauthen missed out to Pat Eddery, who had 176, the following season, but bounced back to take the 1987 title with a total of 197 winners.

Quality went hand in hand with quantity, for 1987 was the year of Reference Point. The colt missed the 2,000 Guineas because of a sinus operation, but after taking the Mecca-Dante he gave Cauthen his second Epsom Derby triumph. But there was tragedy for the American in the Oaks when Cecil's Scimitarra broke her off-fore cannon bone when well-placed to win.

Reference Point went on to take the King George VI and Queen Elizabeth Stakes before becoming the first Derby hero since Nijinsky (1970) to win the Doncaster St Leger. Failure in the Arc de Triomphe, for which an abscessed foot was blamed, was one of Cauthen's greatest disappointments. His thousandth success in Britain was scored on Picnicing at Brighton on 5 August. Cecil did not have a Derby runner for the American in 1988, but the ever-popular combination

American Steve Cauthen relaxes before the action. A superb horseman and tactician, he won America's Triple Crown on Affirmed before hitting champion form in Britain to become one of the world's top riders.

came in Queen Elizabeth II's Jubilee Year, 1977, after taking over from Joe Mercer at Major Dick Hern's Berkshire stables. It was the Oaks triumph of the Queen's fine filly Dunfermline, who went on to win the St Leger, that gave him so much pleasure. Jockeys' championship glory (182 winners) came the following year and, in 1979, Troy won for him the 200th Epsom Derby, Irish Derby, King George VI and Queen Elizabeth Stakes, and the Benson and Hedges Gold Cup. Niniski put icing on the cake by taking the Irish St Leger and the Prix Royal-Oak.

Henbit gave Carson the 1980 Epsom Derby, Bireme won the Oaks, and Known Fact was awarded the 2,000 Guineas prize on the controversial disqualification of Nureyev. These English Classic successes were backed up by Policeman (French Derby), Shoot a Line (Irish Oaks) and Ela-Mana-Mou (Eclipse Stakes and King George VI and Queen Elizabeth Stakes). Carson was champion again, with 166 winners. Swiftfoot gave him the 1982 Irish Oaks and, in 1983, Sun Princess (Epsom Oaks, St Leger and Yorkshire Oaks) and Little Wolf (Ascot Gold Cup) helped him towards a title-winning 159 winners.

Carson kept the winners flowing, notably: Circus Plume (Yorkshire Oaks, 1984), Helen Street (Irish Oaks, 1985), Petoski (King George VI and Queen Elizabeth Stakes, 1985), Longboat (Ascot Gold Cup, 1986) and Don't Forget Me (English and Irish 2,000 Guineas, 1987). In 1988, he had the chance to become the first jockey to win the Epsom Derby on a horse he had bred (Minster Son), but was unplaced. Ample consolation came with the pair's St Leger triumph and Carson ended the season as runner-up in the jockeys' championship with 130 successes.

brought off the English-Irish Oaks double with Diminuendo. Cauthen came close to disaster in a horrific fall at Goodwood on 26 August of that year, when he had scored 104 winners. He did not ride for the rest of the season, but recovered well.

Since his arrival in England, Cauthen's other major triumphs include: **Champion Stakes**: Cormorant Wood (1983); **Matchmaker International**: Cormorant Wood (1984) and Triptych (1987); **Eclipse**: Pebbles (1985); **Ascot Gold Cup**: Gildoran (1984), Paean (1987), **French St Leger**: El Cuite (1986). His big winners in the USA include: Affirmed (Hopeful Stakes, 1977; Kentucky Derby, Preakness Stakes, Belmont Stakes and Hollywood Derby, all 1978); Johny D (Washington DC International, 1977); Nearly On Time (Whitney Stakes, 1977).

Sam CHIFNEY
b.1753 d.1807

Acknowledged as one of the most unscrupulous jockeys of his time, Sam Chifney was also the best. An insufferably arrogant character, he pulled off the 1789 Epsom Classic double with Skyscraper (Derby) and Tag (Oaks). He lost whatever money he might have had and died in a debtors' prison.

Ray COCHRANE
b.1957

Ten years after struggling for winners over the jumps, Ray Cochrane scored a 1988 English-Irish Derby double with Kahyasi and was already established as a top-class jockey on the Flat. After being taught to ride in County Down, Ireland, at the age of nine, he joined Barry Hills as an apprentice in 1973 and rode his first winner, Roman Way, at Windsor in September 1974. During five years with Hills, Cochrane was lucky enough to ride the speedy two-year-old, Nagwa, to nine victories in 1975. Then a broken pelvis laid him up and his weight increased. He turned to jumping with encouragement from Duncan Sasse, who provided the jockey's first success over hurdles, on Wanlockhead, at Newton Abbott in August 1977.

Cochrane then joined Kim Bailey, but after three more winners moved to Ron Sheather at Newmarket. It was in Sheather's yard that Cochrane was kicked on the head by a horse called Monief, and while he was recovering from a fractured skull his weight fell away, never to return. Two wins on Hawkins in 1980 signalled his return to the Flat but, after a 1981 Lincoln Handicap

triumph with Saher, it was Chief Singer, the 1984 winner of the St James's Palace Stakes, July Cup, and Sussex Stakes, who put him among the big prizes. Even after Kahyasi's Derby double, he maintained that Chief Singer was the best horse he had ridden.

In 1986, the suspension of Pat Eddery let Cochrane in for victory in the 1,000 Guineas on Midway Lady. Trainer Ben Hanbury kept him aboard for the filly's Oaks triumph. Luca Cumani was so impressed that he signed up Cochrane for the 1987 season, in which he was third in the jockeys' list, with 111 winners. His total included five consecutive successes at Goodwood's main meeting and Royal Ascot wins on Half a Year (St James's Palace Stakes) and Then Again (Queen Anne Stakes). In 1988 he slipped to fourth place in the table, but increased his final score to 120.

Felix COETZEE
b.1959

Set to become one of the most successful jockeys in South African racing history, Felix Coetzee set two national riding records for the 1987–8 racing season. During easily the most successful season yet enjoyed by any jockey in South Africa, he won the national championship with 266 winners, shattering the previous record of 204 wins in a season.

Coetzee, Number 1 stable rider to top trainer Terrance Millard, comes from one of South Africa's foremost racing families. His grandfather and no fewer than four uncles

Ray Cochrane was given his big chance by trainer Luca Cumani, and has never looked back.

were all trainers. He rode his first winner in July 1974 and has twice captured the South African jockeys' championship. He also has the distinction of having twice ridden six winners at one meeting. He has won most of the major races on the South African racing calendar, including the country's premier event, the Rothmans July Handicap.

The ambitious young rider would like to follow in the footsteps of Michael Roberts and achieve fame overseas. But he is unlikely to leave South Africa in the foreseeable future as this would jeopardize his incredibly successful partnership with Millard.

Angel Cordero (right) has been cleaning up prizes in the United States for more than 25 years. His triumphs include three Kentucky Derbys, and he was the third jockey to beat Johnny Longden's record of 6,032 winners.

Bill
COOK
b.1910 d.1985

One of Australia's greatest jockeys, Bill Cook was a tremendous favourite with the public. His first winner was in 1925 at Canterbury, on Pigeon Pie. His first major success came on Crusis in the 1929 Sydney Cup.

Cook's father was a butcher and Bill learned to ride while delivering meat on horseback. He rode for King George VI in England and accumulated more than 2,400 winners in a career that included six Sydney titles. He was runner-up in the premiership seven times. His best season was 1939–40, when he had 150 winners.

Cook took the Melbourne Cup on Skipton (1941) and Rainbird (1945). This feat was equalled by his son, Peter, who won the big race on Just A Dash (1981) and Black Knight (1985). Bill's last ride was on Chc Sara at Rosehill on 25 July 1979, when he went out with a winner.

Patricia
COOKSEY
b.1958

A childhood dream came true for Patricia Cooksey when, in 1984, she became only the second woman to ride in the Kentucky Derby. She finished eleventh on So Vague. But Cooksey, whose ambition was inspired at the age of six after watching the race on television, could never have imagined that she would ever ride more winners than any other woman in the world. That day dawned for the 5 ft (1.52 m), 110 lb (50 kg) jockey on 28 February 1988, at Turfway Park, when she beat Patti Barton's record of 1,202, which had stood since 1984. But Cooksey could hardly have foreseen that her reign as Queen of the Turf would last for only a week, for Michigan-born Julie Krone took over the crown at Aqueduct on 6 March.

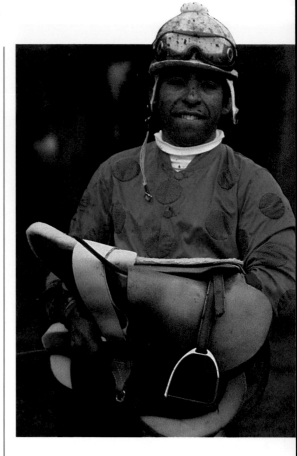

Angel
CORDERO Jr
b.1942

Born in Puerto Rico, Angel Cordero rode his first winner in 1960 at his local El Commandante track, where his father, who was first a jockey then a trainer, had taught him to groom horses as a child. In 1961, Angel was leading jockey there with 124 winners. His first New York victory was scored on Counterate in July 1962, and he went on to become only the third jockey to beat Johnny Longden's record of 6,032, at Belmont in September 1987.

Cordero celebrated the hundredth Kentucky Derby, in 1974, with a triumph on Cannonade and was back to win the 'Run for the Roses' on Bold Forbes (1976) and Spend A Buck (1985). He was the first rider to exceed 11 times (1977–87) purse earnings of $5 million in a season. Second only to Laffit Pincay in career earnings, with more than $121 million, Cordero's life was threatened after a fall with Highfalutin at Aqueduct in March 1986. He underwent four-and-a-half hours of surgery to repair a lacerated liver and fractured tibia. He was out of the saddle for four months, spending his convalescence helping his fiancé, trainer Marjorie Clayton, around the barn, picking up tips that will help when he takes up training himself.

One of the highlights of 1987 for this forceful rider was to get through a whole year without suspension. It was the first year in a decade in which he had steered clear of trouble.

Jean CRUGUET
b.1939

Born in Agen, France, Jean Cruguet went to the USA in 1965 and, apart from spending 1972–5 back in his home country, has been there ever since. While based in France, he was booked to ride the Irish-trained Hurry Harriet in England's 1973 Champion Stakes and her 33–1 triumph over Allez France was one of the biggest shocks in the long history of the race.

Cruguet was unlucky to miss the winning Prix de l'Arc de Triomphe ride on San San, at Longchamp, in 1972. Angel Penna would have given him the mount, but he broke both hands before the race. The leading rider at Deauville in 1972 and 1973, he arrived back in the USA in good time to partner Seattle Slew in his 1977 Triple Crown triumph.

Pat DAY
b.1953

It took a plane ride on a rainy New Year's Eve for Pat Day to become the USA's leading jockey of 1982. He flew from Fair Grounds to Delta Downs and rode the two winners needed to beat Angel Cordero Jr 399–397 for the title. From that time, Day was in the national spotlight, leading the field again in 1983 with 455 winners and in 1984 with 400. In 1987, he was runner-up, with 391 successes. He was top jockey at every meeting he attended in 1983, except Keeneland, and rewrote the records book at Churchill Downs, including a devastating 169 winners there in 1983.

Born in Brush, Colorado, where his father farmed, the young Day wanted to be a rodeo rider. But, at 4 ft 11 in (1.5 m) and 100 lb (45.5 kg), he saw that the racecourse was a wiser choice and went on to take Eclipse Awards as the USA's outstanding rider in 1984, 1986, and 1987. This born-again Christian cannot remember the last time he went to the cinema. 'But my least favourite movies are those the stewards invite you to see,' he claims.

Pierre DELFARGUIEL
b.1925

'Pierrot' Delfarguiel was arguably the greatest-ever French jump jockey and certainly the most famous. Apprenticed to an uncle at Maisons-Laffitte, Delfarguiel was schooling National Hunt horses over fences at the age of five, with great style and vigour. At eight, he won his first race. It was an event for junior riders over the straight course at Maisons-Laffitte, and he weighed in at 28 kg (62 lb), with his saddle! From 1943 to 1962 he won over 600 races, including the big events at Auteuil and Enghien.

Delfarguiel is particularly remembered for riding nine consecutive winners, starting with the last race on Thursday 8 December 1955, at Auteuil. The following meeting (Sunday 11 December) found him without a ride in the first race, so he won the following six instead. The next day, he took the first two races.

Franco DETTORI
b.1941

Born in Sardinia, the son of a building worker, Gianfranco Dettori was 18 years old before he saw a race horse. On leaving school he tried several jobs. He helped his father at bricklaying, tried his hand as a mechanic, and even became a barber's assistant. At 18, tiny Dettori went to Rome to work in stables exercising trotters. He was 19 before he became an apprentice and was 20 when he rode his first winner. Four years later he was Italy's champion jockey, a position he held for five seasons.

Dettori was unknown in Britain before he won the 1975 2,000 Guineas on the Italian-owned Bolkonski. He finished that season

Franco Dettori had already won most of the big races in Italy when he went to England to land a 2,000 Guineas double on Bolkonski (1975) and Wollow (1976).

Steve Donoghue was Britain's champion jockey on ten consecutive occasions and won four Epsom Derbys in five years. He went through a brilliant career without committing a single riding offence. 'Come on Steve' was a call he answered in 14 English Classics.

with 14 wins from 42 rides in England. By 1976, when he took the 2,000 Guineas again, on 11–10 Epsom Derby failure Wollow, he had been successful in almost all Italy's feature races and in his best season there rode 186 winners. In 1977, he won the Irish 2,000 Guineas on Pampapaul, by a short head from Lester Piggott on The Minstrel.

In 1983, Dettori scored three big home successes in quick succession — on Right Bank (Oaks d'Italia), Celio Rufo (Gran Premio d'Italia), and Bold Run (Premio Emilio Turati). That was the year he was disqualified after finishing second on Tolomeo in the Champion Stakes at Newmarket. Pat Eddery was aboard Tolomeo for the colt's Budweiser Million triumph later in the season. Dettori won the Oaks d'Italia four times in the five years from 1980 to 1984 and completed a hat-trick in the Gran Criterium (1977, 1978, and 1979).

Steve
DONOGHUE
b.1884 d.1945

The son of a Lancashire iron-worker, Steve Donoghue was a charmer who could talk his way into, and out of, any situation. He worked with a few English stables briefly, but had his first winner in France in 1905, before a period in Ireland. His first retainer was with Atty Persse in 1911. It was this stable that produced The Tetrarch, one of the best horses Donoghue ever rode.

'Come on Steve!' was a popular call in the

1920s, when the jockey dominated the Derby with Humorist (1921), Captain Cuttle (1922), Papyrus (1923), and Manna (1925). He was a rider with sensitive hands and bottomless courage and nowhere did he show these qualities to better effect than at Epsom. He was also aboard wartime Derby winners, Pommern and Gay Crusader, at Newmarket. In all, he had 14 English Classic triumphs and won four Irish Derbys. He was champion jockey for ten consecutive years (1914–23).

At the age of 52, and only months before his retirement, Donoghue brought off the 1937 1,000 Guineas-Oaks double with Exhibitionnist. It was a fitting farewell for one of the greatest of all jockeys. When he left Castle Irwell, Manchester, after his very last ride, he could look back on 33 blameless years in the saddle. In all that time he never committed a single riding offence. Donoghue's wealth was shared around and there was little left of his fortune when he died suddenly. But the memory of him is rich enough.

Pat
EDDERY
b.1952

Eddery's first winner was Alvaro, at Epsom in 1969, but it was in August of the following year that he really sparkled, with five winners from seven rides at Haydock Park.

The leading apprentice in 1971 with 71 successes, Eddery became a fully-fledged jockey in September 1972. The next eight years with Peter Walwyn, the most loyal of trainers, brought four jockeys' championships — and the partnership with the 1975 star, Grundy, who won eight of 11 races. Chief among these were the Epsom Derby, Irish Derby, Irish 2,000 Guineas, and the King George VI and Queen Elizabeth Stakes. Eddery was reluctant to leave Walwyn after riding more than 800 winners for the yard, but was finally wrenched away to succeed Lester Piggott as Vincent O'Brien's stable jockey for 1981.

In 1980, Eddery won his first Arc de Triomphe on Detroit, trained by Frenchman Olivier Douieb and owned by O'Brien's powerful syndicate member, Robert Sangster. Two years later Eddery scored O'Brien's sixth Epsom Derby triumph on Golden Fleece and in 1985 was back at Longchamp for another 'Arc' success with Rainbow Quest, trained by Jeremy Tree. In the autumn of 1985 he had other notable successes with Pebbles, who won both the Champion Stakes and Breeders' Cup Turf race at Aqueduct, New York.

The growing demand for Eddery's services was never more strongly emphasized than at Royal Ascot in 1986 when, without an O'Brien runner at the meeting, he was booked for all

24 races and won six of them. He went on in that championship-winning season to score with the unlucky Derby loser Dancing Brave in both the King George VI and Queen Elizabeth Stakes and the 'Arc'. He took the 'King George' ride when Dancing Brave's Epsom jockey, Greville Starkey, was reported unfit. But Eddery was first choice for the Paris race and at the end of the season left O'Brien to take a very substantial retainer to ride for Dancing Brave's owner Prince Khalid Abdullah.

For Eddery, 1987 was marked by his desperate championship battle with Steve Cauthen and his fourth 'Arc' victory (Trempolino) in eight years. His 1988 season got off to a bad start when Warning, a winter favourite for the 2,000 Guineas, missed the Classic. There was no Abdullah runner in the Epsom Derby, but winners came thick and fast, and he reached his fastest century on 20 July, at Brighton. This total was achieved in 101 days — two fewer than in 1987 — and was scored after 481 rides. Without a challenge from the injured Steve Cauthen, he romped away with the jockeys' title, his 183 winners putting him 53 ahead of his closest rival, Willie Carson.

Other big winners for Eddery include: **2,000 Guineas**: Lomond (1983), El Gran Señor (1984); **Oaks**: Polygamy (1974), Scintillate (1979); **St Leger**: Moon Madness (1986), **Ascot Gold Cup**: Erimo Hawk (1972); **Eclipse Stakes**: Coup de Feu (1974), Solford (1983), Sadlers Wells (1984); **Champion Stakes**: Vitiges (1976); **Irish 2,000 Guineas**: King's Lake (1981); **Irish Derby**: El Gran Señor (1984), Law Society (1985); **Irish Oaks**: Colorspin (1986); **Irish St Leger**: Leading Counsel (1985).

Charlie ELLIOTT
b.1904 d.1979

The rider of 14 English Classic winners, Charlie Elliott was the apprentice who, in 1924, put a stop to Steve Donoghue's domination of the jockeys' championship. Elliott was still apprenticed to Jack Jarvis at Newmarket when he ended Donoghue's ten-year reign, which started in 1914. The two riders tied for the 1923 title with 89 winners, but the following year the talented youngster took it outright with 106 successes. He was born into a Newmarket racing family. His father, 'Darkie' Elliott, worked for Lord Dundas, while his brother, Jock, was apprenticed to George Lambton.

A very accomplished and forceful jockey, Elliott rode Nimbus to a thrilling head triumph over Amour Drake in the 1949 Epsom Derby. Swallow Tail was only a head farther back in third place. He had already shown his strength in a classic finish that year, when Nimbus beat Abernant by a short head in the 2,000 Guineas. Elliott became a popular figure in France, too, his winners there including the 1939 French Derby hero, Pharis. The unbeaten colt was owned by Marcel Boussac, whom he joined as a trainer in 1953 as the replacement for Charles Semblat. Elliott saddled the 1954 Ascot Gold Cup winner, Elpenor, but the Boussac empire was beginning to crumble and, in 1958, Elliott moved back to Newmarket, where he trained until retiring in 1962.

Elliott's English Classic winners were:

Irishman Pat Eddery is a British champion with international status. An all-action jockey with great power in the saddle, he is much admired abroad, especially in France, and won the Prix de l'Arc de Triomphe four times in eight years.

Derby: Call Boy (1927), Bois Roussel (1938), and Nimbus (1949); **2,000 Guineas**: Ellangowan (1923), Flamingo (1928), Djebel (1940), Lambert Simnel (1941), and Nimbus (1949); **1,000 Guineas**: Plack (1924), Four Course (1931), Kandy (1932), and Picture Play (1944); **Oaks**: Brulette (1931) and Why Hurry (1943).

George FORDHAM
b.1837 d.1887

Cambridge-born George Fordham weighed only 54 lb (24.5 kg) when he won the 1852 Cambridgeshire Handicap. He developed into a strong jockey and won the 1,000 Guineas seven times, the Oaks five times, and the 2,000 Guineas three times. Although he had many fancied rides in the Derby, it was a race that eluded him before his retirement. He failed in business before money problems forced him back into the saddle and, in 1879, he won the Derby at last, on the 20–1 outsider Sir Bevys.

Unlike many jockeys of his time, Fordham was against gambling. He loved horses and was firmly opposed to giving a two-year-old a hard race first time out. He seldom used the whip, but was very effective in driving his horse home with his hands.

John Francome pictured on his retirement with his guv'nor, Fred Winter, left behind a trail of 1,138 winners. A superb horseman with a ready wit, he claims not to miss riding winners. But the sport in Britain misses Francome.

John FORTH
b.1769 d.1848

The oldest jockey to win an Epsom Derby was probably John Forth, who was in his sixties when he rode and trained Frederick, to take the Classic in 1829.

John FRANCOME
b.1952

The most successful jump jockey of all time, John Francome rode a total of 1,138 winners from his first success, on Multigrey, at Worcester in 1970, to his retirement in 1985. An accomplished junior show-jumper, he joined Fred Winter's stable in 1969 and took over the Number 1 job in 1975. Three years later he won the Cheltenham Gold Cup on Midnight Court, followed in 1981 by a Champion Hurdle triumph with Sea Pigeon. On 29 February 1984, he rode his thousandth winner on Observe at Worcester, and on 28 May of that year passed Stan Mellor's record total of 1,035, on Don't Touch, at Fontwell.

Francome was champion jockey seven times: 1975–6, 1978–9, 1980–1, 1981–2, 1982–3, 1983–4, and 1984–5. That equalled the record set up by Gerry Wilson between 1932–3 and 1940–1. The other big successes of this outstanding horseman included: Tote Gold Trophy (Donegal Prince, 1982); Hennessy Cognac Gold Cup (Brown Chamberlin, 1983 and Burrough Hill Lad, 1984); King George VI Chase (Wayward Lad, 1982 and Burrough Hill Lad, 1984).

Francome took out a trainer's licence in September 1985, but after only moderate success — That's Your Lot was his best horse — he retired in 1985 and became a television commentator.

Bill HARTACK
b.1932

Born in Edensburg, Pennsylvania, Bill Hartack led America's riders in 1955, with 417 winners, to become only the second jockey ever to top 400 in one season. The following year, he was top again, with 347, and pulled in a record $2,343,955 purse money. In 1957, he took both titles again and his new record of $3,060,501 was not surpassed for ten years.

Hartack's first winner, at West Virginia's Waterford Park in 1952, was the foundation of a career total of 4,272 spanning 22 years in the USA. He won five Kentucky Derbys (an achievement equalled only by Eddie Arcaro), two of them in record times for the track. The Preakness Stakes (three times) and the Belmont were among other major triumphs that put him aboard such champions as Kelso, Round Table, Northern Dancer, Tim Tam, Jewel's Reward, Carry Back, Dedicate, Barbizon, Ridan, Idun, Royal Native, and Airman's Guide. Hartack claims that the 1957 Florida Derby hero, Gen. Duke, was his best-ever horse.

Sandy HAWLEY
b.1949

The seventh jockey to win 5,000 races, Sandy Hawley rode while being treated for skin cancer. Born in Canada, he started as a hot walker and groom in Toronto. The leading North American jockey for winners in 1970, 1972, 1973, and 1976, Hawley was the first jockey to top 500 winners in a year, with 515 in 1973. He twice won seven races in one day at Woodbine, Canada, and had two six-win days at Santa Anita Park in 1976. He took five consecutive Canadian Oaks (1970–4) and was successful four times in the Queen's Plate. The jockey's other major victories include: Washington DC International: Nobiliary (1975), Youth (1976); Rothmans International: Youth (1976), Golden Act (1979).

Freddie HEAD
b.1947

Frédéric (Freddie) Head was apprenticed to his grandfather, William Head, but also spent five months in Australia learning his craft under the top trainer Tommy Smith. He rode for the first time in France, on Rayon de Soleil, at Le Tremblay. Head's first winner, on his third ride, was Zamboanga in October 1964, and his 2,000th success was scored aboard Marie de Litz at Deauville in August, 1984. His early career was helped greatly by having a famous grandfather and a trainer-father, Alec, who is now a legendary figure.

Not the most admired foreign jockey in Britain, Head must nevertheless be considered one of the top two in France. Unhappily for him, after years of playing a close second fiddle to Yves Saint-Martin (Head lost 15–6 in their jockeys' championship battles) he was then faced with tough opposition from the American Cash Asmussen. Head has won the Prix de l'Arc de Triomphe four times, with Bon Mot (1966), San San (1972), Ivanjica (1976), and Three Troikas (1979). He was only 19 when Bon Mot triumphed

and San San was picked up as a spare ride.

Among Head's 22 French Classic successes are four French Derby heroes — Goodly (1969), Roi Lear (1973), Val de l'Orne (1975), and Youth (1976). He also won three French 2,000 Guineas (Green Dancer, Red Lord, and Blushing John); six French 1,000 Guineas (Ivanjica, Riverqueen, Dancing Maid, Three Troikas, Silvermine, and Miesque); four French Oaks (Pistol Packer, Reine de Saba, Harbour and Lacovia); and the French St Leger five times.

The jockey's reputation in Britain still suffers from his dreadful experience with Lyphard in the 1972 Epsom Derby, but his successes with Zino (2,000 Guineas, 1982), Ma Biche (1,000 Guineas, 1983) and Miesque (1,000 Guineas, 1987) have helped to re-establish him. Head is an international jockey, whose wins farther afield include the USA's Breeders' Cup Turf Mile double, with Miesque (1987 and 1988).

Roy HIGGINS
b.1938

Weight problems forced Australian jockey Roy Higgins to retire at the age of 45, after 30 glorious years in the saddle. He was champion of the State of Victoria 11 times between the seasons 1964–5 and 1977–8. He rode in his first race on 28 August 1953, and has never looked back. As an apprentice he rode five winners in one day, three times — twice at Benalla and once at Holbrook.

Higgins never did things by halves. He had five triumphs at Flemington on 11 March 1972, and at the Victoria Racing Club three-day fixture rode 12 winners to beat the record of 11 set by Tommy Hales. Another remarkable feat was his eight consecutive city winners between 28 December 1976 and 8 January 1977. Bill Duncan is the only other jockey to have won the Victoria championship 11 times.

Not only one of Australia's greatest jockeys but also one of its most popular, Higgins won several Cups: Melbourne Cup (twice), Caulfield Cup (once), Sydney Cup (twice), Brisbane Cup (three times), Australian Cup (twice), Sandown Cup (three times), and Moonee Valley Cup (three times).

Higgins's other major successes include the George Adams (five times), Futurity Stakes (seven times), VATC Invitation Stakes (three times), AJC Doncaster (twice), Victoria Derby (twice), VRC Oaks Stakes (four times), VRC St Leger Stakes (three times), VRC Sires' Produce Stakes (seven times), AJC Oaks Stakes (six times), Blue Diamond Stakes (three times), and the Golden Slipper Stakes (twice).

Higgins suffered from chronic hay fever for the last few years of his career.

Roy Higgins could beat almost anything except a weight problem. His procession of winners through the years made him a popular hero, especially in Victoria, where he was leading jockey 11 times.

Charley KURTSINGER
b.1907 d.1946

One of the few riders to have won the coveted Triple Crown — on War Admiral in 1937 — Charley Kurtsinger learned his trade from his jockey-father, and from Roscoe Goose and Mack Garner. He was aboard Twenty Grand when the colt beat Equipoise in the 1930 Kentucky Jockey Club Stakes in a time of 1 minute 36 seconds. That was then the fastest mile (1.6 km) ever recorded by a two-year-old. The following year, the same partnership took the Kentucky Derby, Belmont Stakes, Wood Memorial, Dwyer, Lawrence Realisation, and Jockey Club Gold Cup.

Kurtsinger retired to take up training in 1939 and died in 1946 at the age of 39. He was inducted to the Hall of Fame in 1967.

Julie KRONE
b.1963

Julie Krone is a United States pace-setter. She was only the third woman ever to ride more than 1,000 winners, and then broke the record.

Julie Krone, whose mother was a very advanced dressage rider, was raised among horses on a Michigan farm. She rode at shows and on local bush tracks. The top

woman rider of 1986, with earnings of $2,357,136, she won six races on one card, at Monmouth Park on 19 August 1987. She was America's 18th most successful jockey, with earnings of $4,514,961 in 1987, when she came sixth in races won, with 324 successes. She was the first woman to capture riding titles at major tracks when, in 1987, she scored 130 wins at Monmouth Park and 124 at Meadowlands.

Krone was only the third woman ever to top 1,000 career victories when she joined Patty Barton and Patricia Cooksey in August 1987. And on 6 March 1988, she became the world's most successful female jockey ever by overtaking Cooksey, who in turn, had overhauled Barton's 1,202 record only the previous week.

Bobby LEWIS
b.1878 d.1947

The winner of four Melbourne Cups on The Victory (1902), Patrobas (1915), Artilleryman (1919), and Trivalve (1927), Bobby Lewis was riding in pony races at the age of ten. His first success as a jockey was on Rizpam at Caulfield in 1894 when a month short of his sixteenth birthday. He rode winners of 18 Derbys, 13 St Legers, and seven Oaks, and was aboard Phar Lap in the 1929 Melbourne Cup. When Lewis retired in 1938, he enjoyed the magnificent record of having been suspended only once in his career.

Marina LEZCANO
b.1957

The accomplishments of Marina Lezcano entitle her to take her place among the leading jockeys of Argentinian racing history and lay claim to the title of the world's leading woman rider. Born in San Vincente, a small town 40 miles (64 km) from Buenos Aires, she is known as 'The Doll'. It was her association with trainer Juan Bianchi that gave her the chance to display her talent as a jockey. Standing 4 ft 10 in (1.5 m) tall and riding at 98 lb (44.5 kg), her retainer with Bianchi took her to triumphs in all the Argentinian Classics, with the exception of the 1,000 Guineas.

Lezcano has been successful in three of her country's 2,000 Guineas (Cipayo, Telescópico, and El Asesor), two Jockey Club Stakes (Telescópico and Fort de France) and two Argentine Derbys (Sorxono and Telescópico). Fort de France's Jockey Club Stakes win established a world record for 2.0 km (10 furlongs) on turf. The jockey's partnership with Telescópico is famous. The colt was the first horse since Forli to land the Argentine Quadruple Crown (1978). His triumph in the last leg, the Carlos Pellegrini, Argentina's premier weight-for-age race, is one of his rider's three wins in the event.

In 1981, Lezcano scored in an international jockeys' challenge at San Isidro, beating such great riders as Steve Cauthen, Willie Carson, and Pat Eddery. In 1988, she married trainer Hugo Gutierrez. She rides for her husband, but plans to retire and have children.

Johnny **LONGDEN**
b.1907

Born in Wakefield, England, Johnny Longden spent his working life in the USA. Nicknamed 'The Pumper' for his vigorous urgings from the saddle, he rode until the age of 59, gathering a long list of records on the way. When he retired from the saddle in 1966, he was undisputed champion of the world, with 6,032 winners. Ten years earlier, he had overtaken Sir Gordon Richards, and in 1966 became the first jockey to top 6,000 winners. He capped his career by taking the 1966 San Juan Capistrano on George Royal, a great moment in Santa Anita's history.

Longden rode his first winner in Utah, in 1927. In 1938, he claimed his first jockey's championship, with 236 triumphs. In 1943, he was leading money earner, with $573,276, the most for any rider since Earl Sande's 1927 season. He led with $981,977 in 1945 and was top again in 1947 and 1948 in races won. The jockey rated the 1943 Triple Crown hero, Count Fleet, the best horse he ever rode. His other major winners included Noor, Busher, Swaps, Whirlaway, T. V. Lark, Your Host, Real Good Deal, Four-and-Twenty, and On Trust. Longden who began training in 1967, is the only man ever to have ridden and trained winners of the Kentucky Derby. He followed his riding triumph on Count Fleet by saddling Majestic Prince (1969) to score with Bill Hartack aboard.

Chris **McCARRON**
b.1955

The youngest jockey ever to reach $90 million in prize money, Chris McCarron set up a world record in his very first season (1974) by riding 546 winners in one year. In 1975 and 1980 he topped the list again, and in 1981, ($8,397,604) and 1984 ($12,045,813) was the highest prize-money earner. He joined the exclusive 4,000-win club on Hawkley, at Santa Anita Park in 1985.

Johnny Longden's Yorkshire grit took him to the top in the United States. His record 6,032 winners is still a milestone passed only by the elite.

Chris McCarron began his career by setting a world record in his first season, and has never looked back. He responded to an eight month lay-off through injury by riding the Kentucky Derby winner.

McCarron was the regular partner of all-time prize-money leader, John Henry, during his 1984 Horse of the Year campaign. He rates that experience one of the great highlights of a career which was briefly halted by a crashing fall from Aboard Variety at Santa Anita, in October 1986. But he was back in the saddle in less than eight months to win the 1987 Kentucky Derby, Preakness Stakes, and Super Derby on Alysheba, hero of the 1988 Breeders' Cup Classic. In 1986 he became the first rider since Eric Guerin (1955) to finish first, second, or third on different horses in each of the Triple Crown events.

Danny
MAHER
b.1881 d.1916

A top-class jockey on two continents, Danny Maher started his career in the USA in 1895 at the age of 14. Born in Connecticut, he served his apprenticeship under Bill Daly and scored his first success on his second ride. He won some notable races on Ethelbert, Banaster, Lothario, and Oneck Queen before arriving in England in 1900. He took his first English Classic the following year with Aida in the 1,000 Guineas. In 1903, Rock Sand won the Derby and St Leger for him, followed by two more Derby triumphs, with Cicero (1905) and Spearmint (1906). He completed the Epsom double with Keystone II in the 1906 Oaks. Other Classics came his way with a second St Leger, on Bayardo (1909), and the 2,000 Guineas with Neil Gow (1910) and Sweeper II (1912).

Maher won the Eclipse Stakes five times, the Ascot Gold Cup twice, and the Irish Derby with Civility (1912). He was naturalized British when he became champion jockey in 1913. Three years later, he contracted tuberculosis and died. In 21 years (1895–1915) he had won 1,771 races.

Joe
MERCER
b.1934

One of the best jockeys never to ride a Derby winner, Joe Mercer had his first success with Eldoret at Bath on 13 September 1950. Mercer was to ride for Jack Colling, Major Dick Hern, Henry Cecil, and Peter Walwyn. He was champion apprentice in 1952 and again in 1953, when Oaks winner Ambiguity gave him the first of 12 Classic successes in Europe. Provoke provided the second in the 1965 St Leger, a race he was to win again with Bustino (1974), Light Cavalry (1980), and Cut Above (1981). Outstanding among

Joe Mercer was the stylish partner of the great Brigadier Gerard. His career brought him 2,810 riding triumphs in Britain.

Mercer's many good horses was Brigadier Gerard, whose 17 triumphs in 18 races included the 2,000 Guineas of 1971 and the King George VI and Queen Elizabeth Stakes in 1972.

Always proud to wear the Royal colours, Mercer got a special kick out of a Classic double in 1974, when the Queen's Highclere took both the English 1,000 Guineas and the French Oaks. But there were storm clouds ahead and it came as a great shock to the racing world when it was announced that Mercer would be succeeded in the Hern job by Willie Carson at the end of 1976. Not that the change did Mercer much harm, for he was quickly signed on by Henry Cecil and in 1979 won not only the 1,000 Guineas on One in a Million, but became champion jockey with his best-ever total of 164. Another move took him to Peter Walwyn's stable in 1981, and in 1985 he retired after scoring on the 20–1 November Handicap winner Bold Rex on his very last ride in Britain.

Mercer had won 2,810 races in his home country, and on retiring became an agent for jockeys Brent Thomson and Tony McGlone before being appointed racing manager to Maktoum Al Maktoum.

Martin
MOLONY
b. 1925

One of the most skilled and versatile jockeys of our time, Martin Molony's brilliant career was cut short by a crashing fall at Thurles on 18 September 1951. His skull was fractured

and he was forced to retire at the age of 26.

Molony left Ireland at 13 to join a number of Irish apprentices at Martin Hartigan's Wiltshire stable. Gordon Richards and his brother Cliff rode in gallops with him. He was sent home at the start of World War II, and while with Kilmallock trainer George Harris rode his first winner, Chitor, at The Curragh, in October 1939. He then moved on to Ginger Wellesley's stable and from there to Captain Cyril Harty. As he became heavier he took more to combining jumping with Flat racing. His first winner over hurdles was Prince John, at Rathkeale, on 19 March 1942. His first Flat winner in England was Sugar Palm, at Liverpool, in 1948.

Molony's versatility shows up clearly in his achievements. He won the 1951 Cheltenham Gold Cup on Silver Fame and in the same year took both the Phoenix Park '1,500' on Abadan and the Irish 2,000 Guineas on Signal Box. He was third with Signal Box in the Epsom Derby, a position he filled on Stella Polaris in the Epsom Oaks (1950). Twice winner of the Irish Cesarewitch (1949 and 1950) on triple Champion Hurdle hero Hatton's Grace, he also took the Irish Grand Nationals of 1944, 1946, and 1950. The jockey retired to own and manage the Rathmore Stud, in County Limerick.

Tim
MOLONY
b.1919

Champion jump jockey in Britain for four consecutive seasons (1948–9 to 1951–2), and in the 1954–5 season, Irishman Tim Molony is the elder brother of Martin. Winner of four successive Champion Hurdles, on Hatton's Grace (1951) and Sir Ken (1952, 1953, and 1954), Tim also took the Cheltenham Gold Cup on Knock Hard (1953). He won on both Freebooter (Champion Chase, 1949) Wot No Sun (Grand Sefton 1952, and Emblem Chase 1949), but was on neither when they finished first and second in the 1950 Aintree Grand National. Successful in about 900 races, Tim was undoubtedly a top-class jockey, but when the talented Molony brothers are discussed, it is usually Martin who is given the edge.

George
MOORE
b.1923

Recognized internationally as one of the world's greatest jockeys, Australian George Moore had the lives of himself and his family threatened in his 1967 season, when he was

riding for Noel Murless in England. His London flat was broken into after menacing telephone calls. That was in September, by which time he had won three of the five English Classics, on Royal Palace (2,000 Guineas and Derby) and the 1,000 Guineas on Fleet. His 72 winners in 1967 also included his King George VI and Queen Elizabeth Stakes triumph with Busted.

Moore, who took over the job with Murless from Lester Piggott, rode his first winner in 1940. In Australia, the only major race to elude him was the Melbourne Cup, in which he had 19 rides. From 1956 he rode five winners at a meeting five times, four winners 18 times, and scored 83 trebles. One of his greatest performances was at the 1969 Australian Jockey Club carnival at Randwick, Sydney. There were 29 races over the four days and Moore rode 15 winners. An investment of $A 10 on each of his 3,403 mounts at 730 meetings would have shown a profit of $1,830 from 1,040 winners.

In 1959, the first of two seasons he rode for Aly Khan in France, Moore scored his first English Classic success with Taboun in the 2,000 Guineas. His other triumphs include the French Derby and Grand Prix (Charlottesville); the Arc de Triomphe and Eclipse (Saint Crespin III); the Ascot Gold Cup and Grand Prix de Saint-Cloud (Sheshoon); the French 1,000 Guineas (Ginetta); and the Irish 1,000 Guineas (Fiorentina).

When he retired from the saddle, Moore trained in France and Hong Kong. He now lives on Queensland's Gold Coast and his son, Gary, is a successful jockey in Europe.

Australian George Moore's spectacular stay in England ended with threats to the lives of himself and his family.

Darby **MUNRO**
b.1913 d.1966

The son of the Australian trainer, Jim Munro, Darby began riding at the age of 14. His first winner was Release (20–1) at Warwick Farm in 1927. He was disqualified for two years over his handling of Vagabond. The English Jockey Club claimed he had not obtained a clearance certificate before he left Australia in 1953 and refused to let him ride in Britain. But Munro was able to take mounts in France and America during the same trip. He won the Melbourne Cup on Peter Pan (1934), Sirius (1944), and Russia (1946). Darby's brother, Jim, a top jockey in India and Germany, also took the Melbourne Cup on Statesman (1928).

Darby had many big race triumphs before he retired in 1955 to train, with moderate success, until his death 11 years later.

Isaac **MURPHY**
b.1861 d.1896

Isaac Murphy, the son of a former slave, is regarded as one of the greatest American jockeys of all time. Loyal to long-time patrons like Lucky Baldwin and Ed Corrigan, he was incorruptible. It is on record that he refused big bribes offered by gamblers to lose the 1879 Kenner Stakes on the champion, Falsetto.

Year after year, Murphy's win rate was better than one in three, and in 1886 he scored on 40 per cent of his rides. He won the Kentucky Derby three times, on Buchanan (1884), Riley (1890), and Kingman (1891). And he was aboard four of the first five winners of the American Derby, when it was the richest three-year-old race in the country.

Murphy was taught to ride on a Kentucky horse farm, and his mounts included the champions Emperor of Norfolk, Kingston, Firenze, and Salvator. A badly judged race on Firenze, in 1890, brought adverse publicity, but he continued to ride for five more years, at the same time owning and training horses. When he died of pneumonia, he had won 530 of his 1,538 races. He was the first rider to be voted into the Hall of Fame.

Jonjo **O'NEILL**
b.1952

All the courage and determination shown by Jonjo O'Neill during a spectacular National Hunt riding career were shown to the full in his successful fight against cancer, which struck soon after he retired from the saddle in 1986. The Irishman, who rode his first winner at The Curragh in 1970, joined Gordon Richards at Penrith in 1973. He stayed there (from late 1975 as first jockey) until turning freelance for the 1977–8 season. He was much in demand immediately, and after passing Ron Barry's record of 125 winners, went on to score 149. The closest any jockey has come to it is Peter Scudamore, with 132 in 1987–8.

O'Neill, champion again in 1979–80, rode some exceptional horses, including Dawn Run, with whom he completed a unique double in the Champion Hurdle (1984) and Cheltenham Gold Cup (1986). He rode the remarkable Sea Pigeon in the first of his two Champion Hurdle victories (1980) as well as riding him to triumphs on the Flat. Alverton, his winner of the 1979 Cheltenham Gold Cup, was killed under him in that year's Grand National. Now, as a trainer, his thirst for racing remains unquenched.

John **PARSONS**
b.— d.—

Credited with being the youngest rider to win the Epsom Derby, John Parsons is believed to have been only 16 when he scored on Caractacus in 1862.

Jonjo O'Neill set a riding record in 1978 with 149 winners in the season. After retiring to become a trainer, he was struck by cancer, but fully recovered.

Lester PIGGOTT
b.1935

The three-year jail sentence imposed on Lester Piggott in October 1987 for tax evasion could do nothing to diminish the vast contribution he made as a jockey to racing around the world. Momentarily obscured by the big black cloud that rolled over him as he left the dock in Ipswich Crown Court were the mostly blue skies that stretched from his first success, at the age of 12, to his last ride in Britain, at Nottingham, on 29 October 1985.

The boy Piggott was a favourite with women. And so he remained, as the rounded cheeks of childhood gave way to a face pinched by self-deprivation and starved of colour. Partially deaf, he saw everything and said very little. He was his own man; a loner. But despite his reticence and unsmiling lips, the public adored him. To them, he was simply the most brilliant, individualistic jockey of them all. Piggott kept his admirers at arm's length by declining most invitations to visit their homes via television interviews.

It was against this background that Piggott, by now an established trainer at Newmarket, went to prison. Many faithful followers attacked the sentence as unfair or too harsh. More emotion was displayed than ever Piggott himself had shown, as he walked away from freedom on that sad October afternoon. And when the OBE he had so richly deserved was stripped from him in June 1988, there was yet more sympathy.

Piggott was born into racing. His grandfather, Ernest Piggott, who married Margaret, the daughter of trainer Tom Cannon (also the rider of 13 Classic winners) and sister of winning Derby jockeys Mornington and Kempton Cannon, rode two Grand National winners. His father, Keith, was a tough jump jockey before becoming a trainer, and his mother, Iris, came from the famous Rickaby racing family.

His father's apprentice, Piggott was only 12 and weighed 5 stone (32 kg) when he rode the first of his 4,349 winners in Britain on The Chase at Haydock on 18 August 1948. Reckless on the track, despite domestic reprimands from, among others, his experienced and respected jockey-cousin Bill Rickaby, he fell foul of the stewards four times before taking his first apprentice title at fifteen.

Piggott won the 1954 Epsom Derby at the age of eighteen, when he scored his first of nine record triumphs, on Never Say Die. But only a fortnight later, the stewards lost their patience after his riding of the same horse in the King Edward VII Stakes at Royal Ascot. He was stood down and reported to the Jockey Club, who in turn suspended him for the rest of the season. In their statement, the stewards said that they had taken notice of

The face of fame – Lester Piggott. The deeply furrowed brow and pinched cheeks reveal some of the deprivation suffered in the quest for winners all over the world. Probably the greatest jockey of all time, he tried to dodge the tax man and ended up in prison.

Piggott's dangerous and erratic riding in 1954 and in previous seasons, and that 'in spite of continuous warnings he continued to show complete disregard for the Rules of Racing and the safety of other jockeys.' It was stipulated that before any application for the renewal of Piggott's licence could be entertained, he must be attached to some trainer other than his father for six months.

Piggott went to work for Jack Jarvis at Newmarket, but never served his full sentence. He got his licence back in September and although his weight had soared ominously to 9 stone 7 lb (60.5 kg), he stripped himself down to 8 stone (51 kg) six days later to win on Cardington King at Newmarket. There were to be rare flashbacks to his early indiscretions, but generally Piggott took a pull on his daredevil instincts and without ever losing an ounce of his driving will to win, took a safer route to the top of the world. With his leathers shorter than could be safely negotiated by most jockeys, Piggott's backside was carried high in the air when his horse was in cruising gear. To watch him hold this position while other jockeys were scrubbing their horses along was a great comfort to his backers!

Noel Murless was the first trainer to sign up Piggott as stable jockey. The stable soon reaped a harvest, notably with a 1957 Epsom Classic double with Crepello (Derby) and the Queen's Carrozza (Oaks). And there was the great filly Petite Etoile, who took the 1959 1,000 Guineas under Doug Smith before Piggott jumped aboard for triumphs in the Oaks, Yorkshire Oaks, Champion Stakes, Sussex Stakes, and Coronation Cup (1960 and 1961). The Murless connection, which included Derby winner St Paddy (1960), was broken in 1966. Piggott went freelance until, in 1968, Irish trainer Vincent O'Brien stepped in to put the jockey up on his all-conquering classic collection of Derby winners Sir Ivor, Nijinsky, Roberto, and The Minstrel. Nijinsky was the first to take the Triple Crown since Bahram, in 1935.

Out of a job in 1980, Piggott teamed up with Henry Cecil in 1981. The outcome was two more jockeys' titles, bringing his score to 11. Geoffrey Wragg supplied Piggott's ninth Derby hero, Teenoso (1983), and Luca Cumani's American contract rider, Darrell McHargue, was 'jocked off' 1984 St Leger winner Commanche Run to give Lester a record twenty-eighth English Classic. Shadeed (2,000 Guineas, 1985) made it 29 before the 'Long Fella' called it a day and turned successfully to training. After the imprisonment, Piggott's wife Susan was granted a licence to train at Eve Lodge Stables, which produced 30 winners in 1986 and 31 in 1987. Lester was released on parole from Highpoint Prison in October of that year, having served one third of his sentence.

Piggott's 29 Classic winners were: **Derby**: Never Say Die (1954), Crepello (1957), St Paddy (1960), Sir Ivor (1968), Nijinsky (1970), Roberto (1972), Empery (1976), The Minstrel (1977), Teenoso (1983); **Oaks**: Carrozza (1957), Petite Etoile (1959), Valoris (1966), Juliette Marny (1975), Blue Wind (1981), Circus Plume (1984); **2,000 Guineas**: Crepello (1957), Sir Ivor (1968), Nijinsky (1970), Shadeed (1985); **1,000 Guineas**: Humble Duty (1970), Fairy Footsteps (1981); **St Leger**: St Paddy (1960), Aurelius (1961), Ribocco (1967), Ribero (1968), Nijinsky (1970), Athens Wood (1971), Boucher (1972), Commanche Run (1984).

Piggott's big successes abroad include the Irish Sweeps Derby (five times), Grosser Preis von Berlin (three), Prix de l'Arc de Triomphe (three), Washington DC International (three). He rode at least 822 winners abroad and had 20 successes over hurdles.

Laffit Pincay, the Mr Moneybags of American racing, is the jockey with the golden touch. He has opened more purse strings than any rider in the world and his total earnings are close to $130 million.

Jim PIKE
b.1893 d.1969

Jim Pike began his career at the age of 12, but he was soon banned by the Stewards for being too young. His first winner was Victoria Cross, at Maitland, in 1906. When he was 17, Pike left Australia with his master, Bill Kelso, for England, where he landed winners for Lord Carnarvon at Newmarket and Manchester. Both were homesick and soon returned. Pike scored five wins at the 1909 Melbourne Carnival, including the Champion Stakes and Australian Cup.

He ended his career with triumphs in 165 feature races, the most rewarding of them being Phar Lap's 1930 Melbourne Cup victory under 9 stone 12 lb (62.5 kg).

Laffit PINCAY Jr
b.1946

No jockey in the world has won as much purse money as the Panamanian Laffit Pincay. The son of a jockey, he would follow his father to the track and do jobs for free in the hope that somebody would give him the opportunity to ride.

Pincay was 18 when he first took out a licence. His second ride, Huelen, was a winner at his home track, Remon, in Panama. He rode there for two years before being taken to the USA by owner Fred Hooper in 1966. Pincay rates his main achievements as winning five Eclipse titles and taking the Belmont Stakes three years in a row with 1982 Horse of the Year Conquistador Cielo and then with Caveat and Swale. Pincay was only the second jockey ever to bring off the Belmont treble (James McLaughlin was the first) and he trails only Bill Shoemaker in the number of races won.

Successful in the 1984 Kentucky Derby on Swale, Pincay was the first jockey to have seven winners on one Santa Anita programme (1987). His successes in million-dollar races include the Arlington Million (Perrault) and Jersey Derby (Spend A Buck). His national championships for prize-money earnings include the five straight years 1970–4. Pincay's 1985 winnings of almost $13.5 million were an all-time record for one year. His total earnings are approaching $130 million.

Robin PLATTS
b.1949

Born in Leicester, England, Robin Platts has not missed out on many big races on the Ontario Jockey Club circuit. He is one of only three riders to have won Woodbine's Queen's Plate four times. He shares the record with Sandy Hawley and the late Avelino Gomez. Platts has ridden many of Canada's best horses, including Bessarabian, Overskate, Key to the Moon, and Frost King.

Roger POINCELET
b.1921 d.1977

To say Roger Poincelet was a Parisian is like saying a Cockney is a Londoner. Born in the French capital, he was, until the end, a real 'Parigot' with an enduring and tumultuous love affair with Montmartre.

During an amazing career, Poincelet rode over 2,500 winners, beginning with the Aly Khan's two-year-old, Manchuria, in May 1937. He lost his apprentice allowance three seasons later and went on to 20 years of stardom. His victories include three Prix de l'Arc de Triomphe (Coronation, Nuccio, and Prince Royal II); three Grand Prix de Paris (Altipan, San Roman, and Sanctus); two French Derbys (Sandjar and Right Royal V); three Grand Prix de Saint-Cloud (Un Gaillard, Goyama, and Chingacgook); two French Oaks (Corteira and Crepallana); and seven Grands Critériums.

In Great Britain he won the Derby with Psidium (1961) and took the Oaks with Never Too Late (1960) and the 1952 2,000 Guineas with Thunderhead. He was French champion jockey nine times. Poincelet became Marcel Boussac's jockey soon after World War II and he stayed with this great owner-breeder for almost all his career. The millionaire industrialist and his 'Parigot' jockey had an amazing relationship, using the familiar 'tu' to each other in public, like father and son.

In 1970, Boussac set Poincelet up as trainer at his Villa Djebel stable, where he replaced René Emery, and although the Boussac horses were by then drifting from the crest of the wave towards the doldrums, Poincelet did very well with them despite poor health, until losing the battle against cancer on 1 November (All Saints' Day) 1977.

Pat REMILLARD

b.1906 d.—

North America's oldest jockey when he retired in 1966 at the age of 60, Pat Remillard won 1,922 races and a fantastic total of $2,644,365. Such prize-money earnings were staggering at the time.

Avelino Gomez, who remembered riding against him with mixed feelings, said, 'Pat rode long, and one of his best tricks was to boot your horse in the chest when he tried to edge by. The trick wasn't illegal, it was just his way of riding.'

Sir Gordon RICHARDS

b.1904 d.1986

The only professional jockey to be honoured with a knighthood, Sir Gordon Richards received the accolade five days before his one and only Epsom Derby triumph. It was a magnificent double to top up Coronation celebrations for Britain's sporting public.

The son of a miner, Nathan Richards, and one of 12 children, Richards was born in Shropshire. His first winner, Gay Lord, at

Sir Gordon Richards was riding high as British champion no less than 26 times. He rode an amazing 269 winners in one season and was admired as much for his integrity as his relentless will to win.

Leicester in 1921, was followed by 4,869 more in a glittering career spanning 35 years. He was champion jockey 26 times, rode an astounding 269 winners in one year (1947), and in 1933 scored 12 in a row in his last ride at Nottingham and 11 more over two days at Chepstow. Two hundred winners in a season, which is such a barrier for jockeys nowadays, were collected no fewer than 12 times. Richards, who rode with a loose rein, was always perfectly balanced and horses ran their hearts out for him. Gordon Richards was fortunate in enjoying the trust and affection of the public, who coupled their appreciation of his skill with admiration for his honesty and determination.

Two of Richards's 27 beaten Derby horses started odds on: Big Game (sixth at 4–6 in 1942) and Tudor Minstrel (fourth at 4–7 in 1947). When Pinza (1953) finally ended the famine, in Richards's last ride in the Classic, he was a popular choice with punters at 5–1 joint favourite.

Richards, who began his working life as a clerk in an engineering works, was apprenticed to Martin Hartigan and had a total of ten winners in his first three years. But 1923 brought 49, and in 1925, when he was out of his apprenticeship and riding for Tommy Hogg's stable, 118 winners were enough to give him the championship for the first time. In 1926, he was taken ill with tuberculosis and missed most of the season. But he was back on top the following year with 164.

In 1932, Richards joined Fred Darling at his training yard at Beckhampton, west of Lambourn. He remained there when Noel Murless took over the establishment in 1948, and moved to Newmarket with him four years later. A bad fall from the Queen's Abergeldie as the filly reared on leaving the paddock left Richards with a broken pelvis at Sandown in 1954. He had planned to complete the season, but instead retired and in 1955 returned briefly to Beckhampton with a trainer's licence. After a season there he switched first to Ogbourne Maisey and then to Whitsbury, from where he retired in 1970 to manage horses for Sir Michael Sobell and Lady Beaverbrook.

Richards was a truly remarkable man of boundless energy. Let it not be forgotten that he did not have motorways or the bonus of helicopter dashes to evening meetings to help him on his way. Among his big-race wins were: **2,000 Guineas**: Pasch (1938), Big Game (1942), Tudor Minstrel (1947); **1,000 Guineas**: Sun Chariot (1942), Queenpot (1948), Belle of All (1951); **Derby**: Pinza (1953); **Oaks**: Rose of England (1930), Sun Chariot (1942); **St Leger**: Singapore (1930), Chulmleigh (1937), Turkhan (1940), Sun Chariot (1942), Tehran (1944); **King George VI and Queen Elizabeth Stakes**: Pinza (1953); **Ascot Gold Cup**: Felicitation (1934), Owen Tudor (1942), Ujiji (1943), Umiddad (1944), Aquino (1952).

Britain's Jockey of the Year in 1988, South African born Michael Roberts was regular rider of Racehorse of the Year, Mtoto.

Michael
ROBERTS
b.1954

South African lightweight Michael Roberts has become a most popular and successful jockey since he joined Alec Stewart's Newmarket stables in 1986.

Born in Cape Town, Roberts had five years with the Summerveld Jockeys' Academy before joining Herman Brown. His first winner was Smyrna, at Pietermaritzburg in 1968, and since then he has been champion jockey of South Africa no fewer than 11 times. Roberts also became the first rider in his home country to achieve more than 200 winners (1981–2), and the only feature race to have eluded him in South Africa is the Rothmans July Handicap. His major successes include the South African 2,000 Guineas, which he has won eight times, and the South African Derby (six times).

Roberts at first experienced some difficulty in getting established on the English racing scene during his 1978 visit, but two of Stewart's good horses, Mtoto and Waajib, helped to put him in the spotlight on his return. In 1988, Mtoto became the first horse since Polyphontes (1924–5) to win the Eclipse Stakes in consecutive years, and he went on to a thrilling triumph in the King George VI and Queen Elizabeth Stakes. Waajib's triumphs included the valuable Schweppes Golden Mile (1987). In 1988 Roberts took Britain's Jockey of the Year award. His 121 winners from 777 rides won him third place in the jockeys' championship.

Yves SAINT-MARTIN
b.1941

When Yves Saint-Martin rode in his last race at Bay Meadows, USA, on 17 January 1988, in the International Jockeys' Cup, he had long been one of racing's cult figures. Since his first win on Royalic at Le Tremblay in 1958, he had ridden 3,313 winners.

Saint-Martin arrived in François Mathet's stable as an apprentice. The dark good looks he had then went a long way to making him a favourite with French women in the years that followed. He remembers little or nothing of his first ride, at the now defunct Soissons track. He fell off and woke up in an ambulance. Then there was the horrific fall at Chantilly's 1983 Diane meeting which nearly resulted in a life in a wheelchair.

Saint-Martin, stable jockey to Mathet, Daniel Wildenstein, and the Aga Khan, was champion jockey 15 times. He won 29 French Classics, including nine French Derbys and six French Oaks. He took four Prix de l'Arc de Triomphe (Sassafras, Allez France, Akiyada, and Sagace) and triumphed abroad as well. In England, he took the Derby (Relko); the Oaks (Monade and Pawneese); the St Leger (Crow); the 1,000 Guineas (Altesse Royale and Flying Water); and the 2,000 Guineas (Nonoalco). Other victories included the King George VI and Queen Elizabeth Stakes (Match III and Pawneese) and the Champion Stakes (Flying Water, Vayrann, and Palace Music).

Saint-Martin's major successes in the USA were with Match III (Washington DC International); and Lashkari (53–1) and Last Tycoon (36–1) in Breeders' Cup turf races.

When he retired at the age of 46, Saint-Martin had nothing else to prove. His son, Eric, was beginning to make a name for himself as a jockey, but his father had no intention of taking up training. A post with a bloodstock agency and the possibility of becoming a television personality beckoned.

Earl SANDE
b.1899 d.1968

Earl Sande's track achievements earned him a place in racing history. The leading money winner in 1921, 1923, and 1927, he won 196 stakes races, including three Kentucky Derbys, five Belmonts, five Jockey Club Gold Cups, and four Withers.

Born in South Dakota, Sande did the rounds of fairs in the western USA and in his first year of riding thoroughbreds, 1918, won 18 stakes, four of them on champion horse Billy Kelly. In 1923, he took 39 stakes, ten of them on Zev, who included among his triumphs the Kentucky Derby, Belmont, and a match with the English Derby winner Papyrus. His champions included Sir Barton, Grey Lag, Sarazen, Crusader, and Mad Hatter, but he regarded Man O' War as the greatest horse he ever rode.

Sande retired, but was persuaded by William Woodward Sr to return to ride Gallant Fox in 1930, and the partnership triumphed in the Triple Crown. He retired for the second time in 1932, and after taking up training went right to the top in 1938. Sande was elected to the Hall of Fame in 1955.

Peter SCUDAMORE
b.1958

The most successful British jump jockey since the retirement of John Francome in 1985, Peter Scudamore rode 132 winners in 1987–8. Only Jonjo O'Neill has ridden more in one season. Scudamore shared the title with Francome in 1981–2, but won it outright in 1985–6, 1986–7, and 1987–8. His biggest success was aboard Celtic Shot in the 1988 Champion Hurdle. He was top jockey at the Cheltenham Festival in 1986 and 1987. In 1988 he scored the fastest 50 winners in National Hunt history when Wolfhangar obliged at Fakenham on 24 October. It broke John Francome's record set on 9 November 1984. At the end of 1988 Scudamore set a record for the fastest century.

Peter Scudamore made a sensational start to the 1988–9 jumping season by riding his first 100 winners in record time.

Otto SCHMIDT
b.1896 d.1964

Otto Schmidt, usually known as 'Otto-Otto', was both the most successful German jockey of all time and the most popular character of the German racing scene. That was at a time when racing, especially in Berlin, enjoyed tremendous public appeal.

In the early part of this century, most jockeys in Germany were imports from the English-speaking world, but partly as a result of World War I, the inter-war period was dominated by local-born riders, led by Schmidt. Apprenticed to Fred Taral, who was private trainer to Gestüt Waldfried, one of the most successful owner-breeders of the period, Schmidt won the 1916 Derby in Waldfried's fourth colours on Amorino, only nine months after riding his first winner. This marked the beginning of a spectacular career, with almost unbroken success until he retired in 1952 with a total of 2,216 wins. He won every big German race, including seven German Derbys and 22 other Classics.

Neville SELLWOOD
b.1922 d.1962

Apprenticed to Jim Shean in Brisbane at the same time as George Moore was a junior there, Neville Sellwood made his racing debut on 12 October 1938, and his first winner, Ourimbah, came 15 rides later.

Sellwood, whose thousandth winner was at Warwick Farm, Sydney, in May 1966, took the Melbourne Cup on Delta (1951) and Toparoa (1955). He partnered the great horses, Tulloch and Todman, in a number of successes. He had an Epsom Derby triumph for the Irish trainer Vincent O'Brien on Larkspur (1962) and, at home, three Sydney Cups, two Caulfield Cups, and two AJC Derbys led a procession of big race victories.

The jockey rode until he was 39, when he was tragically killed in a fall from Lucky Seven at Maisons-Laffitte, near Paris. At the time of his death he should have been in Australia to fulfil a commitment to ride in the Melbourne Cup, but had stayed in France to cement his place at the top of the jockeys' list.

Neville Sellwood should have been in his native Australia when he was killed in a fall at Maisons-Laffitte, in France.

Don SEYMOUR
b.1961

Canada's leading rider from 1981 to 1986, a period when he was the best in the West, Don Seymour moved to eastern Canada for the 1987 season and received the Sovereign Award for jockey of the year. Seymour, who grew up within sight of the Woodbine track, won 105 races in Ontario in 1987 and his mounts earned more than $2 million.

Bill SHOEMAKER
b.1931

With his 8,700th winner long since home and hosed, the USA's Bill Shoemaker had no thought of retirement as he approached his fortieth year in the saddle. 'Charlie Whittingham is still training those good horses and I want to keep on riding them. I want to win as many races as possible so that the record can stand for a while,' he said at the time. But in October 1988, after only 60 wins at that point in the season, he announced that 1989 would be his last year in the saddle and that he would turn to training and television work.

At 4 ft 11 in (1.5 m) and 95 lb (43 kg), 'Shoe' has ridden more winners than any man in the world. He broke Johnny Longden's record with success number 6,033 at Del Mar in September 1970, and 11 years later passed the 8,000 mark. In 1985, he became the first rider to reach $100 million in career earnings. He has led North American jockeys five times in the number of races won and ten times in purse earnings.

Shoemaker, who was elected to racing's Hall of Fame in 1958, spent part of his youth with his grandfather, a ranch foreman, in Winters, Texas. There, he rode a pony at a very early age and, despite his size, boxed and wrestled in high school before being introduced to racing by Wallace 'Bud' Bailey, a jockey at Santa Anita Park, California. His first monthly pay packet was $75 for working at Suzy Q Ranch, in La Puente. He left after two years for Bay Meadows and became an apprentice in 1949. Two years later, he won his first $100,000 race, at Santa Anita, and in 1981 he became the first rider to land a $1 million event, the Arlington Million.

The Texan swept through American racing after laying the foundations of a brilliant career on the filly, Shafter V, in April 1949, at Golden Gate Fields. By the end of that year he had won 219 races, to finish second to Gordon Glisson for the championship. His first Kentucky Derby win, on Swaps (1955), was followed by Tommy Lee (1959) and Lucky Debonair (1965). He became the oldest rider to win the great event when, at the age of 54, he was cheered home on Ferdinand (1986). There should have been a fifth Churchill Downs triumph. He admits: 'I misjudged the finish line of the 1957 race with Gallant Man and lost because of that.'

(James) Tod SLOAN
b.1874 d.1933

Jaunty American James Sloan, always known as Tod, claimed to have set the pattern for a new style of riding — the body crouched above short leathers — during his stay in England. But it has been claimed that a black American called Simms, who won four races from 19 rides at Newmarket in 1895 before vanishing from the scene, was the first. The jibe 'monkey up a stick' did not worry Sloan. His streamlined style was eminently more effective on a racecourse than the upright, straight-legged posture of his English contemporaries.

Encouraged by Lord William Beresford to come to England in 1897, Sloan soon made his mark. The 'monkey up a stick' made a monkey out of jockeys who had laughed at him, for they soon aped his style. There is no doubt that Sloan had genius and that his effect on racing all around the world was profound. He was out on his own, and a young hero, so it was no surprise that he found himself, cigar in mouth, surrounded by a group of seedy characters who had made their way across the Atlantic.

In 1900 the axe fell. Although Sloan was never warned off, it was made clear to him by the English and French authorities that he need not bother applying for a licence the following year. Betting was his 'crime', but he stayed in England for another 15 years in the vain hope that his licence would one day be renewed and that he could add to his 254 winners. But he was finally deported for breaking the gaming laws, and when he died there was nothing left of the $500,000 he claimed to have been worth 33 years before.

Doug SMITH
b.1917

Sir Gordon Richards rated Newmarket's Rowley Mile the best of all courses, but perhaps even he did not handle it better than Doug Smith, who had been riding winners since 1931 when he retired in 1967 to take up training. Apprenticed to Major F. B. Sneyd, Smith became a very successful jockey, but

American Bill Shoemaker had ridden many more winners than any man in the world when he announced plans for retirement.

also knew what it felt like to lose, for in 1938 he had a run of 111 rides without a winner.

It was at Newmarket that Smith had two royal Classic victories — the 1,000 Guineas of 1946 for King George, with Hypericum, and the 2,000 Guineas of 1958 for Queen Elizabeth, on Pall Mall. He also won these races with Our Babu (2,000 Guineas, 1955) and Petite Etoile (1,000 Guineas, 1959). Scobie Breasley was the only rider to interrupt a run of jockeys' championships for Smith, who took the title every year from 1954 to 1959, with the exception of 1957. But his best season for winners (173 in 1947) had already gone. That was the year Gordon Richards excelled himself with 269.

A master at riding staying races, Smith had five of his six Cesarewitch successes between 1954 and his retirement. That race was generally regarded as his speciality, but he also won the Doncaster Cup seven times. He rates Lord Derby's Alycidon, winner of the 'Cup Triple Crown' as perhaps the best stayer of all time. The Lord Derby retainer brought Smith more than 350 winners after he took the job in 1946.

The jockey's worst accident of several came on the last day of the 1964 season, at Liverpool, when he was thrown from Miracle Man during a race. Flying hooves fractured his skull and he remembers nothing of the fall that so seriously endangered his life. He retired from riding with 3,112 winners.

Greville
STARKEY
b.1939

Controversy still surrounds Greville Starkey's narrow defeat on the 2,000 Guineas hero Dancing Brave in the 1986 Epsom Derby. Although Britain's senior jockey since the

Greville Starkey, Britain's senior jockey, caused a storm of controversy when he was beaten on Dancing Brave in the Epsom Derby in 1986.

retirement of Lester Piggott in 1985, he was accused by some of riding an ill-judged race.

Starkey rode his first winner at Pontefract in 1956, when apprenticed to Tom Jones. He was leading apprentice in 1957 and, two years after joining John Oxley, rode the stable's Homeward Bound to take the 1964 Oaks. From Oxley, he went to Henry Cecil, but after four years left in April 1974.

Success for the German trainer Theo Greiper with Star Appeal in both the Eclipse Stakes (at 20–1) and the Arc de Triomphe (at 119–1) of 1975 followed Starkey's move to Guy Harwood's stable. A strong field, including Allez France, produced one of the 'Arc's' roughest races, but Starkey kept out of trouble to weave through beaten runners with a burst of finishing speed that stunned the Longchamp crowd.

John Dunlop's Shirley Heights won the Derby with Starkey in 1978, and Dancing Brave went off the 2–1 favourite to give him a second triumph in 1986. The Form Book remarks that the colt, who came with a strong, late run from a long way back, was given 'too much to do'. The partnership then won the Eclipse Stakes, but the jockey was unfit for the King George VI and Queen Elizabeth Stakes. Pat Eddery took the ride on Dancing Brave and was called back again for both the 'Arc' and the Breeders' Cup after Starkey's success on the colt at Goodwood.

Dancing Brave's owner, Prince Khalid Bin Abdullah, who is a leading patron in the Harwood yard, signed up Eddery to ride all his horses world-wide from the start of 1987. It was made clear that stable jockey Starkey would be asked to partner the Saudi prince's horses when Eddery was not available.

Starkey's big winners include: **Derby**: Shirley Heights (1978); **2,000 Guineas**: To-Agori-Mou (1981), Dancing Brave (1986); **Oaks**: Homeward Bound (1964), Fair Salinia (1978); **Prix de l'Arc de Triomphe**: Star Appeal (1975); **French 2,000 Guineas**: Recitation (1981), Soviet Star (1987); **Irish Sweeps Derby**: Shirley Heights (1978); **Irish Oaks**: Fair Salinia (1978).

George
STEVENS
b.1833 d.1871

Such was the fame of George Stevens that a fire was lit on Cleeve Hill, Cheltenham, to celebrate the Gloucestershire-born rider's five Grand National triumphs, on Freetrader (1856), Emblem (1863), Emblematic (1864), and The Colonel (1869 and 1870).

Stevens first rode at Aintree in 1852 and never fell in 15 Grand Nationals. He was killed at the age of 38 when, riding along at the foot of Cleeve Hill, his hat blew off and caused his horse to shy. Stevens was thrown head-first against a stone, which fractured his skull.

A memorial stone stands by the side of the road at Southam to mark the spot where the fatal accident occurred. The inscription reads: 'In memory of George Stevens the rider of the winners of five Grand National steeplechases who, after riding for twenty years with no serious accident, was here killed by a fall from his hack only three months after riding The Colonel in the Grand National of 1871.'

Walter SWINBURN
b.1961

It has not been a smooth road to the top for Walter Swinburn since his first winner on Paddy's Luck at Kempton Park in 1978. Apprenticed first to Frenchie Nicholson, then to Reg Hollinshead, he took on a big challenge when he became stable jockey to Newmarket trainer Michael Stoute in 1981. A good, strong rider with great determination to win, Swinburn was suspended for more than 50 days in his first seven years in the job.

Suspensions cost Swinburn two Classic winners — his 1981 Epsom Derby hero Shergar, in the Irish Derby, and Shadeed in the 2,000 Guineas in 1985. Lester Piggott picked up both rides. But it was Piggott's rejection of Daniel Wildenstein's All Along that let Swinburn in for a 1983 Arc de Triomphe victory on the filly, followed by an amazing treble with her in North America's big autumn races. Swinburn was to have partnered his Irish Derby winner, Shareef Dancer, in that 'Arc', but was left without a ride when the colt worked badly in his preparation for the Paris race.

Swinburn brought off a 1986 Classic double with Shahrastani in the English and Irish Derbys. His ride at Epsom, where he beat Dancing Brave, was particularly memorable. But he had trouble picking between Stoute's four fillies in that year. When the stable ran more than one in a race he was invariably unlucky in his choice of ride. This cost him the Irish Oaks, when he was only third on Untold to stablemate Colorspin, ridden by Pat Eddery. He had no choice in the 1987 Epsom Oaks, which he won easily on Unite.

Other big winners for Swinburn include: **King George VI and Queen Elizabeth Stakes**: Shergar (1981); **Irish 1,000 Guineas**: Prince's Polly (1982), Sonic Lady (1986); **Irish Oaks**: Blue Wind (1981), Unite (1987).

A publicized incident in a London drinking club seemed to put Swinburn out of favour with Stoute in the late autumn of 1987, but he was back with the stable's 2,000 Guineas winner, Doyoun, in 1988.

Pat TAAFFE
b.1930

One of Ireland's most successful jump jockeys of all time, Pat Taaffe will always be best remembered as the rider of Arkle. But before he retired from the saddle in 1970, he won two Aintree Grand Nationals and six Irish Grand Nationals. He rode his first winner as a 17-year-old amateur when he picked up a spare ride on Ballincorona at Phoenix Park on the afternoon of the race. After four successes at a two-day Christmas meeting at Leopardstown, he turned professional in 1950.

Taaffe scored a Cheltenham Gold Cup hat-trick on the immortal Arkle in 1964, 1965, and 1966. Fort Leney gave him a fourth triumph in 1968. His six Irish Grand National wins came in a space of 13 years. The first was Royal Approach (1954), followed by Umm (1955), Zonda (1959), Fortria (1961), Arkle (1964), and Flyingbolt (1966).

The jockey rode Vincent O'Brien's third Aintree Grand National hero, Quare Times (1955), and it was injury to Fred Rimell's jockey, Terry Biddlecombe, that let him in for the mount on the 1970 winner, Gay Trip. Arkle carried him to triumphs in the King George VI Chase (1965), the Hennessy Cognac Gold Cup (1964 and 1965), and the Whitbread Gold Cup (1965). The Queen Mother Champion Chase was a great race for him. He scored on Fortria (1960 and 1961), Ben Stack (1964), Flyingbolt (1966), and Straight Fort (1970).

Taaffe's worst fall was on a horse called

Pat Taaffe, seen here on Flyingbolt, was a great horseman. Arkle was by far his most famous partner, but he won most of the big steeplechases in England and Ireland.

Jorge Velasquez played second fiddle in 1978's three Triple Crown races, but won both the 1981 Kentucky Derby and Preakness Stakes on Pleasant Colony.

Ireland in 1955, before helmets were compulsory. When he was recovering, after being unconscious for a week, he warned trainer Tom Dreaper that he might not be able to do justice to his good horses. Dreaper replied: 'If you don't ride them, I don't run them!' Taaffe was back in the saddle just over three months later. He retired soon after Gay Trip's Aintree success in 1970. He took up training and provided jockey Bobby Beasley with the ride on Captain Christy to score a unique double in the Sweeps Hurdle (1972) and Cheltenham Gold Cup (1974).

Ron
TURCOTTE
b.1941

As an out-of-work 18-year-old roofer, Ron Turcotte caught the racing bug after watching the Kentucky Derby on television in his rooming house. He graduated to riding and had his first winner, at Fort Erie, Canada, in 1962. Eventually, he went to New York and in his 18 seasons rode 3,032 winners, accumulating $28,606,490 in prize money.

Turcotte won the 1973 Triple Crown on Secretariat (Smokey Saunders was the only other Canadian to do it) and took the 1972 Kentucky Derby with Riva Ridge. In 1973, he was the first person from thoroughbred racing ever to be appointed a member of the Order of Canada. Tragically, the jockey was paralysed from the waist down when injured in a fall at Belmont Park on 13 July 1978.

Jacinto
VASQUEZ
b.1944

Panamanian jockey Jacinto Vasquez won the 1980 Kentucky Derby on the filly Genuine Risk, who went on to be second in the two other Triple Crown races, the Preakness Stakes and the Belmont Stakes. Genuine Risk was the first filly to win the Derby since Regret in 1915 and the first of her sex to run in all three events.

One of ten children, Vasquez was brought up among horses on a farm. He entered the racing scene at Remon racecourse, in Panama, where he worked without pay. Eventually, his chance came and he won his first race at the age of sixteen. He moved to the USA at that age and after starting in New York rode in Arizona, Nebraska, Colorado, and New Mexico.

Among the top 20 jockeys of all time for races won, and in the top ten for prize-money earnings, Vasquez had his 4,000th success on 28 October 1983 with Sunshine o' My Life. He is the only jockey to have beaten Secretariat twice — on Angle Light in the 1973 Wood Memorial, and Onion in the 1973 Whitney. He rode six consecutive winners at Atlantic City in 1967, but one of his best spells was 11 winners out of 15 races in Panama. In 1975, he was aboard Ruffian in her Filly Triple Crown triumph. Jacinto Vasquez regards this achievement as the highlight of his career. By contrast, the biggest disappointment of the jockey's career occurred when Ruffian broke down.

Jorge
VELASQUEZ
b.1946

Second to Affirmed on Alydar in all three races for the 1978 Triple Crown, the Panamanian jockey Jorge Velasquez was a hot walker before becoming leading apprentice in his native country, where he shattered all fellow-countryman Braulio Baeza's records. He went to the USA in 1965 and his link with the jockeys' agent, Vic Gilardi, became one of the longest and most successful ever. Velasquez was top rider, with 438 winners, in 1967 and money leader in 1969, with earnings of $2,542,315.

He won the 1981 Kentucky Derby and Preakness Stakes with Pleasant Colony, and in 1987 spent less than a year in France riding for Mahmoud Fustok, before returning to the USA. A year later, Velasquez became the fourth jockey, following in the footsteps of Bill Shoemaker, Laffit Pincay Jr, and Angel Cordero Jr, to exceed prize-money earnings of $100 million.

Liam WARD
b.1930

Born in County Limerick, Ireland, Liam Ward won six races, including the Irish Derby, on Triple Crown hero Nijinsky. The dedicated rider took nine other Irish Classics and the 1962 French St Leger.

Ward was one of the small band of jockeys to have been successful in all five Irish Classics. His first winner, at the age of 16, was Andorra, at Phoenix Park; his last (Cambrienne) came from his final ride, at Leopardstown, in October 1971. Having served his apprenticeship with Roderick More O'Ferrall and E. M. Quirke, Ward was very successful during the seasons 1953–5 with Paddy (P. J.) Prendergast at Rossmore Lodge.

However, it was during his long association with Mrs Anne Bullitt-Biddle's horses that Ward became Irish champion in 1959 and 1961. It was for her that he rode such stars as Sindon (Irish Derby), Zenobia (Irish 1,000 Guineas), Partholon, and Ionian. Ward also won three Irish Oaks (Amante, Aurabella, and Gaia) and three Irish St Legers (Do Well, White Gloves, and Reindeer). He had the satisfaction of providing Morny Wing and J. M. 'Mickey' Rogers with their first Classic triumphs, with, respectively, Do Well and D.C.M.

Under a gentleman's agreement, Ward rode for six years (1965–70) for Vincent O'Brien and four of his Classic triumphs came from that stable. He is now a successful breeder of thoroughbreds and a member of the Irish Turf Club.

Bill WILLIAMSON
b.1922 d.1979

Heavy-lidded eyes and an apparently 'laid-back' approach to life earned Australian Bill Williamson the nickname 'Weary Willie'. But in the saddle he was an action man of brilliance.

Born into racing — Bobby Lewis and F. H. 'Dan' Lewis were uncles — Williamson had his first ride in 1937 on Diablot, at the age of fifteen. His fourth ride, Lilirene, was a winner. He won six Victoria jockeys' titles between 1952 and 1958, the most notable of them in the 1953–4 season when his 67.5 winners created a record that stood until 1972, when it was overtaken by Roy Higgins. Williamson won the 1952 Melbourne Cup on Dalray, but regarded Rising Fast as the best horse he rode during his career in Australia.

In 1960, the jockey went to Ireland, where he rode winners of the Oaks and St Leger, before switching to Britain two years later. He continued to have much success for Irish trainers after the move, including more Classics, as well as the 1969 Ascot Gold Cup on Levmoss.

In England, Abermaid (1962) and Night Off (1965) gave Williamson 1,000 Guineas successes, but his greatest triumphs were in the Prix de l'Arc de Triomphe, which he won with Vaguely Noble (1968) and Levmoss (1969). Lester Piggott, who was second to him in both of the French races, later replaced Williamson in a blaze of controversy on 1972 Epsom Derby hero Roberto.

Williamson retired in 1973 and became racing manager to Ravi Tikkoo before going home to Australia in 1976. He was an assistant starter in Melbourne before he died in 1979.

Gerry WILSON
b.1904 d.1969

The outstanding British jumps jockey of the 1930s, Gerry Wilson rode the fabulous steeplechaser Golden Miller. The partnership completed the Cheltenham Gold Cup–Grand National double in 1934, and went on to take the Gold Cup again in 1935, when Wilson also took the Champion Hurdle with Lion Courage.

Wilson was champion jockey in the six consecutive seasons 1932–3 to 1937–8 and

Bill Williamson was an Australian who captivated Europe. His quiet lifestyle and brilliant riding earned him many admirers among fellow professionals.

Frank Wootton, British champion four times on the Flat, turned successfully to riding jumpers when his weight became a problem.

with the best in Britain had he remained there. He rode over 2,000 winners, the majority of these from the time he linked up with Colonel A. J. Blake's stable in 1931. He also rode in England, Spain, and India, where he went through the card once. He rode eight consecutive winners at a three-day Tramore meeting and on three occasions rode five winners.

Wing, who had six Irish Derby successes, retired in 1949 to take up training. He saddled only one Classic winner, Do Well, in the 1951 Irish St Leger. He died in 1965, several years after the death of his son Wally, who was killed in a riding accident in India.

George
WOOLF
b.1909 d.1946

They called George Woolf the 'Iceman' because of his nerves of steel. Some say he was the greatest money-rider of them all. Born on a ranch in southern Alberta, Canada, he was riding bareback before he could walk. Although he rode on recognized tracks for only 13 years before he was killed in a race at Santa Anita Park in 1946, he was the most sought-after stakes rider in the world.

Woolf's terms to take a ride were $1,000 in advance plus 10 per cent of the purse — and owners were happy to pay. He had only 263 rides in 1942, but still led North American jockeys in prize-money earnings. In 1944, when diabetes was making him weak, he had only 227 mounts, yet again was the continent's money leader. He won four top American races three times — the Belmont Futurity, Hollywood Gold Cup, Havre de Grace Handicap, and American Derby. The jockey's one regret was never to win the Kentucky Derby, in which he finished second twice.

Woolf was killed in a fall from Please Me in the fourth race at Santa Anita Park on 3 January 1946.

again in 1940–1. He retired to take up training and won the Champion Hurdle with Brains Trust (1945) before becoming the landlord of a public house near Newbury.

Morny
WING
b.1897 d.1965

The son of a Yorkshire horse-dealer, Morny Wing was named after his father's jockey idol, Mornington Cannon. Wing was not just a fine jockey — he was also a superb horseman who used the whip sparingly. At his best in sprints, he excelled at handling two-year-olds.

The Yorkshireman rode his first winner in 1911 when apprenticed to W. Walters Jr. In 1914, he was third to Steve Donoghue in the jockeys' list. In 1917 Bert Lines invited Wing to Ireland for two mounts, which both won. He fell in love with the country and stayed on. Along with Joe Canty, Willie Parkinson, Tommy Burns, and Martin Quirke, he revolutionized riding in Ireland to a large degree.

Wing won 22 Classics in his adopted country. He was champion jockey overall in 1928, 1937, 1938, and 1941–5 and never rode under National Hunt Rules. He was a masterly judge of pace and would have been on a par

Frank
WOOTTON
b.1893 d.1940

A man for all seasons, Australian Frank Wootton was Britain's champion jockey on the Flat and a leading rider over jumps. Son of the trainer Richard Wootton, he rode his first winner at Folkestone in 1906, soon after his arrival in England. He was then only 12, and it took him just three more years to establish himself as the top jockey on the Flat. He was champion in 1909, 1910, 1911 (187 winners), and 1912. His successes included the Oaks (Perola, 1909), the St Leger (Swynford, 1910), and seven winners at Royal Ascot in 1912.

On his return from military service in World War I, Wootton was too heavy to continue a brilliant career on the Flat. He turned to jumping, and in his best season (1921) gave Dick Rees (65 winners) a close fight for the title. Wootton retired to take up training at Epsom and returned home to Australia in 1933.

Harry WRAGG
b.1902 d.1985

When Harry Wragg, who was apprenticed to Bob Colling in 1919, finally retired at the age of 80, he had given more than 60 years of his life to racing. He rode 13 Classic winners in Britain and trained six more before handing over to his son, Geoffrey, in 1983.

Gordon Richards was tough opposition in his riding days, but Wragg did step in to take the 1941 championship, with 71 winners, when Richards was injured. His tactic of holding his horse back for a fast late run earned him the nickname the 'Head Waiter'.

Wragg's first Classic success was on Felstead in the 1928 Epsom Derby, a race he won again on Blenheim (1930) and Watling Street (1942). Garden Path (1944) provided his only 2,000 Guineas success, but he took the 1,000 Guineas three times, with Campanula (1934), Herringbone (1943), and Sun Stream (1945). He rode Epsom well and brought home Rockfel (1938), Commotion (1941), and Steady Aim (1946) to take the Oaks. His St Leger winners were Sandwich (1931) and Herringbone (1943). Sun Stream won the 1945 Oaks, run at Newmarket.

In 1946, Wragg ended his riding career with a treble at Manchester on his last day in the saddle. The following year he started training at Abington Place, Newmarket, with such distinguished owners as Lord Derby, the Aga Khan, Sir Percy Lorraine, Sir Hugo Cunliffe-Owen, Lord Stanley, and Maharajah Gaekwar of Baroda as his first patrons.

Wragg went to The Curragh for his first Classic winner, Fraise du Bois II (1951 Irish Derby) and in 1954 saddled Darius (2,000 Guineas) for his first Classic triumph in England. More home winners followed with Psidium (Derby, 1961), Intermezzo (St Leger, 1969), and 1,000 Guineas heroines, Abermaid (1962), Full Dress II (1969), and On The House (1982). The trainer's best year for winners in Ireland was 1956, when he scored a treble with Lucero (2,000 Guineas), Talgo (Derby), and Garden State (Oaks). Other Irish Classic successes were: **1,000 Guineas**: Lacquer, (1967), Favoletta (1971); Derby: Fidalgo (1959); **Oaks**: Discorea (1959), Ambergris (1961).

Harold 'Tiger' WRIGHT
b.1921

Ranked one of the best South African jockeys ever to don silks, 'Tiger' Wright could barely walk when his father, Tiny, taught him to ride on a Shetland pony. Wright was a master of timing and finesse and, unlike most of today's jockeys, used the whip sparingly. He preferred to ride horses out 'hands and heels' in a finish.

Wright rode for nearly 30 years, from 1935 until 1964, and booted home 2,454 winners from 12,540 mounts, a winning average of nearly one in five. He rode 100 or more winners in a season nine times and won the South African Jockeys' championship 11 times, a feat that was equalled by Michael Roberts. His best season was in 1951 when he rode a then record 175 winners. Although that figure pales into insignificance when compared with the current record of 269, it must be remembered that Wright rode in an era when fewer races were staged every year.

Wright's era was also the golden age of jockeyship in South Africa. In those days, apprentices lived in the homes of the trainers they were indentured to and, although life was hard for the young men, the system produced many great jockeys. Nowadays, apprentices live in the South African Jockeys' Academy during their indentures.

Wright is the only jockey in the long history of South Africa's premier race, the Rothmans July Handicap, to have ridden four winners — Silver Phantom (1942), Brookhill (1947), Milesia Pride (1949), and Preto's Crown (1955). He retired from race riding on medical advice after injuring his back in a fall at his home.

Harry Wragg was a brilliant judge of pace. His skill at holding a horse back for a late run earned him the title of 'The Head Waiter'. He used his brain and became a clever tactician.

The Betting Angle

Gambling is traditionally a pursuit for the needy and the greedy: either you don't have enough and want more or you have more already, but want more still.

Those two extremes of the human race do indeed bet on a roll of the dice, the turn of a card, or the speed of a horse, but for millions around the world, gambling is no more than an entertaining and pleasurable pastime. The punters are neither destitute nor rich, and they do not seek to earn a lifetime of comfort from their bets. Yet that does not mean that the concentration is not fierce, the research not intense, the cheers not loud.

Much gambling is a matter of chance, but not betting on a horserace. If you know enough, you will win, but that trite definition of the magic key to success can hide a lifetime's work. No one would say that top players of chess or bridge need to be gamblers. But the methods they employ to achieve their triumphs are not significantly different from those of the successful horse player. Like them, he studies all the variables, evaluates as many permutations of possibilities as he can, and makes a decision based on personal judgement.

It is easy to see where the money went at this race meeting in Tokyo. Losing tickets litter the ground as punters search their newspapers for guidance to the next winner.

Bet on a horse for a place in Britain and, if your choice finishes third in a field of eight or more runners, you will collect your money; achieve the same in North America and you could lose. 'Place' in the USA refers only to the first two horses home, while the term for finishing in the first three is 'show'.

Such technical differences may exist, but in general the language of the horserace gambler is international. You place a bet on a horse to win and, if it passes the post ahead of its field without infringing the rules, you experience the unique and delightful feeling of collecting money for very nearly nothing. Why very nearly nothing? Well, there is the risk, of course. A 10–1 winner returns a 1,000 per cent profit on your investment – far higher than bank interest, as well as far quicker and a great deal more exciting, but, if you are wrong, you lose all. Banks, by contrast, offer a steady return.

Pari-mutuel betting

Whether you bet with bookmakers, pari-mutuel, or any other mechanical system, the odds you are offered contain an element of profit for the operator. In pari-mutuel systems, a percentage (which varies from country to country and from bet to bet) is deducted. Bookmakers also offer odds which, if they can operate efficiently, will give them a profit whichever horse wins. It is not difficult to understand how a betting profit margin is achieved. Suppose backers place a total of £100,000 in pool betting on a race. The organizer deducts perhaps 20 per cent and, if there are 8,000 winners each holding identical stakes of £1, their total return would be £10 – £80,000 divided by 8,000.

Bookmakers provide a different service, offering prices which the individual can take if he finds the odds acceptable. Suppose, in a five-horse race, each horse is offered at 4–1

A punter, who has been shopping around the bookmakers for the best odds, strikes his bet.

and a bookmaker takes an equal amount for each horse, he will show no profit, merely sharing the losers' money among the winners. Here is a simple example:

Horse	Price	Stake
A	4–1	£100
B	4–1	£100
C	4–1	£100
D	4–1	£100
E	4–1	£100

The bookmaker holds total stakes of £500, but no matter which horse passes the post in front he has to pay out winnings of £400 and return stakes of £100. He has therefore worked for nothing.

Changing the prices

However, the effect of changing the prices is dramatic. Suppose our bookmaker offers 3–1 against all five runners. He still (in theory) takes £100 for each runner (£500), but now has to pay out only £400 (£300 winnings + £100 stake), leaving himself a profit of £100.

Here is a more complicated example: With total stakes of £950, if horse B wins, the

Horse	Price	Stake	Payout (winnings + stake)
A	3–1	£200	£800
B	2–1	£400	£1,200
C	4–1	£150	£750
D	5–1	£100	£600
E	10–1	£50	£550
F	10–1	£50	£550

bookmaker loses £250. However, if any other horse wins, he makes a profit, and if either horse E or F is successful, he makes a clear margin of £400. Some races are easier to win on than others. If a heavily-backed favourite wins, sometimes the bookmaker loses, whereas if a long-odds outsider beats his rivals, then the bookmaker may have a 'skinner' – a race in which not one of his clients is entitled to a return – and he retains all the stakes.

There is a simple way to calculate whether the overall odds offered in any race are fair, or licensed larceny. In a three-horse race, a bookmaker offers the following prices: Now the theoretical odds are 2–1 against

Horse	Price
A	Evens
B	6–4
C	4–1

each horse, but we can quickly work out the bookmaker's profit by imagining that he keeps all his bets for a race in one large bag. Then we calculate how much he is required to take for each horse to remove £100 out of the bag if successful.

Horse	Odds	Stake to Return £100 (including winnings)
A	Evens	£50
B	6–4	£40
C	3–1	£25

Whichever horse wins removes £100 from the bookmaker's take, but leaves him with a profit of £15 from the total of £115 staked, or 15 per cent, civilized by any standards, but the outcome is not always so reasonable.

The bookmaker's safeguards

Of course, making a successful book is by no means as simple as the above examples suggest. If a horse attracts a lot of money, the price on offer is reduced. This helps to deter any other backers, and to lessen further liability if they continue to support that runner. Conversely, the prices of rival horses are lengthened, in order to attract money for them, and thus balance the book. Clerks, wizards with figures, can tell a bookmaker at a glance how he stands about each horse.

Most British bookmakers accept that their business has changed in recent years. Until the 1960s it was possible to attract money for several, if not all, the horses in a race, with a view to making a profit if any won. But the last 30 years have seen an explosion in information. Since the 1960s punters in Britain have benefited from the compulsory declaration of runners on the previous day, so that fields could be studied in depth. Before, only lists of 'probables' were available and the strength of the race was not known until three-quarters of an hour before the event was due to be run.

Better specialist newspapers, offering the latest reports of home gallops, computerized race analyses, and expert forecasts of starting prices, have made the average punter far more aware of the relative ability of horses in any race. Consequently, punters tend to favour the form horses at the shortest prices, and bookmakers find their liabilities completely unbalanced. They still survive, though, and while there may be some races on which they lose, they continue to make high profits when a completely unfancied outsider romps home.

Only in a few countries do backers have the luxury of choosing between bookmakers and pari-mutuel. Britain offers the widest range of opportunities, and for each race two sets of prices are returned: the starting price, which is paid out by bookmakers, or the Tote (Horserace Totalisator Board), Britain's pari-mutuel.

Early bookmaking

Bets were struck between individual owners before the advent of the first recognized bookmaker, a Mr Ogden, who began laying against more than one horse in a race, towards the end of the 18th century. By the

1820s the bookmaking fraternity had become an established part of the racing scene. On the course they operated from horseback, forming a ring (still a common term for the betting arena) until grandstands became commonplace, when an area in front was reserved for their activities.

Richard Tattersall, the first bloodstock auctioneer, conducted his business from premises at Hyde Park Corner, in London's West End. Bookmakers (although illegal) used to congregate there until the police banished them farther afield, usually to private gaming and drinking clubs. Tattersalls, then a set of rooms in London frequented by bookmakers and backers, was the scene of many a momentous gamble, and in 1856 the Committee of Tattersalls was made officially responsible by the Jockey Club for settling all disputes between wagering parties. Those who could not meet their liabilities were 'warned off' Newmarket Heath and all other official racecourses.

But such strictures were not common. Bookmakers were generous in offering their wealthy clients credit, and the nobility who betted with them had a cavalier attitude towards payment. As long as a proportion of the outstanding losses was met, bookmakers were prepared to continue to accept bets. Indeed, one layer said that a client who settled promptly and in full was far from ideal, suggesting that if a backer owed him money he could offer less attractive prices, whereas the man with no debt would want the 'top of the market'.

Punters at Aintree place their Grand National bets with the Tote. If they are lucky, they will be paid out at better odds than the official starting price.

Credit betting

By the early part of this century credit betting offices were gradually becoming a feature off-course, but cash betting away from the course was illegal. Naturally, this did not stop gambling, and street-corner bookmakers, although regularly prosecuted by the police, flourished. Before the 1930s many rich owners wanted to bet but, not caring to suffer the hurly-burly of the ring, they employed agents to place bets for them. The shrewd agent, once he had placed the money, would make no secret of the confidence behind the horse and consequently the price would shrink further, thus enabling him to report to the owner that the bets had been struck at good odds, but not the best available. If the horse won, the agent pocketed the difference.

A betting tax was introduced by Winston Churchill in 1926, but collection proved notoriously difficult and it was abandoned three years later. In 1928 the Tote came into being, initially at 13 courses. Although it has been a part of the British racing scene for 60 years, only very recently has its popularity increased significantly. In 1987 British punters bet a total of £3.4 billion, the Tote accounting for £146 million.

How the Tote works

The Tote offers simple win bets, and the place pool pays out for the first two horses in races of five, six, and seven runners, and three places for eight runners or more. However, in handicap races of 16 or more horses, the first four past the post are paid. Dual-forecast bets (nominating first and second in either order) are available on races of three or more runners. The Tote jackpot requires the backer to nominate the winner of the first six races. Near-misses are given minor consolation dividends if the pool is not won, and the balance is carried over to the next meeting. The better has to select horses placed in all of the first six races at a meeting to land the placepot.

The most significant change in British betting this century came with the Betting and Gaming Act of 1960, which legalized betting shops. On 1 May 1961, high-street betting shops opened and put out of business overnight all but a handful of illegal street-corner bookmakers. The number of betting shops peaked at 15,000 in the 1970s, but rationalization over more than a decade had reduced this figure by 1988 to 9,500, nearly half of which are controlled by bookmaking's 'Big Four' – Ladbrokes, William Hill, Corals, and Mecca.

As well as offering simple win and place bets, the major firms compete to provide all manner of exotic bets, exhorting the punters to play more often. Such wagers do, of course, offer higher rewards, but are far more difficult and inevitably result in a greater profit for the bookmaker. Each-way betting, in which the stake is divided between a win and a place bet, is permitted on races of

Women have taken their place in all departments of British racing, but it is rare to find a female tic-tac signalling the latest odds.

five or more runners, although fields of five, six, or seven runners only reward backers of the first two horses, at a quarter of the win odds. Generally, three places at one-fifth of the odds are paid on eight or more runners, although for handicap races (in which the horses are allocated different weights to equalize their chances) four places at one quarter the odds are paid in races of 16 or more runners. The minor details will vary between bookmakers, but all can supply a copy of the regulations.

Betting options

On England's racecourses betting with bookmakers is offered in three different areas: the 'rails', Tattersalls, and the Silver Ring. Rails bookmakers (who are sited in Tattersalls but who stand on the rails delineating the areas, and face the exclusive Members' Enclosure) do not put prices on a board, but offer them to clients who approach them, and generally lay the biggest bets. Tattersalls bookmakers chalk their prices on a board, and turn over much larger sums than their colleagues in the Silver Ring, who bet in relatively small amounts to racegoers in the cheapest enclosure.

Weight of money for a horse shortens its price and, as we have seen, as some prices

shorten, others are lengthened to make them more attractive to backers. These movements are relayed from one bookmaker to another through the tic-tac, a man employed by one or more bookmaking firms. Wearing white gloves, which can easily be seen as he stands on a box to raise himself above the crowd, the tic-tac uses a system of hand and arm signals to convey, across the ring, details of betting transactions . There are two dozen competent operators, working up and down the country and, despite the speed with which the system works, there are remarkably few disagreements.

Nowadays rails bookmakers take cash bets, although until the 1970s all business was in credit, with a weekly or fortnightly settlement. Most wagers are struck at the prevalent odds offered, but some are recorded (at the better's request) at starting price – the odds generally available at the time the field leaves the starting stalls. In Britain these odds are decided by employees of *The Sporting Life*, one of two daily racing newspapers, and by the Press Association news agency. One representative of each organization is usually present, and they confer after each race, often arriving at what they regard as a fair compromise. If half the bookmakers were offering 2–1 against a horse and the remainder 7–4, the reporters would split the difference and return a starting price of 15–8.

Satellite information

Odds, and changes to prices, are relayed to betting shops either via an audio commentary service or, since 1986, by Satellite Information Services, which also provide live pictures from two race meetings a day. Since the arrival of satellite broadcasting, betting-shop turnover on horseracing has increased by about 20 per cent, and turnover on greyhounds by more.

Betting tax was reintroduced in 1966 and is collected by Her Majesty's Customs and Excise department. Off-course tax stands at 8 per cent deducted from winnings, but most bookmakers have to pay a 1 per cent levy to the racing industry, and round up the deduction to 10 per cent. Punters can opt to pay 10 per cent with their stake and receive their winnings in full. If they are winners, it saves a little: if they are losers, it adds more to the bill. A tax of 4 per cent used to be taken from on-course bets, but this requirement was rescinded in 1987.

Illegal gambling exists but, while its detection is difficult, it is unlikely that unregistered trade accounts for more than 10 per cent of the industry. With the abolition of on-course tax, a handful of illegal racecourse bookmakers have all but disappeared, and the majority of illegal betting is conducted either at large factories with a work-force of thousands or in bars, clubs, and pubs.

While total turnover of betting in Britain has risen steadily, it has probably declined in real terms. Certainly the carefree gamblers who enlivened the scene during the 19th century and up to the 1950s are no longer present. Betting has become a pastime, with relatively small sums staked, although one of the biggest coups landed in recent years was when Rotherfield Greys won the 1988 William Hill Stewards' Cup at Goodwood, considered to be the most competitive sprint handicap of the season. The gelding's owner Tony Gleeson and his family backed the six-year-old to win over £½ million, their confidence being rewarded when the grey came late to land the gamble by two lengths.

Ireland and the Continent

The Irish enjoy the same opportunities to bet as can be found in Britain – on and off-course bookmakers and Tote facilities. At one time, government taxes on betting were so high that a healthy trade in illegal wagering blossomed, but since the mid-1980s a more benign attitude on the part of the authorities has restored turnover to its former level.

Elsewhere in Europe punters have few alternatives to betting on pari-mutuel systems. The best racing, and highest betting turnover, is in France, where the Tiercé is a national institution. All over the country tickets are sold, not only in betting shops, but in corner *tabacs*, the aim of the punters being to select the first three home in the big race of the day.

Ensuring high dividends

Occasionally, as with the Prix de l'Arc de Triomphe, a major championship event will be selected as being competitive enough to make the task of Tiercé punters sufficiently difficult, but the authorities usually rely on a handicap with a big field to ensure that dividends are kept high. The Tiercé operates during selected days of the week, but the major interest is on Sunday, when the race is shown on national television.

In 1957, in a handicap chase at Auteuil, the Tiercé pool amounted to FF324,598, but, with no one forecasting the correct order, the prize was shared among those who had found the first three past the post, whatever the order they predicted. At Enghien in 1984 1,400,916 Tiercé players got it right, but received only a fraction more than their stake in return. It is possible to bet off-course on the major designated meeting of the day, and occasionally regional racing festivals will warrant off-course facilities, but such occasions are infrequent.

There are no legal bookmakers in France. They exist in small numbers in Germany and Italy, offering ante-post odds on major races, multiple bets not available on the pari-mutuel system, and facilities to bet on racing in other European countries (notably France). However, the turnover is meagre and most betters use the pari-mutuel system.

Eastern bloc disincentives

Behind the Iron Curtain there is elementary pool betting, but the authorities' take-out percentage is high enough to discourage all but those desperate enough to try for a quick profit in a determinedly non-capitalist society.

The US betting scene

In the earliest days of American racing, all wagering was done on a man-to-man basis, the owner asserting that his colt was the fastest and backing his words with his money. But just before the Civil War, auction pools were developed. A betting interest on each horse in a race was auctioned to the highest bidder, with the most likely winner commanding the highest price. The auctioneer took his commission and the remainder of the pool went to the one fortunate enough to have bid on the winning horse.

Peace brought the horses back on to the tracks, and the post-war gambling fervour that followed demonstrated the need for more than the limited gambling pools. This need was met by professional on-track bookmakers, who offered odds for each horse and an organized form of wagering that helped fuel racing's expansion. But this situation did not last long. An anti-gambling sentiment

'Fifty thousand francs for 20 cents!' That is the nineteenth century seller's cry as he offers French lottery tickets.

swept the nation and, by 1908, there were just 25 racetracks left in the USA. The sport did not recover until betting returned under state regulations and developed into its present form.

The twin centres of American racing are the New York and Southern California tracks. In the East, Belmont Park, Aqueduct, and Saratoga offer impressive facilities, equalled in the West by Santa Anita, Hollywood Park, and Del Mar. On these major tracks the finest riders – Angel Cordero Jnr., Bill Shoemaker, Laffit Pincay Jnr., Jorge Velasquez – compete, along with the best horses in the nation. Good purses range from $50,000 to $100,000, while a purse of $1 million is no longer uncommon and highest prize on offer is $3 million.

In other big cities, the racing, while not the best, is still good. Chicago boasts Arlington Park, while San Francisco has Bay Meadows and Golden Gate Fields. In Philadelphia they run at the safely named Philadelphia Park. And then there is the USA's 'leaky-roof' circuit – those small, seedy, out-of-the-way tracks where the prizes are small, the crowds thin, and both horses and riders have limited talent.

A wealth of choice

In all, there are 83 thoroughbred racetracks in the United States and as many as 40 might operate on the busiest days. Unlike their European counterparts, American tracks run five or six days a week and remain open for months on end. Some offer year-round sport – dirt-racing surfaces, which are resistant to constant use, providing this luxury. Only a small proportion of American races is run on the turf and the majority of racetracks do not have turf courses. But, no matter what the surface, the location, or the standard of the action, the aim is universal – to find more winners, fewer losers, and to go home with that unique feeling of satisfaction, knowing that your wealth has increased while you have been enjoying yourself.

By 1940, New York had banned the last of the country's legalized bookmakers and all gambling was from that time conducted on the pari-mutuel system, first tried in Kentucky in 1870. Under this system, patrons are not betting against the house, but against each other. From every dollar wagered, a portion, usually 83 per cent, is returned to those selecting a winning wager. The track retains the remaining portion of the pool for profits, expenses, and prize money.

During the early years, the bets offered were straightforward – win, place, and show. A win bet is self-explanatory; a successful place bet is paid to those selecting a horse who runs either first or second; and a show bet is a winner if the horse finishes first, second, or third. For the truly daring, there was only one alternative, the Daily Double. The idea is to pick the winner of both the first and second races on the day's racing card.

The betting boom

In the late 1960s, betting opportunities blossomed. This was the age of the 'exotic' wagers: exactas, perfectas, quinellas, big exactas, double exactas, trifectas, triples, twin triples, pick fours, pick sixes, pick sevens, pick nines, superfectas, superbets, win threes, and so on. The aim was to give the punter a chance to make a fortune for a modest investment. The chances of winning were, of course, reduced.

The most common of the exotic bets are the exacta (also called the perfecta), the trifecta (also called triples), and the Pick Six (also called virtually unwinnable).

The exacta is the simplest. You must select the horses that finish first and second in the correct order. To win a quinella, you must select, in either order, the horses that finish first and second. The trifecta requires the selection, in their correct order, of the horses that finish first, second, and third. Exacta and trifecta pay-offs were lucrative, but soon they, too, became outmoded. The American horseplayers' dreams were not satisfied by winning trifectas paying $61,000. They wanted big money.

In the early 1980s wagering took another step forward. 'Multiple Exotic' wagers were born, designed to yield huge pay-offs, rewarding only a handful of punters who were either abundantly skilful or abundantly lucky. To win the Pick Six, the most common of

such bets, you must pick six consecutive winners. If no one successfully completes the challenge, a large proportion (usually 75 per cent) of the pool is 'carried over' and added to the next day's Pick Six wagering until someone achieves the target. In New York, pools have grown in the late 1980s to $2.4 million and single pay-offs have flirted with the $1-million mark.

The need for expansion

In the early part of the century in the USA legal betting could only be conducted within the narrow environment of the racetrack and public demand was not satisfied with just one betting medium. Lotteries, casinos, greyhounds, harness racing, and illegal gambling on other sports have, over the years, made a major dent in racing's once dominant command of the American dollar. There were problems, and simple solutions, to bring the sport to the public.

In 1971 New York, the city with the country's most influential racing market, offered the first legal off-track betting. Within a few years neighbourhood betting shops sprouted from nothing as thousands of self-interested fans unwilling to make the traffic-ridden trek to Aqueduct or Belmont walked to their local Off-Track Betting (OTB) shops and pumped further millions of dollars into the day's turnover.

By 1988 there were 238 OTB branches

There are no legal bookmakers in France, so the pari-mutuel machine at Longchamp does all the business.

throughout New York State, 106 of them in the city itself. In recent years, off-track betting has been implemented in Connecticut, Illinois, Louisiana, and the State of Washington. Once the monster had begun to grow, there was no stopping development. The next wave of expansion brought 'simulcasting', a system that allows racetracks to accept betting on races from other courses. Major events, such as the Kentucky Derby, are simulcast to as many as 80 tracks throughout North America, boosting the day's turnover to previously unbelievable levels.

The success of simulcasting

Even an ordinary day at the races has become a simulcasting bonanza. In the summer of 1988 daily wagering on the nine races offered at Saratoga typically reached $10 million, yet only a quarter of that amount was bet on track. Glamorous Saratoga, where the best East-coast racing is staged each August, is too remote for most punters, and 200 miles away at Aqueduct, at the harness track at Yonkers Raceway, they can bet on the action. Of the $10 million bet daily at Saratoga, at least half comes from OTB, a remarkable testimony to the Americans' willingness to tolerate just about anything to bet.

New York OTB is run by the federal government. Under a nightmare reign of bureaucracy, the employees excel in rudeness, the shops are filthy and uncomfortable, and the returns are lower than they are on-track. New York OTB has no competition for the off-track betting dollar and no in-

centive to improve its service, so it does not.

Among the drawbacks to New York OTB is the five per cent surcharge. All winning wagers made at OTB automatically pay five per cent less than they do if purchased on-track. The only exceptions are a handful of plush OTB teletheatres, which are clubs that show the races live on wide-screen televisions or movie screens. There is, however, an admission charge of $5.

A move towards legality

In New York, the once-flourishing business of illegal bookmaking on racing was hit by OTB. Elsewhere, lack of interest did the same damage. Bookies began to concentrate on the estimated $19-billion market on sports betting and they offered racing bets mainly as a rare convenience for their customers.

Legal bookmaking is conducted only in Nevada, a state in which it is hard to find anything which transgresses the law. Amid the pervasive glitter of Las Vegas, Reno, and Lake Tahoe are a number of 'racebooks', some dazzling facilities themselves, which offer betting on as many as five or six tracks at the same time. For the true racing junkie it is a smorgasbord that cannot be matched. Lined across the wall of the 'book' are a show of movie screens which display the action from their assigned track. It is possible to bet on – and watch – three or four live races being run simultaneously.

Horserace betting has prospered, to become big business. Over $13 billion was legally wagered on- and off-track in 1987, with another $365 million being poured into the Nevada racebooks. And, when such money is at stake, there are inevitably those who want to ensure some of it finds its way into their own pockets. One Tony Ciulla, a self-proclaimed race-fixer, claimed he altered the outcome of hundreds of races in the 1970s. He pointed the finger at several of the most prominent jockeys, selling his story – once he had gained immunity – to a national magazine. But little illegal activity was proved and only a few minor characters were punished.

Another to fall foul of the authorities was Dr Mark Girard, a New York veterinarian who imported two horses from South America in the early 1970s. One could gallop, the other could not. Dr Girard switched them and collected over $70,000 in bets. The two horses, Libon and Cinzano, are still commonplace in the vocabulary of every horseplayer.

Success at Saratoga

One famous gambler, Art Rooney, the former owner of the National Football League's Pittsburgh Steelers, built his fortune with the help of a miraculous run of luck at Saratoga, when he all but swept the card one day in the late 1930s, taking the bookies for $105,000. Legend has it that he named his son Jim, current President of Yonkers

Racing at Sha Tin attracts punters to a Hong Kong betting shop.

Raceway, after a bookmaker he had consistently beaten in the year of his son's birth.

The dreamers of success include the army of sophisticated professional gamblers that has developed in recent years. With names like Big Richie, Al the Wise Guy, and The Source, they apply the most sophisticated methods, particularly comprehensive sets of figures that estimate a horse's ability on the basis of times. Such men have been known to bet $40–50,000 in one afternoon. But everyone who bets is a dreamer: the $2 'show' better as much as the $10,000 pick-six player. For them all the goal is the same: to win easy money at this most difficult game.

Betting in the Far East

The countries of the Far East have an appetite for gambling unsurpassed anywhere in the world. But since the concept of a pre-determined fate is central to various Eastern religions, those who choose to bet are not necessarily using their skill and judgement to pick a winner, but merely putting down their money, in the knowledge that fate will reward them as and when it chooses.

Nowhere is this gambling fever better demonstrated than in the tiny colony of Hong Kong, which will be handed back to the Chinese authorities by the British government in 1997. Here, apart from a weekly lottery, the only legal gambling in a country hungry for action is horseracing, virtually a national sport for its five million-plus inhabitants.

Because of the wealth of the Royal Hong Kong Jockey Club, brought about by a level of betting turnover almost beyond the comprehension of the more conservative European and American populations, the sport is superbly organized, and popular both with the local population and expatriates. There are only two racecourses, Sha Tin (built on land reclaimed from the sea and opened in 1978) and Happy Valley. When the latter, situated in the middle of high-rise buildings on Hong Kong Island, is full a red flag is hoisted so that racegoers who have not yet arrived can turn round and go home.

A nation of gamblers

In 1987 the Royal Hong Kong Jockey Club reported an annual turnover of HK$28,267 billion, or almost US$4 billion. This is equivalent to an annual average betting sum of HK$5,000 per capita for the whole population, including every bed-ridden grandmother and infant. It has been calculated that, if horse racing were to cease in Hong Kong, income tax would have to be increased by two per cent to rectify the shortfall in revenue. Nor are the punters short of help: on racedays more than 50 Chinese newspapers offer their readers advice.

The majority of turnover is from off-course betting shops throughout the colony, but 18 per cent of the total is on-course money, while only slightly less comes from betting on the telephone, using deposit accounts. Originally, 100,000 betting accounts were envisaged, but such was the demand that, when applications for new customers were invited, numbers had to be limited until a telephone system of higher capacity could be introduced. Nowadays almost 300,000 inhabitants have telebet accounts. Each year brings new records for betting turnover and, such is the voracity for betting, that the boom seems set to continue.

Over half the total amount of money bet is on the 'quinella', or dual forecast, so it is nearly as important to the punter for a horse to finish second as it is to win. In the late 1970s, in order to try to curb the betting explosion, the authorities decided not to progress to exotic bets resulting in high dividends, but that philosophy changed. Now, one of the largest computer installations in Asia offers punters opportunities to find six winners or six quinellas at a meeting, with jackpot payouts and consolation dividends for those who just miss out.

Telephone betting

While betting by telephone is encouraged, it is only permitted to those who have already deposited money with the official club. Credit is not allowed. This restriction gives illegal bookmakers an edge, and much of the large amount of money spent on preserving the integrity of racing goes towards seeking out and prosecuting illegal bookmakers. They operate on-course, using a constantly changing cast of helpers, and away from the action offer a sophisticated, computer-recorded

Hong Kong suffered a major scandal, but this does not deter punters at Happy Valley racecourse.

Japanese place their wagers in a computerized Tokyo betting shop. The machine does not tip winners, but it does say 'thank you' to customers.

duals from the racing society were held, among them Y. L. Yang, a textile magnate, who was found guilty of corruption and given a suspended sentence. Jockeys who were tight-lipped suddenly became loquacious, turning Queen's Evidence, and only one rider, the Australian David Brosman, served a prison sentence. Later, when released, he made remarks in public to a juror during a second trial, which then had to be abandoned.

The Japanese betting scene

Although Japan has a higher turnover from betting than Hong Kong – not surprising in view of its massive population – gambling on horses is not as widespread. Horseracing has to compete with other sports, including cycling, motorcycling, and powerboat racing, for the punter's yen. Even so, in 1987 the Japanese Racing Association, which runs thoroughbred horseracing and betting, reported a turnover of 1,973 billion yen, or US$14 billion. The JRA operates 21 off-course betting centres, located mainly around Tokyo and Osaka, and 200,000 telephone betting accounts, which together are responsible for 80 per cent of turnover. As in Hong Kong, betting is fully computerized, even down to the purchase of tickets, which can be bought from a polite machine which thanks you for your bet when the transaction is completed.

Again, the quinella is the most popular wager, although there is a crucial difference. In Hong Kong and most other countries, all runners can be chosen in any combination, but the Japanese authorities, in the hope that preventing jackpot payouts will keep gambling fever to an acceptable level, limit the numbers to be combined for first and second place to eight per race. If the field contains more than eight runners, as it usually does, some are grouped together. In a nine-runner race, for example, numbers 1 and 2 would be paired, and the remainder available to be chosen for quinella bets. In a field of sixteen, eight pairs of runners are available.

The quinella

The groupings are quite clearly shown in the racecards, and each group is recognizable by the colour of the jockeys' caps. Thus, those with a quinella of groups 2 and 6 might be betting on runners 3,4, and 5, coupled with 18 and 19, and if one from each group occupies the first two places home, the bet is successful. However, if two from one group fight out the finish, the bet is lost. Of course, with only eight groupings, the combinations of the quinella bet are limited. This reduces the complexity of the computer programs required to run the system, a bonus in view of the size of the pool.

By far the biggest betting shop in the world is the Japanese Racing Association centre at Korakuen, in Tokyo. A yellow-and-orange building with thirteen floors to

service which, in many cases, changes location weekly. Somehow the punters know where to go and law and order tries to follow. But illegal bookmakers continue to make high profits and are experts at avoiding detection, proving a constant headache to the authorities.

Betting fraud

Of course, with such large sums at stake, there are many who seek to affect the result of a race beforehand to give them an edge. Professional race-stewards, aided by half-a-dozen colour video cameras strategically placed around the course, manage to identify the jockeys who do not ride to win, but that does not stop sophisticated, wide-ranging attempts to corrupt.

In 1985 some jockeys were found guilty of betting and were punished. Most authorities forbid jockeys to bet in any way at all. A few allow them to bet on their own mounts but, invariably, if a jockey wishes to put money on his horse, there are plenty of willing helpers.

A major scandal rocked Hong Kong in 1986. Dawn raids by investigating officers of the International Council Against Corruption (ICAC) swooped and arrested trainers, jockeys, and owners. At one time 20 indivi-

accommodate the tide of eager punters, it is a modern temple to betting. On a busy day the noise as the field approaches the line would crack all but the toughest eardrums. Year after year the turnover increases, estimates having to be revised upwards, and no one will predict when the bonanza is likely to end.

Singapore, too, has sophisticated pari-mutuel betting, but recent tax increases have made the dividends less attractive, and have boosted the trade of illegal bookmakers.

Australian betting

One man who made his mark in the betting ring both in England and Australia during the late-19th and early-20th centuries was Robert Sievier, a flamboyant man whose chief claim to fame was to own the peerless Sceptre, one of the greatest fillies in racing history.

The Winning Post, Sievier's newspaper, cost him dear through a series of libel actions, but there is no doubt that Sievier, who made his money from horses and cards, was a highly successful gambler in his day, and shook up the Australians when he arrived in 1882 at the age of 22. Until then local bookmakers walked around the course, taking down bets in their notebooks, and settling later in the day. They discouraged backers from betting on single horses, and most would accept doubles only on 'this race and the next' at odds disadvantageous to the punter.

Sievier cut a swathe through all this. At the major tracks he stood at a regular pitch with a clerk, issued numbered tickets bearing the initials of the horse backed, called out the odds for each horse and, to his clients' delight, paid out immediately after the race. He was quite happy to accept single bets on all races and soon 'The Englishman', as he was known, had such impact that on his first day at Adelaide he took three quarters of the business at the racecourse.

Soon he needed three clerks to help him, but when he ventured to Randwick, Sydney, for the Spring Carnival of 1882, he met with fierce opposition from his rivals. They dvanced on Sievier and his team, but a band of punters formed a protective ring around them, and it was not long before Sievier was in business.

Nowadays, Australia has the best betting system in the world, with pari-mutuel betting contributing to the wealth of racing and on-course bookmakers adding colour to the occasion. In England, most of the profit from betting, particularly off-course, remains with the large bookmakers, with the result that the sport is not as healthy as it should be.

The unpredictability of betting

Even the most sophisticated computers cannot tell a punter what his return is certain to be; last-minute money changes the odds, and there are both surprises and disappointments, but a bookmaker offers firm odds, and when a bet is struck both sides know the extent of the liability. Bookmakers do not necessarily offer the same odds for each horse, allowing backers to shop around for the best price, and there is nothing more satisfying than taking a price about a horse and watching the odds tumble, knowing that your investment is guaranteed.

In England bookmakers do not have to offer a price about each horse. When there is a rumour that a particular runner is likely to attract considerable support, they leave the price blank, perhaps eventually putting up an artificially short price, in order to discourage would-be backers. They are under no obligation to accept any bet, and can refuse punters or offer them a smaller wager than requested.

None of this applies in Australia. The major racing centres have a very strong betting market and bookmakers are not only obliged to put up a price for every horse in a race but, according to their position in the betting ring, must guarantee to lay a horse to lose a specified amount. On the rails the figure is A$2,000, in the stand A$400, and in the minor rings A$200. However, these figures have remained static for a long time and, with turnover increasing every year, their revision is overdue.

Illegal betting

Until the 1960s most money in Australia was wagered with illegal bookmakers off the course. As in England before the betting shops, they operated in pubs, clubs, and on street corners, often controlled by organized

The Melbourne Cup is one of the world's most treasured racing trophies. The race brings big business to the betting industry.

Colourful crowds pack Flemington racecourse on Melbourne Cup day. On-course bookmakers and pari-mutuel machines help to give Australia the best betting system in the world.

crime syndicates, and no sooner had one man been put out of business by the authorities, than another took his place. But Sir Chester Manifold changed all that: having looked at systems round the world, his drive and enthusiasm led to the creation of Australia's Totalisator Agency Board (TAB).

Originally stark betting shops, with no form displayed, announcements of scratchings and changes of jockey delayed until five minutes before the 'off', dividends not declared until after the last race, and winnings not paid out until the following working day, the new facilities hardly appealed at first to discerning punters. Illegal bookmakers, offering their clients the opportunity to bet, listen to races, and be paid immediately, did not suffer unduly.

Racing had to compete with other leisure activities and, after an initial surge of interest, turnover began to fall. A new attitude on the part of the authorities revived the TAB: betting deadlines were cut to the 'off' time, price movements were shown on television monitors, after-race payouts began, and races were shown live on direct telecasts. Formerly dark, uninviting premises, TAB parlours started to provide tables, chairs, racing newspapers, and food and drink. The turnover rose dramatically as a result.

Inevitably, on-course bookmakers have suffered as a result and their numbers are not as great now as they were twenty years ago. Then, almost anyone with a pitch was guaranteed a profit, but this is no longer so, because of competition from the TAB. Each state has its own TAB, which produces different dividends, but before each race the monies already bet around the state are added to the pool. Bookmakers' runners note the odds, signal them quickly to the pitch, and the odds are amended accordingly to approximate with TAB dividends.

Reduced profits

The 'easy' money – that is, bets from those who are at the races simply for a day out and know little of the intricacies of form – is now mostly taken by the TAB. Punters, including professionals with videos and computers, are much better informed than they used to be, with the result that bookmakers' profit margins have been trimmed.

Australia has had more than its fair share of legendary bookmakers and gamblers, but the recent duel between media magnate Kerry Packer and Sydney 'rails' bookmaker Bruce McHugh beat all previous records. In the autumn of 1988 they clashed regularly for huge sums, McHugh just getting the better of his rival most of the time.

The struggle reached its climax in the Sydney Cup, Packer betting A$11 million to win A$8 million that his horse would triumph. However, Myocard was narrowly beaten by Major Drive, owned in partnership by Melbourne businessman Lloyd Williams and – Kerry Packer! After the race McHugh was so wound up that he had an accident in his car, and not long afterwards, retired from the fray. Taking Packer on was good business all the time he was ahead but, if his rival had enjoyed a long winning run, it would have put McHugh into the bankruptcy court.

Changing horses

One of the biggest scandals of recent years concerned the seemingly moderate sprinter Fine Cotton. The defrauders had originally planned to run a substitute for Fine Cotton in a race at Eagle Farm, Brisbane, in August 1984, but the horse was injured while being sent up from Sydney. With all the plans laid, the conspirators pressed ahead and secured a useful sprinter, Bold Personality, as a replacement.

With the horse opening as high as 33–1, the correct odds for Fine Cotton, money poured in and, as the field left the stalls, he started at 9–4. Those who had set up the fraud had their hearts in their mouths as Fine Cotton's stand-in scraped home by a short half-head. But they never collected their money, for angry punters demanded that the stewards inquire into the running of the horse before it had weighed in. The authorities found that Bold Personality, who had had white paint daubed on his legs to make him resemble Fine Cotton, had been substituted, and they disqualified the winner. Several leading racing personalities in Sydney were warned off, including the legendary bookmaker Bill Waterhouse and his son, Robbie.

Such attempts to organize races are rare and Australian betting flourishes. The country's biggest race, the Melbourne Cup, is the jewel in the betting crown, and over A\$38 million was wagered on the race, the highest TAB turnover being recorded in Sydney.

Betting on the major meetings is popular at the minor country racetracks, which may themselves stage only modest events with small fields. On Saturdays up to forty such meetings will be held, and punters from miles around will congregate, betting most of their money on the big races at Sydney or Melbourne, accommodated by local bookmakers and listening to an audio commentary broadcast direct to the course.

A nationwide network

However, the popularity of the country meetings is under threat. 'Pubtabs' have been introduced in New South Wales and Victoria, in which punters can drink and bet at the same time. Live racing is broadcast via television and satellite and, while these latest extensions of the TAB's arm are confined to the more populous areas, they have proved so successful that expansion to all parts of Australia seems inevitable.

If the standard of racing in New Zealand is not far short of that in Australia, the betting does not bear comparison. Bookmakers are banned and pool betting is tame compared to that of Australia.

The African betting scene

In most African countries betting is conducted very much at the whim of the political leader. A coup can bring an end to racing, but it will take more than a revolution to upset the betting habits of South Africans. They not only race the best horses on the continent, but the per capita turnover from betting in South Africa is comparable with that of any western country.

Punters are offered betting almost identical to that in Australia, with on-course bookmakers and a thriving Tote, on- and off-course. Bookmakers do bet away from the course, but only in private Tattersalls Clubs in the major centres – Johannesburg, Durban, and Capetown. During the week they take bets on the major races run at the weekend, but the real action is at the racecourse.

There are 'rails' bookmakers, a Gold Ring (equivalent to Tattersalls in England) and a Silver Ring. Some bookmakers offer bets at other meetings, and the racecard for, say, Durban will also carry the runners for the principal races at Capetown and Johannesburg if they are staging fixtures. The Tote, a wholly-owned subsidiary of racing clubs, offers a full range of exotic bets.

Betting in India

In India there are plenty of illegal bookmakers operating away from the track, but on racecourses bookmakers are an established part of the scene, co-existing happily with the official pool-betting facilities, which are wholly-owned subsidiaries of the race clubs.

Bombay is the major centre for racing and betting, and high turnovers are regularly recorded at Calcutta, Delhi, Madras, Bangalore, and Hyderabad. Bookmakers must be licensed both by the government and the local racing clubs before they can set up in business. Betting is banned away from racecourses, but many punters have illegal telephone accounts. As in Australia and South Africa, bookmakers can bet at other meetings, and even if there is, for example, a blank racing day in Madras, the bookmakers and punters will go to the track and wage war over events at Bombay.

Racing ended in Sri Lanka during the 1960s, but illegal bookmakers do a healthy trade on English racing. Punters bet on English races in the morning before going to the races in the afternoon.

Racing in South America

In South America there are no legal bookmakers and in some countries political uncertainty tends to colour the betting scene. Argentina and Venezuela have the most competitive racing, and offer Tote facilities with a limited range of wagers. However, the revenue from Totes is valuable to the racecourses and races are often delayed until Tote betting has ended.

Blackboards at San Isidro, one of Argentina's two main tracks, give a mass of information – but backers are offered only a limited selection of wagers.

The Great Horses

'Great' is a much devalued word. Nowadays almost any sporting achievement of note is classified as a 'great performance' and consequently the epithet has become almost commonplace. Fortunately, with racehorses we can be a little more exact in our judgement. The great performances are there for all to see in the record books — the races won, the quality of the defeated opposition, the time of the race, the weight the horse shouldered and, to a certain extent, the merit of the particular horse relative to the achievements of its forebears.

Certain horses stand out in any discussion of great racehorses. Phar Lap, Carbine, Man O'War, Secretariat, Sea Bird, Ribot, Arkle, and Golden Miller would be automatic runners in the 'Greatness Stakes', while others have achieved their place in racing's Hall of Fame through sheer guts and the indomitable will to win. Sea Pigeon, Brown Jack, Red Rum, and Citation are such horses. Add to these the eighteenth- and nineteenth-century stars — Flying Childers, Eclipse, Lexington, and Kincsem, all of whose training schedules and racing feats modern trainers would look upon with horror, and it becomes clear that there is no foolproof recipe for greatness in a horse.

Breeding plays its part, as do jockeyship, the skills of the trainer, and the care of the stable-lad, in producing champions of the turf. But there is, in addition to the human element, an indefinable ingredient provided by the horse. Call it aura, presence, or the will to win, it comes to the same thing — great racehorses know that they are great.

Unbeaten in 18 races, and sire of three of the first five Epsom Derby winners, the great Eclipse was so named because he was born during a total eclipse of the sun.

USA
AFFIRMED
1975
Chestnut colt by Exclusive Native out of Won't Tell You

Despite winning the American Triple Crown in 1978, Affirmed will always be remembered for the great battles he had with his arch-rival Alydar during the 1977–8 season.

In looks, Alydar was clearly superior, Affirmed being rather tall and unfurnished, but on the racecourse there was never very much in it. Affirmed's first defeat was by Alydar and they were to meet on another four occasions as two-year-olds, the score being 3–2 to Affirmed.

Both horses were aimed at the 1978 Triple Crown, and Affirmed had a thorough preparation for the Classics by winning the Grade One Hollywood Derby, as well as the Santa Anita Derby and the San Felipe Handicap. In the Classics, Affirmed swept the board, beating Alydar in all three races. The distance in the Kentucky Derby was one and a half lengths, in the Preakness Stakes it was a neck, and in the Belmont Stakes it was a head. Alydar got his revenge in the Travers Stakes, but only on the disqualification of Affirmed, who was adjudged to have hampered his rival.

As a four-year-old, Affirmed won seven of his nine starts, including the Jockey Club Gold Cup, in which he beat Spectacular Bid, and the Hollywood Gold Cup. He became the first horse to win $2 million and his career record reads 22 wins, including 14 Grade One races, from 29 starts. At stud Affirmed has not been as successful as Alydar, although he sired the Dante Stakes winner Claude Monet.

IRELAND
ALLEGED
1974
Bay colt by Hoist The Flag out of Princess Pout

Originally bought by Robert Sangster to race on dirt in California, Alleged was rerouted to Vincent O'Brien's yard at Ballydoyle. He was backward as a two-year-old, only running and winning once, in November 1976. He first showed signs that he was something out of the ordinary when he won the 1977 Royal Whip at The Curragh as the 33–1 outsider in a field of three, beating his stablemate, the hot favourite Valinsky. He added victory over Voltigeur and was aimed at the St Leger, for which he started favourite. It was to be his only defeat in ten starts — he did not stay the trip and was beaten by the Queen's Dunfermline.

Alleged got his revenge in the Prix de l'Arc de Triomphe three weeks later, over his ideal distance of 1½ miles (2.4 km), beating Balmerino by one and a half lengths. A second 'Arc' was the ultimate target for Sangster's colt the following season, but he had an interrupted preparation and it was only as a result of O'Brien's legendary training skills that he started to come right again in the autumn. Piggott rode a masterful race on Alleged, who won by two lengths, the first horse since the mighty Ribot to win Europe's greatest race in consecutive years.

Alleged was retired to stud in Kentucky with a syndication value of $13 million.

FRANCE
ALLEZ FRANCE
1970
Bay filly by Sea-Bird II out of Priceless Gem

Allez France, like Dahlia, was one of the best fillies to have raced in France this century. Out of 21 starts, she won 13 — beating her great rival Dahlia on all six occasions they met — and the climax of her career was her victory in the 1974 Prix de l'Arc de Triomphe. She was owned by art dealer Daniel Wildenstein and trained at Chantilly, first by Albert Klimscha and, after his retirement, by Angel Penna.

As a three-year-old, Allez France won the Poule d'Essai des Pouliches (French 1,000 Guineas), the French Oaks (beating Dahlia), and the Prix Vermeille, a traditional 'prep' race for the 'Arc'. In the big race, however, she was no match for Rheingold (ridden by Lester Piggott), who had finished second in the 1972 Derby behind Roberto. The following season she was unbeaten and crowned it by winning the 'Arc' by a head from Comtesse de Loir. Kept in training as a five-year-old, Allez France could never recapture her former brilliance and in her last race, a championship event at Santa Anita, California, she finished last. She was retired to the paddocks in the USA, but proved a dismal failure as a brood-mare.

ENGLAND
ALYCIDON
1945
Chestnut colt by Donatello II out of Aurora

A truly great stayer, Alycidon was the first horse since Isonomy in 1879 to win the stayers' 'triple crown' of the Ascot Gold Cup and the Goodwood and Doncaster Cups, a feat he achieved in 1949. In those days the Cup races were still held in esteem by owners and breeders and were contested by top-class middle-distance horses as well as true out-and-out stayers.

Alycidon was extremely difficult to train. He was lazy and had a mind of his own when it came to work on the gallops — so much so that his trainer Walter Earl had to devise all sorts of schemes to keep his attention on the job. He raced in blinkers and usually with one or two pacemakers, as he did in the 1949 Gold Cup. In addition to his Cup treble, Alycidon also won the Jockey Club Stakes and the Prince of Wales Stakes in 1948 and the 1949 Ormonde Stakes.

Alycidon was a success at stud, being Champion sire in 1955, when his daughter Meld won three Classics. He also sired Twilight Alley, who showed exactly the same quirks as his father and who, like him, went on to win the Ascot Gold Cup, in 1963.

USSR
ANILIN

1961
Bay colt by Element out of
Analogichnaya

With few exceptions, the Eastern Bloc is not renowned for the quality of its racehorses, but in the mid-1960s the USSR produced in Anilin a worthy champion. He had four seasons of racing, in which he notched up the impressive record of 22 wins from 28 starts. He was unbeatable in his native country and won races in Hungary and in both East and West Germany, including the Group 1 Preis von Europa at Cologne, where he beat top-class European opposition.

In 1964, after winning the Soviet Derby, he travelled to the USA to contest the Washington DC International at Laurel. He put up a good performance to finish third to American champion Kelso, being beaten by about 13 lengths. Behind him were Belle Sicambre (1964 French Oaks winner), Biscayne (1964 Irish St Leger winner), and Italian Classic winner Veronese.

The following year Anilin became the first challenger from the USSR for Europe's most prestigious all-aged middle-distance prize, the Prix de l'Arc de Triomphe. It was one of the classiest international fields ever assembled for the race and, although he was unable to cope with the mighty Sea Bird, Anilin ran a most creditable race to finish fifth, beaten by about 12 lengths. Behind him that day were such top-class animals as the American horse Tom Rolfe and Irish Derby winner Meadow Court.

Anilin had another crack at the 'Arc' in 1967, but could manage only eleventh place behind Topyo. He was retired to stud.

Allez France won 13 races for Paris art dealer Daniel Wildenstein, but the climax of her career was her success in the 1974 Prix de l'Arc de Triomphe.

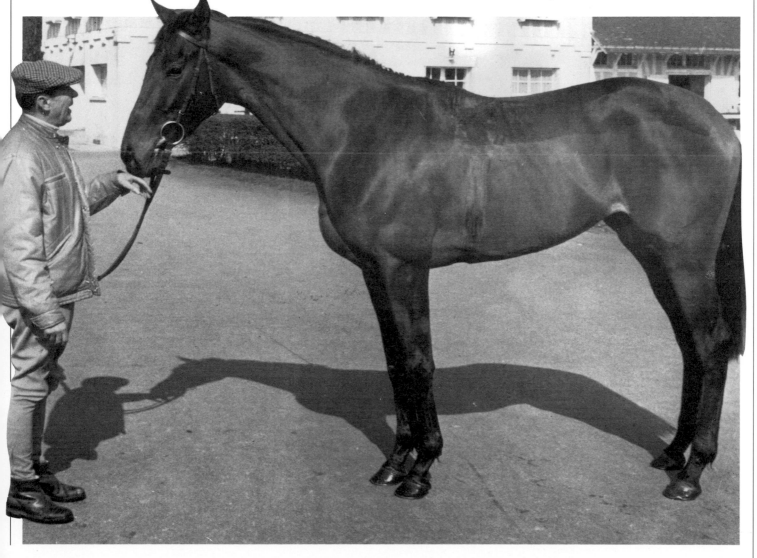

IRELAND
ARKLE
1957
Bay gelding by Archive out of Bright Cherry

Bred in County Dublin, Arkle was bought by Anne, Duchess of Westminster, for 1,150 guineas at Goff's sales in 1960 and put into training with Tom Dreaper.

Arkle was not an impressive-looking animal and was not, at first, highly regarded, but he was to show in his first few races that ability to accelerate instantly which is the hallmark of all great racehorses. Add to that a fast, economical, and clean method of jumping and you have the recipe for a champion. He started off hurdling, but as he put on condition it was obvious that chasing was to be his forte, and he was soon sent to England to take on the best of the novice chasers in the Honeybourne Novices' Chase at Cheltenham in November 1962. He won by 20 lengths.

An impressive win in the Broadway Chase at the Cheltenham Festival meeting the following year established Arkle's credentials, and he ended the 1962–3 season with seven wins from seven starts. His great English rival, Mill House, had meanwhile won the Gold Cup that year and rivalry between them was to thrill jumping fans for the next two seasons. They first met in the 1963 Hennessy Gold Cup. Mill House had to concede 5 lb (2.5 kg) to Arkle, who slipped on landing over the final ditch. Mill House won by eight lengths, with Arkle just beaten in third place.

Mill House went on to win that season's King George VI Chase at Kempton and went to Cheltenham a hot favourite for the 1964 Gold Cup. But he had no answer to Arkle's finishing burst and was beaten by five lengths. The issue was settled — Arkle could beat the best that England could offer and from then on he was almost unbeatable. He added two more Gold Cups, beating Mill House by 20 lengths in 1965, a King George VI Chase, another 'Hennessy', and an Irish Grand National.

Arkle's owner refused to let him run in the Aintree Grand National for fear of injury, but there can be no doubt that, had he run, he would have gone close to emulating Golden Miller's achievement of winning the Gold Cup and the National.

The gelding won the Whitbread Gold Cup at Sandown in 1965 by five lengths, giving 2 stone 7 lb (16 kg), or more, to his rivals. Arkle was not only beating top-class chasers at level weights, but also giving lumps of weight away to handicappers. The situation was such that the handicap rules were changed to give his challengers some sort of a chance, the Irish setting two handicaps for races in which Arkle was entered — one to be used if he ran, the other if he was absent.

Arkle ran his last race in England on 27 December 1966, in the King George VI Chase, when he injured a pedal bone in his off-fore and was beaten by a length by Dormant. He never recovered from the injury and was retired to the Duchess's farm in County Kildare. He was put down in May 1970. He had won over £75,000 — a colossal sum for a chaser in those days and his fame had spread far beyond the world of racing.

Proud and arrogant, Arkle (trained by Pat Taaffe) was loved by racegoers in both England and Ireland. He had style to match his unrivalled ability, and his enforced retirement after injury was a bitter blow to the sport.

AUSTRALIA/ENGLAND
BALMERINO
1972
Bay colt by Trictrac out of Dulcie

Probably the best horse to come out of New Zealand, Balmerino proved he was top-class not only in Australia and New Zealand, but also in the USA and Europe.

He burst on the scene in the 1975–6 season, winning 14 out of his 18 races, including the New Zealand Derby and the 2,000 Guineas, the Wellington Derby, and, in Australia, the Rawson Stakes over nine furlongs (1.8 km) and the Brisbane Cup (2 miles/3.2 km). He was the first horse to head the three-year-old Free Handicap in both countries. After four more wins the following season, Balmerino was sent to race in California where, despite taking time to become acclimatized, he managed to pick up one race out of the four he contested.

In August 1977 Balmerino was sent to the more sedate atmosphere of John Dunlop's stables at Arundel, in Sussex, to be prepared for a European campaign that was to culminate in a tilt at the Prix de l'Arc de Triomphe, the most prestigious race in the European calendar.

Balmerino's 'prep' race was the Valdoe Stakes at Goodwood, which he won easily. In Paris he ran the race of his life, coming late on the scene to finish second to the brilliant Irish colt Alleged. He was beaten by one and a half lengths despite not having the best of luck in running. This was to be his best performance.

Balmerino raced until the autumn of 1978, winning the Group 1 Gran Premio del Jockey Club in Milan, only to be relegated to second place after a stewards' inquiry. He also finished second in the Eclipse Stakes and the Coronation Cup, and fourth in the Washington DC International. Balmerino returned to New Zealand to stand at the Middlepark Stud.

USA
BOLD RULER

1954
Brown colt by Nasrullah out of Miss Disco

Many would consider Bold Ruler to be the greatest sire to stand in the USA. A son of the fiery Nasrullah, Bold Ruler was bred by Ogden Phipps and competed in the highest company in a generation that included such stars as Round Table, Gallant Man, and Iron Liege.

Bold Ruler was placed second in the Free Handicap as a two-year-old, having won seven of his ten races. The following season he raced 16 times, winning 11 races, including the Preakness Stakes from Kentucky Derby winner Iron Liege, and set new track records in both the Flamingo Stakes at Hialeah and the Vosburgh Handicap. He was named Horse of the Year, beating for the title his arch-rival Gallant Man, the brilliant winner of the Belmont Stakes by eight lengths.

As a four-year-old he won the Toboggan, Carter, Stymie, Suburban, and Monmouth Handicaps, but injured an ankle in his last race, the Brooklyn Handicap, and was retired to the Claiborne Stud at Paris, Kentucky.

Bold Ruler lacked stamina as a racehorse and most of his success at stud was in siring exceptionally fast juveniles. He led the American juvenile sires' list in 1963, 1964, 1966, 1967, and 1968, and for seven consecutive years, from 1963 to 1969, was the leading sire in America. He recaptured that title in 1973, when his son Secretariat won the Triple Crown. Indeed, between 1963 and 1973 his male line supplied seven of the ten winners of the Kentucky Derby. He was put down in July 1971 because of cancer.

ENGLAND
BRIGADIER GERARD

1968
Bay colt by Queen's Hussar out of La Paiva

One of the great milers of all time in British racing, Brigadier Gerard was unfashionably bred by his owner John Hislop but boasted a career record of 17 wins from 18 starts, his only defeat was to Roberto in the 1972 Benson and Hedges Gold Cup at York.

The field for the 1971 2,000 Guineas was one of the best in post-war years and included Mill Reef and My Swallow, who dominated the betting. But over a mile (1.6 km) they were no match for the colt, who won by three lengths. Hislop believed his colt would not stay the Derby trip and Brigadier Gerard's season revolved around the top mile (1.6 km) races, the colt winning the St James's Palace Stakes, the Sussex Stakes, the Queen Elizabeth II Stakes, and the Champion Stakes. The following season he stepped up in distance to add the Eclipse and the 'King George' to his tally. He also won the Champion Stakes for the second time as well as a second Queen Elizabeth II Stakes and the Prince of Wales's Stakes.

Brigadier Gerard and his jockey Joe Mercer won their first 15 races together before Panamanian jockey Braulio Baeza came from the United States to beat them with brave front-running tactics on Roberto.

He retired to stud, and although his breeding record does not match that of his great rival Mill Reef, he did sire some useful performers, including the St Leger winner Light Cavalry, the Champion Stakes winner Vayrann, and the Champagne Stakes winner R. B. Chesne.

ENGLAND
BROWN JACK
1924
Brown gelding by Jackdaw out of Querquidella

Probably the most famous gelding in the history of the English Turf — certainly the most popular — Brown Jack, and his regular rider Steve Donoghue, monopolized long-distance Cup races in the early 1930s.

Unlike many geldings who start off on the Flat and then revert to hurdling, Brown Jack did it the other way round. He was bought for 750 guineas by the Hon Aubrey Hastings for his patron Sir Harold Wernher with the long-term plan in mind of winning the Champion Hurdle. This Brown Jack did in 1928 and watching the race was champion Flat jockey Steve Donoghue, who persuaded Hastings to race the gelding on the Flat. The rest is history: Brown Jack won the Ascot Stakes in 1928, the Goodwood and Doncaster Cups in 1930, and the Ebor Handicap and Chester Cup in 1931.

The gelding raced at Royal Ascot in seven consecutive seasons, winning the Queen Alexandra Stakes six times in succession, from 1929 to 1934. The last such success was followed by scenes of celebration rarely, if ever, seen at the Royal meeting. Brown Jack was much loved by the general public, who flocked to see him run. The gelding raced 65 times, between 1927 and 1934, winning 25 times.

Brown Jack was such a popular horse that he was put on show at London's Olympia in 1935. He won seven years in a row at Royal Ascot, a feat that has never been equalled.

USA
BUCKPASSER
1963
Bay colt by Tom Fool out of Busanda

Bred and owned by Ogden Phipps, Buckpasser proved himself one of the very best American champions since World War II, and he did it the hard way — without contesting any of the American Classics, because of injury.

He kicked off his racing career by winning nine of his 11 starts as a two-year-old, earning his connections $568,000. An elegant, perfectly formed colt, Buckpasser never did more than was necessary to win. He was only unplaced once in 31 starts and, as a three-year-old, won 13 consecutive races, nine of them by less than a length.

In his second season, Buckpasser was virtually unbeatable. He won 13 of his 14 races and set a world record for a mile (1.6 km) in the Arlington Classic, clocking 1 minute 32 ⅗ seconds. He was unanimously voted Horse of the Year. He missed the Classics because of an arthritic ankle, which proved troublesome throughout his career, and as a four-year-old he picked up another three wins from six starts.

He retired to stud at Claiborne, the winner of 25 of his 31 races and was syndicated for a then record $4,800,000. Among his offspring were the 1980 1,000 Guineas winner Quick As Lightning. He died in the covering yard at Claiborne from a heart attack on 6 March 1978.

AUSTRALIA
CARBINE
1885
Bay colt by Musket out of Mersey

Carbine was the first great Australian racehorse. He was bred, as most Australian champions were at that time, in New Zealand.

The lure of greater prize money in Australia proved irresistible to the unbeaten colt's owner and Carbine left the South Island in 1888. But his three-year-old career did not get off to an auspicious start and, after losing the VRC Derby, he was sold for 3,000 guineas. However, from then on he showed himself to be near-unbeatable. At the four-day Easter meeting at Randwick, Sydney, he won four races out of five over distances ranging from 1 mile (1.6 km) to 2¼ miles (3.6 km), and the following year went one better by winning all five.

Carbine's reputation was by now legendary, but the best was yet to come, in the 1890 Melbourne Cup. A record field of 39 horses lined up for a prize of over £10,000. Carbine seemed to have an impossible task

with his huge weight of 10 stone 5 lb (66 kg), but at the line he was two-and-a-half lengths clear of the second, Highborn, to whom he was conceding almost 4 stone (25.5 kg). His time of 3 minutes 28¼ seconds set a new record. At the end of his five-year-old season he had notched up ten wins out of 11 races to give him a career total of 43 races, 33 wins, six seconds, and three thirds.

'Old Jack', as Carbine was sometimes known, started his stud career in Australia, siring Wallace, who won the AJC St Leger and the Sydney Cup, but in 1895 he was bought by the Duke of Portland for 31,000 guineas, then a record price for an Australian horse. He stood, at a fee of 200 guineas, alongside the Duke's great stallion St Simon at Welbeck Stud and sired the 1906 Derby winner Spearmint. He was also the grandsire of two more Derby winners, Spion Kop and Felstead. Carbine died at the age of 27 and his remains were shipped back to Australia.

Like most great horses, Carbine had considerable character. The Duke of Portland, in his autobiography *Memories of Racing and Hunting*, mentions that the horse could not bear to get his ears wet; so much so that his trainer Higginbotham had a leather protector made resembling a small umbrella, which was attached to the bridle to keep his ears dry. It was not until Phar Lap burst on to the scene 40 years later that Australians had a hero to compare with Carbine.

USA
CITATION

1945
Bay colt by Bull Lea out of Hydroplane II

Until the arrival of Secretariat in 1973, no horse had won the American Triple Crown since Citation in 1948. However, his standing as a true champion of the American Turf has been tarnished by the persistence of his owners in racing him up to the age of six in an effort to break two records — Stymie's record-winning prize money total of $918,000 and the $1 million mark.

Citation won 19 of his 20 races in his first two seasons. These successes included taking the Triple Crown by capturing the Kentucky Derby by three and a half lengths, the Preakness Stakes by five and a half lengths, and the Belmont by eight, all of which were won easily. After winning the Jersey Stakes by 11 lengths in record time, Citation was sent to California to beat Stymie's earnings record, but was foiled by an injury.

On his return he had the misfortune to come up against Noor, who beat him repeatedly. Citation finished second in seven of his eight races, but he eventually passed the magic million mark at the age of six. He won 32 of his 45 starts.

Carbine's record in Australia was unrivalled until the arrival of Phar Lap 40 years later.

IRELAND
COTTAGE RAKE

1939
Bay or brown gelding by Cottage out of Hartingo

Cottage Rake's three successive wins in the Cheltenham Gold Cup between 1948 and 1950 laid the foundations for one of the greatest training careers ever — that of Dr Vincent O'Brien.

O'Brien started training in 1941 and had landed a few notable touches for his first owner, Frank Vickerman. It was Vickerman who was to buy Cottage Rake, a useful stayer on the Flat, in November 1946 and the horse, despite some initial doubts as to his soundness, was to prove a bargain at £1,000.

Cottage Rake soon showed himself to be a natural recruit to the jumping game. He was quick and economical at his fences and possessed a blistering turn of foot. O'Brien was to use this ability to good advantage in training the gelding to win his races from the last fence to the winning post. Cottage Rake lined up for the 1948 Gold Cup a relative novice in a field that was brimful with top-class, experienced chasers. Ridden with cool precision by Aubrey Brabazon, he used his finishing speed to good effect to beat Happy Home by a length and a half.

Cottage Rake won the King George VI Chase at Kempton on his way to a second crack at the Gold Cup, for which he started an odds-on chance. In a similar race to the previous year's, the 'Rake' had to again rely on his finishing speed to see off Cool Customer, the distance being two lengths.

The third Gold Cup was even easier, despite the presence in the field of Finnure,

an up-and-coming young chaser who had beaten Cottage Rake in that season's King George VI Stakes. The two horses managed to frighten off most of the opposition and only six lined up at Cheltenham. Brabazon rode a clever tactical race, kicking on at the top of the hill and soon opening up a considerable lead. The others never pegged him back and the 'Rake' had ten lengths to spare at the line.

CHILE/USA
COUGAR II

1966
Bay colt by Tale Of Two Cities out of Cindy Lou II

The best horse ever bred in Chile, Cougar II's early career in his native country gave no indication of the heights he was to scale in his adopted country, the USA. He finished third in the Chile Derby and was then bought by Mrs Mary Jones for $135,000 in 1970, to be trained on the West Coast by Charlie Whittingham. He picked up a couple of small races that year, but came into his own the following season, proving himself to be an extremely tough performer on grass by winning six races from 12 starts, including the Oak Tree Invitational, the Californian Stakes, and the San Juan Capistrano (1¾ miles/2.8 km) at Santa Anita.

In 1972 Cougar II was voted Champion Grass Horse by winning the Century Handicap, the Californian Stakes, the Carlton Burke Handicap, and the Oak Tree Stakes.

Cougar II went to the Spendthrift Farm Stud with a record of 20 wins from 50 starts, including nine Grade 1 Stakes races.

*Dancing Brave's incredible win in the 1986 Prix de l'Arc de Triomphe (**right**) and his defeat in the Epsom Derby will be talking points for years to come.*

FRANCE
DAHLIA

1970
Chestnut filly by Vaguely Noble out of Charming Alibi

Dahlia's racing career lasted five seasons, during which she raced 48 times, winning 15 races, including Group 1 races in five different countries. She was inconsistently brilliant, never really coming to herself in the early part of the season, but then suddenly putting up breathtaking performances, not only in her native France, but also in England, Ireland, Canada, and America.

She never beat her great rival Allez France, who was foaled in the same year, but she won the Irish Oaks in 1973 and a week later put up a scintillating performance under Australian jockey Bill Pyers to win Ascot's King George VI and Queen Elizabeth Stakes. In this race she came from last to first, to win by six lengths from Rheingold.

Dahlia travelled to Washington that November to win the Washington DC International from Big Spruce. After a slow start as a four-year-old, she soon got into top gear to gain her second King George VI and Queen Elizabeth Stakes, as well as the Benson and Hedges Gold Cup at York, a race she was to win again the following season. An autumn campaign in America followed, and Dahlia, although flopping in the Washington DC International, did manage to win the Man O'War Stakes and the Canadian International Championship.

She retired to the paddocks in 1976, and unlike Allez France, was a success as a brood-mare, foaling Group winners.

ENGLAND
DANCING BRAVE

1983
Bay colt by Lyphard out of Navajo Princess

Owned by Prince Khalid Bin Abdullah and trained by Guy Harwood, Dancing Brave set the 1986 season alight with a series of brilliant displays in the Craven Stakes, the 2,000 Guineas, the Eclipse, the King George VI and Queen Elizabeth Stakes, and the 'Arc', although he will probably be best remembered as the horse who lost the Derby.

Dancing Brave won twice in his first season and, following a successful reappearance in the Craven Stakes, lined up for the 2,000 Guineas a warm favourite. He won by three lengths from Green Desert and was then aimed at the Derby. There were worries that he would not get the trip, but his stable jockey Greville Starkey was confident he would win and so were the public.

Dropped out towards the rear at the beginning of the race, Dancing Brave was still only third from last coming down Tattenham Hill and, when switched to make his challenge, he became momentarily unbalanced. He got going again and came with a storming run in the final two furlongs (0.4 km), catching Shahrastani hand over fist, but in the end he was beaten by half a length.

Starkey's riding came in for a torrent of criticism and although he kept the ride in the 'Brave's' following race, the Eclipse Stakes at Sandown, his place on the colt was taken by Pat Eddery in both the 'King George' and the 'Arc'. The latter was Dancing Brave's finest moment. He came with an astonishing late burst to win by a length and a half in record time from one of the finest 'Arc' fields ever assembled. Shahrastani finished fourth. It was then decided to let Dancing Brave take on the best American horses in the Breeders' Cup Turf at Santa Anita, but he could manage only fourth to Manila.

Dancing Brave retired to the Dalham Hall Stud at Newmarket.

IRELAND
DAWN RUN

1978
Bay mare by Deep Run out of Twilight Slave

Dawn Run will go down in history as the first horse ever to win both Cheltenham's Champion Hurdle and Gold Cup. The latter she won when barely out of the novice stage.

Owned by the indomitable Mrs Charmian Hill (who rode Dawn Run in races in Ireland at the age of 62), the mare started off running

Dawn Run and her jockey Jonjo O'Neill are given an overwhelming reception after their 1986 Cheltenham Gold Cup triumph. The mare was following up her Champion Hurdle success of two years earlier.

in 'bumpers' — Irish National Hunt flat races — graduating to handicaps and eventually winning the 1984 Champion Hurdle. She ended that campaign by beating the best the French could offer in the Grande Course de Haies at Auteuil.

Steeplechasing was next on the agenda and Dawn Run won her first race over fences at Navan in November 1984. She bounced back in December 1985 with a win at Punchestown, when ridden by trainer Paddy Mullins's son Tony. All sights were now set on attempting the unique double and, following a disastrous expedition to Cheltenham in January 1986, when Mullins was unseated, the owner insisted on an experienced jockey for chasing's greatest crown. Jonjo O'Neill was chosen for the task.

In the Gold Cup, the mare cut out the early running, but jumped the last fence in third place and looked held. However, she fought back on the run-in to win by a length from Wayward Lad in a record time. There were scenes of bedlam in the stands and the unsaddling enclosure, caused by the vast Irish contingent, who had backed her as though defeat were out of the question. History had been made.

Desert Orchid, Britain's most popular steeplechaser of the 1980s, on his way to victory in the 1988 Whitbread Gold Cup.

Dawn Run returned to England for the Liverpool meeting only to fall at the first fence, and then won a match with top Irish chaser Buck House at Punchestown before her fateful mission to France for a repeat win in the French Champion Hurdle. Ridden by French jockey Michel Chirol, she misjudged a hurdle in the back straight, fell, and died almost instantly.

Some critics have devalued the mare's Gold Cup win, pointing to the mandatory 5 lb (2.5 kg) sex allowance for fillies and mares introduced in the 1983–4 season. But there is no doubting that she was brilliant on her day. She won the Gold Cup after only four races over fences, a feat only two other horses have achieved.

at their own game and then defeat the best of the three-mile (4.8 km) chasers.

Desert Orchid has a strong preference for bowling along in front, but he has a marked dislike of left-handed tracks.

When he started out on his 1988–9 campaign, 'Dessie' had won more than £200,000, with 14 victories over fences and seven over hurdles. Of these, the 1986 King George VI Chase and the 1988 Whitbread Gold Cup were outstanding.

ENGLAND
DESERT ORCHID
1979
Grey gelding by Grey Mirage out of Flower Child

There is not a steeplechaser in Britain who can moisten an eye and warm a heart more readily than Desert Orchid. His arrogance, boldness and beauty in action have made him a winter idol.

In full flow, 'Dessie' is a stirring sight. With ears pricked in front and a tail streaming out behind, he shows obvious enjoyment of the job in hand. His jumping seems to be more like flying.

Unlike most horses, he can tackle races of varying distances with devastating effect. He can beat so-called two-mile (3.2 km) specialists

---

ENGLAND
DIOMED
1777
Chestnut colt by Florizel out of a Spectator mare

Diomed was the winner of the first Derby, in 1780. He was owned by Sir Charles Bunbury and after an impressive win at Newmarket, he started favourite for the Epsom race, which he won from Boudrow, the property of Dennis O'Kelly, the owner of Eclipse.

Diomed was unbeaten as a three-year-old, but deteriorated thereafter and was retired to stud, standing at a fee of ten guineas. He was not a great success and was eventually exported to the USA in 1798, at the age of 21. The change of scenery gave him a new lease of life and he excelled at stud.

squarely on top of it. Straddling the fence and unable to move, he caused the rest of the field either to refuse it or to take evasive action, with the result that only nine horses jumped Valentine's.

After the disappearance of Lowenstein, Easter Hero was bought by the American millionaire Jock Whitney and put into training with Jack Anthony. A 20-length win in the 1929 Gold Cup was followed by another tilt at the National. This time Easter Hero, carrying top weight of 12 stone 7 lb (79.5 kg), jumped superbly, led until the penultimate fence, but was then run out of it by Cregalach, who was in receipt of 17 lb (7.5 kg), and beaten by six lengths. It was one of the greatest losing performances ever seen at Aintree, a feat made more creditable by the discovery that Easter Hero had spread a plate at Valentine's the second time around.

Another 20-length win in the Gold Cup followed in 1930, but the gelding missed the National because of a tendon injury.

ENGLAND
ECLIPSE
1764
Chestnut colt by Marske out of Spiletta

The second great racehorse, after Flying Childers, Eclipse was foaled on 1 April 1764 during a total eclipse of the sun — hence the name. He was bred by the Duke of Cumberland, on whose death the colt was bought for 75 guineas by William Wildman, a Smithfield meat salesman.

Eclipse did not make his racecourse debut until May 1769, when he contested two heats of a race at Epsom. After the colt had won the first heat, the well-known Irish gambler Dennis O'Kelly predicted the outcome of the second: 'Eclipse first, the rest nowhere'. The colt won by a distance.

O'Kelly had bought a half share in the horse for 650 guineas and later owned him outright. Eclipse was never beaten in 18 recorded races and at stud he sired three of the first five Derby winners — Young Eclipse, Saltram, and Serjeant.

ENGLAND
EASTER HERO
1920
Chestnut gelding by My Prince out of Easter Week

Bred in Ireland, Easter Hero was brilliantly fast and a natural and extravagant jumper who, between 1926 and 1931, had no peer on the park courses. With the exception of Prince Regent and Crisp, he was probably the best horse never to have won the Grand National, although he picked up two Gold Cups on the way.

Originally owned by an Irish textile magnate, Frank Barbour, Easter Hero was sold on the eve of his first Gold Cup in 1928 for £7,000, with a contingency of £3,000 should the horse win the National. His new owner was a Belgian financier, Captain Alfred Lowenstein, who was later to disappear mysteriously from his private plane.

Easter Hero lined up for the 1928 Grand National, a race that was to prove as dramatic as any. Forty-two horses started, but only two finished and, of those the second, Billy Barton, had to be remounted after falling at the last fence. The catastrophe was due in part to the heavy going, but mainly to Easter Hero's failure to jump the Canal Turn, which, in those days, was an open ditch. Easter Hero misjudged the fence and landed

---

BRAZIL
EMERSON
1958
Bay gelding by Coaraze out of Empeñosa

The unbeaten champion of Brazil and one of the best horses that country has produced in recent decades. Emerson raced only as a three-year-old, winning all five of his races at distances which ranged from seven furlongs

(1.4 km) to just over 1½ miles (2.4 km).

Bred in Brazil, out of an Argentinian mare by the 1945 French Derby winner Coaraze, Emerson's most notable victory was in the Brazilian Derby and the Gran Premio Derby Sulamericano at São Paulo. He broke down after that race and was sold to stand at stud in Normandy, where his best season was in 1972, when his daughter Rescousse won the French Oaks.

FRANCE
EXBURY
1959
Chestnut colt by Le Haar out of Greensward

Baron Guy de Rothschild's Exbury was trained at Chantilly by Geoffrey Watson and raced for three seasons, with increasing success. One win out of four runs as a two-year-old was followed by two wins out of seven the next season, including the Prix Daru and the Prix Foy.

But it was not until 1963 that Exbury produced his best performances. After winning the Prix Ganay by four lengths from Val de Loir, who had beaten him in the previous year's French Derby, Exbury travelled to Epsom for the Coronation Cup, which he had no trouble in winning by six lengths from the 1962 St Leger winner Hethersett.

To prove he was the best middle-distance horse in Europe, Exbury was aimed at the Prix de l'Arc de Triomphe, in which, using his decisive finishing speed, he took up the running a furlong (0.2 km) out and soon had two lengths to spare at the line. That year's Derby winner Relko was back in sixth place. He was retired to the Haras de Meautry stud at Deauville.

ENGLAND
FLYING CHILDERS
1714
Bay colt by the Darley Arabian out of Betty Leedes

The first truly great racehorse in the history of the turf was Flying Childers whose sire, the Darley Arabian, was one of the three foundation sires of the modern thoroughbred.

Flying Childers was owned during his racing and stud career by the Duke of Devonshire, who originally bought him for hunting. Little record remains of the colt's racing feats, but it is known that he won all his races with considerable ease. He beat Fox, a leading horse of the time, in a match in 1772, by nearly two furlongs (0.4 km) while conceding a stone (6.5 kg). He also accounted for the Duke of Bolton's good horse Speed-

---

well in a match over 4 miles (6.4 km) in 1721.

Flying Childers stood at his owner's stud at Chatsworth, Derbyshire, but although siring numerous winners, he was not a great sire of sires. He does appear, however, in the pedigrees of the early Derby winners Saltram and Sir Peter Teazle.

ARGENTINA/USA
FORLI
1963
Chestnut colt by Aristophanes out of Trevisa

Forli was bred in Argentina, where he won the Argentinian equivalent of Britain's Triple Crown in 1966. A resolute galloper who usually made all the running, he won the Polla de Potrillos (2,000 Guineas), winning by 12 lengths in record time, the Premio del Jockey Club, the Gran Premio Nacional (the Argentinian Derby) and the Gran Premio Carlos Pellegrini.

Forli was sold to an American syndicate who won two races with him at Hollywood Park. His only defeat was in the Citation Handicap at Arlington. He stood at stud at Claiborne Farm, where he sired 30 Stakes winners, including Forego, the American champion of 1974, 1975 and 1976.

AUSTRALIA
GALILEE
1963
Bay colt by Alcimedes out of Galston

Bred, like Tulloch, by Seton Otway at the Trelawney Stud, on New Zealand's North Island, Galilee was the undisputed star of the 1966–7 Australian racing scene. Trained by Bart Cummings, he started his career in South Australia, gaining his first important win against the top milers in the Toorak Handicap a week before contesting the Caulfield Cup, for which he started favourite. He won easily enough under 8 stone 7 lb (54 kg) and was then aimed at the Melbourne Cup.

With John Miller as jockey, Galilee carried 8 stone 13 lb (56.5 kg) for the big race and got up in the final furlong to beat stablemate Light Fingers, who had won the race the year before. He had some tremendous duels with Tobin Bronze that season, culminating in a brave win in the ten-furlong (2 km) Queen's Plate at Flemington in the autumn of 1967.

Galilee won the Sydney Cup over 2 miles (3.2 km) the following season, but struck into himself during the race, rupturing a blood vessel in his foreleg, which resulted in him missing another attempt at the Melbourne Cup. In total, he raced 36 times, winning 18.

ENGLAND
GIMCRACK
1760
Grey colt by Cripple out of Miss Elliot

Along with Eclipse, Gimcrack was one of the most famous racehorses of eighteenth century England. A small horse who stood only 14.0¼ hands, Gimcrack made his debut at Newmarket in 1765, winning easily for his owner William Wildman (who also owned Eclipse), but was sold a few weeks later to Viscount Bolingbroke.

It was for the Viscount that Gimcrack ran his most famous race, a match against Sir James Lowther's Ascham, with a prize of 1,000 guineas, which Gimcrack won easily. He was sold again in October 1765 to the Comte de Lauraguais, after the first defeat of his career. His new owner subjected the colt to some severe tests, such as running 22½ miles (36 km) in an hour in a ruthless time trial. Sir Charles Bunbury bought Gimcrack in October 1768 and in the spring of 1770 the colt won the prestigious Newmarket Whip. He was retired to stud soon after.

Gimcrack won 27 times in a career spanning seven seasons. Most of his races were run in heats over distances of 4–6 miles (6.4–9.6 km). Horses were tough in those days.

FRANCE
GLADIATEUR
1862
Bay colt by Monarque out of Miss Gladiator

Triple Crown winner Gladiateur was the first French-owned and -bred horse to win the Derby and, because he shattered the supposed invincibility of English-bred horses, he was nicknamed 'The Avenger of Waterloo'.

Trained at Newmarket by Tom Jennings, private trainer to the colt's owner-breeder, Count Frédéric de Lagrange, Gladiateur always had trouble with his legs, but this did not prevent Jennings from preparing the colt for an ambitious campaign in the English Classics.

Lightly raced as a two-year-old, Gladiateur won the 2,000 Guineas after an interrupted preparation and then went on to win the Derby by two lengths. He returned to France to win the Grand Prix de Paris, after which he travelled to Doncaster to land the St Leger. Gladiateur won all four of his races as a three-year-old, and these included Ascot's prestigious Gold Cup.

At stud Gladiateur was not a great success and he died of navicular disease in 1876. His statue stands at the entrance to Longchamp racecourse.

A painting of Gimcrack by George Stubbs, in 1770. Although the grey still has a race at York named after him, none of his 27 successes was recorded there.

ENGLAND
GOLDEN MILLER

1927
Bay gelding by Goldcourt out of Miller's Pride

Bred in Ireland and bought in 1931 by the redoubtable Dorothy Paget, Golden Miller dominated the jumps scene between 1932 and 1936, winning five Gold Cups in succession and a Grand National.

As with most great horses, there was little to suggest when he arrived at trainer Basil Briscoe's stables that Golden Miller was going to be anything out of the ordinary. Nevertheless, he won his first Gold Cup in 1932 with only four chases under his belt. He followed up in the 1932–3 season by winning his second and then contesting the Grand National which, in those days, was of considerably more prestige and importance than the Cheltenham race. He made a mistake at Becher's and unseated his rider at the Canal Turn.

The Grand National was again Golden Miller's main target the next season. On the way, he picked up his third Gold Cup by six lengths and went to Aintree with the welter burder of 12 stone 2 lb (77 kg) on his back. He started 8–1 second favourite and won by five lengths, shattering the record time for the race by eight seconds. He is still the only horse to have completed the Gold Cup-Grand National double in the same year.

Golden Miller, with ears pricked and eyes alert, seems to be on the look-out for more glory. King of the steeplechasers in the 1930s, his ability was unmatched until the arrival of peerless Arkle.

The 1935 Gold Cup was hotly contested, with Golden Miller getting the better of a prolonged battle with Thomond II (who had finished third in the 1934 National) to win by three-quarters of a length. Again the course record was beaten — this time by 27 seconds — and it looked as though Golden Miller only had to jump round Liverpool to win his second National. He topped the handicap with 12 stone 7 lb (79.5 kg) and started at 2–1, the shortest price of any National favourite. But disaster struck two fences after Valentine's, when he unseated Gerry Wilson. This failure led to a row between the eccentric Miss Paget and Briscoe, with the result that all her horses were transferred to Owen Anthony.

Golden Miller never forgot that incident at Liverpool. The following season, after winning his sixth Gold Cup, he returned to Aintree, was brought down at the first, remounted, and then refused at the eleventh, the same fence where disaster had struck the previous year. There was no Gold Cup in 1937, but Golden Miller returned once more for another crack at the National. He again refused at his 'jinx' fence.

Never returning to Aintree, Golden Miller contested one more Gold Cup in 1938, finishing second to Morse Code, and ran his last race in February 1939. He ran 52 times under the rules of racing, winning 28 races.

No horse is ever likely to emulate Golden Miller's Gold Cup record, for steeplechasing is much more competitive now and many of today's top chasers shun the Grand National.

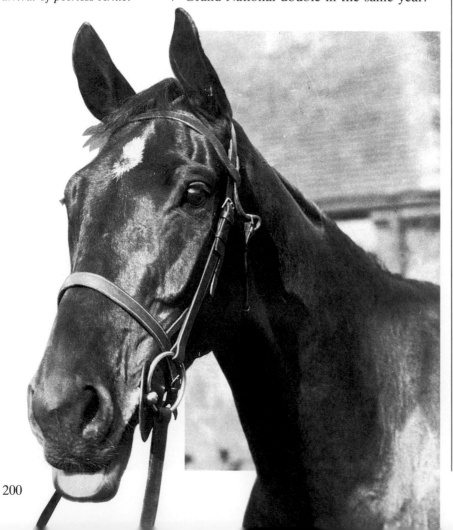

IRELAND
HATTON'S GRACE

1940
Bay gelding by His Grace out of Hatton

Bred in Tipperary, Hatton's Grace was initially sold at Goff's Sales for 18 guineas, becoming the property of Moya Keogh, whose husband, Harry, was a fearless punter. The gelding ran with some measure of success before going into training with Vincent O'Brien in the summer of 1948. It was O'Brien who was to transform him into a triple Champion Hurdle winner.

Hatton's Grace won his first Champion Hurdle by six lengths at the age of nine, when most hurdlers are beginning to lose their speed. He had had only three runs for O'Brien before that win. Among his victims was National Spirit, who had won the last two runnings of the race. Less than a month later Hatton's Grace won the Irish Lincoln over a mile (1.6 km), added the Irish Cesarewitch by beating stablemate Knock Hard (who was to win the Cheltenham Gold Cup in 1953), and added a second Champion Hurdle by beating Harlech by a length and a half.

The following year, Hatton's Grace became the first horse to win three Champion Hurdles after National Spirit had fallen at the last when slightly in the lead. Hatton's Grace then turned his attention to steeplechasing, winning one race from four starts. He was retired to spend the rest of his days at O'Brien's Ballydoyle stables.

SOUTH AFRICA/USA
HAWAII

1964
Bay colt by Utrillo out of Ethane

Hawaii was the first South African racehorse to make his mark on the international scene. His owner, the American millionaire Charles Engelhard, who was to win the Triple Crown with Nijinsky in 1970, bought him as a yearling and put him in training with George Azzie. Hawaii was an immediate success, winning his first three races as a two-year-old by an aggregate of 23 lengths.

The bay raced 12 times as a three- and four-year-old, winning ten races, including the South African Guineas and a number of important handicaps. He ran only twice over distances in excess of a mile (1.6 km) in his homeland and was twice beaten. He was therefore considered to be a non-stayer, a false impression bolstered by the predominance in South African racing at that time of sprints and handicaps at the expense of middle-distance weight-for-age races.

Engelhard sent Hawaii to America to race over longer distances, and the colt repaid his owner's faith in his ability to stay well in top-class company by winning the Group 1 Man O'War Stakes and finishing a length second to British challenger, Karabas, in the Washington DC International, both over 1½ miles (2.4 km). Hawaii went on to become Champion Grass Horse of 1969 in the USA.

Hawaii was retired to the Claiborne Stud, in Kentucky, where he sired Henbit, the winner of the 1980 Derby, as well as Hawaiian Sound, who was beaten by a head by Shirley Heights in the 1978 Epsom Classic.

ENGLAND
HYPERION

1930
Chestnut colt by Gainsborough out of Selene

Hyperion was not only a great racehorse, but also one of the most influential sires this century. He stood only 15.1½ hands, but made up for his lack of size with a perfect conformation and majestic action. Owned and bred by Lord Derby, Hyperion raced for

three seasons, winning nine of his 13 starts. He was trained for most of his career by the Hon George Lambton, but Lord Derby moved him to Colledge Leader's stable at the end of the 1933 season, much to Lambton's annoyance.

Hyperion was bone idle at home, but once on a racecourse there were not many horses who could get near him. He won the Derby by four lengths and, on the way to winning the St Leger, picked up the Prince of Wales Stakes at Royal Ascot. His four-year-old career was a little disappointing, mainly because his new trainer did not realize how much work Hyperion needed on the gallops. He was beaten in the Ascot Gold Cup and soon retired to stud.

As a stallion, Hyperion enjoyed wonderful success. Champion sire on six occasions, his offspring won a total of 752 races at a time when the war severely interrupted racing. He sired seven Classic winners and his son Aureole became the top Classic sire of the next generation. As a sire of brood-mares he was outstanding: Alycidon, Carrozza, Citation, and Ribocco all trace back to him and his influence spread to American and European bloodlines. He was at stud for 25 years and was eventually put down in 1960, at the age of 30.

It does not take long to size up Hyperion. One of the smallest horses to achieve true greatness, he was a star stallion after a magnificent racing career as a three-year-old.

ENGLAND
IROQUOIS

1878
Bay colt by Leamington out of Maggie B.B.

Iroquois' place in history is assured — he was the first American-bred horse to win the Epsom Derby, putting the USA on the map in terms of international racing. His owner was Pierre Lorillard, a rich tobacco merchant who in 1879 decided to try his luck in England. He sent over a six-year-old called Parole, who caused a sensation by winning the City and Suburban and the Grand Metropolitan, both ridden by Fred Archer, on successive days at Epsom.

Lorillard then sent over some yearlings, among them Iroquois and his trainer, Jacob Pincus. The colt was not fully fit in the 2,000 Guineas and could manage only second to Peregrine, who was immediately installed a strong favourite for the Derby.

Peregrine, however, was a heavy-topped colt who came down the Epsom Hill badly, letting Archer on Iroquois through on the inside, to win by half a length at 11–2. This was the result all America had been waiting for. A message was telegraphed to New York, reading 'Iropertow' — Iroquois 1, Peregrine 2, Town Moor 3. There were scenes of pandemonium and trading was suspended on Wall Street and the London Stock Exchange. Fred Archer immediately became a national hero in the USA.

Iroquois consolidated his position as the top three-year-old in England by winning the St Leger, but it was to be 73 years before another American-bred colt, Never Say Die, captured the Blue Riband of the Turf.

Kincsem did the rounds of European racing to establish herself as one of the greatest fillies of all time.

USA
KELSO
1957
Brown gelding by Your Host out of Maid Of Flight

Kelso must hold sound claims to the title of the best gelding ever to have raced. He certainly dominated American racing in the early 1960s in a way that no other horse had done before or since.

His record speaks for itself, for he was: Horse of the Year five years running, from 1960 to 1964; winner of 39 of his 63 starts (favourite on 53 occasions) for earnings of just under $2 million; Jockey Club Gold Cup hero on five occasions; and winner of the 1964 Washington DC International in the fastest time ever clocked in the USA for 1½ miles (2.4 km) on any surface — a fifth of a second faster than Secretariat's 31-length Belmont win in 1973.

Owned and bred by Mrs Allaire du Pont, Kelso raced for seven seasons over distances ranging from six furlongs (1.2 km) to 2 miles (3.2 km), mainly on the New York circuit, but also in California and Florida. He travelled everywhere with a dog as a companion and with specially bottled supplies of Arkansas spring water. He was a national institution,

with his own fan club and weekly fan mail delivered to his personal letterbox on his yellow-painted stable. He always raced with a yellow ribbon on his forelock and attracted great crowds wherever he appeared.

On his retirement, Kelso took up jumping and dressage and his owner rode him regularly in the local hunt. He was in great demand for public appearances and indeed was working right up to the end, appearing at Belmont Park for charity the day before he died of colic, at the age of 26.

HUNGARY
KINCSEM

1874
Chestnut filly by Cambuscan
out of Water Nymph

One of the most remarkable racehorses of all time, the Hungarian filly Kincsem was the unbeaten winner of 54 races on 13 different courses all over Europe, in an age when travelling was much slower and complicated than it is now.

Owned and bred by Erno Blaskovich and trained by Yorkshireman Robert Hesp, the filly failed to attract a bidder as a yearling because of her size (16.1 hands). As a two-year-old, in 1876, she was successful ten times on ten different courses in Germany, Austria, and Hungary, winning by an aggregate of 33½ lengths. As a three-year-old Kincsem added another 17 wins, including the 1,000 Guineas, 2,000 Guineas, Oaks, and St Leger in Hungary, the Emperor's Prize and the Derby in Austria, as well as the Grosser Preis von Baden and the Grosser Preis von Hannover in Germany.

Kincsem had her first race as a four-year-old at Becs in late April 1878 over a mile (1.6 km). She added another eight wins at distances ranging from a mile (1.6 km) to 1¾ miles (2.8 km) before she made her only appearance in Britain, to contest the Goodwood Cup over 2½ miles (4 km) on 1 August. The mare had only two opponents that day, the Chester Cup winner Pageant, who started favourite, and Lady Golightly, owned by Lady Falmouth. Kincsem started as the outsider at 5–2 and, unused to the undulating track, was kept steadied in the rear. A furlong (0.2 km) out she shot clear for a two-length win.

On her way home Kincsem stopped off at Deauville to win the Grand Prix by half a length from Fontainebleau, and then added four more races to her tally to round off the season. In one of these she ran a dead-heat with the best German colt of the time, Prince Giles I. In those days there was the choice of sharing the prize or re-running the race. Kincsem's owner asked for a re-run, which she won by five lengths.

The mare's final season was in 1879, when she won 12 more races, including the prestigious Grosser Preis von Baden for the third time. She was ridden in most of her races by Manchester-born Herbert Madden.

AUSTRALIA
KINGSTON TOWN

1976
Black gelding by Bletchingley
out of Ada Hunter

One of the great all-rounders in Australian racing and the top three-year-old of the 1979–80 season, Kingston Town had a rare blend of speed and stamina that stood him in good stead as a two-year-old, when he won two of his three starts. His abundant stamina and strength also took him to the top of the tree as a three-year-old.

Kingston Town proved difficult to train as a two-year-old and was gelded during the winter. This worked wonders and he reached his peak in the second half of the 1979–80 season, when he won three Grade One races on the Sydney circuit: the Rosehill Guineas (1¼ miles/2 km), the Australian Jockey Club Derby (1½ miles/2.4 km) and the Sydney Cup (2 miles/3.2 km), when he beat the previous year's winner Double Century by three-quarters of a length.

AUSTRALIA
LEILANI

1970
Brown filly by Oncidium out of Lei

Trained by Bart Cummings, Leilani was unraced as a two-year-old but, until an accident at Sydney airport cut short her career, she proved herself to be one of the toughest and most consistent mares to have raced in Australia.

The second foal of a speedy dam, Lei, and that great sire of classic horses in New Zealand, Oncidium, Leilani did not race as a two-year-old and only had a light spring campaign the following season. It was not until the autumn that she really proved to have outstanding prospects by winning the VATC St Clair Handicap at Caulfield and the AJC Oaks in a canter on heavy ground. This established her as the best middle-distance filly of her year.

The following season she showed herself to be the best racehorse in Australia when, on returning following a fracture of the hock sustained in the Oaks, she had as her main targets the Caulfield Cup and the Melbourne Cup. She had only a light preparation for the former — two starts over sprint distances and then a length-and-a-quarter defeat of the St Leger winner Herminia in the Turnbull

Man O' War was arguably America's greatest racehorse. He captivated a nation in only two seasons.

Stakes over 1¼ miles (2 km) at Flemington.

A week before the Caulfield Cup, she beat the New Zealand-bred mare Bellota by three lengths. For the Cup, she appeared to be well handicapped with 8 stone 2 lb (52 kg) and the only worry was her ability to last out the 1½ mile (2.4 km) distance. Ridden by R. Malyon and not by her usual jockey Roy Higgins, who could not make the weight, Leilani started favourite. With the race run on heavy ground, which suited her, she accelerated from the turn into the straight to leave her field floundering. She won by two and three-quarter lengths from Broadway Hit in the slowest time for 58 years.

After this triumph, Leilani was allotted 8 stone 10 lb (55.5 kg) in the Melbourne Cup, a weight that no mare had carried to victory and it was the weight, rather than the expected lack of stamina, that proved Leilani's undoing.

The race had attracted tough opposition in the top stayer Battle Heights, who had previously been beaten by Leilani in the Mackinnon Stakes at Flemington. But it was Leilani's stablemate Think Big who took Leilani's measure on the outside to win by a length.

Leilani proved her strength five days later, when she landed the Queen's Cup. She finished the season by winning another four races, including the Queen's Plate by half a length from Forest Boy, and the Australian Cup. But by then the long season had taken its toll on the mare.

Leilani's career came to a premature end when she was injured at Sydney airport after slipping on the tarmac *en route* for Melbourne. She made a comeback and won a race, but was then retired. Her 13 wins from 23 starts earned her connections over A$250,000.

LEXINGTON
1850
Bay colt by Boston out of Alice Carneal

Lexington was the first great American racehorse. But he was an even greater sire, with an all-pervasive influence on American breeding. He started his racing career under the name Darley but, after winning his first two races, he was sold to Richard Ten Broeck, a well-known gambler and breeder. Races in the USA at that time consisted mainly of a series of private matches, much as had occurred in England in the eighteenth century. These were generally run over 4 miles (6.4 km) in a series of heats, a sphere in which Lexington excelled.

The colt's great rival at this time was his own half-brother, Lecomte, and they first met as four-year-olds at Metairie racecourse, New Orleans, in 1854. Lexington proved too strong in the heats and for the first time Lecomte was beaten. But he got his revenge shortly after, when he won the Jockey Club Purse in straight heats.

The two horses met once more in the same race in 1855, Lexington winning the first heat and walking over in the second, after the withdrawal of Lecomte on health grounds. On 2 April 1855 Lexington raced against the clock at the Metairie track over 4 miles (6.4 km) after his owner had wagered that his horse would beat Lecomte's time of 7 minutes 26 seconds. Lexington, with the aid of pacemakers, completed the distance in 7 minutes 19¾ seconds and scooped the $20,000 prize.

After the trial, Richard Ten Broeck sold Lexington for the then record price of $15,000 and left for England. Lexington took up stud duties at Medway, Kentucky, and quickly became one of the greatest sires in the history of the American Turf. He was champion sire on 16 occasions, 14 in succession.

MAN O'WAR
1917
Chestnut colt by Fair Play out of Mahubah

Secretariat, Seattle Slew, and Kelso have their supporters, but for most American racing enthusiasts there has only ever been one true champion — Man O'War.

Standing 16.2¼ hands, weighing 1,150 lb (522.5 kg) and with a girth of 74 in (1.9 m), the fiery chestnut soon acquired the nickname 'Big Red'. He was bred by August Belmont II, the chairman of the New York Jockey Club, who had owned the 1908 2,000 Guineas winner Norman III and the 1912 St Leger winner Tracery. At the age of 65,

Belmont enlisted in the US Army to fight in Europe and put all his yearlings up for sale at Saratoga in 1918.

Man O'War (originally named My Man O'War by Belmont's wife Eleanor in honour of her husband) was bought by textile manufacturer Samuel D. Riddle for $5,000 and put into training with Louis Feustel. The colt raced for only two seasons. As a two-year-old he ran ten times, winning nine. His sole defeat came in the Sanford Memorial Stakes at Saratoga, where he lost ground after a bad start and then found himself boxed in. Switched to the outside, he failed by half a length to beat Upset. 'Big Red' got his revenge when beating Upset by a length in the Grand Union Hotel Stakes, ten days later.

As a three-year-old, nothing could touch Man O'War. He won the Preakness and Belmont Stakes, the latter by 20 lengths from his sole opponent in a record time. He was denied the chance of becoming the first horse to win the American Triple Crown because his owner did not enter him for the Kentucky Derby. The race was won by Paul Jones, whom Man O'War beat decisively in the Potomac Handicap later in the season.

Only one horse, John P. Grier, ever gave him a decent race. In a head-to-head battle for the Dwyer Stakes at Aqueduct, Man O'War regained the lead close to home, to win by a length and a half in a record time for the course. 'Big Red' set six more course records that season. His winning distances ranged from a length and a half to 100 lengths, and he started odds-on at every race.

Man O'War's owner retired him at the end of his three-year-old campaign, as there was nothing left for Man O'War to prove and he would have been asked to carry impossible weights as a four-year-old. He began his stud duties at the Hinata Stock Farm at Lexington, and then moved to the specially built Faraway Stud, also at Lexington.

Man O'War was never given the opportunity to shine at stud, as his owner restricted him to only 25 mares a season and most of those were Riddle's own mares. He sired 220 winners and was champion sire in 1926.

FRANCE
MIESQUE
1984
Bay filly by Nureyev out of Pasadoble

Miesque, owned initially by Greek shipping magnate Stavros Niarchos and trained in France by François Boutin, proved herself one of the great fillies over a mile (1.6 km) with brilliant victories over top-class opposition in France, England and the USA.

After winning three out of her four races as a juvenile, in her homeland, Miesque was favourite to win the 1987 English One

Thousand Guineas which she duly did in impressive style by one and a half lengths.

She added the French equivalent and two more top-class races in France over a mile and, despite finishing second in both the Queen Elizabeth II Stakes at Ascot and to Henry Cecil's Indian Skimmer in the Prix de Diane (French Oaks) at Chantilly, she later beat a strong field at Hollywood Park in November in the Breeders' Cup Mile.

The highlights of her four-year-old career were a second win in the Prix du Jacques Le Marois at Deauville, beating the champion English miler Warning by a length and retaining her Breeders' Cup Mile crown in decisive fashion at Churchill Downs, Kentucky, winning effortlessly by four lengths to notch her ninth win in Group One (championship) company in her last 12 starts. In an age of increasingly tough international competition, that is a record of a champion.

ENGLAND
MILL HOUSE
1957
Bay gelding by King Hall out of Has Na Riogh

Mill House had the extreme misfortune to be born in the same year as the great Arkle and, to some extent, his achievements on the racecourse were, and have remained, overshadowed by those of the Irish wonderhorse.

Bred, like Arkle, in Ireland, Mill House was bought by the Epsom trainer Syd Dale for the wealthy patron Bill Gollings. Gollings, despite the somewhat erratic jumping of his

Miesque brought off the English-French 1,000 Guineas double before winning the Breeders' Cup Mile in 1987 and again in 1988.

Mill House (right) and his old enemy, Arkle, take a fence together in the 1965 Cheltenham Gold Cup.

Nearco, unbeaten on the track and a star at stud, was one of the two best racehorses to come out of Italy.

new purchase early on, was convinced he had a champion on his hands. He backed Mill House to win over £25,000 in the 1963 Gold Cup and the horse was transferred to Fulke Walwyn's stable. He won two races at Sandown and then the great freeze of 1962–3 set in. From Christmas until early March there was no racing in England and Mill House went to Cheltenham poorly prepared. He was made the 9–2 favourite and easily outpointed a rather substandard field, winning by ten lengths.

Mill House first met Arkle in the 1963 Hennessy Gold Cup. Giving Arkle 5 lb (2.5 kg), Mill House beat him by eight lengths, and although Arkle had slipped at the last ditch, most observers were of the opinion that the English champion was the better horse. Mill House went on to land the King George VI Chase with ease and was now hailed as the greatest since Golden Miller.

The 1963 'Hennessy' was to be the last time that Mill House ever beat Arkle. The Irish horse beat him by five lengths in the 1964 Gold Cup and by 20 lengths the following year. Mill House lost the 1964 'Hennessy' to Arkle by 10 lengths in receipt of 3 lb (1.5 kg), and on their last meeting Arkle destroyed his old adversary in the Gallagher Gold Cup at Sandown in a record time for the course. Mill House returned in April 1967. Ridden by David Nicholson, he won the Whitbread Gold Cup carrying 11 stone 11 lb (75 kg).

In any normal period Mill House would have been the undisputed champion. He had immense presence, standing 17.2 hands. His jumping was extravagant and carefree — sometimes too carefree — and he galloped his rivals into the ground.

> ### ENGLAND
> # MILL REEF
> #### 1968
> #### Bay colt by Never Bend out of Milan Mill

The best middle-distance horse trained in England since the war, Mill Reef was bred in the USA by his owner, Paul Mellon, and trained at Kingsclere by Ian Balding. A small, compact colt with a marvellous action, Mill Reef raced 14 times over three seasons and was beaten only twice — once as a two-year-old by My Swallow in the Prix Robert Papin after a terrible cross-Channel journey, and then in the 2,000 Guineas by another outstanding performer and specialist miler, Brigadier Gerard.

Mill Reef won the Derby by two lengths and followed it up by beating the top-class French colt Caro by four lengths in the Eclipse. He 'hacked up' in the 'King George', beating Ortis by six lengths.

Kept in training as a four-year-old, Mill Reef ran only twice. He won the Prix Ganay by ten lengths and then struggled to beat Homeric by a neck in the Coronation Cup at Epsom. The colt then went down with a virus and, while being prepared for a second 'Arc', shattered his near foreleg on the gallops. He was operated on immediately and retired to stand at the National Stud. Right up to his death in 1986, Mill Reef proved to be an outstanding sire, among his offspring being the Classic winner Fairy Footsteps, and the Derby winners Shirley Heights and Reference Point.

ITALY
NEARCO
1935
Bay colt by Pharos out of Nogara

Owned and bred by Federico Tesio, one of the greatest breeders of thoroughbreds, Nearco ranks alongside Ribot as the greatest racehorse to have come out of Italy. He not only reigned supreme on the track, winning all 14 of his races, but also had a permanent and highly influential career at stud, numbering amongst his progeny such champions as Dante, Sayajirao, Nimbus, Neartic, and Nasrullah. Among his male descendants are Sir Ivor, Habitat, Nonoalco, Northern Dancer, Nijinsky, Mill Reef, Roberto, The Minstrel, Shirley Heights, Secretariat, Spectacular Bid, and Bold Ruler.

Nearco was unbeaten on the racecourse, winning all seven of his races as a two-year-old, including the Gran Criterium, before going on to greater achievements the following season. In 1938 he swept all before him, capturing the Italian 2,000 Guineas and the Derby Italiano, followed by the Gran Premio di Milano and the Gran Premio d'Italia.

Nearco proved he was the champion of Europe in the Grand Prix de Paris over 3 km (1 mile 7 furlongs), when he took on the English Derby winner Bois Roussel, French Derby winner Cillas, as well as the winners of the French 1,000 Guineas and the Oaks. It was 'no contest', with Nearco taking the lead and drawing away for a length-and-a-half win from Canot, with Bois Roussel third.

The horse was sold to the English bookmaker Martin Benson for the then colossal figure of £60,000, to stand at Newmarket's Beech House Stud. He made an immediate impact at stud and for 15 consecutive years he was in the top ten list of sires.

IRELAND
NIJINSKY
1967
Bay colt by Northern Dancer out of Flaming Page

Owned by Charles Engelhard and trained by Vincent O'Brien in Tipperary, Nijinsky was sired by the great Canadian stallion Northern Dancer. Nijinsky was always rated by O'Brien to be one of the greatest he had ever trained, along with Sir Ivor, and in 1970 he became the first horse since Bahram in 1935 to win the Triple Crown.

Nijinsky was unbeaten as a two-year-old. He started a short-priced favourite for the 2,000 Guineas, which he won comfortably by two and a half lengths, and then demolished a small but high-class field for the Derby. The Irish Derby was a formality and next it was

Ascot, for the King George VI and Queen Elizabeth Stakes, which he won hard held by six lengths from the previous year's winner, Blakeney.

Nijinsky then fell ill with ringworm and had not fully recovered by the time the St Leger came around. Engelhard was desperate to win the Triple Crown and, even though the 'Arc' was Nijinsky's ultimate target, it was reasoned that the St Leger would be a suitable 'prep' race. He won it, but it took a lot out of him and when he went to France for the 'Arc' he lost by a head to Sassafras.

It was decided to end Nijinsky's career on a winning note and he was sent to Newmarket for the Champion Stakes. However, the pressures of a long season's racing in the highest company all over Europe, as well as the mid-season setback, had taken their toll, and the colt was again beaten by a length and a half into second place by Lorenzaccio.

Nijinsky took up stud duties at Claiborne Stud in Kentucky. His winners include Ile De Bourbon, Golden Fleece, Shadeed, Caerleon, King's Lake, and Shahrastani.

USA/CANADA
NORTHERN DANCER
1961
Bay colt by Nearctic out of Natalma

Northern Dancer was the greatest racehorse to come out of Canada and at stud the most influential stallion of the second half of this century. A small colt, standing less than 15.3 hands, he failed to reach his reserve at the yearling sales and his breeder E. P. Taylor put him in training with Horatio Luro. He was a precocious sort, winning seven of his nine races in his first season.

Bill Shoemaker had taken over the ride on Northern Dancer after his original jockey had been sacked by Luro for misuse of the whip. However, Shoemaker decided to ride Californian challenger Hill Rise in the Kentucky Derby and the ride on Northern Dancer was given to Bill Hartack. Hill Rise started favourite on the day, but lost ground round the turn and was beaten by a neck by Northern Dancer who set a track record of two minutes dead.

The winning margin between the two had grown to two and a quarter lengths by the time the little Canadian colt had won the Preakness Stakes, but the third leg of the Triple Crown, the Belmont Stakes, was to prove too far for Northern Dancer, who did not stay the 1½ miles (2.4 km). He returned to Canada, to win the Queen's Plate by a wide margin, but soon afterwards at exercise he injured a tendon and was retired to stud with a racing record of 14 wins from 18 starts.

He started his stud career in Canada, before moving to Taylor's Windfields Farm, in Maryland. He was syndicated for $2,400,000, but nominations to him have

Nijinsky with Lester Piggott aboard won Britain's Triple Crown, but his St Leger success left him below par for the Arc de Triomphe.

Trainer John Porter admires his great colt Ormonde, who contributed the 2,000 Guineas, Derby and St Leger to his stable's total of 23 English Classics.

reached astronomical proportions. In 1986, a year before he retired from stud duties, his nomination figure was $700,000. Among his offspring are such champions as Nijinsky, The Minstrel, Lyphard, El Gran Señor, Secreto, Nureyev, Sadler's Wells, Storm Bird, and Try My Best. Not bad for an unsold yearling!

ENGLAND
OH SO SHARP

1983
Chestnut filly by Kris out of Oh So Fair

The first filly since Meld in 1955 to win the fillies' Triple Crown — the 1,000 Guineas, the Oaks, and the St Leger — Oh So Sharp was owned and bred by Sheikh Mohammed al Maktoum and trained by Henry Cecil. Three wins from three starts as a two-year-old, including the Solario Stakes and the Hoover Fillies' Mile (1.6 km) at Ascot, proved that Oh So Sharp was a staying filly of the highest calibre, and this she confirmed the following season when, after winning the Nell Gwyn Stakes, she produced a devastating late burst to land the 1,000 Guineas by a short head.

Those critics who doubted Oh So Sharp's ability to stay the 1½ miles (2.2 km) of the Oaks — her sire Kris had never raced beyond a mile (1.6 km) — were quickly silenced at Epsom when she ran her best-ever race to beat French filly Triptych by six lengths under the new stable jockey Steve Cauthen. Following the setback of her stablemate

Slip Anchor in midsummer, Oh So Sharp deputized for him in the King George VI and Queen Elizabeth Stakes, but could manage only second to Petoski. The filly started odds-on for the Benson and Hedges Gold Cup at York, but again filled second spot behind Commanche Run.

ENGLAND
ORMONDE

1883
Bay colt by Bend Or out of Lily Agnes

One of the greats of the English Turf, Ormonde was bred and owned by the First Duke of Westminster and trained at Kingsclere by John Porter. A backward two-year-old, Ormonde was slow to mature and it was not until the autumn of 1885 that he made his mark by winning the Dewhurst Stakes. He beat a top-class field for the following year's 2,000 Guineas and went on to win the Derby and the St Leger, as well as the St James's Palace Stakes and the Hardwicke Stakes at Royal Ascot on successive days, the Champion Stakes, and the Free Handicap.

Kept in training as a four-year-old, Ormonde added another Hardwicke Stakes to his tally, as well as winning the six-furlong (1.2 km) Imperial Gold Cup at Newmarket. In all, Ormonde raced 16 times and was unbeaten, a record made all the more remarkable by the fact that in the later stages of his career he was wrong in his wind.

Ormonde spent two seasons at stud in England and was then exported, amid considerable outcry, to Argentina for £12,000. In 1894 he changed hands again and was sent to California. He was never particularly fertile, however, siring few good-quality foals.

ENGLAND
PEBBLES

1981
Chestnut filly by Sharpen Up out of La Dolce

Pebbles, the winner of ten of her 15 races, is the top stakes winner trained in Europe, her total prize money amounting to £1,402,994. Trained at Newmarket by Clive Brittain, Pebbles was a tough, genuine filly of the highest quality. After a variable juvenile campaign, she reappeared as a three-year-old to win the Nell Gwyn Stakes at Newmarket before following up in the 1,000 Guineas, which she won easily by three lengths.

While being trained for the Oaks, Pebbles was sold by her breeder, Captain Marcos Lemos, to Sheikh Mohammed, who already had two other fancied fillies in the race.

Pebbles was accordingly switched to the Coronation Stakes at Royal Ascot, but found Katie's one-and-a-half lengths too good. An injury forced her to rest until the Champion Stakes at Newmarket in the autumn, in which she put up a game display to go down by a neck to Palace Music.

Pebbles was kept in training as a four-year-old — a decision which paid dividends. She won her first race, the Trusthouse Forte Mile (1.6 km) at Sandown, in April and then became the first filly ever to win the Eclipse Stakes. A three-month rest was followed by an ambitious autumn campaign, starting with the Champion Stakes, which she won in brilliant style by three lengths from that season's seven-length Derby winner Slip Anchor. She then crossed the Atlantic for a tilt at the Breeders' Cup Turf at Aqueduct, which she won by a neck from Strawberry Road in a record time for the course.

ENGLAND
PERSIAN WAR

1963
Bay gelding by Persian Gulf out of Warning

Bred by Sir John Astor and trained on the Flat by Dick Hern, Persian War was probably the toughest triple Champion Hurdle winner since the war. He was owned by Henry Alper, who thought the world of his horse, but not of his trainers, and so Persian War had five different handlers after Alper bought him from Tom Masson in January 1967.

Brian Swift trained Persian War to win the Victor Ludorum and the Triumph Hurdle that season, but Alper and Swift parted company soon afterwards and the horse was sent to Colin Davies, who was to train him during his spell as triple Champion Hurdler. Before winning the first of his hurdling crowns, Persian War won the toughest handicap hurdle in the calendar — the Schweppes at Newbury — with 11 stone 13 lb (69.5 kg) on his back. A month later he won the Champion Hurdle by four lengths.

Persian War's build-up to his defence of the title the next season was interrupted by an injury incurred at Worcester, but he was fully fit on the day, winning again by four lengths. More disasters occurred the following season. Lameness was followed by a respiratory problem and the gelding went to Cheltenham without a win for a year. And yet he was still too good for his rivals, beating Major Rose by a length and a half.

Arthur Pitt took over the training reins and produced Persian War to win a Sweeps Hurdle and to run second, behind Bula, in the 1971 Champion Hurdle. Two more changes of stables occurred, but by this time the horse was in decline and his racing days were over.

ENGLAND
PETITE ETOILE

1956
Grey filly by Petition out of Star Of Iran

Petite Etoile was a fiery, temperamental filly owned by Prince Aly Khan and, following his death, by his son the present Aga Khan. Trained by Sir Noel Murless and ridden to all her important successes by stable jockey Lester Piggott, she inherited blinding speed from her dam's side, which reached back to the late Aga Khan's foundation mare Mumtaz Mahal.

After winning the Free Handicap under top weight, Petite Etoile then ran in the 1,000 Guineas, winning by a length. Next stop was the Oaks, but many felt that with her breeding she would not stay the trip. Piggott rode her for the first time and she won in a canter by three lengths.

The filly went on to win the Sussex Stakes, Yorkshire Oaks and the Champion Stakes that season. She took the Coronation Cup at Epsom the following season, effortlessly beating the 1959 Derby winner Parthia. Made favourite for the King George VI and Queen Elizabeth Stakes at Ascot, Petite Etoile was outclassed by Aggressor.

On the death of Aly Khan, Petite Etoile was kept in training by the young Aga Khan and, although winning a second Coronation Cup, she never really showed the same sparkle as she had done in her three-year-old days. She won 14 of her 19 starts.

Persian War was kept on the move between stables by restless owner Henry Alper, but he stayed long enough with trainer Colin Davies to win three Champion Hurdles.

AUSTRALIA
PHAR LAP
1926
Chestnut gelding by Night Raid
out of Entreaty

To many Australians Phar Lap was quite simply the greatest racehorse ever — certainly 'down under', if not in the world. His feats on the racecourse were legendary and, unlike many great Australasian racehorses, he had the chance to prove his worth outside the subcontinent.

Phar Lap's early story reads like that of the Ugly Duckling. Bred at Timaru, on the South Island of New Zealand, Phar Lap was so unprepossessing that he was bought for the paltry sum of 160 guineas by a small-time trainer, Harry Telford, on behalf of owner David Davis. The horse having been shipped over to Australia, Davis had second thoughts when confronted with him, and backed down from the deal. Telford could not afford to keep Phar Lap on his own and he leased the horse for three years, with Davis taking a third of any prize money.

The yearling was gelded and did not show much promise in his first season. He was trained on the sandhills outside Sydney and did manage to win the Rosehill Maiden Juvenile Handicap over six furlongs (1.2 km). But it was the following season that he struck form in no uncertain fashion, winning the Rosehill Guineas, the AJC Derby and St Leger, and the Victoria Derby and St Leger, and nine other races. He was third in the 1929 Melbourne Cup, but made no mistake the following year when, carrying the welter burden of 9 stone 12 lb (62.5 kg) and starting at 11–8 on (the only time a horse has started at odds-on for Australia's greatest race) he won by three lengths, giving the best of his three-year-old rivals 15 lb (7 kg) more than weight-for-age.

Phar Lap won his first eight races the following season and was then allotted the impossible burden of 10 stone 10 lb (68 kg) for the 1931 Melbourne Cup. He was not fully fit that day and was eased to finish eighth behind White Nose when all chance of victory had gone. That race was his last in Australia and two months later he was sent to California to continue his career. He was sent into Mexico to run in the Agua Caliente Handicap which he won in spectacular style, in a course record time under top weight of 9 stone 3 lb (58.5 kg).

The Mexican race was to be Phar Lap's last, for, after returning to California, he died of poisoning at Menlo Park on 5 April 1932. Many hold that he was poisoned deliberately, but it is more likely that he died as a result of ingesting grass which had been treated with a toxic spray.

In all Phar Lap won 37 races from 51 starts, most of them against top-class opposition, and with great ease. He broke eight course records and usually gave away substantial amounts of weight. He was extremely difficult to settle in a race and often forged well clear of his rivals from the off.

ENGLAND
PRETTY POLLY
1901
Chestnut filly by Gallinule out
of Admiration

Just as the great filly Sceptre was retiring, another outstanding filly was making her debut at Sandown Park in June 1903. She was Pretty Polly, owned and bred by Major Eustace Loder and trained by Peter Gilpin.

With nine wins from nine races as a two-year-old, Pretty Polly was the undisputed champion juvenile and when she reappeared the following season for the 1,000 Guineas she was the 4–1-on hot favourite. She won the race, without coming out of a canter, by three lengths in record time.

By the time the Oaks came around, Pretty Polly had frightened away most of the opposition and she again had no trouble in beating her three opponents easily at long odds-on. The Coronation Stakes at Royal Ascot and the Nassau Stakes at Goodwood

followed before she completed the fillies' Triple Crown by winning the St Leger.

Pretty Polly stayed in training as a four- and five-year-old, adding six more wins to her credit, her only defeat coming in the 1906 Ascot Gold Cup. At stud she produced nothing of note on the male side, but her fillies are responsible for the families from which Psidium, St Paddy, and Brigadier Gerard originate.

AUSTRALIA
RAIN LOVER
1964
Bay colt by Latin Lover out of Rain Spot

Rain Lover's main claim to fame was that he was the first horse since Archer in 1862 to win the Melbourne Cup in successive years. He achieved this feat in 1968 and 1969.

Trained by Mick Robins, Rain Lover first showed he was a stayer of the highest class when he won the 1967 Adelaide Cup at Morphettville and three more races that season. Set to carry 8 stone 2 lb (51.5 kg) in the Melbourne Cup, he proved far too strong for his rivals. The race was a rough one, AJC Derby winner Wilton Park falling after

scrimmaging, but Jim Johnson took Rain Lover to the front as he entered the straight and had eight lengths to spare at the line.

In the autumn of 1969, Rain Lover won the VRC Queen's Plate and the Queen Elizabeth Stakes and then won a second Melbourne Cup in a photo-finish from Alsop, to whom he was conceding 2 stone (12.5 kg).

Rain Lover ran 46 times, winning 17 starts and being placed on 18 occasions.

ENGLAND
RED RUM
1965
Bay gelding by Quorum out of Mared

Red Rum was the epitome of a Grand National horse — courageous, blessed with abundant stamina, a circumspect, unflamboyant jumper, and well-balanced and nimble. On park courses he was always in the top of the second division — not as classy as the Gold Cup winners — but at Aintree he had no peer.

Red Rum was not bred for chasing. His pedigree is that of a Flat racer and that is precisely how he started his career, coincidentally winning his first race in a dead-heat at Liverpool in spring 1967. He was

Making a bit of a splash . . . Red Rum, hero of three Aintree Grand Nationals, goes for a paddle in the sea after exercising on Southport sands. The beach was his regular training ground.

bought by his trainer Donald 'Ginger' McCain at the August 1972 Doncaster Sales for 6,000 guineas on behalf of the millionaire businessman, Noel le Mare, after winning five chases and three hurdles. McCain then transformed the gelding, who was suffering from pedalostitis, by working him on the sands at Southport, Lancashire, where the sea air and water cured his ailment.

Red Rum won all his five chases in 1973 and was aimed at the National. It was to be an unforgettable race. The Australian horse, Crisp, carrying joint top weight of 12 stone (76.5 kg), forged clear and set a blistering gallop, soaring over the fences as though they were hurdles. He was still in the lead 20 yards (18 m) from the winning post, but his exertions had taken their toll and, exhausted, he had no answer to Red Rum's late challenge and was beaten by three-quarters of a length. The time of the race was a record 9 minutes 1.9 seconds, beating Golden Miller's 39-year-old record by almost 19 seconds.

'Rummy', back the following year, and with no Crisp to share the limelight, stole the show when he won by seven lengths carrying top weight of 12 stone (76.5 kg). He was the first horse since Reynoldstown in 1935–6 to win successive Nationals. He added the Scottish National that same year. Then, after finishing second to Gold Cup winner L'Escargot in 1975 and filling the same spot behind Rag Trade in 1976, Red Rum won the Grand National for an unprecedented third time in 1977, ridden by his former trainer Tommy Stack.

Red Rum was withdrawn from the 1978 running of the Grand National at the last moment, after injuring his foot in training, and retired a national hero.

Ribot ranks among the greatest. Yet he was not even entered for the Italian Classics.

ITALY
RIBOT
1952
Bay colt by Tenerani out of Romanella

The supreme achievement of Federico Tesio's brilliance as a breeder was an insignificant little bay called Ribot, who was nicknamed by his stable lad 'Il Piccolo', the little one. Tesio never saw Ribot race — he died two months before the horse's first race at Milan on 4 July 1954 — but even geniuses make mistakes and Ribot, who was an unprepossessing individual as a yearling, had not even been entered for the Italian Classics.

Ribot never really faced a stern test on the racecourse until the autumn of his three-year-old career when, after defeating the best in Italy, he was pitched in at the deep end in the 1955 Prix de l'Arc de Triomphe against the cream of Europe. Taking the lead at the turn into the straight, Ribot forged ahead and beat Beau Prince by three lengths, with French Derby winner Rapace, Irish Derby victor Zarathustra, and French Classic winners Douve and Macip in arrears.

Ribot's main target as a four-year-old was a second crack at the 'Arc'. His dress rehearsal for Europe's most prestigious race was to win four more races at Milan and to tackle the best that England had to offer in the King George VI and Queen Elizabeth Stakes at Ascot. He beat Queen Elizabeth's High Veldt by five lengths on the sort of going he hated.

An eight-length win at Milan also preceded Ribot's second 'Arc' attempt but, even so, he went to Paris with a stiff task on his hands. Lined up against him were the winners of the English and French Oaks, the winner of the Grand Prix, the French St Leger winner, two Irish Derby winners, a winner of the Washington DC International, and the runner-up in the Belmont Stakes.

Enrico Camici, who rode Ribot in all his races, kept the Italian wonderhorse in touch throughout, and in the end had six lengths to spare at the line over Irish Derby winner Talgo. He became the sixth horse to win the 'Arc' twice, but he did so in an era when international racing was far more competitive. On his return to Italy, Ribot staged two exhibition gallops at Milan and Rome, where he rounded off his final public performance by throwing his regular jockey Camici in front of a huge crowd at the Capannelle.

Ribot retired the unbeaten winner of 16 races and started his stud career at Lord Derby's Woodland Stud at Newmarket, where he stayed for two seasons before returning to Italy. He was then sent to the Derby Dan Stud in Kentucky, where he died in 1972. Ribot sired seven individual winners of 10 Classics in England, Ireland, the USA, and Italy. Among his offspring are two 'Arc' winners, Molvedo and Prince Royal II, top American horses Tom Rolfe, Arts And Letters, and Graustark, and English Classic winners Ribocco, Ribero, Boucher, Ragusa, and Long Look.

What made Ribot one of the greatest horses of this century? Like all champions he combined superb speed with stamina.

AUSTRALIA
RISING FAST

1951
Bay colt by Alonzo out of Faster

Distantly related to the great 19th-century stallion Musket (sire of Carbine), Rising Fast came from relatively lowly stock and was sold as a yearling for only 325 guineas. He was slow to come to hand and it was not until he was four that he started to show the class that stamped him a top performer in Australia.

He won the Caulfield Cup and the Melbourne Cup in 1954, the latter under top weight of 9 stone 5 lb (59.5 kg), as well as the valuable W. S. Cox Plate. The following year he came close to pulling off a unique double by landing the Caulfield Cup for the second year running under 9 stone 10 lb (61.5 kg).

Not since Archer's successes in 1861 and 1862 had any horse won the Melbourne Cup in successive years, and Rising Fast faced a stiff task under top weight of 10 stone (63.5 kg). Ridden by Bill Williamson, Rising Fast met with interference in the race and, unable to show his usual finishing burst on the soft ground, ran second to Toparoa, to whom he was conceding 34 lb (15.5 kg). The stewards inquired into possible interference between Toparoa and Rising Fast and ruled that Toparoa had interfered with the latter. The jockey Neville Sellwood was suspended, but Toparoa was allowed to keep the race.

Rising Fast had 24 wins from 68 races.

FRANCE/ENGLAND
SAGARO

1971
Chestnut colt by Espresso out of Zambara

Bred in Ireland by his owner Gerry Oldham, Sagaro was trained in France by François Boutin. As a stayer he was in a class of his own, with a rare combination of limitless stamina and the ability to quicken at the end of a race. He used both these assets to good effect in winning the Ascot Gold Cup three times in succession — a feat no other horse has achieved since the race was founded in 1807.

Sagaro first made his mark in the 3 km (1 mile 7 furlongs) Grand Prix de Paris at Longchamp in 1974. He won the Gold Cup in

1975, and the following season proved he was the best stayer in Europe by winning the Prix du Cadran, the Prix de Barbeville, and a second Gold Cup.

Oldham then decided to sell Sagaro as a stallion, but did not receive a single offer. Kept in training as a six-year-old, he won his third Gold Cup against a top-class field, and was then bought by the National Stud for £175,000 — a price that some breeding purists thought excessive for a stayer.

ENGLAND
St SIMON

1881
Bay colt by Galopin out of St Angela

Bred by the Hungarian aristocrat Prince Batthyany, St Simon was bought by the Duke of Portland on the sudden death of his breeder at Newmarket on the morning of the 1883 2,000 Guineas. The Duke paid 1,600 guineas for the backward-looking colt, which was to prove one of the greatest bargains in the history of the turf.

St Simon was put into training with Mat Dawson and won all five of his starts as a two-year-old. He was never entered for the Classics but proved unbeatable the following season, winning the Ascot Gold Cup by 20 lengths and beating the St Leger winner Ossian by the same distance in the Goodwood Cup.

All distances were alike to St Simon — he won over six furlongs (1.2 km) and 2½ miles (4 km) — although he tended to be very

St Simon was unbeaten in his nine races and, at stud, sired the winners of 17 Classics.

highly-strung and temperamental in training.

St Simon retired to stud the unbeaten winner of nine races. At stud he proved an outstanding success. He was champion sire nine times, seven of those in succession between 1890 and 1897, and was probably the greatest sire of sires that ever stood. Ten of his offspring won 17 Classics, among them Persimmon, Diamond Jubilee, and St Frusquin.

ENGLAND
SCEPTRE

1899
Bay filly by Persimmon out of Ornament

Sceptre established a record in 1902 that will never be beaten: she won four out of the five Classics outright. Her only failure was in the Derby, when she was given an appalling ride by Herbert Randall and could finish only an unlucky fourth. In 1868, another filly, Formosa, had won the same four races, but had dead-heated in the 2,000 Guineas.

Bred by the First Duke of Westminster, Sceptre was sold on the death of the Duke to the disreputable American gambler Bob Sievier, who planned to use her as a medium for some enormous gambles. She had a hard race in the Lincoln Handicap when not fully fit and was then aimed at both the 1,000 and 2,000 Guineas. She won both and was then sent to Epsom, to finish fourth to Ard Patrick in the Derby. She turned out again two days later to win the Oaks by three lengths.

Sceptre was then shipped off to Paris to tackle the Grand Prix, in which she finished unplaced. On returning to England, she contested the Coronation Stakes, in which she was unplaced, and the St James's Palace Stakes, which she won. More races followed, but at the end of the season Sievier was broke and tried to sell the filly. She failed to make her reserve at auction and Sievier put her away with a view to training her for the Lincoln, in an effort to escape bankruptcy.

After she finished fifth in the Lincoln, Sievier finally sold Sceptre to Sir William Bass for 25,000 guineas and she moved to the Manton stables of Alec Taylor, who saddled her to win the 1903 Hardwicke Stakes.

FRANCE
SEA-BIRD II

1962
Chestnut colt by Dan Cupid out of Sicalade

In many racing enthusiasts' minds Sea-Bird ranks alongside Ribot as the greatest horse to have raced in the post-war years, and evidence for this proposition can be seen in his achievements in the Derby and 'Arc' of 1965.

Trained at Chantilly by Etienne Pollet, Sea-Bird II was by a sire who had finished second in the French Derby in 1959, while his dam never won a race and ended up in the knackers' yard. He was beaten for the only time as a two-year-old, but the following season, after easy wins in the Prix de Greffulhe and the Prix Lupin, was installed favourite for the Derby. Sea-Bird II turned the race into a procession, cruising into the lead off the bit just over a furlong (0.2 km) out to win as he pleased by four lengths.

He went to Paris for the 'Arc' after winning the Grand Prix de Saint-Cloud. Lining up were the winners of the French, Irish, and Russian Derbys, French Oaks winner Blabla, and Tom Rolfe, one of America's top horses, who had already won the Preakness Stakes and the American Derby. Pouring with sweat, Sea-Bird II simply annihilated his field by six lengths.

In his first season at stud, Sea-Bird II sired Gyr, who was to finish second to Nijinsky in the 1970 Derby, and he was later to sire the great filly Allez France, as well as the popular dual-purpose gelding Sea Pigeon.

SOUTH AFRICA
SEA COTTAGE

1962
Bay colt by Fairthorn out of Maritime

Owned and trained by Sydney Laird, Sea Cottage was virtually unbeatable in four seasons of racing in his native South Africa. He was bred at the most famous stud in the country, the Vogelvlei Stud, founded by the Birch family, and rapidly made his mark on the South African racing scene, especially in the Cape and Natal provinces.

The colt's victories included the South African Guineas, the Cape of Good Hope Derby, the Champion Stakes (twice) and the Rothmans July Handicap, one of the great betting races in the South African season. It was in the build-up to his first crack at the Rothmans July Handicap that Sea Cottage was the victim of a nobbling attempt. A gunman fired a bullet into his hind quarters, which vets could not extract. However, the incident put only a temporary halt to Sea Cottage's career, and two months later he was back to finish a courageous third in the Champion Stakes at Greyville, Durban.

Sea Cottage started at odds-on for the following year's try at the July Handicap, for which he carried top weight of 9 stone 1 lb (57.5 kg). He came with a strong late run to catch the lightweight Jollify, to whom he was conceding almost 2 stone (12.5 kg). They flashed past the post together to record the first ever dead-heat in the history of the race.

Although he never raced outside South

Sea-Bird II was such a commanding winner of both the Epsom Derby and Arc de Triomphe that he is often rated Europe's best horse since World War II.

Africa, there is evidence of how good Sea Cottage really was in terms of international standing. In the last appearance he made in the Champion Stakes at Greyville, as a five-year-old in 1967, he took on the French challenger Alyscamps, who had won the Prix Jean Prat at Longchamp and finished fourth in the Prix du Cadran the previous year. The colt ran his prestigious rivals ragged, winning by nine lengths.

ENGLAND
SEA PIGEON

1970
Brown gelding by Sea-Bird II out of Around The Roses

The oldest winner of the Champion Hurdle, Sea Pigeon endeared himself to Flat and jumping fans alike. Most will remember him for his hurdling prowess — he won two Champion Hurdles (1980 and 1981), two Scottish Champion Hurdles (1977 and 1978), a Welsh Champion Hurdle (1980) and two Fighting Fifths (1979 and 1980) — but he was also a top-class handicapper on the Flat.

Sea Pigeon started life with expectations of a successful Flat career at the highest level. Bred to win a Derby, he actually competed in one, finishing seventh to Morston in 1973, but his Flat career was disappointing and he was bought out of Jeremy Tree's yard at the end of his three-year-old campaign. Having been gelded, he was sent to Gordon Richards and then to Peter Easterby at the start of the 1976–7 National Hunt season.

The gelding won the Champion Hurdle at his fourth attempt, beating his old rival Monksfield by seven lengths, and followed up this success the next year when ridden by John Francome, who was deputizing for the injured Jonjo O'Neill. Sea Pigeon was a difficult ride — he had to be covered up and produced for a late burst — and Francome employed these tactics to perfection, sprinting past his rivals close to home to win by a length and a half.

On the Flat, Sea Pigeon was just as tough. He won the Chester Cup twice in successive years, and put up his best performance when winning the highly competitive Ebor Handicap at York's August meeting in 1979 under 10 stone (63.5 kg) by a short head.

Sea Pigeon was retired just before the 1982 Cheltenham Festival. He had won 21 races from 40 starts over jumps and 16 races from 45 starts on the Flat.

USA
SEATTLE SLEW

1974
Bay or brown colt by Bold Reasoning out of My Charmer

There were three winners of the American Triple Crown in the 1970s — Secretariat in 1973, Seattle Slew in 1977, and Affirmed in 1978 — but Seattle Slew holds the unique distinction of being the only undefeated winner of the American Classics.

Bought for the bargain price of $17,500 at the 1975 Fasig-Tipton July sale by a young couple, Mickey and Karen Taylor, in partnership with vet Jim Hill and his wife, Seattle

The USA's Triple Crown hero, Secretariat, showed the mark of greatness when he won the Belmont Stakes by 31 lengths in world-record time.

Slew was put into training with Billy Turner. There were no immediate signs of outstanding ability until the colt contested the top two-year-old race the Champagne Stakes over a mile (1.6 km) at Belmont. He won it effortlessly by ten lengths in a new record time for the race. The young connections now knew that they had a champion on their hands and, following a stiff preparation, Seattle Slew went to post for the Kentucky Derby undefeated in six races.

He missed the break out of the gate and soon found himself behind a wall of horses. A gap appeared on the rail and Seattle Slew scooted through. Once he was in front, the race was as good as over for a horse of his speed and class, and he had two lengths to spare at the line. He won the Preakness Stakes by a length and a half in near-record time, and clinched the treble by winning the Belmont easily by four lengths.

The pressures on his owners were now great, and they succumbed to the idea of running him in California in the Swaps Stakes at Hollywood Park. Here he met with his first defeat. Arguments then broke out between the trainer and the owners, with the result that the colt was sent to a new trainer, Doug Peterson. Peterson soon fell out with the 'Slew's' regular jockey, Jean Cruguet, and the ride was given to Angel Cordero.

The next season Seattle Slew had to prove himself against the current Classic champions, in particular the new Triple Crown winner Affirmed and the top-class former European racer Exceller. He beat Affirmed in the first-ever meeting of the two Triple Crown winners in the Marlboro Cup. Seattle Slew made all to win by three lengths in an exceptionally fast time.

Exceller was the next victim. He was beaten in the Woodward Stakes by four lengths in a time that equalled the great Kelso's record. Exceller, however, got his revenge in the Jockey Club Gold Cup in a thrilling battle.

Seattle Slew retired to stud after that heroic effort, standing at the Spendthrift Farm in Kentucky. He had won 14 races from 17 starts, usually by setting an unbeatable pace.

ENGLAND

SHERGAR

1978
Bay colt by Great Nephew out of Sharmeen

Bred by the Aga Khan and trained at New-market by Michael Stoute, Shergar proved that he was one of the very best middle-distance horses to have raced in England by winning the Derby by a record ten lengths. Add to this a ten-length win in the Guardian Classic Trial at Sandown, a 12-length win in the Chester Vase, and victories in the Irish

Derby and the 'King George', both by four lengths, and it becomes obvious that Shergar was something special.

His only bad race was in the St Leger, when he finished fourth, beaten by nine lengths by Mill Reef's son Glint Of Gold.

Instead of running in the 'Arc', Shergar retired to his owner's Ballymany Stud in County Kildare, from where on 9 February 1983 he was kidnapped, reputedly by IRA terrorists, never to be seen again.

USA

SECRETARIAT

1970
Chestnut colt by Bold Ruler out of Somethingroyal

Secretariat's place in racing's Hall of Fame is assured by his capture of the 1973 Triple Crown. But it was the manner of his win in the final leg, the Belmont Stakes, that left an indelible impression of greatness on all those who witnessed it.

The huge chestnut, son of champion American sire Bold Ruler, was bred and raced by Meadow Stables. He won seven of his nine starts as a two-year-old, being disqualified once. On the death of C. T. Chenery, the owner of the stable, Secretariat was syndicated for the then record price of just over $6 million.

Trained by Lucien Laurin, the colt swept all before him the following season, winning the Kentucky Derby by two and a half lengths from Sham in a track record time. He followed up in the Preakness Stakes by defeating that same opponent by the same margin and the stage was then set for the Belmont Stakes (1½ miles/2.4 km).

Sham took Secretariat on again and set off at a breakneck speed in an effort to run him into the ground. The two clocked 46.2 seconds for the first half mile (0.8 km) and at half-way the pace told on Sham, who dropped away. Secretariat quickly opened up a clear lead, with nothing to race against but the clock. With nearly 70,000 spectators cheering him on, Secretariat flashed over the winning line 31 lengths clear in a time of 2 minutes 24 seconds, slashing 2.6 seconds off the old record and in the process setting a new 1½ mile (2.4 km) record on dirt. His jockey, Ron Turcotte, was unable to pull him up, with the result that he also beat the world record for 13 furlongs (2.6 km).

Another world record fell to Secretariat in the Marlboro Cup over nine furlongs (1.8 km), when he clocked 1 minute 45⅝ seconds, beating older horses Onion, the 1972 Kentucky Derby winner Riva Ridge, and Cougar. Secretariat was retired to stud with a career record of 16 wins from 21 starts. The best of his offspring so far have been Lady's Secret and, in Britain, Dactylographer.

IRELAND
SIR IVOR
1966
Bay colt by Sir Gaylord out of Attica

Bought as a yearling at the Keeneland Sales for $42,000 for Raymond Guest, the US Ambassador to Ireland, Sir Ivor was sent to Ballydoyle to be trained by Vincent O'Brien. He made his racecourse debut in June and finished sixth that day but went on to win the Grand Critérium in France, and two other races. Lester Piggott chose him in preference to the crack English three-year-old Petingo in the following season's 2,000 Guineas, and Sir Ivor proved Piggott's judgement to be sound by winning by a length and a half.

Guest had backed Sir Ivor at 100–1 for the Derby and the colt went to the post as the 4–5 favourite. In one of the most exciting Derbys ever seen, Sir Ivor, whose stamina was suspect, was held up by Piggott until the last possible moment and then pounced on Connaught to win by a length and a half.

A shock defeat in the Irish Derby when ridden by Liam Ward (ironically at the hands of Piggott on Ribero) was followed by another defeat in the Eclipse when Piggott, reunited with Sir Ivor, could finish only third to Royal Palace on firm going. A crack at the 'Arc' was the main autumn target and, despite running a brave race, Sir Ivor was beaten by a true mile-and-a-half (2.2 km) horse in Vaguely Noble. Sir Ivor returned to his ideal trip in the Champion Stakes (1¼ miles/2 km), which he won before taking on the best of the Americans in the Washington DC International at Laurel. Piggott excelled that day, winning by three-quarters of a length from Czar Alexander on atrocious going.

Sir Ivor was retired to stud, standing one year in Ireland before standing at the Claiborne Stud in Kentucky. Among the best of his offspring is the 'Arc' winner Ivanjica.

ENGLAND
SIR KEN
1947
Bay gelding by Laeken out of
Carte Grise II

Since World War II there have been four triple winners of the Champion Hurdle — Hatton's Grace, Sir Ken, Persian War and See You Then. Sir Ken was bred in France and bought privately by Willie Stephenson. He won his first race in England by five lengths at Liverpool and landed his first Champion Hurdle in 1952, beating Noholme by two lengths.

No trace has even been found of kidnapped Shergar, who won the 1981 Epsom Derby by a record ten lengths.

Sir Ken was unbeaten in his first 16 races in England, picking up a second Champion Hurdle in 1953, when he started at 5–2-on, the shortest-priced favourite in the history of the race. He was beaten for the first time in England at Uttoxeter on firm going, but bounced back at Cheltenham to land his third title, this time by a length from Impney.

Sir Ken then tried his luck over fences and the transition resulted in some good wins, notably in the Cotswold Chase at the Cheltenham Festival and the Mildmay Chase at Liverpool. He started joint second favourite for the 1957 Gold Cup, won by Linwell.

USA
SPECTACULAR BID
1976
Grey colt by Bold Bidder out of Spectacular

Harry Meyerhoff, a Baltimore businessman, certainly picked up a bargain when he successfully bid $37,000 for Spectacular Bid as a yearling at the Keeneland Fall Sales. The grey was to win 26 of his 30 races, including the first two legs of the 1979 American Triple Crown, earning over $2 million. He was eventually syndicated at stud for $22 million.

Spectacular Bid lost only two of his nine starts as a two-year-old and went to post for the Kentucky Derby a hot favourite at 3–5, to defeat the top colt from the West Coast, Flying Paster, by three lengths.

The Preakness Stakes was next and the grey won it in near record time by five lengths, to go into the final leg, the Belmont Stakes as 3–10 favourite. But the Triple Crown was to elude him, for he finished third to Coastal. However, after the race it was discovered that Spectacular Bid had trodden on a nail that morning, causing an injury that kept the colt off the track for two months. The Marlboro Cup was the next meeting of the two and the grey won easily, by five lengths. They met again in the Jockey Club Gold Cup, but the four-year-old Affirmed, beat Spectacular Bid by three-quarters of a length.

As a four-year-old Spectacular Bid was unbeaten in nine starts, and he retired to stud with 22 Grade races to his credit. Among his offspring are the top French milers Spectacular Joke and Legal Bid.

AUSTRALIA
STAR KINGDOM
1946
Chestnut colt by Stardust out of Impromptu

The most influential stallion in post-war Australian breeding, Star Kingdom was bred in Ireland in 1946 and raced as a two-, three-, and four-year-old in England under the name Star King. A small colt, Star Kingdom was nevertheless brilliantly fast, winning five of his six races, including the Gimcrack Stakes. The only race he lost was by a head to the top-class sprinter Abernant.

Star Kingdom won the Hungerford and Greenham Stakes at Newbury the following season, as well as the Jersey Stakes at Royal Ascot. He was bought by Australian-born Stanley Wootton, the Epsom trainer. Wootton sent Star Kingdom to the Baramul Stud near Sydney, where the stallion made an immediate impact on the breeding scene. From his first crop he sired Kingster, rated the best two-year-old in Australia, and in his third crop was the exceptionally fast Todman who beat the great Tulloch by six lengths in the six-furlong (1.2 km) Champagne Stakes.

Star Kingdom had his first success as a Classic-winning sire when Skyline won the AJC Derby in 1958 and followed up when Skyline's brother, Sky High, won the Victoria Derby. He was leading sire of winners five times, his offspring winning nearly 850 races in Australia, and he left an indelible impression on the Australian breeding scene with his ability to transmit a unique blend of precocious speed and stamina. He died of a twisted gut at the Baramul Stud in April 1967, aged 21.

ENGLAND
THE TETRARCH
1911
Grey colt by Roi Herode out of Vahren

Known as 'The Spotted Wonder' because his iron-grey coat was splashed with large patches of white, The Tetrarch was one of the fastest horses ever to have raced in England. He was a fluke on breeding, his sire being a one-paced out-and-out stayer. An injured fetlock curtailed his career to one season, but in that time The Tetrarch proved an outstanding sprinter and a great favourite with racegoers.

His trainer Atty Persse realized he had something special on his hands after The Tetrarch had worked with older horses and, giving them weight, had beaten them out of sight. After winning on his debut at Newmarket, The Tetrarch went on to land six more two-year-old races, including the Champagne Stakes and the National Produce Breeders' Stakes at Sandown, where he was left at the start but still won by a neck.

Persse was adamant that The Tetrarch would stay the Derby trip and his subsequent career at stud indirectly confirmed the trainer's conviction, for the horse sired three winners of the St Leger — Caligula, Polemarch, and Salmon Trout. He headed the sires' list in 1919, but eventually became sterile. Speed was the main ingredient he gave his offspring, his best being Mumtaz Mahal.

AUSTRALIA
TOBIN BRONZE

1962
Bay colt by Arctic Explorer out of Amarco

Tobin Bronze was trained by Graham Heagney and won the Victoria Derby in 1965 and the AJC Doncaster Handicap the following year. He suffered a virus at the start of his five-year-old campaign, but put up a great show to win the Caulfield Cup under 9 stone 10 lb (61.5 kg).

After winning the W. S. Cox Plate — Australia's most valuable weight-for-age race — for the second time, Tobin Bronze was sent to America where he ran his best race in defeat, finishing third in the Washington DC International to Fort Marcy and Damascus. He won four of his 16 races in the United States and his overall record was 24 wins from 44 starts. He was retired to stud.

AUSTRALIA
TULLOCH

1954
Bay colt by Khorassan out of Florida

Probably the greatest horse to have raced in Australia since World War II, Tulloch was bred at the Trelawney Stud, on New Zealand's North Island. An unimpressive-looking yearling, Tulloch was sold at the sales to top trainer Tommy Smith for 750 guineas, which proved a great bargain.

He was rated the equal-best two-year-old of 1956–7, sharing the honours with his great rival, the extremely fast Todman. As a three-year-old he stepped up in distance to out-point the best older horses in Australia, most notably in the AJC Derby and the Victoria and Queensland Derbys.

Tulloch's best race was in the Caulfield Cup over 1½ miles (2.4 km), which attracts the best weight-for-age horses in Australia and New Zealand. He carried 7 stone 8 lb (48 kg), started at 6–4 on (the first horse ever to be quoted at odds-on for the race), and won, beating the course record by nearly a second in the time of 2 minutes 26.9 seconds.

A mysterious viral infection kept Tulloch off the racecourse for almost two years, but he returned from a long course of treatment to win all five of his races as a five-year-old and ten races as a six-year-old, including a gutsy effort in the two-mile (3.2 km) Brisbane Cup, carrying 9 stone 12 lb (62.5 kg).

Tulloch's illness prevented him from competing in England as a four-year-old, so it is hard to judge his relative merits with the best international horses. His trainer once suggested that Tulloch would easily have beaten the top American horse of the day, Round Table. He certainly had the class and courage to hold his own in the very highest company. In all, he won 36 of his 53 races and was only once unplaced out of the first three.

The Major Records

The records listed below include historic horses such as Phar Lap, Man O'War, and Tudor Minstrel along with modern champions like Ribot, Kelso, Sea Bird, Mill Reef, Brigadier Gerard, Secretariat, Seattle Slew, Kingston Town, and many others. Included too, are the leading Classic races: England's 1,000 Guineas, 2,000 Guineas, Derby, Oaks, and St Leger; the USA's Kentucky Derby, Preakness Stakes, and Belmont Stakes; the Queen's Plate from Canada; and the Derbys of Ireland, Australia, and France (the Prix du Jockey Club).

Any list of major horse racing records would be incomplete without coverage of the foremost all-aged championship events, and so also included in this section are the Melbourne Cup and W. S. Cox Plate from Australia, England's King George VI and Queen Elizabeth Diamond Stakes, France's Prix de l'Arc de Triomphe (Europe's most prestigious race) and the USA's Jockey Club Gold Cup.

Jumping is a poor second to Flat racing in terms of prize money, but the excitement generated by a top-class steeplechase cannot be equalled.

For this reason, the results of the Grand National, the world's greatest such race, as well as those of the Cheltenham Gold Cup, the Champion Hurdle, and the King George VI Chase, will all be found below, completing this world survey of the major records of the Turf.

Edouard Manet's 1875 painting of racing at Longchamp.

AUSTRALIA

AJC DERBY
Randwick: 2,400 m (1½ miles). *Three-year-olds. First run*: 1861

YEAR	HORSE	TRAINER	JOCKEY	YEAR	HORSE	TRAINER	JOCKEY
1861	Kyogle	–	–	1897	Amberite	W. Duggan	M. Harris
1862	Regno	–	–	1898	Picture	M. Thompson	A. Delaney
1863	Remornic	–	–	1899	Cranberry	S. Fielder	F. Fielder
1864	Yattendon	–	–	1900	Maltster	J. Scobie	R. Lewis
1865	Clove	J. Tait	F. Martineer	1901	Hautvilliers	J. Scobie	R. Lewis
1866	The Bart	J. Tait	C. Stanley	1902	Abundance	P. McGrath	J. Barden
1867	Fireworks	J. Tait	C. Stanley	1903	Belah	J. Burton	W.H. Smith
1868	The Duke	–	J. Bishop	1904	Sylvanite	J. Scobie	R. Lewis
1869	Charon	W. Filgate	J. Morrison	1905	Noctuiform	R.J Mason	L.H. Hewitt
1870	Florence	J. Tait	C. Stanley	1906	Poseidon	I. Earnshaw	T. Clayton
1871	Javelin	J. Burton	J. Keen	1907	Mountain King	J. Burton	F. Hickey
1872	Loup Garou	Owner	T. Brown	1908	Parsee	I. Earnshaw	T. Clayton
1873	Benvolio	H. Tothill	T. Brown	1909	Prince Foote	F. McGrath	B. McCarthy
1874	Kingsborough	T. Lamond	W. Yeomans	1910	Tanami	F. McGrath	W. Foulsham
1875	Richmond	E. Jellett	T. Hales	1911	Cisco	T.F. Scully	W. Osborne
1876	Robinson Crusoe	W. Filgate	J. Morrison	1912	Cider	T. Payten	P.J. Foley
1877	Woodlands	–	B. Colley	1913	Beragoom	Owner	J.E. Pike
1878	His Lordship	E. de Mestre	J. Morrison	1914	Mountain Knight	H. Rayner	W.H. McLachlan
1879	Nellie	T. Lamond	B. Colley	1915	Cetigne	E. Green	A. Wood
1880	Grand Flaneur	T. Brown	T. Hales	1916	Kilboy	J.H. Prosser	W.H. McLachlan
1881	Wheatear	T. Lamond	W. Yeomans	1917	Biplane	R.J. Mason	B. Deeley
1882	Navigator	E. de Mestre	T. Hales	1918	Gloaming	R.J. Mason	B. Deeley
1883	Le Grand	J. Monaghan	B. Colley	1919	Artilleryman	P.T. Heywood	G. Harrison
1884	Bargo	M. Fennelly	T. Hales		*and* Richmond Main	F.J. Marsden	A. Wood
1885	Nordenfeldt	M. Fennelly	R. Ellis	1920	Salitros	F. Williams	M. Connell
1886	Trident	M. Fennelly	T. Hales	1921	Cupidon	R.J. Mason	G. Young
1887	Abercorn	T. Payten	T. Hales	1922	Rivoli	I.H. Andrews	P. Brown
1888	Melos	R. Raynor	E. Power	1923	Ballymena	F.D. Jones	M. McCarten
1889	Singapore	T. Payten	E. Huxley	1924	Heroic	C.T. Godby	H. Cairns
1890	Gibraltar	J. Allsop	T. Nerriker	1925	Manfred	H. McCalman	W. Duncan
1891	Stromboli	T. Payten	E. Huxley	1926	Rampion	F. Williams	S. Cracknell
1892	Camoola	T. Payten	E. Huxley	1927	Trivalve	J. Scobie	R. Lewis
1893	Trenchant	J. Allsop	H. Gardiner	1928	Prince Humphrey	J.T. Jamieson	J. Munro
1894	Bonnie Scotland	P. Martin	W. Morrison	1929	Phar Lap	H.R. Telford	J. Pike
1895	Bob Ray	Owner	E. Huxley	1930	Tregilla	C.O. Battye	E. Bartle
1896	Charge	T. Lamond	M. Harris	1931	Ammon Ra	J.T. Jamieson	M. McCarten

CAULFIELD CUP
Caulfield: 2,400 m (1½ miles). *Three-year-olds and up. First run*: 1879

YEAR	HORSE	TRAINER	JOCKEY	YEAR	HORSE	TRAINER	JOCKEY
1879	Newminster	W.E. Dakin	W. Yeomans	1909	Aborigine	H. Raynor	W. McLachlan
1880	Tom Kirk	–	R. Walker		*and* Blue Book	J.A. Mayo	M. Connell
1881	Blue Ribbon	H. Yeend	R. Walker	1910	Flavinius	J. Siely	F. Hickey
1881	Master Avenel	T. Ivory	P. Piggot	1911	L'y Medallist	J.W. Noud	W. Barnett
1882	Little Jack	J. Wilson	C. Moore	1912	Uncle Sam	M.P. Whitty	G. Lambert
1883	Calma	P.T. Heywood	M. O'Brien	1913	Aurifer	J. Siely	W.H. Smith
1884	Blink Bonny	–	A. Blair	1914	Uncle Sam	M.P. Whitty	J. Ettershanl
1885	Grace Darling	–	J. Williams	1915	Lavendo	L. Robertson	F. Dempsey
1886	Ben Holt	–	M. O'Brien	1916	Shepherd King	C. Wheeler	R. Lewis
1887	Oakleigh	T. Wilson	E. Gorry	1917	Bronzetti	J. Smith	F. Dempsey
1888	Chicago	–	J. Campbell	1918	King Offa	R. Bradfield	F. Bullock
1889	Boz	J. Cripps	R. Ramage	1919	Lucknow	R. Bradfield	F. Bullock
1890	Vengeance	–	P. McGowan	1920	Eurythmic	J. Holt	F. Dempsey
1891	G'Naroo	I. Foulsham	W. Morrison	1921	Violoncello	C.H. Bryans	W. Foulsham
1892	Paris	–	G. Parker	1922	Whittier	H. McCalman	E. Simmons
1893	Sainfoin	I.T. Carslake	C. Ettridge	1923	Wynette	H.W. Torr	E. Simmons
1894	Paris	–	J. Fielder	1924	Purser	C.T. Godby	G. Young
1895	Waterfall	M. Thompson	W. Delaney	1925	Whittier	H. McCalman	J. Pike
1896	Cremorne	J. Allsopp	E. Huxley	1926	Manfred	H. McCalman	R. Lewis
1897	Amberite	–	M. Harris	1927	Textile	E.J. O'Dwyer	W. Scanlon
1898	Hymettus	P.T. Heywood	N. Leek	1928	Maple	J. Holt	W. Duncan
1899	Dewey	T. Payten	L. Kuhn	1929	High Syce	J. Holt	W. Duncan
1900	Ingliston	J. Leek	C. Cooper	1930	Amounis	F. McGrath	W. Cook
1901	Hymettus	P.T. Heywood	W. Powell	1931	Denis Boy	F. McGrath	A. Knox
1902	Lieut. Bill	D. Harris	W. Daniels	1932	Rogilla	L. Haigh	G. Robinson
1903	Sweet Nell	J. Scobie	A. Richardson	1933	Gaine Carrington	C. T. Godby	J. Pike
1904	Murmur	F. Musgrave	S.D. Fisher	1934	Journal	J.T. Cush	A. Knox
1905	Marvel Loch	J. Burton	A. Hood	1935	Palfresco	C. Brown	N. Percival
1906	Poseidon	I. Earnshaw	T. Clayton	1936	Northwind	C.T. Godby	H. Badger
1907	Poseidon	I. Earnshaw	T. Clayton	1937	The Trump	S.W. Reid	A. Reed
1908	Maranui	D. O'Brien	M. McLachlan	1938	Buzalong	A. Leftwich	F. Shean

YEAR	HORSE	TRAINER	JOCKEY
1932	Peter Pan	F. McGrath	J. Pike
1933	Hall Mark	J. Holt	D. Munro
1934	Theo	F. Williams	M. McCarten
1935	Allunga	J.F. Munro	D. Munro
	and Homer	G. Price	A. Knox
1936	Talking	A.G. Papworth	A. Knox
1937	Avenger	J. Holt	E. Bartle
1938	Nuffield	J. Holt	D. Munro
1939	Reading	J.T. Cush	D. Munro
1940	Pandect	F. McGrath	W. Cook
1941	Laureate	H. Freedman	M. McCarten
1942	Main Topic	M.T. McGrath	D. Munro
1943	Moorland	R. Lamond, Jnr	E. Bartle
1944	Tea Rose	A.G. Anderson	H. Darke
1945	Magnificent	A.S. Croall	R. Heather
1946	Concerto	D. Lewis	W. Cook
1947	Valiant Crown	A.J. Doyle	N. McGrowdie
1948	Carbon Copy	D.S. McCormick	A. Breasley
1949	Playboy	T.J. Smith	G. Moore
1950	Alister	H. Wolters	R. Heather
1951	Channel Rise	W. Chaffe	B. Smith
1952	Deep River	M. McCarten	N. Sellwood
1953	Prince Morvi	E. Fellows	N. Sellwood
1954	Prince Delville	S. Lamond	R. Selkrig
1955	Caranna	E. Hush	A. Mulley
1956	Monte Carlo	F. Dalton	J. Thompson
1957	Tulloch	T. Smith	G. Moore
1958	Skyline	J. Green	M. Schumacher
1959	Martello Towers	E. Lawson	G. Podmore
1960	Persian Lyric	J. Cook	A. Mulley
1961	Summer Fair	L. O'Sullivan	T. Hill
1962	Summer Prince	T. Smith	G. Moore
1963	Summer Fiesta	T. Smith	G. Moore
1964	Royal Sovereign	J. Page	R. Selkrig
1965	Prince Grant	T. Smith	R. Dawkins
1966	El Gordo	L. O'Sullivan	N. Campton

YEAR	HORSE	TRAINER	JOCKEY
1967	Swift Peter	A. Beuzeville	R. Selkrig
1968	Wilton Park	M. Anderson	H. Cope
1969	Divide And Rule	N. Begg	R. McCarthy
1970	Silver Sharpe	T. Smith	N. Voigt
1971	Classic Mission	S. Brown	G. Moore
1972	Gold Brick	T. Kennedy	R. Selkrig
1973	Imagele	T. Smith	K. Langby
1974	Taras Bulba	G. Hanlon	J. Stocker
1975	Battle Sign	T. Millard	D. Messingham
1976	Great Lover	T. Smith	K. Langby
1977	Belmura Lad	J.B. Cummings	N. Voigt
1978	no race		
1979	Dulcify	C. Hayes	B. Thomson
1980	Kingston Town	T. Smith	M. Johnston
1981	Our Paddy Boy	C. Hayes	R. Mallyon
1982	Rose Of Kingston	R. Hoysted	G. Willetts
1983	Strawberry Road	D. Bougoure	L. Dittman
1984	Prolific	J.B. Cummings	J. Marshall
1985	Tristarc	R. McDonald	W. Treloar
1986	Bonecrusher	F. Ritchie	G. Stewart
1987	Myocard	Dr.G. Chapman	M.De Montford
1988	Beau Zam	J.B. Cummings	J. Marshall

YEAR	HORSE	TRAINER	JOCKEY
1939	Rivette	H. Bamber	E. Preston
1940	Beaulivre	G. Price	A. Dewhurst
1941	Velocity	S.B. Ferguson	J. Purtell
1942	Tranquil Star	R. Cameron	A. Breasley
1943	St. Warden (1st Div.)	J. Nicholson	H. White
1943	Skipton (2nd Div.)	J. Fryer	A. Breasley
1944	Counsel	R. Webster	A. Breasley
1945	St. Fairy	T. Lewis	A. Breasley
1946	Royal Gem	G.R. Jesser	R. Heather
1947	Columnist	M. McCarten	H. Badger
1948	Red Fury	J. Flannery	W. Briscoe
1949	Lincoln	L. Robertson	N. Eastwood
1950	Grey Boots	H. Cooper	N. Sellwood
1951	Basha Felika	E. Fisher	N. Sellwood
1952	Peshawar	P. Quinlan	A. Breasley
1953	My Hero	O. Watson	N. Eastwood
1954	Rising Fast	I. Tucker	A. Ward
1955	Rising Fast	F. Hoysted	W. William
1956	Redcraze	T. Smith	A. Ward
1957	Tulloch	T. Smith	N. Sellwood
1958	Sir Blink	J. Godby	A. Yeomans
1959	Regal Wrench	W. Murrell	T. Dyer
1960	Illumquh	E. Ropiha	W. Williamson
1961	Summer Fair	L. O'Sullivan	W. Smith
1962	Even Stevens	A. McGregor	L. Coles
1963	Sometime	L. Patterson	W. Pyers
1964	Yangtze	R. Dini	J. Stocker
1965	Bore Head	R. Dillon	F. Clarke
1966	Galilee	J.B. Cummings	J. Miller
1967	Tobin Bronze	H. Heagney	J. Johnson
1968	Bunratty Castle	K. Wynne	R. Mallyon

YEAR	HORSE	TRAINER	JOCKEY
1969	Big Philou	J.B. Cummings	R. Higgins
1970	Beer Street	D. Judd	B. Gilders
1971	Gay Icarus	C. Beechey	R. Mallyon
1972	Sobar	K. Hilton	H. White
1973	Swell Time	W. Winder	B. Andrews
1974	Leilani	J.B. Cummings	R. Mallyon
1975	Analight	C. Beechey	P. Trotter
1976	How Now	C. Hayes	J. Stocker
1977	Ming Dynasty	J.B. Cummings	H. White
1978	Taksan	T. Smith	J. Duggan
1979	Mighty Kingdon	T. Smith	M. Johnston
1980	Ming Dynasty	J.B. Cummings	E. Didham
1981	Silver Bounty	G. Carson	E. Didham
1982	Gurner's Lane	G. Murphy	B. Thomson
1983	Hayai	J. Lee	N. Voigt
1984	Affinity	J. Moloney	P. Hyland
1985	Tristarc	R. McDonald	W. Treloar
1986	Mr Lomondy	N. Eales	D. Walsh
1987	Lord Reims	C. Fenwick	B. Thomson
1988	Impofera	R. McDonald	B. York

AUSTRALIA

MELBOURNE CUP
Flemington: 3,200 m (2 miles). *Handicap*: Three-year-olds and up

YEAR	HORSE	HANDICAP	TRAINER	JOCKEY	YEAR	HORSE	HANDICAP	TRAINER	JOCKEY
1861	Archer	5–9–7	E. de Mestre	J. Cutts	1931	White Nose	5–6–12	E. Hatwell	N. Percival
1862	Archer	6–10–2	E. de Mestre	J. Cutts	1932	Peter Pan	3–7–6	F. McGrath	W. Duncan
1863	Banker	3–5–4	S. Waldock	H. Chifney	1933	Hall Mark	3–7–8	J. Holt	J. O'Sullivan
1864	Lantern	3–6–3	S. Mahon	S. Davis	1934	Peter Pan	5–9–10	F. McGrath	D. Munro
1865	Toryboy	8–7–0	P. Miley	E. Cavanagh	1935	Marabou	4–7–11	L. Robertson	K. Voitre
1866	The Barb	3–6–11	J. Tait	W. Davis	1936	Wotan	4–7–11	J. Fryer	O. Phillips
1867	Tim Whiffler	5–8–11	E. de Mestre	J. Driscoll	1937	The Trump	5–8–5	S. Reid	A. Reed
1868	Glencoe	4–9–1	J. Tait	C. Stanley	1938	Catalogue	8–8–4	A. McDonald	F. Shean
1869	Warrior	6–8–10	R. Sevoir	J. Morrison	1939	Rivette	6–7–9	H. Bamber	E. Preston
1870	Nimblefoot	7–6–3	W. Lang	J. Day	1940	Old Rowley	7–7–12	J. Scully	A. Knox
1871	The Pearl	5–7–3	J. Tait	J. Cavanagh	1941	Skipton	3–7–7	J. Fryer	W. Cook
1872	The Quack	6–7–10	J. Tait	W. Enderson	1942	Colonus	4–7–2	F. Manning	H. McCloud
1873	Don Juan	4–6–12	J. Wilson	W. Wilson	1943	Dark Felt	6–8–4	R. Webster	V. Hartney
1874	Haricot	4–6–7	S. Harding	P. Piggott	1944	Sirius	4–8–5	E. Fisher	D. Munro
1875	Wollomai	6–7–8	S. Moon	R. Batty	1945	Rainbird	4–7–7	S. Evans	W. Cook
1876	Briseis	3–6–4	J. Wilson	P. St Albans	1946	Russia	6–9–0	E. Hush	D. Munro
1877	Chester	3–6–12	E. de Mestre	P. Piggott	1947	Hiraji	4–7–11	J. McCurley	J. Purtell
1878	Calamia	5–8–2	E. de Mestre	T. Brown	1948	Rimfire	6–7–2	S. Boyden	R. Neville
1879	Darriwell	5–7–4	W. Dakin	S. Cracknell	1949	Foxzami	4–8–8	D. Lewis	W. Fellows
1880	Grand Flaneur	3–6–10	T. Brown	T. Hales	1950	Comic Court	5–9–5	J.B. Cummings	T.P. Glennon
1881	Zulu	4–5–10	T. Lamond	J. Gough	1951	Delta	5–9–5	M. McCarten	N. Sellwood
1882	The Assyrian	5–7–13	J. Savill	C. Hutchens	1952	Dalray	4–9–8	C. McCarthy	W. Williamson
1883	Martini Henry	3–7–5	M. Fennell	Williamson	1953	Wodalla	4–8–4	R. Sinclair	J. Purtell
1884	Malua	5–9–9	I. Foulsham	A. Robertson	1954	Rising Fast	5–9–5	I. Tucker	J. Purtell
1885	Sheet Anchor	7–7–11	T. Wilson	M. O'Brien	1955	Toparoa	7–7–8	T. Smith	N. Sellwood
1886	Arsenal	4–7–5	H. Rayner	W. English	1956	Evening Peal	4–8–0	E. Lawson	G. Podmore
1887	Dunlop	5–8–3	J. Nicholson	T. Sanders	1957	Straight Draw	5–8–5	J. Mitchell	M. McGrowdie
1888	Mentor	4–8–3	W. Hicken-botham	M. O'Brien	1958	Baystone	6–8–9	J. Green	M. Schumacher
					1959	MacDougal	6–8–11	R. Roden	T.P. Glennon
1889	Bravo	6–8–7	T. Wilson	J. Anwin	1960	Hi Jinx	5–7–10	T. Knowles	W. Smith
1890	Carbine	5–10–5	W. Hicken-botham	R. Ramage	1961	Lord Fury	4–7–8	F. Lewis	R. Selkrig
					1962	Even Stevens	5–8–5	A. McGregor	L. Coles
1891	Malvolio	4–8–4	J. Redfearn	G. Redfearn	1963	Gatum Gatum	5–7–12	H. Heagney	J. Johnson
1892	Glenloth	5–7–13	M. Carmody	G. Robson	1964	Polo Prince	6–8–3	J. Carter	R. Taylor
1893	Tarcoola	7–8–4	J. Cripps	H. Cripps	1965	Light Fingers	4–8–4	J.B. Cummings	R. Higgins
1894	Patron	4–9–3	R. Bradfield	H. Dawes	1966	Galilee	4–8–13	J.B. Cummings	J. Miller
1895	Auraria	3–7–4	J. Hill	J. Stevenson	1967	Red Handed	5–8–9	J.B. Cummings	R. Higgins
1896	Newhaven	3–7–13	W. Hicken-botham	H. Gardiner	1968	Rain Lover	4–8–2	M. Robins	J. Johnson
					1969	Rain Lover	5–9–7	M. Robins	J. Johnson
1897	Gaulus	6–7–8	W. Forrester	S. Callinan	1970	Baghdad Note	5–8–7	R. Heasley	E. Didham
1898	The Grafter	5–9–2	W. Forrester	J. Gough	1971	Silver Knight	4–8–9	E. Templeton	R. Marsh
1899	Merriwee	3–7–6	J. Wilson	V. Turner	1972	Piping Lane	6 48 kg	G. Hanlon	J. Letts
1900	Clean Sweep	3–7–0	J. Scobie	A. Richardson	1973	Gala Supreme	4 49 kg	R. Hutchins	F. Reys
1901	Revenue	5–7–10	H. Munro	F. Dunn	1974	Think Big	4 53 kg	J.B. Cummings	H. White
1902	The Victory	4–8–12	R. Bradfield	R. Lewis	1975	Think Big	5 58.5 kg	J.B. Cummings	H. White
1903	Lord Cardigan	3–6–8	A. Cornwell	N. Godby	1976	Van Der Hum	5 54.5 kg	L. Robinson	R. Skelton
1904	Acrasia	7–7–6	A. Wills	T. Clayton	1977	Gold And Black	5 57 kg	J.B. Cummings	J. Duggan
1905	Blue Spec	6–8–0	W. Hicken-botham	F. Bullock	1978	Arwon	5 50.5 kg	G. Hanlon	H. White
					1979	Hyperno	6 56 kg	J.B. Cummings	H. White
1906	Poseidon	3–7–6	I. Earnshaw	T. Clayton	1980	Beldale Ball	5 49.5 kg	C. Hayes	J. Letts
1907	Apologue	5–7–9	I. Earnshaw	W. Evans	1981	Just A Dash	4 53.5 kg	T. Smith	P. Cook
1908	Lord Nolan	3–6–10	E. Mayo	J. Flynn	1982	Gurner's Lane	4 56 kg	G. Murphy	L. Dittman
1909	Prince Foote	3–7–8	F. McGrath	W. McLachlan	1983	Kiwi	6 52 kg	E. Lupton	J. Cassidy
1910	Comedy King	4–7–11	J. Lynch	W. McLachlan	1984	Black Knight	5 50 kg	G. Hanlon	P. Cook
1911	The Parisian	6–8–9	C. Wheeler	R. Cameron	1985	What A Nuisance	7 52.5 kg	J. Meagher	P. Hyland
1912	Piastre	4–7–9	R. O'Connor	A. Shanahan	1986	At Talaq	6 54.5 kg	C. Hayes	M. Clarke
1913	Posinatus	5–7–10	J. Chambers	A. Shanahan	1987	Kensei	5 51.5 kg	L. Bridge	L. Olsen
1914	Kingsburgh	4–6–12	I. Foulsham	G. Meddick	1988	Empire Rose	—	L. Laxon	T. Allan
1915	Patrobas	3–7–6	C. Wheeler	R. Lewis					
1916	Sasanof	3–6–12	M. Hobbs	F. Foley					
1917	Westcourt	5–8–5	J. Burton	W. McLachlan					
1918	Night Watch	5–6–9	R. Bradfield	W. Duncan					
1919	Artilleryman	3–7–6	P. Heywood	R. Lewis					
1920	Poitrel	6–10–0	H. Robinson	K. Bracken					
1921	Sister Olive	3–6–9	J. Williams	E. O'Sullivan					
1922	King Ingoda	4–7–1	J. Scobie	A. Wilson					
1923	Bitalli	5–7–0	J. Scobie	A. Wilson					
1924	Backwood	6–8–2	R. Bradfield	P. Brown					
1925	Windbag	4–9–2	G. Price	J. Munro					
1926	Spearfelt	5–9–3	V. O'Neill	H. Cairns					
1927	Trivalve	3–7–6	J. Scobie	R. Lewis					
1928	Statesman	4–8–0	W. Kelso	J. Munro					
1929	Nightmarsh	4–9–2	A. McAulay	R. Reed					
1930	Phar Lap	4–9–12	H. Telford	J. Pike					

ROSEHILL GUINEAS
Rosehill: 2,000 m (1¼ miles). Three-year-olds. First run: 1910

YEAR	HORSE	TRAINER	JOCKEY	YEAR	HORSE	TRAINER	JOCKEY
1910	Electric Wire	–	McLachlan	1955	Caranna	E. Hush	A. Mulley
1911	Woolerina	–	Barnett	1956	Gay Lover	E. Hush	G. Moore
1912	Burri	–	J. Pike	1957	Tulloch	T. Smith	G. Moore
1913	Beau Soult	–	M. Connell	1958	Bold Pirate	T. Smith	G. Moore
1914	Carlita	–	W. Lillyman	1959	Martello Towers	E. Lawson	G. Podmore
1915	Wallace Isinglass	–	P. Maher	1960	Wenona Girl	M. McCarten	N. Sellwood
1916	Wolaroi	–	A. Wood	1961	King Brian	B. Andrews	K. Smith
1917	Biplane	–	B. Deeley	1962	Bogan Road	K. Montgomery	A. Mulley
1918	Woorawa	–	M. Connell	1963	Castanea	H. Sampson	W. Camer
1919	Elfacre	–	C.O. Davies	1964	Eskimo Prince	C. Rolls	A. Mulley
1920	Wirraway	–	J. Mahoney	1965	Fair Summer	J. Denham	D. Lake
1921	Furious	–	R. Marsden	1966	Dark Briar	T. Smith	S. Spinks
1922	Caserta	–	H. Cairns	1967	Grey Spirit	W. McNabb	J. Johnson
1923	All Sunshine	–	G. Harrison	1968	Royal Account	A. McKenna	R. Selkrig
1924	Nigger Minstrel	–	A. Reed	1969	Portable	T. Smith	N. Voigt
1925	Amounis	–	K. Bracken	1970	Royal Show	T. Smith	K. Langby
1926	Cromwell	–	W. Duncan	1971	Latin Knight	N. Anderson	R. Selkrig
1927	Winalot	–	S. Davidson	1972	Longfella	G. Murphy	P. Cook
1928	Mollison	–	J. Daniels	1973	Imagele	T. Smith	K. Langby
1929	Phar Lap	–	J. Munro	1974	Taras Bulba	G. Hanlon	G. Willetts
1930	Balloon King	–	D. Munro	1975	Battle Sign	T. Millard	D. Messington
1931	Lightning March	–	H. Hornery	1976	Fashion Beau	G. Murphy	P. Cook
1932	Bronze Hawk	–	E. Bartle	1977	Lefroy	G. Murphy	B. Andrews
1933	Blixten	–	M. McCarten	1978	no race		
1934	Silver King	–	D. Webb	1979	Dulcify	C. Hayes	B. Thomson
1935	Hadrian	–	D. Munro	1980	Kingston Town	T. Smith	M. Johnston
1936	Shakespeare	–	R. Parsons	1981	Deck The Halls	R. McGuinness	L. Dittman
1937	Ajax	–	M. McCarten	1982	Isle Of Man	Mrs D. Waddell	P. Cook
1938	Aeolus	–	W. Cook	1983	Strawberry Road	D. Bougoure	L. Dittman
1939	High Caste	–	E. Bartle	1984	Alibhai	T. Smith	L. Dittman
1940	Tidal Wave	–	E. Bartle	1985	Spirit Of Kingston	R. Hoysted	J. Marshall
1941	Laureate	–	M. McCarten	1986	Drawn	L. Bridge	G. Duffy
1942	Hall Stand	–	W. Cook	1987	Ring Joe	G. Tsolakis	J. Marshall
1943	Moorland	–	E. Bartle	1988	Sky Chase	J.B. Cummings	J. Marshall
1944	Tea Rose	–	H. Darke				
1945	Questing	G. Johnson	W. Cook				
1946	Prince Standard	D. Lewis	W. Briscoe				
1947	Conductor	J.W. Cook	E. Fordyce				
1948	Royal Andrew	J.W. Cook	A. Mulley				
1949	Thracian Lad	D. Lewis	A. Ward				
1950	Careless	F. Hood	T. Hill				
1951	Hydrogen	E. Hush	D. Munro				
1952	Idlewild	T. Smith	G. Moore				
1953	Silver Hawk	H. Telford	R. Selkrig				
1954	Pride Of Egypt	E. Hush	W. Cook		Note: For 1910–44, names of trainers not available.		

GOLDEN SLIPPER STAKES
Rosehill: 1,200 m (6 f). Two-year-olds. First run: 1957

YEAR	HORSE	TRAINER	JOCKEY	YEAR	HORSE	TRAINER	JOCKEY
1957	Todman	M. McCarten	N. Sellwood	1979	Century Miss	J.B. Cummings	W. Harris
1958	Skyline	J. Green	A. Mulley	1980	Dark Eclipse	N. Begg	K. Moses
1959	Fine And Dandy	H. Plant	J. Thompson	1981	Full On Aces	A. Armanasco	L. Dittman
1960	Sky High	J. Green	A. Mulley	1982	Marscay	J. Denham	R. Quinton
1961	Magic Night	H. Plant	M. Schumacher	1983	Sir Dapper	L. Bridge	R. Quinton
1962	Birthday Card	R. Ferris	R. Greenwood	1984	Inspired	T. Green	D Beadman
1963	Pago Pago	T. Jenner	W. Pyers	1985	Rory's Jester	C. Hayes	R. Quinton
1964	Eskimo Prince	C. Rolls	A. Mulley	1986	Bounding Away	T. Smith	L. Dittman
1965	Riesling	J. Norman	L. Billet	1987	Marauding	B. Mayfield-Smith	R. Quinton
1966	Storm Queen	J.B. Cummings	R. Higgins				
1967	Sweet Embrace	E. Stanton	C. Clare	1988	Star Watch	T. Smith	M. Dittman
1968	Royal Parma	J. Daniels	N. Campton				
1969	Vain	J. Moloney	P. Hyland				
1970	Baguette	F. Allotta	G. Moore				
1971	Fairy Walk	T. Smith	G. Moore				
1972	John's Hope	T. Smith	K. Langley				
1973	Tontonan	J.B. Cummings	R. Higgins				
1974	Hartshill	T. Smith	K. Langby				
1975	Toy Show	T. Smith	K. Langby				
1976	Vivarchi	J.B. Cummings	J. Duggan				
1977	Luskin Star	M. Lees	J. Wade				
1978	Manikato	N. Haysted	G. Willetts				

AUSTRALIA

VICTORIA DERBY
Flemington: 2,500 m (1 mile, 4½ furlongs). Three-year-olds. First run: 1855

YEAR	HORSE	TRAINER	JOCKEY
1855	Rose Of May	–	S. Holmes
1856	Flying Doe	–	J. Carter
1857	Tricolour	–	Snell
1858	Brown Lock	–	Hutton
1859	Buzzard	–	Henderson
1860	Flying Colours	–	J. Treacy
1861	Camden	–	J. Morrison
1862	Barwon	–	S. Waldock
1863	Oriflamme	–	W. Lang
1864	Lantern	W. Filgate	W. Simpson
1865	Angler	W. Filgate	Redman
1866	Seagull	W. Filgate	J. Morrison
1867	Fireworks	J. Tait	C. Stanley
1868	Fireworks	J. Tait	C. Stanley
1869	My Dream	–	Duffy
1869	Charon	W. Filgate	J. Morrison
1870	Florence	J. Tait	C. Stanley
1871	Miss Jessie	J. Wilson	J. Wilson
1872	Loup Garou	–	T. Brown
1873	Lapidist	W. Filgate	H. Grubb
1874	Melbourne	J. Tait	J. Ashworth
1875	Robin Hood	E. de Mestre	G. Donnelly
1876	Briseis	J. Wilson	T. Hales
1877	Chester	E. de Mestre	P. Piggott
1878	Wellington	–	M. Griffin
1879	Suwarrow	–	R. Walker
1880	Grand Flaneur	T. Brown	T. Hales
1881	Darebin	Owner	E. Power
1882	Navigator	E. de Mestre	T. Hales
1883	Martini Henry	M. Fennelly	Williamson
1884	Rufus	J. Redfearn	M. O'Brien
1885	Nordenfeldt	–	R. Ellis
1886	Trident	–	T. Hales
1887	The Australian Peer	H. Rayner	E. Gorry
1888	Ensign	T. Payten	T. Hales
1889	Dreadnought	T. Payten	T. Hales
1890	The Admiral	Owner	T. Hales
1891	Strathmore	H.R. Munro	H. Cusdin
1892	Camoola	T. Payten	E. Huxley
1893	Carnage	H.R. Munro	J. Gough
1894	The Harvester	Owner	C. Moore
1895	Wallace	H.R. Munro	J. Gough
1896	Newhaven	Hickenbotham	H. Gardner
1897	Amberite	Owner	M. Harris
1898	Cocos	T. Payten	W. Delaney
1899	Merriwee	J. Wilson	V. Turner
1900	Maltster	J. Scobie	R. Lewis
1901	Hautvilliers	J. Scobie	R. Lewis
1902	Abundance	F. McGrath	J. Barden
1903	F.J.A.	J. Scobie	A. Richardson
1904	Sylvanite	J. Scobie	R. Lewis
1905	Lady Wallace	J. Burton	F. Hickey
1906	Poseidon	I. Earnshaw	T. Clayton
1907	Mountain King	J. Burton	F. Picking
1908	Alawa	J. Scobie	R. Lewis
1909	Prince Foote	F. McGrath	D. McCarthy
1910	Beverage	W. Kelso	J.E. Pike
1911	Wilari	J. Wilson	G. Lambert
1912	Wolawa	J. Scobie	R. Lewis
1913	Beragoon	Owner	J.E. Pike
1914	Carlita	J. Moore	R. Lewis
1915	Patrobas	C. Wheeler	W. Smart
1916	Wolaroi	B. Quinn	A. Wood
1917	Biplane	R. Mason	B. Deeley
1918	Eusebius	C. Wheeler	L. Franklin
1919	Richmond Main	F.J. Marsden	A. Wood
1920	Salitros	F. Williams	M. Connell
1921	Furious	F.J. Marsden	R. Lewis
1922	Whittier	H. McCalman	P. Brown
1923	Fran. Tressady	W. Foulsham	F. Dempsey
1924	Spearfelt	V. O'Neill	G. Young
1925	Manfred	H. McCalman	F. Dempsey
1926	Rampion	F. Williams	S. Cracknell
1927	Trivalve	J. Scobie	R. Lewis

W.S. COX PLATE
Moonee Valley: about 2,050 m (about 1¼ miles).*
Three-year-olds and up. First run: 1922

YEAR	HORSE	TRAINER	JOCKEY
1922	Violoncello	C. Bryans	J. King
1923	Easingwold	J. Holt	G. Harrison
1924	The Night Patrol	J. Scobie	G. Young
1925	Manfred	H. McCalman	F. Dempsey
1926	Heroic	J. Holt	H. Cairns
1927	Amounis	F. McGrath	J. Toohey
1928	Highland	J. Holt	W. Duncan
1929	Nightmarch	A. McAulay	R. Reed
1930	Phar Lap	H. Telford	J. Pike
1931	Phar Lap	H. Telford	J. Pike
1932	Chatham	F. Williams	J. Munro
1933	Rogilla	L. Haigh	D. Munro
1934	Chatham	F. Williams	S. Davidson
1935	Garrio	L. Robertson	K. Voitre
1936	Young Idea	J. Holt	H. Skidmore
1937	Young Idea	J. Holt	D. Munro
1938	Ajax	F. Musgrave	H. Badger
1939	Mosaic	J. Abbs	D. Munro
1940	Beau Vite	F. McGrath	E. McMenamin
1941	Beau Vite	F. McGrath	D. Munro
1942	Tranquil Star	R. Cameron	K. Smith
1943	Amana	R. Shaw	A. Dewhurst
1944	Tranquil Star	R. Cameron	A. Breasley
1945	Flight	F. Nowland	J. O'Sullivan
1946	Flight	F. Nowland	J. O'Sullivan
	and Leonard**	L. Robertson	W. Briscoe
1947	Chanak	J. Holt	H. Badger
1948	Carbon Copy	D. McCormick	H. Badger
1949	Delta	M. McCarten	N. Sellwood

Prize distribution after Rubiton's success in the 1987 W.S. Cox Plate at Moonee Valley in Melbourne.

YEAR	HORSE	TRAINER	JOCKEY		YEAR	HORSE	TRAINER	JOCKEY
1928	Strephon	L. Robertson	J.E. Pike		1965	Tobin Bronze	H. Heagney	N. Mifflin
1929	Phar Lap	H.R. Telford	J.E. Pike		1966	Khalif	D. Judd	R. Higgins
1930	Balloon King	R.D. O'Donnell	J.E. Pike		1967	Savoy	K. Hilton	P. Jarman
1931	Johnnie Jason	C. Unwin	J.E. Pike		1968	Always There	C. Waymouth	G. Lane
1932	Liberal	F. Foulsham	J. Munro		1969	Daryl's Joy	S. Brown	W. Skelton
1933	Hall Mark	J. Holt	D. Munro		1970	Silver Sharpe	T. Smith	P. Hyland
1934	Theo	F. Williams	M. McCarten		1971	Classic Mission	S. Brown	G. Moore
1935	Feldspar	L. Robertson	K. Voitre		1972	Dayana	J.B. Cummings	R. Higgins
1936	Talking	A.G. Papworth	A. Knox		1973	Taj Rossi	J.B. Cummings	R. Higgins
1937	Hua	J. Scobie	R. Wilson		1974	Haymaker	C. Hayes	J. Miller
1938	Nuffield	J. Holt	D. Munro		1975	Galena Boy	J. Hawkes	J. Letts
1939	Reading	J.T. Cush	D. Munro		1976	Unaware	C. Hayes	J. Stocker
1940	Lucrative	H. Freedman	M. McCarten		1977	Stormy Rex	J.B. Cummings	R. Higgins
1941	Skipton	J. Fryer	N. Creighton		1978	Dulcify	C. Hayes	B. Thomson
1942	Great Britain	H. Freedman	W. Cook		1979	Big Print	A. White	P. Jarman
1943	Precept	J. Pengilly	E. Preston		1980	Sovereign Red	G. Murphy	M. Goreham
1944	San Martin	L. Robertson	A. Breasley		1981	Brewery Boy	T. Smith	W. Treloar
1945	Magnificent	A.S. Croall	J. O'Sullivan		1982	Grosvenor	G. Murphy	L. Dittman
1946	Prince Standard	D. Lewis	W. Briscoe		1983	Bounty Hawk	J.B. Cummings	H. White
1947	Beau Gem	G.R. Jesser	D. Munro		1984	Red Anchor	T. Smith	L. Dittman
1948	Comic Court	J.M. Cummings	O. Phillips		1985	Handy Proverb	B. Mayfield-Smith	J. Cassidy
1949	Delta	M. McCarten	N. Sellwood		1986	Raveneaux	J. Moloney	R. Quinton
1950	Alister	H. Wolters	R. Heather		1987	Omnicorp	J.B. Cummings	J. Cassidy
1951	Hydrogen	E. Hush	D. Munro		1988	Kings High	C. Hayes	G. Clark
1952	Advocate	F. Allotta	A. Breasley					
1953	Prince Morvi	E. Fellows	N. Sellwood					
1954	Pride Of Egypt	E. Hush	W. Cook					
1955	Sailor's Guide	G. Daniel	N. Sellwood					
1956	Monte Carlo	F. Dalton	J. Thompson					
1957	Tulloch	T. Smith	G. Moore					
1958	Sir Blink	J. Godby	W. Williamson					
1959	Travel Boy	T. Smith	N. Sellwood					
1960	Sky High	J. Green	N. Sellwood					
1961	New Statesman	B. Courtney	G. Lane					
1962	Coppelius	B. Courtney	G. Lane					
1963	Craftsman	A. White	P. Hyland					
1964	Royal Sovereign	J. Page	R. Selkrig					

YEAR	HORSE	TRAINER	JOCKEY		YEAR	HORSE	TRAINER	JOCKEY
1950	Alister	H. Wolters	J. Purcell		1978	So Called	C. Hayes	B. Thomson
1951	Bronton	R. Sinclair	J. Purtell		1979	Dulcify	C. Hayes	B. Thomson
1952	Hydrogen	E. Hush	D. Munro		1980	Kingston Town	T. Smith	M. Johnston
1953	Hydrogen	E. Hush	W. Williamson		1981	Kingston Town	T. Smith	R. Quinton
1954	Rising Fast	I. Tucker	J. Purtell		1982	Kingston Town	T. Smith	P. Cook
1955	Kingster	J. Green	W. Camer		1983	Strawberry Road	D. Bougoure	L. Dittman
1956	Ray Ribbon	G. Barr	J. Purtell		1984	Red Anchor	T. Smith	L. Dittman
1957	Recraze	T. Smith	G. Moore		1985	Rising Prince	Mrs D. Stein	K. Langby
1958	Yeman	H. Wiggins	L. Whittle		1986	Bonecrusher	F. Ritchie	G. Stewart
1959	Noholme	M. McCarten	N. Sellwood		1987	Rubiton	P. Barns	H. White
1960	Tulloch	T. Smith	N. Sellwood		1988	Our Poetic Prince	J. Wheeler	N. Harris
1961	Dhaulagiri	B. Courtney	G. Lane					
1962	Aquanita	R. Shaw	F. Moore					
1963	Summer Regent	R. Cotter	N. Riordan					
1964	Sir Dane	R. Shaw	R. Higgins					
1965	Star Affair	A. Armanasco	P. Hyland					
1966	Tobin Bronze	H. Heagney	J. Johnson					
1967	Tobin Bronze	H. Heagney	J. Johnson					
1968	Rajah Sahib	T. Hill	G. Moore					
1969	Daryl's Joy	S. Brown	W. Skelton					
1970	Abdul	G. Murphy	P. Jarman					
1971	Tauto	R. Agnew	L. Hill					
1972	Gunsynd	T. Smith	R. Higgins					
1973	Taj Rossi	J.B. Cummings	S. Aitken					
1974	Battle Heights	R. Douglas	G. Willetts					
1975	Fury's Order	L. Gestro & W. McEwan	B. Thomson					
1976	Surround	G. Murphy	P. Cook					
1977	Family Of Man	G. Hanlon	B. Thomson					

* 1950–71: 2,050 m (1¼ miles); 1972–3: 2,000 m.
** 1946: run in two divisions.

Sydney's Randwick track (**above**), where both the AJC Derby and the Sydney Cup are run.

First steps towards establishing Randwick racecourse were taken in 1832 when a site was chosen south of Sydney. It was known as 'The Sandy Course on Old Botany Road'.

AUSTRALIA

AJC SYDNEY CUP

Randwick: 3,200 m (2 miles). *Three-year-olds and up. First run*: 1866

YEAR	HORSE	TRAINER	JOCKEY	YEAR	HORSE	TRAINER	JOCKEY
1866	Yattendon	–	–	1937	Mestoravon	R.L. Cashman	J. Duncan
1867	Fishook	–	–	1938	L'Aiglon	D. Lewis	A. Harvey
1868	The Barb	–	–	1939	Mosaic	J.H. Abbs	E. Bartle
1869	The Barb	–	–	1940	Mosaic	J.H. Abbs	D. Munro
1870	Barbelle	–	–	1941	Lucrative	P.H. Fr'dm'n	M. McCarten
1871	Mermaid	–	–	1942	Veiled Threat	J.M. Mitchell	R. Parsons
1872	The Prophet	–	–	1943	Abspear	E. Hush	D. Munro
1873	Vixen	–	–	1944	Veiled Threat	J.M. Mitchell	D. Munro
1874	Speculation	–	–	1945	Craigie	G. Douch	J. Duncan
1875	Imperial	–	–	1946	Cordale	G. Ray	G. Moore
1876	A.T.	–	–	1947	Proctor	D. Lewis	W. Briscoe
1877	Kingfisher	–	–	1948	Dark Marne	D.L. Burke	J. Thompson
1878	Democrat	–	–	1949	Carbon Copy	D.S. McCormick	A. Breasley
1879	Savanaka	–	–	1950	Sir Falcon	J. Mitchell	J. Thompson
1880	Petrea	–	T. Hales	1951	Bankstream	V. Thompson	N. McGrowdie
1881	Progress	–	T. Hales	1952	Opulent	J. Munro	N. McGrowdie
1882	Cunnamulla	–	S. Cracknell	1953	Carioca	P. Hoysted	W. Cook
1883	Darebin	–	R. O'Connor	1954	Gold Scheme	L. Ellis	N. Sellwood
1884	Favo	–	F. Smith	1955	Talisman	C. Hasler	S. Cassidy
1885	Normanby	–	D. Nicholson	1956	Sailor's Guide	G. Daniel	N. Sellwood
1886	Cerise & Blue	–	B. Colley	1957	Electro	J. Haigh	D. Weir
1887	Frisco	–	R. Argall	1958	Straight Draw	J. Mitchell	N. McGrowdie
1888	The Australian Peer	–	E. Power	1959	On Line	F. McGrath	B. Howlett
1889	Carbine	W.S. Hickenbotham	M. O'Brien	1960	Grand Garry	T. Smith	N. Sellwood
1890	Carbine	W.S. Hickenbotham	M. O'Brien	1961	Sharply	W. Elliott	B. Howlett
1891	Highborn	W. Forrester	J. Gough	1962	Grand Print	J. Besanko	R. Higgins
1892	Stromboli		E. Huxley	1963	Maidenhead	K. Cantrell	W. Smith
1893	Realm	–	E. Hodson	1964	Zinga Lee	W. McNabb	R. Royle
1894	Lady Trenton	–	W. Delaney	1965	River Seine	N. Prendergast	G. Podmore
1895	Patroness	–	H. Cook	1966	Prince Grant	T. Smith	G. Moore
1896	Wallace	–	Jas. Gough	1967	Galilee	J.B. Cummings	J. Miller
1897	Tricolor	–	J. McCurley	1968	General Command	W. Wilson	G. Moore
1898	Merloolas	–	W.H. Smith	1969	Lowland	J.B. Cummings	R. Higgins
1899	Diffidence	–	E. Turner	1970	Arctic Symbol	J. Moloney	N. Voigt
1900	La Carabine	–	W. Burn	1971	Gallic Temple	A. Ward	P. Cook
1901	San Fran	–	A. Richardson	1972	Dark Suit	G. Hanlon	J. Duggan
1902	Wakeful	–	F. Dunn	1973	Apollo Eleven	M. Anderson	B. Andrews
1903	Street Arab	–	F. Hickey	1974	Battle Heights	R. Douglas	G. Willetts
1904	Lord Cardigan	–	J. Barden	1975	Gay Master	T. Hughes	A. Trevena
1905	Tartan	–	J. Rodgers	1976	Oopik	D. O'Sullivan	R. Lang
1906	Noreen	–	D. Callinan	1977	Reckless	T. Woodcock	P. Trotter
1907	Realm	W.S. Cox	C. Cooper	1978	My Good Man	R. Verner	D. Peake
1908	Dyed Garments	–	G. Ross	1979	Double Century	R. McDonell	R. Mallyon
1909	Trafalgar	–	W.H. Smith	1980	Kingston Town	T. Smith	M. Johnston
1910	Vavasor	–	W. McLachlan	1981	Our Paddy Boy	C. Hayes	R. Mallyon
1911	Moorilla	–	F. Hood	1982	Azawary	A. Jones	N. Tiley
1912	Saxonite	–	G. Lambert	1983	Veloso	M. Barnes	P. Cook
1913	Cadonia	–	J. McDonald	1984	Trissaro	J.B. Cummings	J. Marshall
1914	Lilyveil	–	W. McLachlan	1985	Late Show	B. Mayfield-Smith	N. Campton
1915	Scotch Artillery	–	F. Hood	1986	Marooned	B. Mayfield-Smith	J. Cassidy
1916	Pr. Bardolph	–	G. Meddick	1987	Major Drive	J. Meagher	G. Hall
1917	The Fortune Hunter	–	A. Wood	1988	Banderol	D. O'Sullivan	P. Cook
1918	Rebus	–	A.O. Davies				
1919	Ian d'Or	–	T.F. McNamara				
1920	Kennaquhair	–	A. Wood				
1921	Eurythmic	J. Holt	F. Dempsey				
1922	Pr. Charles	S.R. Lamond	J. Munro				
1923	David	W. Booth	A. Wood				
1924	Scarlet	–	J. Crowe				
1925	Lilypond	–	W. Duncan				
1926	Murray King	G. Price	S. McNamara				
1927	Piastoon	E. Fisher	S. Davidson				
1928	Winalot	J.W. Cook	J. Toohey				
1929	Crucis	D. Lewis	W. Cook				
1930	Gwillian G.	W.A. Ross	J. Simpson				
1931	The Dimmer	C.P. Barden	E. Bartle				
1932	Johnnie Jason	C. Unwin	R. Wilson				
1933	Rogilla	L. Haigh	G. Robinson				
1934	Broad Arrow	W. McGee	E. Britt				
1935	Akuna	D. Lewis	H. Hanley				
1936	Contact	D. Lewis	M. McCarten				

CANADA

QUEEN'S PLATE

Woodbine: 1¼ miles (2,000 m). *Three-year-olds. First run*: 1860

YEAR	HORSE	TRAINER	JOCKEY	YEAR	HORSE	TRAINER	JOCKEY
1860	Don Juan	–	–	1897	Ferdinand	–	Lewis
1861	Wild Irishman	–	–	1898	Bon Ino	–	R. Williams
1862	Palermo	–	–	1899	Butter Scotch	–	Mason
1863	Touchstone	–	–	1900	Dalmoor	–	Lewis
1864	Brunette	–	–	1901	John Ruskin	–	Vititoe
1865	Lady Norfolk	–	–	1902	Lyddite	–	Wainwright
1866	Beacon	–	–	1903	Thessalon	–	Castro
1867	Wild Rose	–	–	1904	Sapper	–	J. Walsh
1868	Nettie	–	–	1905	Inferno	–	H. Phillips
1869	Bay Jack	–	–	1906	Slaughter	–	Trebel
1870	John Bell	–	–	1907	Kelvin	–	Foley
1871	Floss	–	–	1908	Seismic	–	Fairbrother
1872	Fearnaught	–	–	1909	Shimonese	–	Gilbert
1873	Mignonette	–	–	1910	Parmer	–	J. Wilson
1874	Swallow	–	–	1911	St. Bass	–	E. Dugan
1875	Trumpeter	–	–	1912	Heresy	–	Small
1876	Norah P.	–	–	1913	Hearts Of Oak	–	J. Wilson
1877	Amelia	–	–	1914	Beehive	–	G. Burns
1878	King George	–	–	1915	Tartarean	–	H. Watts
1879	Moss Ross	–	–	1916	Mandarin	–	A. Pickens
1880	Bonnie Bird	–	Leary	1917	Belle Mahone	–	F. Robinson
1881	Vice Chancellor	–	Brown	1918	Springside	–	L. Mink
1882	Fanny Wiser	–	A.E. Gates	1919	Ladder Of Light	–	L. Lyke
1883	Rhody Pringle	–	Smith	1920	St. Paul	–	R. Romanelli
1884	Williams	–	Martin	1921	Herendesy	–	J. Butwell
1885	Willie W.	–	Jamieson	1922	South Shore	–	K. Parrington
1886	Wild Rose	–	C. Butler	1923	Flowerful	–	T. Wilson
1887	Bonnie Duke	–	Wise	1924	Maternal Pride	–	G. Walls
1888	Henry Cooper	–	C.O'Leary	1925	Fairbank	–	C. Lang
1889	Colonist	–	R. O'Leary	1926	Haplite	–	H. Erickson
1890	Kite String	–	Coleman	1927	Troutlet	–	F. Horn
1891	Victorious	–	Gorman	1928	Young Kitty	–	L. Pichon
1892	O'Donohue	–	Horton	1929	Shorelint	–	J.D. Mooney
1893	Martello	–	Blaylock	1930	Aymond	–	H. Little
1894	Joe Miller	–	Booker	1931	Froth Blower	–	F. Mann
1895	Bonniefield	–	Booker	1932	Queensway	–	F. Mann
1896	Millbrook	–	Lewis	1933	King O'Connor	–	E. Legere

All Along, from France, is in good hands as Britain's Walter Swinburn steers her to victory in Canada's 1983 Rothmans International.

YEAR	HORSE	TRAINER	JOCKEY
1934	Horometer	–	F. Mann
1935	Sally Fuller	–	H. Lindberg
1936	Monsweep	–	D. Brammer
1937	Goldlure	–	S. Young
1938	Bunty Lawless	–	J.W. Bailey
1939	Archworth	–	S.D. Birley
1940	Willie The Kid	–	R. Nash
1941	Budpath	–	R. Watson
1942	Ten To Ace	–	C.W. Smith
1943	Paolita	–	P. Remillard
1944	Acara	–	R. Watson
1945	Uttermost	–	R. Watson
1946	Kingarvie	–	J. Dewhurst
1947	Moldy	–	C. McDonald
1948	Last Mark	–	H.R. Bailey
1949	Epic	–	C. Rogers
1950	McGill	P. Keiser	C. Rogers
1951	Major Factor	G. McCann	A. Bavington
1952	Epigram	S. Bowden	G. Robillard
1953	Canadiana	G. McCann	E. Acaro
1954	Collisteo	R. Townrow	C. Rogers
1955	Ace Marine	J. Starr	G. Walker
1956	Canadian Champ	J. Passero	D. Stevenson
1957	Lyford Cay	G. McCann	A. Gomez
1958	Caledon Beau	J. Starr	A. Coy
1959	New Providence	G. McCann	R. Ussery
1960	Victoria Park	H. Luro	A. Gomez
1961	Blue Light	P. McMurray	H. Dittfach
1962	Flaming Page	H. Luro	J. Fitzsimmons
1963	Canebora	G. McCann	M. Ycaza
1964	Northern Dancer	H. Luro	W. Hartack
1965	Whistling Sea	R. Johnson	I. Inouye
1966	Titled Hero	P. MacMurchy	A. Gomez
1967	Jammed Lovely	J. Starr	J. Fitzsimmons
1968	Merger	R. Johnson Houghton	W. Harris
1969	Jumpin Joseph	R. Bateman	A. Gomez

YEAR	HORSE	TRAINER	JOCKEY
1970	Almoner	J. Lavigne	S. Hawley
1971	Kennedy Road	J. Bentley	S. Hawley
1972	Victoria Song	L. Grant	R. Platts
1973	Royal Chocolate	G. Rowntree	T. Colangelo
1974	Amber Herod	G. Rowntree	R. Platts
1975	L'Enjoleur	J. Starr	S. Hawley
1976	Norcliffe	R. Attfield	J. Fell
1977	Sound Reason	G. Rowntree	R. Platts
1978	Regal Embrace	M. Benson	S. Hawley
1979	Steady Growth	J. Tammaro	B. Swatuk
1980	Driving Home	G. Magnusson	W. Parsons
1981	Fiddle Dancer Boy	J. Bentley	D. Clark
1982	Son Of Briartic	J. Lavigne	P. Souter
1983	Bompago	J. Cardella	L. Attard
1984	Key To The Moon	G. Rowntree	R. Platts
1985	La Lorgnette	M. Benson	D. Clark
1986	Golden Choice	M. Tammaro	V. Bracciale
1987	Market Control	R. Attfield	K. Skinner
1988	Regal Intention	J. Day	D. Penna

Note: The records for the years up to 1880 are incomplete, only the names of winners being available. The names of trainers are available from 1950 only.

ROTHMANS INTERNATIONAL
Woodbine: 1 mile 5 f (2,600 m). *Three-year-olds and up. First run*: **1938**

YEAR	HORSE	TRAINER	JOCKEY
1938	Bunty Lawless	–	A. Almers
1939	Sir Marlboro	–	C. McTague
1940	Cerise III	–	H. Meynell
1941	Bunty Lawless	–	T. Almers
1942	Shepperton	–	R. Watson
1943	Shepperton	–	R. Watson
1944	Be Brief	–	R. Watson
1945	Tulachmore	–	P. Remillard
1946	Kingarvie	–	J. Dewhurst
1947	Brown Hostess	–	L. Stroud
1948	Canada's Teddy	–	D. Prater
1949	Arise	–	D. Dodson
1950	Nephisto	A. Brent	P. Remillard
1951	Bull Page	G. McCann	J. Vina
1952	Beau Dandy	R. Anderson	D. Kennedy
1953	Navy Page	C. Shaw	N. Shuk
1954	Resilient	H. Williams	B. Green
1955	Park Dandy	P. Brady	R. Ussery
1956	Eugenia II	H. Luro	J. Sanchez
1957	Spinney	R. Cornell	J. Sanchez
1958	Jack Ketch	H. Trotsek	J. Sellers
1959	Martini II	H. Trotsek	C. Clark
1960	Rocky Royal	P. Kelley	J. Adams
1961	Our Jeep	O. Dubasoff	S. Boulmetis
1962	El Bandido	J. Pierce	R. Broussard
1963	The Axe II	R. Wheeler	J. Rotz
1964	Will I Rule	J. Nash	R. Turcotte
1965	George Royal	D. Richardson	J. Longden
1966	George Royal	D. Richardson	I. Valenzuela
1967	He's A Smoothie	W. Beasley	S. McComb

YEAR	HORSE	TRAINER	JOCKEY
1968	Frenetico	L. Cavalris	R. Platts
1969	Vent Du Nord	A. Scotti	R. Turcotte
1970	Drumtop	R. Laurin	C. Baltazar
1971	One For All	H. Luro	T. Turcotte
1972	Droll Role	T. Kelly	B. Baeza
1973	Secretariat	L. Laurin	E. Maple
1974	Dahlia	M. Zilber	L. Piggott
1975	Snow Knight	M. Miller	J. Velasquez
1976	Youth	M. Zilber	S. Hawley
1977	Exceller	M. Zilber	A. Cordero
1978	Mac Diarmida	F. Schulhofer	J. Cruguet
1979	Golden Act	L. Rettele	S. Hawley
1980	Great Neck	S. Nerud	M. Venezia
1981	Open Call	J. Gaver	J. Velasquez
1982	Majesty's Prince	J. Cantey	E. Maple
1983	All Along	P. Biancone	W.R. Swinburn
1984	Majesty's Prince	J. Cantey	L. Pincay
1985	Nassipour	S. Di Mauro	J. Samyn
1986	Southjet	A. Penna	J. Santos
1987	River Memories	R. Collet	C. McCarron
1988	Infamy	L. Cumani	R. Cochrane

Note: The names of trainers are available from 1950 only.

ENGLAND

THE DERBY
Epsom, Surrey: 1½ miles (2,400 m). *Three-year-olds*

YEAR	HORSE	TRAINER	JOCKEY	YEAR	HORSE	TRAINER	JOCKEY
1780	Diomed	R. Teasdale	S. Arnull	1852	Daniel O'Rourke	J. Scott	F. Butler
1781	Young Eclipse	—	C. Hindley	1853	West Australian	J. Scott	F. Butler
1782	Assassin	F. Neale	S. Arnull	1854	Andover	J. Day	A. Day
1783	Saltram	F. Neale	C. Hindley	1855	Wild Dayrell	J. Rickaby	R. Sherwood
1784	Serjeant	—	J. Arnull	1856	Ellington	T. Dawson	T. Aldcroft
1785	Aimwell	J. Pratt	C. Hindley	1857	Blink Bonny	W. I'Anson	J. Charlton
1786	Noble	F. Neale	J. White	1858	Beadsman	G. Manning	J. Wells
1787	Sir Peter Teazle	Saunders	S. Arnull	1859	Musjid	G. Manning	J. Wells
1788	Sir Thomas	F. Neale	W. South	1860	Thormanby	M. Dawson	H. Custance
1789	Skyscraper	M. Stephenson	S. Chifney	1861	Kettledrum	G. Oates	R. Bullock
1790	Rhadamanthus	J. Pratt	J. Arnull	1862	Caractacus	R. Smith	J. Parsons
1791	Eager	M. Stephenson	M. Stephenson	1863	Macaroni	J. Godding	T. Chaloner
1792	John Bull	J. Pratt	F. Buckle	1864	Blair Athol	W. I'Anson	J. Snowden
1793	Waxy	R. Robson	W. Clift	1865	Gladiateur	T. Jennings	H. Grimshaw
1794	Daedalus	J. Pratt	F. Buckle	1866	Lord Lyon	J. Dover	H. Custance
1795	Spread Eagle	R. Prince	A. Wheatley	1867	Hermit	G. Bloss	J. Daley
1796	Didelot	R. Prince	J. Arnull	1868	Blue Gown	J. Porter	J. Wells
1797	unnamed by Fidget	M. Stephenson	J. Singleton	1869	Pretender	T. Dawson	J. Osborne
1798	Sir Harry	F. Neale	S. Arnull	1870	Kingcraft	M. Dawson	T. French
1799	Archduke	R. Prince	J. Arnull	1871	Favonius	J. Hayhoe	T. French
1800	Champion	T. Perren	W. Clift	1872	Cremorne	W. Gilbert	C. Maidment
1801	Eleanor	J. Frost	J. Saunders	1873	Doncaster	R. Peck	F. Webb
1802	Tyrant	R. Robson	F. Buckle	1874	George Frederick	T. Leader	H. Custance
1803	Ditto	J. Lonsdale	W. Clift	1875	Galopin	J. Dawson	J. Morris
1804	Hannibal	F. Neale	W. Arnull	1876	Kisber	J. Hayhoe	C. Maidment
1805	Cardinal Beaufort	R. Boyce	D. Fitzpatrick	1877	Silvio	M. Dawson	F. Archer
1806	Paris	R. Prince	J. Shepherd	1878	Sefton	A. Taylor	H. Constable
1807	Election	R. Boyce	J. Arnull	1879	Sir Bevys	J. Hayhoe	G. Fordham
1808	Pan	J. Lonsdale	F. Collinson	1880	Bend Or	R. Peck	F. Archer
1809	Pope	R. Robson	T. Goodisson	1881	Iroquois	J. Pincus	F. Archer
1810	Whalebone	R. Robson	W. Clift	1882	Shotover	J. Porter	T. Cannon
1811	Phantom	J. Edwards	F. Buckle	1883	St Blaise	J. Porter	C. Wood
1812	Octavius	R. Boyce	W. Arnull	1884	St Gatien	R. Sherwood	C. Wood
1813	Smolensko	Crouch	T. Goodisson		*and* Harvester	J. Jewitt	S. Loates
1814	Blucher	R. Boyce	W. Arnull	1885	Melton	M. Dawson	F. Archer
1815	Whisker	R. Robson	T. Goodisson	1886	Ormonde	J. Porter	F. Archer
1816	Prince Leopold	W. Butler	W. Wheatley	1887	Merry Hampton	M. Gurry	J. Watts
1817	Azor	R. Robson	J. Robinson	1888	Ayrshire	G. Dawson	F. Barrett
1818	Sam	T. Perren	S. Chifney	1889	Donovan	G. Dawson	T. Loates
1819	Tiresias	R. Prince	W. Clift	1890	Sainfoin	J. Porter	J. Watts
1820	Sailor	W. Chifney	S. Chifney	1891	Common	J. Porter	G. Barrett
1821	Gustavus	Crouch	S. Day	1892	Sir Hugo	T. Wadlow	F. Allsopp
1822	Moses	W. Butler	T. Goodisson	1893	Isinglass	J. Jewitt	T. Loates
1823	Emilius	R. Robson	F. Buckle	1894	Ladas	M. Dawson	J. Watts
1824	Cedric	J. Edwards	J. Robinson	1895	Sir Visto	M. Dawson	S. Loates
1825	Middleton	J. Edwards	J. Robinson	1896	Persimmon	R. Marsh	J. Watts
1826	Lap-dog	R. Stephenson	G. Dockeray	1897	Galtee More	S. Darling	C. Wood
1827	Mameluke	J. Edwards	J. Robinson	1898	Jeddah	R. Marsh	O. Madden
1828	Cadland	R. Boyce	J. Robinson	1899	Flying Fox	J. Porter	M. Cannon
1829	Frederick	J. Forth	J. Forth	1900	Diamond Jubilee	R. Marsh	H. Jones
1830	Priam	W. Chifney	S. Day	1901	Volodyovski	J. Huggins	L. Reiff
1831	Spaniel	J. Rogers	W. Wheatley	1902	Ard Patrick	S. Darling	J. Martin
1832	St Giles	J. Webb	W. Scott	1903	Rock Sand	G. Blackwell	D. Maher
1833	Dangerous	I. Sadler	J. Chapple	1904	St Amant	A. Hayhoe	K. Cannon
1834	Plenipotentiary	G. Payne	P. Conolly	1905	Cicero	P. Peck	D. Maher
1835	Mundig	J. Scott	W. Scott	1906	Spearmint	P. Gilpin	D. Maher
1836	Bay Middleton	J. Edwards	J. Robinson	1907	Orby	F. MacCabe	J. Reiff
1837	Phosphorus	J. Doe	G. Edwards	1908	Signorinetta	O. Ginistrelli	W. Bullock
1838	Amato	R. Sherwood	J. Chapple	1909	Minoru	R. Marsh	H. Jones
1839	Bloomsbury	W. Ridsdale	S. Templeman	1910	Lemberg	A. Taylor	B. Dillon
1840	Little Wonder	J. Forth	W. Macdonald	1911	Sunstar	C. Morton	G. Stern
1841	Coronation	Painter	P. Connolly	1912	Tagalie	D. Waugh	J. Reiff
1842	Attila	J. Scott	W. Scott	1913	Aboyeur	T. Lewis	E. Piper
1843	Cotherstone	J. Scott	W. Scott	1914	Durbar	T. Murphy	M. MacGee
1844	Orlando	W. Cooper	E. Flatman	1915	Pommern	C. Peck	S. Donoghue
1845	The Merry Monarch	J. Forth	F. Bell	1916	Finfinella	R. Dawson	J. Childs
				1917	Gay Crusader	A. Taylor	S. Donoghue
1846	Pyrrhus The First	J. Day	S. Day	1918	Gainsborough	A. Taylor	J. Childs
1847	Cossack	J. Day	S. Templeman	1919	Grand Parade	F. Barling	F. Templeman
1848	Surplice	J. Kent	S. Templeman	1920	Spion Kop	P. Gilpin	F. O'Neill
1849	The Flying Dutchman	J. Fobert	C. Marlow	1921	Humorist	C. Morton	S. Donoghue
				1922	Captain Cuttle	F. Darling	S. Donoghue
1850	Voltigeur	R. Hill	J. Marson	1923	Papyrus	B. Jarvis	S. Donoghue
1851	Teddington	A. Taylor	J. Marson	1924	Sansovino	G. Lambton	T. Weston

YEAR	HORSE	TRAINER	JOCKEY
1925	Manna	F. Darling	S. Donoghue
1926	Coronach	F. Darling	J. Childs
1927	Call Boy	J. Watts	E. C. Elliott
1928	Felstead	O. Bell	H. Wragg
1929	Trigo	R. Dawson	J. Marshall
1930	Blenheim	R. Dawson	H. Wragg
1931	Cameronian	F. Darling	F. Fox
1932	April the Fifth	T. Walls	F. Lane
1933	Hyperion	G. Lambton	T. Weston
1934	Windsor Lad	M. Marsh	C. Smirke
1935	Bahram	Frank Butters	F. Fox
1936	Mahmoud	Frank Butters	C. Smirke
1937	Mid-day Sun	Fred Butters	M. Beary
1938	Bois Roussel	F. Darling	E. C. Elliott
1939	Blue Peter	J. Jarvis	E. Smith
1940	Pont l'Eveque	F. Darling	S. Wragg
1941	Owen Tudor	F. Darling	W. Nevett
1942	Watling Street	W. Earl	H. Wragg
1943	Straight Deal	W. Nightingall	T. Carey
1944	Ocean Swell	J. Jarvis	W. Nevett
1945	Dante	M. Peacock	W. Nevett
1946	Airborne	R. Perryman	T. Lowrey
1947	Pearl Diver	P. Carter	G. Bridgland
1948	My Love	R. Carver	R. Johnstone
1949	Nimbus	G. Colling	E. C. Elliott
1950	Galcador	C. Semblat	R. Johnstone
1951	Arctic Prince	W. Stephenson	C. Spares
1952	Tulyar	M. Marsh	C. Smirke
1953	Pinza	N. Bertie	Sir G. Richards
1954	Never Say Die	J. Lawson	L. Piggott
1955	Phil Drake	F. Mathet	F. Palmer
1956	Lavandin	A. Head	R. Johnstone
1957	Crepello	N. Murless	L. Piggott
1958	Hard Ridden	J. Rogers	C. Smirke
1959	Parthia	C. Boyd-Rochfort	W.H. Carr
1960	St Paddy	N. Murless	L. Piggott
1961	Psidium	H. Wragg	R. Poincelet
1962	Larkspur	M.V. O'Brien	N. Sellwood
1963	Relko	F. Mathet	Y. Saint-Martin
1964	Santa Claus	J. Rogers	A. Breasley
1965	Sea-Bird	E. Pollet	T.P. Glennon
1966	Charlottown	G. Smyth	A. Breasley
1967	Royal Palace	N. Murless	G. Moore
1968	Sir Ivor	M.V. O'Brien	L. Piggott
1969	Blakeney	A. Budgett	E. Johnson
1970	Nijinsky	M.V. O'Brien	L. Piggott
1971	Mill Reef	I. Balding	G. Lewis
1972	Roberto	M.V. O'Brien	L. Piggott
1973	Morston	A. Budgett	E. Hide
1974	Snow Knight	P. Nelson	B. Taylor
1975	Grundy	P. Walwyn	P. Eddery
1976	Empery	M. Zilber	L. Piggott
1977	The Minstrel	M.V. O'Brien	L. Piggott
1978	Shirley Heights	J. Dunlop	G. Starkey
1979	Troy	W. Hern	W. Carson
1980	Henbit	W. Hern	W. Carson
1981	Shergar	M. Stoute	W.R. Swinburn
1982	Golden Fleece	M.V. O'Brien	P. Eddery
1983	Teenoso	G. Wragg	L. Piggott
1984	Secreto	D.V. O'Brien	C. Roche
1985	Slip Anchor	H. Cecil	S. Cauthen
1986	Shahrastani	M. Stoute	W.R. Swinburn
1987	Reference Point	H. Cecil	S. Cauthen
1988	Kahyasi	L. Cumani	R. Cochrane

CHAMPION STAKES
Newmarket, Suffolk: 1¼ miles (2,000 m).
Three-year-olds and up. First run: 1930

YEAR	HORSE	TRAINER	JOCKEY
1930	Rustom Pasha	R. Dawson	H. Wragg
1931	Goyescas	B. Jarvis	E.C. Elliott
1932	Cameronian	F. Darling	G. Richards
1933	Dastur	F. Butters	M. Beary
	and Chatelaine	F. Templeman	G. Richards
1934	Umidwar	F. Butters	F. Fox
1935	Wychwood Abbot	T. Leader	R. Perryman
1936	Wychwood Abbot	T. Leader	P. Perryman
1937	Flares	C. Boyd-Rochfort	P. Beasley
1938	Rockfel	O. Bell	H. Wragg
1940	Hippius	J. Jarvis	E. Smith
1941	Hippius	J. Jarvis	E. Smith
1942	Big Game	F. Darling	G. Richards
1943	Nasrullah	F. Butters	G. Richards
1944	Hycilla	C. Boyd-Rochfort	W. Nevett
1945	Court Martial	J. Lawson	C. Richards
1946	Honeyway	J. Jarvis	E. Smith
1947	Migoli	F. Butters	G. Richards
1948	Solar Slipper	H. Smyth	E. Smith
1949	Djeddah	C. Semblat	E.C. Elliott
1950	Peter Flower	J. Jarvis	W. Rickaby
1951	Dynamiter	C. Semblat	E.C. Elliott
1952	Dynamiter	J. Glynn	E.C. Elliott
1953	Nearula	C. Elsey	E. Britt
1954	Narrator	H. Cottrill	F. Barlow
1955	Hafiz II	A. Head	R. Poincelet
1956	Hugh Lupus	N. Murless	W. Johnstone
1957	Rose Royale II	A. Head	J. Massard
1958	Bella Paola	F. Mathet	G. Lequeux
1959	Petite Etoile	N. Murless	L. Piggott
1960	Marguerite Vernaut	U. Penco	E. Camici
1961	Bobar II	R. Corme	M. Garcia
1962	Arctic Storm	J. Oxx	W. Williamson
1963	Hula Dancer	E. Pollet	J. Deforge
1964	Baldric II	E. Fellows	W. Pyers
1965	Silly Season	I. Balding	G. Lewis
1966	Pieces of Eight	M.V. O'Brien	L. Piggott
1967	Reform	Sir G. Richards	A. Breasley
1968	Sir Ivor	M.V. O'Brien	L. Piggott
1969	Flossy	F. Boutin	J. Deforge
1970	Lorenzaccio	N. Murless	G. Lewis
1971	Brigadier Gerard	W. Hern	J. Mercer
1972	Brigadier Gerard	W. Hern	J. Mercer
1973	Hurry Harriet	P. Mullins	J. Cruguet
1974	Giacometti	H. Price	L. Piggott
1975	Rose Bowl	R. Johnson-Houghton	W. Carson
1976	Vitiges	P. Walwyn	P. Eddery
1977	Flying Water	A. Penna	Y. Saint-Martin
1978	Swiss Maid	P. Kelleway	G. Starkey
1979	Northern Baby	F. Boutin	P. Paquet
1980	Cairn Rouge	M. Cunningham	A. Murray
1981	Vayrann	F. Mathet	Y. Saint-Martin
1982	Time Charter	H. Candy	W. Newnes
1983	Cormorant Wood	B. Hills	S. Cauthen
1984	Palace Music	P. Biancone	Y. Saint-Martin
1985	Pebbles	C. Brittain	P. Eddery
1986	Triptych	P. Biancone	A. Cruz
1987	Triptych	P. Biancone	A. Cruz
1988	Indian Skimmer	H. Cecil	M. Roberts

ENGLAND

GRAND NATIONAL
Aintree, Liverpool: 4½ miles (7,200 m). *First run*: 1837

YEAR	HORSE	HANDICAP	TRAINER	JOCKEY	YEAR	HORSE	HANDICAP	TRAINER	JOCKEY
1839	Lottery	9–12–0	G. Dockeray	J. Mason	1877	Austerlitz	5–10–8	R. l'Anson	Mr F. Hobson
1840	Jerry	10–12–0	–	Mr B. Bretherton	1878	Shifnal	9–10–12	J. Nightingall	J. Jones
1841	Charity	11–12–0	–	H.N. Powell	1879	The Liberator	10–11–4	J. Moore	Mr G. Moore
1842	Gaylad	8–12–0	–	T. Oliver	1880	Empress	5–10–7	H. Linde	Mr T. Beasley
1843	Vanguard	8–11–10	–	T. Oliver	1881	Woodbrook	7–11–3	H. Linde	Mr T. Beasley
1844	Discount	6–10–12	–	H. Crickmere	1882	Seaman	6–11–6	J. Jewitt	Lord Manners
1845	Cure-all	a–11–5	–	Mr W. Loft	1883	Zoëdone	6–11–0	W.H.P. Jenkins	Graf K. Kinsky
1846	Pioneer	6–11–12	–	W. Taylor	1884	Voluptuary	6–10–5	W. Wilson	Mr E.P. Wilson
1847	Mathew	9–10–6	J. Courtenay	D. Wynne	1885	Roquefort	6–11–0	A. Yates	Mr E.P. Wilson
1848	Chandler	12–11–12	–	Mr J. Little	1886	Old Joe	7–10–9	G. Mulcaster	T. Skelton
1849	Peter Simple	11–11–0	T. Cunningham	T. Cunningham	1887	Gamecock	8–11–0	Jordan	W. Daniels
1850	Abd-el-Kader	8–9–12	–	Mr C. Green	1888	Playfair	7–10–7	T. Cannon	G. Mawson
1851	Abd-el-Kader	9–10–4	–	T. Abbott	1889	Frigate	11–11–4	M. Maher	Mr T. Beasley
1852	Miss Mowbray	8–10–4	G. Dockeray	Mr A. Goodman	1890	Ilex	6–10–5	J. Nightingall	A. Nightingall
1853	Peter Simple	15–10–10	T. Oliver	T. Oliver	1891	Come Away	7–11–12	H. Beasley	Mr H. Beasley
1854	Bourton	a–11–12	H. Wadlow	Tasker	1892	Father O'Flynn	7–10–5	–	Capt R. Owen
1855	Wanderer	10–9–8	–	J. Hanlon	1893	Cloister	9–12–7	A. Yates	W. Dollery
1856	Freetrader	7–9–6	W. Holman	G. Stevens	1894	Why Not	13–11–13	W. Moore	A. Nightingall
1857	Emigrant	a–9–10	C. Boyce	C. Boyce	1895	Wild Man from Borneo	7–10–11	J. Gatland	Mr J. Widger
1858	Little Charley	10–10–7	W. Holman	W. Archer	1896	The Soarer	7–9–13	W. Moore	Mr D. Campbell
1859	Half Caste	6–9–7	C. Green	C. Green	1897	Manifesto	9–11–3	W. McAuliffe	T. Kavanagh
1860	Anatis	10–9–10	W. Holman	Mr T. Pickernell	1898	Drogheda	6–10–12	R.C. Dawson	J. Gourley
1861	Jealousy	7–9–12	C. Balchin	J. Kendall	1899	Manifesto	11–12–7	W. Moore	G. Williamson
1862	Huntsman	9–11–0	H. Lamplugh	H. Lamplugh	1900	Ambush	6–11–3	J. Hunter	A. Anthony
1863	Emblem	7–10–10	E. Weever	G. Stevens	1901	Grudon	11–10–0	B. Bletsoe	A. Nightingall
1864	Emblematic	6–10–6	E. Weever	G. Stevens	1902	Shannon Lass	7–10–1	J. Hackett	D. Read
1865	Alcibiade	5–11–4	Cornell	Capt H. Coventry	1903	Drumcree	9–11–3	Sir C. Nugent	P. Woodland
1866	Salamander	7–10–7	J. Walters	Mr A. Goodman	1904	Moifaa	8–10–7	W. Hickey	A. Birch
1867	Cortolvin	8–11–13	H. Lamplugh	J. Page	1905	Kirkland	9–11–5	E. Thomas	F. Mason
1868	The Lamb	6–10–7	B. Land	Mr G. Ede	1906	Ascetic's Silver	9–10–9	A. Hastings	Mr A. Hastings
1869	The Colonel	6–10–7	R. Roberts	G. Stevens	1907	Eremon	7–10–1	T. Coulthwaite	A. Newey
1870	The Colonel	7–11–12	R. Roberts	G. Stevens	1908	Rubio	10–10–5	F. Withington	H. Bletsoe
1871	The Lamb	9–11–5	C. Green	Mr T. Pickernell	1909	Lutteur	5–10–11	H. Escott	G. Parfrement
1872	Casse Tête	7–10–0	Cowley	J. Page	1910	Jenkinstown	9–10–5	T. Coulthwaite	R. Chadwick
1873	Disturbance	6–11–11	J.M. Richardson	Mr J.M. Richardson	1911	Glenside	9–10–3	R. Collis	Mr J. Anthony
1874	Reugny	6–10–12	J.M. Richardson	Mr J.M. Richardson	1912	Jerry M.	9–12–7	R. Gore	E. Piggott
					1913	Covertcoat	7–11–6	R. Gore	P. Woodland
1875	Pathfinder	8–10–11	W. Reeves	Mr T. Pickernell	1914	Sunloch	8–9–7	T. Tyler	W. Smith
1876	Regal	5–11–3	J. Cannon	J. Cannon	1915	Ally Sloper	6–10–6	A. Hastings	Mr J. Anthony

KING GEORGE VI CHASE
Kempton Park, Middlesex: 3 miles (4,800 m). *First run*: 1947

YEAR	HORSE	HANDICAP	TRAINER	JOCKEY	YEAR	HORSE	HANDICAP	TRAINER	JOCKEY
1950	Manicou	5–11–8	P. Cazalet	B. Marshall	1976	Royal Marshal II	9–11–7	T. Forster	G. Thorner
1951	Statecraft	6–11–11	P. Cazalet	A. Grantham	1977	Bachelor's Hall	7–11–7	P. Cundell	M. O'Halloran
1952	Halloween	7–11–13	W. Wightman	F. Winter	1978	Gay Spartan	7–11–10	A. Dickinson	T. Carmody
1953	Galloway Braes	8–12–6	A. Kilpatrick	R. Morrow	1979	Silver Buck	7–11–10	A. Dickinson	T. Carmody
1954	Halloween	9–11–10	W. Wightman	F. Winter	1980	Silver Buck	8–11–10	M. Dickinson	T. Carmody
1955	Limber Hill	8–11–13	W. Dutton	A. Power	1981	abandoned			
1956	Rose Park	10–11–7	P. Cazalet	M. Scudamore	1982	Wayward Lad	7–11–10	M. Dickinson	J. Francome
1957	Mandarin	6–12–0	F. Walwyn	P. Madden	1983	Wayward Lad	8–11–10	M. Dickinson	R. Earnshaw
1958	Lochroe	10–11–7	P. Cazalet	A. Freeman	1984	Burrough Hill Lad	8–11–10	Mrs J. Pitman	J. Francome
1959	Mandarin	8–11–5	F. Walwyn	P. Madden	1985	Wayward Lad	10–11–10	Mrs M. Dickinson	G. Bradley
1960	Saffron Tartan	9–11–7	D. Butchers	F. Winter					
1961	abandoned				1986	Desert Orchid	8–11–10	D. Elsworth	S. Sherwood
1962	abandoned				1987	Nupsala	8–11–10	F. Doumen	A. Pommier
1963	Mill House	6–12–0	F. Walwyn	G. Robinson	1988	Desert Orchid	–	D.Elsworth	S. Sherwood
1964	Frenchman's Cove	9–11–7	H.T. Jones	S. Mellor					
1965	Arkle	8–12–0	T. Dreaper	P. Taafe					
1966	Dormant	9–11–0	J. Wells-Kendrew	J. King					
1967	abandoned								
1968	abandoned								
1969	Titus Oates	7–11–10	G. Richards	S. Mellor					
1970	abandoned								
1971	The Dikler	8–11–7	F. Walwyn	B. Brogan					
1972	Pendil	7–12–0	F. Winter	R. Pitman					
1973	Pendil	8–12–0	F. Winter	R. Pitman					
1974	Captain Christy	7–12–0	P. Taafe	R. Coonan					
1975	Captain Christy	8–12–0	P. Taafe	G. Newman					

YEAR	HORSE	HANDICAP	TRAINER	JOCKEY	YEAR	HORSE	HANDICAP	TRAINER	JOCKEY
1916	Vermouth	6–11–10	J. Bell	J. Reardon	1960	Merryman	9–10–12	N. Crump	G. Scott
1917	Ballymacad	10–9–12	A. Hastings	E. Driscoll	1961	Nicolaus Silver	9–10–1	F. Rimell	H. Beasley
1918	Poethlyn	8–11–6	H. Escott	E. Piggott	1962	Kilmore	12–10–4	H. Price	F. Winter
1919	Poethlyn	9–12–7	H. Escott	E. Piggott	1963	Ayala	9–10–0	K. Piggott	P. Buckley
1920	Troytown	7–11–9	A. Anthony	Mr J. Anthony	1964	Team Spirit	12–10–3	F. Walwyn	G. Robinson
1921	Shaun Spadah	10–11–7	G. Poole	F.B. Rees	1965	Jay Trump	8–11–5	F. Winter	Mr C. Smith
1922	Music Hall	9–11–8	O. Anthony	L.B. Rees	1966	Anglo	8–10–0	F. Winter	T. Norman
1923	Sergeant Murphy	13–11–3	G. Blackwell	Capt G. Bennet	1967	Foinavon	9–10–0	J. Kempton	J. Buckingham
1924	Master Robert	11–10–5	A. Hastings	R. Trudgill	1968	Red Alligator	9–10–0	D. Smith	B. Fletcher
1925	Double Chance	9–10–9	F. Archer	Maj J. Wilson	1969	Highland Wedding	12–10–4	G. Balding	E.P. Harty
1926	Jack Horner	9–10–5	H. Leader	W. Watkinson	1970	Gay Trip	8–11–5	F. Rimell	P. Taafe
1927	Sprig	10–12–4	T.R. Leader	T.E. Leader	1971	Specify	9–10–13	J. Sutcliffe	J. Cook
1928	Tipperary Tim	10–10–0	J. Dodd	Mr W. Dutton	1972	Well To Do	9–10–1	T. Forster	G. Thorner
1929	Gregalach	7–11–4	T.R. Leader	R. Everett	1973	Red Rum	8–10–5	D. McCain	B. Fletcher
1930	Shaun Goilin	10–11–7	F. Hartigan	T. Cullinan	1974	Red Rum	9–12–0	D. McCain	B. Fletcher
1931	Grakle	9–11–7	T. Coulthwaite	R. Lyall	1975	L'Escargot	12–11–3	D. Moore	T. Carberry
1932	Forbra	7–10–7	T.R. Rimell	J.H. Hamey	1976	Rag Trade	10–10–12	F. Rimell	J. Burke
1933	Kellsboro' Jack	7–11–9	I Anthony	D. Williams	1977	Red Rum	12–11–8	D. McCain	T. Stack
1934	Golden Miller	7–12–2	A.B. Briscoe	G. Wilson	1978	Lucius	9–10–9	G. Richards	B.R. Davies
1935	Reynoldstown	8–11–4	N. Furlong	Mr F. Furlong	1979	Rubstic	10–10–0	J. Leadbetter	M. Barnes
1936	Reynoldstown	9–12–2	N. Furlong	Mr F. Walwyn	1980	Ben Nevis	12–10–12	T. Forster	Mr C. Fenwick
1937	Royal Mail	8–11–13	I. Anthony	E. Williams	1981	Aldaniti	11–10–13	J. Gifford	R. Champion
1938	Battleship	11–11–6	R. Hobbs	B. Hobbs	1982	Grittar	9–11–5	F. Gilman	Mr C. Saunders
1939	Workman	9–10–6	J. Ruttle	T. Hyde	1983	Corbiere	8–11–4	Mrs J. Pitman	B. de Haan
1940	Bogskar	7–10–4	Lord Stalbridge	M. Jones	1984	Hallo Dandy	10–10–2	G. Richards	N. Doughty
1941–1945 no race					1985	Last Suspect	11–10–5	T. Forster	H. Davies
1946	Lovely Cottage	9–10–8	T. Rayson	Capt R. Petre	1986	West Tip	9–10–11	M. Oliver	R. Dunwoody
1947	Caughoo	8–10–0	H. McDowell	E. Dempsey	1987	Maori Venture	11–10–13	A. Turnell	S.C. Knight
1948	Sheila's Cottage	9–10–7	N. Crump	A.P. Thompson	1988	Rhyme 'N' Reason	9–11–0	D. Elsworth	B. Powell
1949	Russian Hero	9–10–8	G.R. Owen	L. McMorrow					
1950	Freebooter	9–11–11	R. Renton	J. Power					
1951	Nickel Coin	9–10–1	J. O'Donoghue	J. Bullock					
1952	Teal	10–10–12	N. Crump	A. Thompson					
1953	Early Mist	8–11–2	M.V. O'Brien	B. Marshall					
1954	Royal Tan	10–11–7	M.V. O'Brien	B. Marshall					
1955	Quare Times	9–11–0	M.V. O'Brien	P. Taafe					
1956	E.S.B.	10–11–3	F. Rimell	D. Dick					
1957	Sundew	11–11–7	F. Hudson	F. Winter					
1958	Mr What	8–10–6	T. Taafe	A. Freeman					
1959	Oxo	8–10–13	W. Stephenson	M. Scudamore					

Note: 'a' indicates a horse over six years in age.
'Mr' denotes an amateur jockey.

KING GEORGE VI AND QUEEN ELIZABETH DIAMOND STAKES
Ascot, Berkshire: 1½ miles (2,400 m). *Three-year-olds and up*

YEAR	HORSE	TRAINER	JOCKEY	YEAR	HORSE	TRAINER	JOCKEY
1951	Supreme Court	E. Williams	E.C. Elliott	1976	Pawneese	A. Penna	Y. Saint-Martin
1952	Tulyar	M. Marsh	C. Smirke	1977	The Minstrel	M.V. O'Brien	L. Piggott
1953	Pinza	N. Bertie	Sir G. Richards	1978	Ile De Bourbon	R. Johnson Houghton	J. Reid
1954	Aureole	C. Boyd-Rochfort	E. Smith	1979	Troy	W. Hern	W. Carson
1955	Vimy	A. Head	R. Poincelet	1980	Ela-Mana-Mou	W. Hern	W. Carson
1956	Ribot	U. Penco	E. Camici	1981	Shergar	M. Stoute	W.R. Swinburn
1957	Montaval	G. Bridgland	F. Palmer	1982	Kalaglow	G. Harwood	G. Starkey
1958	Ballymoss	M.V. O'Brien	A. Breasley	1983	Time Charter	H. Candy	J. Mercer
1959	Alcide	C. Boyd-Rochfort	W.H. Carr	1984	Teenoso	G. Wragg	L. Piggott
				1985	Petoski	W. Hern	W. Carson
1960	Aggressor	J. Gosden	J. Lindley	1986	Dancing Brave	G. Harwood	P. Eddery
1961	Right Royal	E. Pollet	R. Poincelet	1987	Reference Point	H. Cecil	S. Cauthen
1962	Match	F. Mathet	Y. Saint-Martin	1988	Mtoto	A. Stewart	M. Roberts
1963	Ragusa	P.J. Prendergast	G. Bougoure				
1964	Nasram	E. Fellows	W. Pyers				
1965	Meadow Court	P.J. Prendergast	L. Piggott				
1966	Aunt Edith	N. Murless	L. Piggott				
1967	Busted	N. Murless	G. Moore				
1968	Royal Palace	N. Murless	A. Barclay				
1969	Park Top	B. van Cutsem	L. Piggott				
1970	Nijinsky	M.V.O'Brien	L. Piggott				
1971	Mill Reef	I. Balding	G. Lewis				
1972	Brigadier Gerard	W. Hern	J. Mercer				
1973	Dahlia	M. Zilber	W. Pyers				
1974	Dahlia	M. Zilber	L. Piggott				
1975	Grundy	P. Walwyn	P. Eddery				

ENGLAND

CHELTENHAM GOLD CUP
Cheltenham, Gloucestershire: 3¼ miles (5,200 m). *First run*: 1924

YEAR	HORSE	AGE	TRAINER	JOCKEY	YEAR	HORSE	AGE	TRAINER	JOCKEY
1924	Red Splash	5	F.E. Withington	F.B. Rees	1943	no race			
1925	Ballinode	9	F. Morgan	T.E. Leader	1944	no race			
1926	Koko	8	A. Bickley	J.H. Hamey	1945	Red Rower	11	Lord Stalbridge	D.L. Jones
1927	Thrown In	11	O. Anthony	Mr H. Grosvenor*	1946	Prince Regent	11	T. Dreaper	T. Hyde
1928	Patron Saint	5	H.S. Harrison	F.B. Rees	1947	Fortina	6	H. Christie	Mr R. Black*
1929	Easter Hero	9	J. Anthony	F.B. Rees	1948	Cottage Rake	9	M.V. O'Brien	A. Brabazon
1930	Easter Hero	10	J. Anthony	T. Cullinan	1949	Cottage Rake	10	M.V. O'Brien	A. Brabazon
1931	no race				1950	Cottage Rake	11	M.V. O'Brien	A. Brabazon
1932	Golden Miller	5	A.B. Briscoe	T.E. Leader	1951	Silver Fame	12	G. Beeb	M. Molony
1933	Golden Miller	6	A.B. Briscoe	W. Stott	1952	Mont Tremblant	6	F. Walwyn	D. Dick
1934	Golden Miller	7	A.B. Briscoe	G. Wilson	1953	Knock Hard	9	M.V. O'Brien	T. Molony
1935	Golden Miller	8	A.B. Briscoe	G. Wilson	1954	Four Ten	8	J. Roberts	J. Cusack
1936	Golden Miller	9	O. Anthony	E. Williams	1955	Gay Donald	9	J. Ford	A. Grantham
1937	no race				1956	Limber Hill	9	W. Dutton	J. Power
1938	Morse Code	9	I. Anthony	D. Morgan	1957	Linwell	9	I. Herbert	M. Scudamore
1939	Brendan's Cottage	9	G. Beeby	G.R. Owen	1958	Kerstin	8	C. Bewicke	S. Hayhurst
1940	Roman Hackle	7	O. Anthony	E. Williams	1959	Roddy Owen	10	D. Morgan	H. Beasley
1941	Poet Prince	9	I. Anthony	R. Burford	1960	Pas Seul	7	R. Turnell	W. Rees
1942	Médoc	8	R. Hobbs	H. Nicholson	1961	Saffron Tartan	10	D. Butchers	F. Winter

1,000 GUINEAS
Newmarket, Suffolk: 1 mile (1,600 m). *Three-year-old fillies*

YEAR	HORSE	TRAINER	JOCKEY	YEAR	HORSE	TRAINER	JOCKEY
1814	Charlotte	T. Perren	W. Clift	1861	Nemesis	W. Harlock	G. Fordham
1815	unnamed by Selim	R. Prince	W. Clift	1862	Hurricane	J. Scott	T. Ashmall
1816	Rhoda	R. Boyce	S. Barnard	1863	Lady Augusta	J. Dawson	A. Edwards
1817	Neva	R. Boyce	W. Arnull	1864	Tomato	J. Hayhoe	J. Wells
1818	Corinne	R. Robson	F. Buckle	1865	Siberia	J. Day	G. Fordham
1819	Catgut	R. Robson	–	1866	Repulse	J. Day	T. Cannon
1820	Rowena	R. Robson	F. Buckle	1867	Achievement	J. Dover	H. Custance
1821	Zeal	R. Robson	F. Buckle	1868	Formosa	H. Woolcott	G. Fordham
1822	Whizgig	R. Robson	F. Buckle	1869	Scottish Queen	J. Day	G. Fordham
1823	Zinc	R. Robson	F. Buckle	1870	Hester	J. Dawson	J. Grimshaw
1824	Cobweb	J. Edwards	J. Robinson	1871	Hannah	J. Hayhoe	C. Maidment
1825	Tontine	R. Robson	–	1872	Reine	T. Jennings	H. Parry
1826	Problem	R. Robson	J. Day	1873	Cecilia	M. Dawson	J. Morris
1827	Arab	R. Robson	F. Buckle	1874	Apology	W. Osborne	J. Osborne
1828	Zoe	R. Pettit	J. Robinson	1875	Spinaway	M. Dawson	F. Archer
1829	Young Mouse	R. Boyce	W. Arnull	1876	Camelia	T. Cunnington	T. Glover
1830	Charlotte West	J. Edwards	J. Robinson	1877	Belphoebe	G. Bloss	H. Jeffery
1831	Galantine	H. Scott	P. Conolly	1878	Pilgrimage	J. Cannon	T. Cannon
1832	Galata	C. Marson	W. Arnull	1879	Wheel Of Fortune	M. Dawson	F. Archer
1833	Tarantella	J. Robinson	W. Wright	1880	Elizabeth	J. Dawson	C. Wood
1834	May-day	J. Doe	J. Day	1881	Thebais	A. Taylor	G. Fordham
1835	Preserve	R. Prince	E. Flatman	1882	St Marguerite	R. Sherrard	C. Wood
1836	Destiny	–	J. Day	1883	Hauteur	T. Jennings	G. Fordham
1837	Chateau d'Espagne	J. Day	J. Day	1884	Busybody	M. Dawson	T. Cannon
1838	Barcarolle	W. Edwards	E. Edwards	1885	Farewell	J. Porter	G. Barrett
1839	Cara	C. Marson	G. Edwards	1886	Miss Jummy	R. Marsh	J. Watts
1840	Crucifix	J. Day	J. Day	1887	Reve D'Or	A. Taylor	C. Wood
1841	Potentia	G. Payne	J. Robinson	1888	Briarroot	J. Ryan	W. Warne
1842	Firebrand	J. Kent	S. Rogers	1889	Minthe	M. Dawson	J. Woodburn
1843	Extempore	R. Pettit	S. Chifney	1890	Semolina	G. Dawson	J. Watts
1844	Sorella	W. Butler	J. Robinson	1891	Mimi	M. Dawson	F. Rickaby
1845	Pic-nic	J. Kent	W. Abdale	1892	La Fleche	J. Porter	G. Barrett
1846	Mendicant	J. Day	S. Day	1893	Siffleuse	J. Day	T. Loates
1847	Clementina	M. Dilly	E. Flatman	1894	Amiable	G. Dawson	W. Bradford
1848	Canezou	J. Scott	F. Butler	1895	Galeottia	J. Ryan	F. Pratt
1849	The Flea	J. Day	A. Day	1896	Thais	R. Marsh	J. Watts
1850	Lady Orford	W. Beresford	F. Butler	1897	Chelandry	W. Walters	J. Watts
1851	Aphrodite	A. Taylor	J. Marson	1898	Nun Nicer	W. Waugh	S. Loates
1852	Kate	J. Woolcott	A. Day	1899	Sibola	J. Huggins	T. Sloan
1853	Mentmore Lass	W. King	J. Charlton	1900	Winifreda	T. Jennings	S. Loates
1854	Virago	J. Day	J. Wells	1901	Aida	G. Blackwell	D. Maher
1855	Habena	W. Butler	S. Rogers	1902	Sceptre	R. Sievier	H. Randall
1856	Manganese	J. Osborne	J. Osborne	1903	Quintessence	J. Chandler	H. Randall
1857	Imperieuse	J. Scott	E. Flatman	1904	Pretty Polly	P. Gilpin	W. Lane
1858	Governess	T. Eskrett	T. Ashmall	1905	Cherry Lass	W. Robinson	B. Lynham
1859	Mayonnaise	T. Taylor	G. Fordham	1906	Flair	P. Gilpin	B. Dillon
1860	Sagitta	J. Scott	T. Aldcroft	1907	Witch Elm	W. Robinson	B. Lynham
				1908	Rhodora	J. Allen	L. Lyne

YEAR	HORSE	AGE	TRAINER	JOCKEY
1962	Mandarin	11	F. Walwyn	F. Winter
1963	Mill House	6	F. Walwyn	G. Robinson
1964	Arkle	7	T. Dreaper	P. Taafe
1965	Arkle	8	T. Dreaper	P. Taafe
1966	Arkle	9	T. Dreaper	P. Taafe
1967	Woodland Venture	7	F. Rimell	T. Biddlecombe
1968	Fort Leney	10	T. Dreaper	P. Taafe
1969	What a Myth	12	H. Price	P. Kelleway
1970	L'Escargot	7	D. Moore	T. Carberry
1971	L'Escargot	8	D. Moore	T. Carberry
1972	Glencarig Lady	8	F. Flood	F. Berry
1973	The Dikler	10	F. Walwyn	R. Barry
1974	Captain Christy	7	P. Taafe	H. Beasley
1975	Ten Up	8	J. Dreaper	T. Carberry
1976	Royal Frolic	7	F. Rimell	J. Burke
1977	Davy Lad	7	M. O'Toole	D. Hughes
1978	Midnight Court	7	F. Winter	J. Francome
1979	Alverton	9	M.H. Easterby	J.J. O'Neill
1980	Master Smudge	8	A. Barrow	R. Hoare

YEAR	HORSE	AGE	TRAINER	JOCKEY
1981	Little Owl	7	M.H. Easterby	Mr A.J. Wilson*
1982	Silver Buck	10	M. Dickinson	R. Earnshaw
1983	Bregawn	9	M. Dickinson	G. Bradley
1984	Burrough Hill Lad	8	Mrs J. Pitman	P. Tuck
1985	Forgive 'N' Forget	8	J. FitzGerald	M. Dwyer
1986	Dawn Run	8	P. Mullins	J.J. O'Neill
1987	The Thinker	9	W. Stephenson	R. Lamb
1988	Charter Party	10	D. Nicholson	R. Dunwoody

Note: 'Mr' denotes an amateur jockey.

YEAR	HORSE	TRAINER	JOCKEY
1909	Electra	P. Gilpin	B. Dillon
1910	Winkipop	W. Waugh	B. Lynham
1911	Atmah	F. Pratt	F. Fox
1912	Tagalie	D. Waugh	L. Hewitt
1913	Jest	C. Morton	F. Rickaby
1914	Princess Dorrie	C. Morton	W. Huxley
1915	Vaucluse	F. Hartigan	F. Rickaby
1916	Canyon	G. Lambton	F. Rickaby
1917	Diadem	G. Lambton	F. Rickaby
1918	Ferry	G. Lambton	B. Carslake
1919	Roseway	F. Hartigan	A. Whalley
1920	Cinna	R. Waugh	W. Griggs
1921	Bettina	P. Linton	G. Bellhouse
1922	Silver Urn	H. Persse	B. Carslake
1923	Tranquil	G. Lambton	E. Gardner
1924	Plack	J. Jarvis	E.C. Elliott
1925	Saucy Sue	A. Taylor	F. Bullock
1926	Pillion	J. Watson	R. Perryman
1927	Cresta Run	P. Gilpin	A. Balding
1928	Scuttle	W. Jarvis	J. Childs
1929	Taj Mah	J. Torterolo	W. Sibbritt
1930	Fair Isle	F. Butters	T. Weston
1931	Four Course	F. Darling	E.C. Elliott
1932	Kandy	F. Carter	E.C. Elliott
1933	Brown Betty	C. Boyd-Rochfort	J. Childs
1934	Campanula	J. Jarvis	H. Wragg
1935	Mesa	A. Swann	R. Johnstone
1936	Tide-way	C. Leader	R. Perryman
1937	Exhibitionnist	J. Lawson	S. Donoghue
1938	Rockfel	O. Bell	S. Wragg
1939	Galatea	J. Lawson	R. Jones
1940	Godiva	W. Jarvis	D. Marks
1941	Dancing Time	J. Lawson	R. Perryman
1942	Sun Chariot	F. Darling	G. Richards
1943	Herringbone	W. Earl	H. Wragg
1944	Picture Play	J. Watts	E.C. Elliott
1945	Sun Stream	W. Earl	H. Wragg
1946	Hypericum	C. Boyd-Rochfort	D. Smith
1947	Imprudence	J. Lieux	R. Johnstone
1948	Queenpot	N. Murless	G. Richards
1949	Musidora	C. Elsey	E. Britt
1950	Camaree	A. Lieux	R. Johnstone
1951	Belle Of All	N. Bertie	G. Richards
1952	Zabara	V. Smyth	K. Gethin
1953	Happy Laughter	J. Jarvis	E. Mercer
1954	Festoon	N. Cannon	A. Breasley

YEAR	HORSE	TRAINER	JOCKEY
1955	Meld	C. Boyd-Rochfort	W.H. Carr
1956	Honeylight	C. Elsey	E. Britt
1957	Rose Royale	A. Head	C. Smirke
1958	Bella Paola	F. Mathet	S. Boullenger
1959	Petite Etoile	N. Murless	D. Smith
1960	Never Too Late	E. Pollet	R. Poincelet
1961	Sweet Solera	R. Day	W. Rickaby
1962	Abermaid	H. Wragg	W. Williamson
1963	Hula Dancer	E. Pollet	R. Poincelet
1964	Pourparler	P.J. Prendergast	G. Bougoure
1965	Night Off	W. Wharton	W. Williamson
1966	Glad Rags	M.V. O'Brien	P. Cook
1967	Fleet	N. Murless	G. Moore
1968	Caergwrle	N. Murless	A. Barclay
1969	Full Dress	H. Wragg	R. Hutchinson
1970	Humble Duty	P. Walwyn	L. Piggott
1971	Altesse Royale	N. Murless	Y. Saint-Martin
1972	Waterloo	J.W. Watts	E. Hide
1973	Mysterious	N. Murless	G. Lewis
1974	Highclere	W. Hern	J. Mercer
1975	Nocturnal Spree	S. Murless	J. Roe
1976	Flying Water	A. Penna	Y Saint-Martin
1977	Mrs McArdy	M.W. Easterby	E. Hide
1978	Enstone Spark	B. Hills	E. Johnson
1979	One In A Million	H. Cecil	J. Mercer
1980	Quick As Lightning	J. Dunlop	B. Rouse
1981	Fairy Footsteps	H. Cecil	L. Piggott
1982	On The House	H. Wragg	J. Reid
1983	Ma Biche	Mme C. Head	F. Head
1984	Pebbles	C. Brittain	P. Robinson
1985	Oh So Sharp	H. Cecil	S. Cauthen
1986	Midway Lady	B. Hanbury	R. Cochrane
1987	Miesque	F. Boutin	F. Head
1988	Ravinella	Mme C. Head	G. Moore

ENGLAND

2,000 GUINEAS
Newmarket, Suffolk: 1 mile (1,600 m). *Three-year-olds*

YEAR	HORSE	TRAINER	JOCKEY	YEAR	HORSE	TRAINER	JOCKEY
1809	Wizard	T. Perren	W. Clift	1857	Vedette	G. Abdale	J. Osborne
1810	Hephestion	R. Robson	F. Buckle	1858	Fitzroland	G. Manning	J. Wells
1811	Trophonius	R. Boyce	S. Barnard	1859	Promised Land	W. Day	A. Day
1812	Cwrw	—	S. Chifney	1860	The Wizard	J. Scott	T. Ashmall
1813	Smolensko	Crouch	H. Miller	1861	Diophantus	J. Dawson	A. Edwards
1814	Olive	R. Boyce	W. Arnull	1862	The Marquis	J. Scott	T. Ashmall
1815	Tigris	R. Boyce	W. Arnull	1863	Macaroni	J. Godding	T. Chaloner
1816	Nectar	R. Boyce	W. Arnull	1864	General Peel	T. Dawson	I. Aldcroft
1817	Manfred	R. Stephenson	W. Wheatley	1865	Gladiateur	T. Jennings	H. Grimshaw
1818	Interpreter	R. Prince	W. Clift	1866	Lord Lyon	J. Dover	R. Thomas
1819	Antar	J. Edwards	E. Edwards	1867	Vauban	J. Day	G. Fordham
1820	Pindarrie	R. Robson	F. Buckle	1868	Moslem	A. Taylor	T. Chaloner
1821	Reginald	R. Robson	F. Buckle		*and* Formosa	H. Woolcott	G. Fordham
1822	Pastille	R. Robson	F. Buckle	1869	Pretender	T. Dawson	J. Osborne
1823	Nicolo	J. Rogers	W. Wheatley	1870	Macgregor	J. Waugh	J. Daley
1824	Schahriar	—	W. Wheatley	1871	Bothwell	T. Dawson	J. Osborne
1825	Enamel	C. Marson	J. Robinson	1872	Prince Charlie	J. Dawson	J. Osborne
1826	Dervise	R. Robson	J. Day	1873	Gang Forward	A. Taylor	T. Chaloner
1827	Turcoman	R. Robson	F. Buckle	1874	Atlantic	M. Dawson	F. Archer
1828	Cadland	R. Boyce	J. Robinson	1875	Camballo	M. Dawson	J. Osborne
1829	Patron	C. Marson	F. Boyce	1876	Petrarch	J. Dawson	H. Luke
1830	Augustus	C. Marson	P. Conolly	1877	Chamant	T. Jennings	J. Goater
1831	Riddlesworth	J. Edwards	J. Robinson	1878	Pilgrimage	J. Cannon	T. Cannon
1832	Archibald	—	A. Pavis	1879	Charibert	M. Dawson	F. Archer
1833	Clearwell	—	J. Robinson	1880	Petronel	J. Cannon	G. Fordham
1834	Glencoe	J. Edwards	J. Robinson	1881	Peregrine	R. Peck	F. Webb
1835	Ibrahim	J. Edwards	J. Robinson	1882	Shotover	J. Porter	T. Cannon
1836	Bay Middleton	J. Edwards	J. Robinson	1883	Galliard	M. Dawson	F. Archer
1837	Achmet	J. Edwards	E. Edwards	1884	Scot-Free	T. Chaloner	W. Platt
1838	Gray Momus	J. Day	J. Day	1885	Paradox	J. Porter	F. Archer
1839	The Corsair	J. Doe	W. Wakefield	1886	Ormonde	J. Porter	G. Barrett
1840	Crucifix	J. Day	J. Day	1887	Enterprise	J. Ryan	T. Cannon
1841	Ralph	W. Edwards	J. Day	1888	Ayrshire	G. Dawson	J. Osborne
1842	Meteor	J. Scott	W. Scott	1889	Enthusiast	J. Ryan	T. Cannon
1843	Cotherstone	J. Scott	W. Scott	1890	Surefoot	C. Jousiffe	J. Liddiard
1844	The Ugly Buck	J. Day	J. Day	1891	Common	J. Porter	G. Barrett
1845	Idas	R. Boyce	E. Flatman	1892	Bona Vista	W. Jarvis	W. Robinson
1846	Sir Tatton Sykes	W. Oates	W. Scott	1893	Isinglass	J. Jewitt	T. Loates
1847	Conyngham	J. Day	J. Robinson	1894	Ladas	M. Dawson	J. Watts
1848	Flatcatcher	H. Stebbing	J. Robinson	1895	Kirkconnel	J. Day	J. Watts
1849	Nunnykirk	J. Scott	F. Butler	1896	St Frusquin	A. Hayhoe	T. Loates
1850	Pitsford	J. Day	A. Day	1897	Galtee More	S. Darling	C. Wood
1851	Hernandez	J. Kent	E. Flatman	1898	Disraeli	J. Dawson	S. Loates
1852	Stockwell	W. Harlock	J. Norman	1899	Flying Fox	J. Porter	M. Cannon
1853	West Australian	J. Scott	F. Butler	1900	Diamond Jubilee	R. Marsh	H. Jones
1854	The Hermit	J. Day	A. Day	1901	Handicapper	F. Day	W. Halsey
1855	Lord Of The Isles	W. Day	T. Aldcroft	1902	Sceptre	R. Sievier	H. Randall
1856	Fazzoletto	J. Scott	E. Flatman	1903	Rock Sand	G. Blackwell	J. Martin

CHAMPION HURDLE
Cheltenham, Gloucestershire: 2 miles (3,200 m). *First run*: 1927

YEAR	HORSE	AGE	TRAINER	JOCKEY	YEAR	HORSE	AGE	TRAINER	JOCKEY
1927	Blaris	6	W. Payne	G. Duller	1945	Brains Trust	5	G. Wilson	T.F. Rimell
1928	Brown Jack	4	A. Hastings	L.B. Rees	1946	Distel	5	M. Arnott	R. O'Ryan
1929	Royal Falcon	6	R. Gore	F.B. Rees	1947	National Spirit	6	V. Smyth	D. Morgan
1930	Brown Tony	4	J. Anthony	T. Cullinan	1948	National Spirit	7	V. Smyth	R. Smyth
1931	no race				1949	Hatton's Grace	9	M.V. O'Brien	A. Brabazon
1932	Insurance	5	A.B. Briscoe	T.E. Leader	1950	Hatton's Grace	10	M.V. O'Brien	A. Brabazon
1933	Insurance	6	A.B. Briscoe	W. Stott	1951	Hatton's Grace	11	M.V. O'Brien	A. Brabazon
1934	Chenango	7	I. Anthony	D. Morgan	1952	Sir Ken	5	W. Stephenson	T. Molony
1935	Lion Courage	7	F. Brown	G. Wilson	1953	Sir Ken	6	W. Stephenson	T. Molony
1936	Victor Norman	5	M. Blair	H. Nicholson	1954	Sir Ken	7	W. Stephenson	T. Molony
1937	Free Fare	9	E. Gwilt	G. Pellerin	1955	Clair Soleil	6	H. Price	F. Winter
1938	Our Hope	9	R. Gubbins	Capt R. Harding	1956	Doorknocker	8	W. Hall	H. Sprague
1939	African Sister	7	C. Piggott	K. Piggott	1957	Merry Deal	7	A. Jones	G. Underwood
1940	Solford	9	O. Anthony	S. Magee	1958	Bandalore	7	J. Wright	G. Slack
1941	Seneca	4	V. Smyth	R. Smyth	1959	Fare Time	6	H. Price	F. Winter
1942	Forestation	4	V. Smyth	R. Smyth	1960	Another Flash	6	P. Sleator	H. Beasley
1943	no race				1961	Eborneezer	6	H. Price	F. Winter
1944	no race				1962	Anzio	5	F. Walwyn	G.W. Robinson

YEAR	HORSE	TRAINER	JOCKEY	YEAR	HORSE	TRAINER	JOCKEY
1904	St Amant	A. Hayhoe	K. Cannon	1952	Thunderhead	E. Pollet	R. Poincelet
1905	Vedas	W. Robinson	H. Jones	1953	Nearula	C. Elsey	E. Britt
1906	Gorgos	R. Marsh	H. Jones	1954	Darius	H. Wragg	E. Mercer
1907	Slieve Gallion	S. Darling	W. Higgs	1955	Our Babu	G. Brooke	D. Smith
1908	Norman	J. Watson	O. Madden	1956	Gilles De Retz	Mrs G. Johnson Houghton	F. Barlow
1909	Minoru	R. Marsh	H. Jones	1957	Crepello	N. Murless	L. Piggott
1910	Neil Gow	P. Peck	D. Maher	1958	Pall Mall	C. Boyd-Rochfort	D. Smith
1911	Sunstar	C. Morton	G. Stern	1959	Taboun	A. Head	G. Moore
1912	Sweeper	H. Persse	B. Carslake	1960	Martial	P.J. Prendergast	R. Hutchinson
1913	Louvois	D. Waugh	J. Reiff	1961	Rockavon	G. Boyd	N. Stirk
1914	Kennymore	A. Taylor	G. Stern	1962	Privy Councillor	T. Waugh	W. Rickaby
1915	Pommern	C. Peck	S. Donoghue	1963	Only For Life	J. Tree	J. Lindley
1916	Clarissimus	W. Waugh	J. Clark	1964	Baldric	E. Fellows	W. Pyers
1917	Gay Crusader	A. Taylor	S. Donoghue	1965	Niksar	W. Nightingall	D. Keith
1918	Gainsborough	A. Taylor	J. Childs	1966	Kashmir	C. Bartholomew	J. Lindley
1919	The Panther	G. Manser	R. Cooper	1967	Royal Palace	N. Murless	G. Moore
1920	Tetratema	H. Persse	B. Carslake	1968	Sir Ivor	M.V. O'Brien	L. Piggott
1921	Craig An Eran	A. Taylor	J. Brennan	1969	Right Tack	J. Sutcliffe	G. Lewis
1922	St Louis	P. Gilpin	G. Archibald	1970	Nijinsky	M.V. O'Brien	L. Piggott
1923	Ellangowan	J. Jarvis	E.C. Elliott	1971	Brigadier Gerard	W. Hern	J. Mercer
1924	Diophon	R. Dawson	G. Hulme	1972	High Top	B. van Cutsem	W. Carson
1925	Manna	F. Darling	S. Donoghue	1973	Mon Fils	R. Hannon	F. Durr
1926	Colorado	G. Lambton	T. Weston	1974	Nonoalco	F. Boutin	Y. Saint-Martin
1927	Adam's Apple	H. Cottrill	J. Leach	1975	Bolkonski	H. Cecil	G. Dettori
1928	Flamingo	J. Jarvis	E.C. Elliott	1976	Wollow	H. Cecil	G. Dettori
1929	Mr Jinks	H. Persse	H. Beasley	1977	Nebbiolo	K. Prendergast	G. Curran
1930	Diolite	F. Templeman	F. Fox	1978	Roland Gardens	D. Sasse	F. Durr
1931	Cameronian	F. Darling	J. Childs	1979	Tap on Wood	B. Hills	S. Cauthen
1932	Orwell	J. Lawson	R. Jones	1980	Known Fact	J. Tree	W. Carson
1933	Rodosto	H. Count	R. Brethes	1981	To-Agori-Mou	G. Harwood	G. Starkey
1934	Colombo	T. Hogg	R. Johnstone	1982	Zino	F. Boutin	F. Head
1935	Bahram	F. Butters	F. Fox	1983	Lomond	M.V. O'Brien	P. Eddery
1936	Pay Up	J. Lawson	R. Dick	1984	El Gran Señor	M.V. O'Brien	P. Eddery
1937	Le Ksar	F. Carter	C. Semblat	1985	Shadeed	M. Stoute	L. Piggott
1938	Pasch	F. Darling	G. Richards	1986	Dancing Brave	G. Harwood	G. Starkey
1939	Blue Peter	J. Jarvis	E. Smith	1987	Don't Forget Me	R. Hannon	W. Carson
1940	Djebel	A. Swann	E.C. Elliott	1988	Doyoun	M. Stoute	W.R. Swinburn
1941	Lambert Simnel	F. Templeman	E.C. Elliott				
1942	Big Game	F. Darling	G. Richards				
1943	Kingsway	J. Lawson	S. Wragg				
1944	Garden Path	W. Earl	H. Wragg				
1945	Court Martial	J. Lawson	C. Richards				
1946	Happy Knight	H. Jelliss	T. Weston				
1947	Tudor Minstrel	F. Darling	G. Richards				
1948	My Babu	F. Armstrong	C. Smirke				
1949	Nimbus	G. Colling	E.C. Elliott				
1950	Palestine	M. Marsh	C. Smirke				
1951	Ki Ming	M. Beary	A. Breasley				

YEAR	HORSE	AGE	TRAINER	JOCKEY	YEAR	HORSE	AGE	TRAINER	JOCKEY
1963	Winning Fair	8	G. Spencer	Mr A. Lillingston	1981	Sea Pigeon	11	M.H. Easterby	J. Francome
1964	Magic Court	6	T. Robson	P. McCarron	1982	For Auction	6	M. Cunningham	Mr C. Magnier
1965	Kirriemuir	5	F. Walwyn	G.W. Robinson	1983	Gaye Brief	6	Mrs M. Rimell	R. Linley
1966	Salmon Spray	8	R. Turnell	J. Haine	1984	Dawn Run	6	P. Mullins	J.J. O'Neill
1967	Saucy Kit	6	M.H. Easterby	R. Edwards	1985	See You Then	5	N. Henderson	S. Smith Eccles
1968	Persian War	5	C. Davies	J. Uttley	1986	See You Then	6	N. Henderson	S. Smith Eccles
1969	Persian War	6	C. Davies	J. Uttley	1987	See You Then	7	N. Henderson	S. Smith Eccles
1970	Persian War	7	C. Davies	J. Uttley	1988	Celtic Shot	5	F. Winter	P. Scudamore
1971	Bula	6	F. Winter	P. Kelleway					
1972	Bula	7	F. Winter	P. Kelleway					
1973	Comedy of Errors	6	F. Rimell	W. Smith					
1974	Lanzarote	6	F. Winter	R. Pitman					
1975	Comedy Of Errors	8	F. Rimell	K. White					
1976	Night Nurse	5	M.H. Easterby	P. Broderick					
1977	Night Nurse	6	M.H. Easterby	P. Broderick					
1978	Monksfield	6	D. McDonogh	T. Kinane					
1979	Monksfield	7	D. McDonogh	D.T. Hughes					
1980	Sea Pigeon	10	M.H. Easterby	J.J. O'Neill					

ENGLAND

ST LEGER

Doncaster, Yorkshire: 1 mile 6 furlongs 127 yards (2,900 m). *Three-year-olds*

YEAR	HORSE	TRAINER	JOCKEY	YEAR	HORSE	TRAINER	JOCKEY
1776	Allabaculia	C. Scaife	J. Singleton	1849	The Flying Dutchman	J. Fobert	C. Marlow
1777	Bourbon	–	J. Cade				
1778	Hollandaise	J. Rose	G. Herring	1850	Voltigeur	R. Hill	J. Marson
1779	Tommy	J. Rose	G. Herring	1851	Newminster	J. Scott	S. Templeman
1780	Ruler	–	J. Mangle	1852	Stockwell	W. Harlock	J. Norman
1781	Serina	J. Lowther	R. Foster	1853	West Australian	J. Scott	F. Butler
1782	Imperatrix	G. Searle	G. Searle	1854	Knight Of St George	H. Stebbing	R. Basham
1783	Phoenomenon	I. Cape	A. Hall				
1784	Omphale	M. Mason	J. Kirton	1855	Saucebox	T. Parr	J. Wells
1785	Cowslip	G. Searle	G. Searle	1856	Warlock	J. Scott	E. Flatman
1786	Paragon	J. Mangle	J. Mangle	1857	Imperieuse	J. Scott	E. Flatman
1787	Spadille	J. Mangle	J. Mangle	1858	Sunbeam	J. Prince	L. Snowden
1788	Young Flora	J. Mangle	J. Mangle	1859	Gamester	J. Scott	T. Aldcroft
1789	Pewett	C. Scaife	W. Wilson	1860	St Albans	A. Taylor	L. Snowden
1790	Ambidexter	G. Searle	G. Searle	1861	Caller Ou	W. I'Anson	T. Chaloner
1791	Young Traveller	J. Hutchinson	J. Jackson	1862	The Marquis	J. Scott	T. Chaloner
1792	Tartar	J. Mangle	J. Mangle	1863	Lord Clifden	E. Parr	J. Osborne
1793	Ninety-three	–	W. Peirse	1864	Blair Athol	W. I'Anson	J. Snowden
1794	Beningbrough	J. Hutchinson	J. Jackson	1865	Gladiateur	T. Jennings	H. Grimshaw
1795	Hambletonian	J. Hutchinson	R. Boyce	1866	Lord Lyon	J. Dover	H. Custance
1796	Ambrosio	–	J. Jackson	1867	Achievement	J. Dover	T. Chaloner
1797	Lounger	G. Searle	J. Shepherd	1868	Formosa	H. Woolcott	T. Chaloner
1798	Symmetry	S. King	J. Jackson	1869	Pero Gomez	J. Porter	J. Wells
1799	Cockfighter	T. Fields	T. Fields	1870	Hawthornden	J. Dawson	J. Grimshaw
1800	Champion	T. Perren	F. Buckle	1871	Hannah	J. Hayhoe	C. Maidment
1801	Quiz	G. Searle	J. Shepherd	1872	Wenlock	T. Wadlow	C. Maidment
1802	Orville	C. Scaife	J. Singleton	1873	Marie Stuart	R. Peck	T. Osborne
1803	Remembrancer	J. Smith	B. Smith	1874	Apology	W. Osborne	J. Osborne
1804	Sancho	B. Atkinson	F. Buckle	1875	Craig Millar	A. Taylor	T. Chaloner
1805	Staveley	B. Atkinson	J. Jackson	1876	Petrarch	J. Dawson	J. Goater
1806	Fyldener	–	T. Carr	1877	Silvio	M. Dawson	F. Archer
1807	Paulina	C. Scaife	W. Clift	1878	Jannette	M. Dawson	F. Archer
1808	Petronius	W. Theakston	B. Smith	1879	Rayon D'Or	T. Jennings	J. Goater
1809	Ashton	W. Theakston	B. Smith	1880	Robert The Devil	C. Blanton	T. Cannon
1810	Octavian	–	W. Clift	1881	Iroquois	J. Pincus	F. Archer
1811	Soothsayer	T. Sykes	B. Smith	1882	Dutch Oven	M. Dawson	F. Archer
1812	Otterington	W. Hesseltine	R. Johnson	1883	Ossian	R. Marsh	J. Watts
1813	Altisidora	T. Sykes	J. Jackson	1884	The Lambkin	M. Dawson	J. Watts
1814	William	W. Theakston	J. Shepherd	1885	Melton	M. Dawson	F. Archer
1815	Filho Da Puta	J. Croft	J. Jackson	1886	Ormonde	J. Porter	F. Archer
1816	The Duchess	J. Croft	B. Smith	1887	Kilwarlin	J. Jewitt	W. Robinson
1817	Ebor	J. Lonsdale	R. Johnson	1888	Seabreeze	J. Jewitt	W. Robinson
1818	Reveller	J. Lonsdale	R. Johnson	1889	Donovan	G. Dawson	F. Barrett
1819	Antonio	J. Lonsdale	T. Nicholson	1890	Memoir	G. Dawson	J. Watts
1820	St Patrick	J. Lonsdale	R. Johnson	1891	Common	J. Porter	G. Barrett
1821	Jack Spigot	I. Blades	W. Scott	1892	La Fleche	J. Porter	J. Watts
1822	Theodore	J. Croft	J. Jackson	1893	Isinglass	J. Jewitt	T. Loates
1823	Barefoot	R. Shepherd	T. Goodisson	1894	Throstle	J. Porter	M. Cannon
1824	Jerry	J. Croft	B. Smith	1895	Sir Visto	M. Dawson	S. Loates
1825	Memnon	R. Shepherd	W. Scott	1896	Persimmon	R. Marsh	J. Watts
1826	Tarrare	S. King	G. Nelson	1897	Galtee More	S. Darling	C. Wood
1827	Matilda	J. Scott	J. Robinson	1898	Wildfowler	S. Darling	C. Wood
1828	The Colonel	J. Scott	W. Scott	1899	Flying Fox	J. Porter	M. Cannon
1829	Rowton	J. Scott	W. Scott	1900	Diamond Jubilee	R. Marsh	H. Jones
1830	Birmingham	T. Flintoff	P. Conolly	1901	Doricles	A. Hayhoe	K. Cannon
1831	Chorister	J. Smith	J. Day	1902	Sceptre	R. Sievier	F. Hardy
1832	Margrave	J. Scott	J. Robinson	1903	Rock Sand	G. Blackwell	D. Maher
1833	Rockingham	R. Shepherd	S. Darling	1904	Pretty Polly	P. Gilpin	W. Lane
1834	Touchstone	J. Scott	G. Calloway	1905	Challacombe	A. Taylor	O. Madden
1835	Queen Of Trumps	J. Blenkhorn	T. Lye	1906	Troutbeck	W. Waugh	G. Stern
1836	Elis	J. Doe	J. Day	1907	Wool Winder	H. Enoch	W. Halsey
1837	Mango	M. Dilly	S. Day	1908	Your Majesty	C. Morton	W. Griggs
1838	Don John	J. Scott	W. Scott	1909	Bayardo	A. Taylor	D. Maher
1839	Charles The Twelfth	J. Scott	W. Scott	1910	Swynford	G. Lambton	F. Wootton
1840	Launcelot	J. Scott	W. Scott	1911	Prince Palatine	H. Beardsley	F. O'Neill
1841	Satirist	J. Scott	W. Scott	1912	Tracery	J. Watson	G. Bellhouse
1842	Blue Bonnet	T. Dawson	T. Lye	1913	Night Hawk	W. Robinson	E. Wheatley
1843	Nutwith	R. Johnson	J. Marson	1914	Black Jester	C. Morton	W. Griggs
1844	Foig A Ballagh	J. Forth	H. Bell	1915	Pommern	C. Peck	S. Donoghue
1845	The Baron	J. Scott	F. Butler	1916	Hurry On	F. Darling	C. Childs
1846	Sir Tatton Sykes	W. Oates	W. Scott	1917	Gay Crusader	A. Taylor	S. Donoghue
1847	Van Tromp	J. Fobert	J. Marson	1918	Gainsborough	A. Taylor	J. Childs
1848	Surplice	R. Stephenson	E. Flatman	1919	Keysoe	G. Lambton	B. Carslake

YEAR	HORSE	TRAINER	JOCKEY
1920	Caligula	H. Leader	A. Smith
1921	Polemarch	T. Green	J. Childs
1922	Royal Lancer	A. Sadler	R. Jones
1923	Tranquil	C. Morton	T. Weston
1924	Salmon-Trout	R. Dawson	B. Carslake
1925	Solario	R. Day	J. Childs
1926	Coronach	F. Darling	J. Childs
1927	Book Law	A. Taylor	H. Jelliss
1928	Fairway	F. Butters	T. Weston
1929	Trigo	R. Dawson	M. Beary
1930	Singapore	T. Hogg	G. Richards
1931	Sandwich	J. Jarvis	H. Wragg
1932	Firdaussi	F. Butters	F. Fox
1933	Hyperion	G. Lambton	T. Weston
1934	Windsor Lad	M. Marsh	C. Smirke
1935	Bahram	F. Butters	C. Smirke
1936	Boswell	C. Boyd-Rochfort	P. Beasley
1937	Chulmleigh	T. Hogg	G. Richards
1938	Scottish Union	N. Cannon	B. Carslake
1939	no race		
1940	Turkhan	F. Butters	G. Richards
1941	Sun Castle	C. Boyd-Rochfort	G. Bridgland
1942	Sun Chariot	F. Darling	G. Richards
1943	Herringbone	W. Earl	H. Wragg
1944	Tehran	F. Butters	G. Richards
1945	Chamoissaire	R. Perryman	T. Lowrey
1946	Airborne	R. Perryman	T. Lowrey
1947	Sayajirao	F. Armstrong	E. Britt
1948	Black Tarquin	C. Boyd-Rochfort	E. Britt
1949	Ridge Wood	N. Murless	M. Beary
1950	Scratch	C. Semblat	R. Johnstone
1951	Talma	C. Semblat	R. Johnstone
1952	Tulyar	M. Marsh	C. Smirke
1953	Premonition	C. Boyd-Rochfort	E. Smith
1954	Never Say Die	J. Lawson	C. Smirke
1955	Meld	C. Boyd-Rochfort	W.H. Carr
1956	Cambremer	G. Bridgland	F. Palmer

YEAR	HORSE	TRAINER	JOCKEY
1957	Ballymoss	M.V. O'Brien	T.P. Burns
1958	Alcide	C. Boyd-Rochfort	W.H. Carr
1959	Cantelo	C. Elsey	E. Hide
1960	St Paddy	N. Murless	L. Piggott
1961	Aurelius	N. Murless	L. Piggott
1962	Hethersett	W. Hern	W.H. Carr
1963	Ragusa	P.J. Prendergast	G. Bougoure
1964	Indiana	J. Watts	J. Lindley
1965	Provoke	W. Hern	J. Mercer
1966	Sodium	G. Todd	F. Durr
1967	Ribocco	R. Johnson Houghton	L. Piggott
1968	Ribero	R. Johnson Houghton	L. Piggott
1969	Intermezzo	H. Wragg	R. Hutchinson
1970	Nijinsky	M.V. O'Brien	L. Piggott
1971	Athens Wood	H. Thomson Jones	L. Piggott
1972	Boucher	M.V. O'Brien	L. Piggott
1973	Peleid	W. Elsey	F. Durr
1974	Bustino	W. Hern	J. Mercer
1975	Bruni	H. Price	A. Murray
1976	Crow	A. Penna	Y. Saint-Martin
1977	Dunfermline	W. Hern	W. Carson
1978	Julio Mariner	C. Brittain	E. Hide
1979	Son of Love	R. Collet	A. Lequeux
1980	Light Cavalry	H. Cecil	J. Mercer
1981	Cut Above	W. Hern	J. Mercer
1982	Touching Wood	H. Thomson Jones	P. Cook
1983	Sun Princess	W. Hern	W. Carson
1984	Commanche Run	L. Cumani	L. Piggott
1985	Oh So Sharp	H. Cecil	S. Cauthen
1986	Moon Madness	J. Dunlop	P. Eddery
1987	Reference Point	H. Cecil	S. Cauthen
1988	Minster Son	N. Graham	W. Carson

A very special moment for Willie Carson as he surges to a 1988 St Leger victory aboard Minster Son, the horse he bred.

ENGLAND

THE OAKS
Epsom, Surrey: 1½ miles (2,400 m). *Three-year-old fillies*

YEAR	HORSE	TRAINER	JOCKEY	YEAR	HORSE	TRAINER	JOCKEY
1779	Bridget	Saunders	R. Goodisson	1853	Catherine Hayes	M. Dawson	C. Marlow
1780	Tetotum	–	–	1854	Mincemeat	W. Goodwin	J. Charlton
1781	Faith	J. Pratt	–	1855	Marchioness	J. Scott	S. Templeman
1782	Ceres	J. Pratt	S. Chifney	1856	Mincepie	J. Day	A. Day
1783	Maid Of The Oaks	J. Pratt	S. Chifney	1857	Blink Bonny	W. l'Anson	J. Charlton
1784	Stella	–	C. Hindley	1858	Governess	T. Eskrett	T. Ashmall
1785	Trifle	J. Pratt	J. Bird	1859	Summerside	T. Taylor	G. Fordham
1786	Yellow Filly	R. Prince	J. Edwards	1860	Butterfly	G. Oates	J. Snowden
1787	Annette	J. Watson	D. Fitzpatrick	1861	Brown Duchess	J. Saxon	L. Snowden
1788	Nightshade	F. Neale	S. Chifney	1862	Feu De Joie	J. Godding	T. Chaloner
1789	Tag	F. Neale	S. Chifney	1863	Queen Bertha	J. Scott	T. Aldcroft
1790	Hippolyta	M. Stephenson	S. Chifney	1864	Fille De l'Air	T. Jennings	A. Edwards
1791	Portia	M. Stephenson	J. Singleton	1865	Regalia	W. Harlock	J. Norman
1792	Volante	J. Pratt	C. Hindley	1866	Tormentor	C. Blanton	J. Mann
1793	Caelia	M. Stephenson	J. Singleton	1867	Hippia	J. Hayhoe	J. Daley
1794	Hermione	Saunders	S. Arnull	1868	Formosa	H. Woolcott	G. Fordham
1795	Platina	F. Neale	D. Fitzpatrick	1869	Brigantine	W. Day	T. Cannon
1796	Parisot	R. Prince	J. Arnull	1870	Gamos	H. Woolcott	G. Fordham
1797	Nike	J. Pratt	F. Buckle	1871	Hannah	J. Hayhoe	C. Maidment
1798	Bellissima	R. Prince	F. Buckle	1872	Reine	T. Jennings	G. Fordham
1799	Bellina	J. Pratt	F. Buckle	1873	Marie Stuart	R. Peck	T. Cannon
1800	Ephemera	F. Neale	D. Fitzpatrick	1874	Apology	W. Osborne	J. Osborne
1801	Eleanor	J. Frost	J. Saunders	1875	Spinaway	M. Dawson	F. Archer
1802	Scotia	R. Robson	F. Buckle	1876	Enguerrande	C. Wetherall	Hudson
1803	Theophania	S. King	F. Buckle		*and* Camelia	T. Cunnington	T. Glover
1804	Pelisse	R. Robson	W. Clift	1877	Placida	J. Marsh	H. Jeffery
1805	Meteora	R. Robson	F. Buckle	1878	Jannette	M. Dawson	F. Archer
1806	Bronze	R. Boyce	W. Edwards	1879	Wheel Of Fortune	M. Dawson	F. Archer
1807	Briseis	R. Robson	S. Chifney	1880	Jenny Howlet	W. l'Anson	J. Snowden
1808	Morel	R. Robson	W. Clift	1881	Thebais	A. Taylor	G. Fordham
1809	Maid Of Orleans	R. Robson	J. Moss	1882	Geheimnis	J. Porter	T. Cannon
1810	Oriana	W. Peirse	W. Peirse	1883	Bonny Jean	J. Cannon	J. Watts
1811	Sorcery	R. Boyce	S. Chifney	1884	Busybody	T. Cannon	T. Cannon
1812	Manuella	W. Peirse	W. Peirse	1885	Lonely	W. Gilbert	F. Archer
1813	Music	R. Robson	T. Goodisson	1886	Miss Jummy	R. Marsh	J. Watts
1814	Medora	R. Boyce	S. Barnard	1887	Reve D'Or	A. Taylor	C. Wood
1815	Minuet	R. Robson	T. Goodisson	1888	Seabreeze	J. Jewitt	W. Robinson
1816	Landscape	–	S. Chifney	1889	L'Abbesse De	R. Sherwood	J. Woodburn
1817	Neva	R. Boyce	F. Buckle		Jouarre		
1818	Corinne	R. Robson	F. Buckle	1890	Memoir	G. Dawson	J. Watts
1819	Shoveler	W. Chifney	S. Chifney	1891	Mimi	M. Dawson	F. Rickaby
1820	Caroline	R. Stephenson	H. Edwards	1892	La Fleche	J. Porter	G. Barrett
1821	Augusta	R. Prince	J. Robinson	1893	Mrs Butterwick	G. Dawson	J. Watts
1822	Pastille	R. Robson	H. Edwards	1894	Amiable	G. Dawson	W. Bradford
1823	Zinc	R. Robson	F. Buckle	1895	La Sagesse	M. Gurry	S. Loates
1824	Cobweb	J. Edwards	J. Robinson	1896	Canterbury Pilgrim	G. Lambton	F. Rickaby
1825	Wings	R. Robson	S. Chifney	1897	Limasol	T. Jennings	W. Bradford
1826	Lilias	J. Forth	T. Lye	1898	Airs And Graces	F. Day	W. Bradford
1827	Gulnare	J. Kent	F. Boyce	1899	Musa	H. Enoch	O. Madden
1828	Turquoise	R. Stephenson	J. Day	1900	La Roche	J. Porter	M. Cannon
1829	Green Mantle	C. Marson	G. Dockeray	1901	Cap And Bells	S. Darling	M. Henry
1830	Variation	R. Pettit	G. Edwards	1902	Sceptre	R. Sievier	H. Randall
1831	Oxygen	R. Stephenson	J. Day	1903	Our Lassie	C. Morton	M. Cannon
1832	Galata	C. Marson	P. Conolly	1904	Pretty Polly	P. Gilpin	W. Lane
1833	Vespa	H. Scott	J. Chapple	1905	Cherry Lass	W. Robinson	H. Jones
1834	Pussy	W. Day	J. Day	1906	Keystone	G. Lambton	D. Maher
1835	Queen Of Trumps	J. Blenkhorn	T. Lye	1907	Glass Doll	C. Morton	H. Randall
1836	Cyprian	J. Scott	W. Scott	1908	Signorinetta	O. Ginistrelli	W. Bullock
1837	Miss Letty	I. Blades	J. Holmes	1909	Perola	G. Davies	F. Wootton
1838	Industry	J. Scott	W. Scott	1910	Rosedrop	A. Taylor	C. Trigg
1839	Deception	W. Treen	J. Day	1911	Cherimoya	C. Marsh	F. Winter
1840	Crucifix	J. Day	J. Day	1912	Mirska	T. Jennings	J. Childs
1841	Ghuznee	J. Scott	W. Scott	1913	Jest	C. Morton	F. Rickaby
1842	Our Nell	T. Dawson	T. Lye	1914	Princess Dorrie	C. Morton	W. Huxley
1843	Poison	R. Fisher	F. Butler	1915	Snow Marten	P. Gilpin	W. Griggs
1844	The Princess	J. Scott	F. Butler	1916	Fifinella	R. Dawson	J. Childs
1845	Refraction	J. Kent	H. Bell	1917	Sunny Jane	A. Taylor	O. Madden
1846	Mendicant	J. Day	S. Day	1918	My Dear	A. Taylor	S. Donoghue
1847	Miami	W. Beresford	S. Templeman	1919	Bayuda	A. Taylor	J. Childs
1848	Cymba	J. Day	S. Templeman	1920	Charlebelle	H. Braime	A. Whalley
1849	Lady Evelyn	T. Taylor	F. Butler	1921	Love In Idleness	A. Taylor	J. Childs
1850	Rhedycina	W. Goodwin	F. Butler	1922	Pogrom	A. Taylor	E. Gardner
1851	Iris	J. Scott	F. Butler	1923	Brownhylda	R. Dawson	V. Smyth
1852	Songstress	J. Scott	F. Butler	1924	Straitlace	D. Waugh	F. O'Neill

Jockey Steve Cauthen and trainer Henry Cecil win the second Epsom Oaks in four years as Diminuendo (1988) follows Oh So Sharp's 1985 success.

YEAR	HORSE	TRAINER	JOCKEY
1925	Saucy Sue	A. Taylor	F. Bullock
1926	Short Story	A. Taylor	R. Jones
1927	Beam	F. Butters	T. Weston
1928	Toboggan	F. Butters	T. Weston
1929	Pennycomequick	J. Lawson	H. Jelliss
1930	Rose of England	T. Hogg	G. Richards
1931	Brulette	F. Carter	E.C. Elliott
1932	Udaipur	F. Butters	M. Beary
1933	Chatelaine	F. Templeman	S. Wragg
1934	Light Brocade	F. Butters	B. Carslake
1935	Quashed	C. Leader	H. Jelliss
1936	Lovely Rosa	H. Cottrill	T. Weston
1937	Exhibitionnist	J. Lawson	S. Donoghue
1938	Rockfel	O. Bell	H. Wragg
1939	Galatea	J. Lawson	R. Jones
1940	Godiva	W. Jarvis	D. Marks
1941	Commotion	F. Darling	H. Wragg
1942	Sun Chariot	F. Darling	G. Richards
1943	Why Hurry	N. Cannon	E.C. Elliott
1944	Hycilla	C. Boyd-Rochfort	G. Bridgland
1945	Sun Stream	W. Earl	H. Wragg
1946	Steady Aim	F. Butters	H. Wragg
1947	Imprudence	J. Lieux	R. Johnstone
1948	Masaka	F. Butters	W. Nevett
1949	Musidora	C. Elsey	E. Britt
1950	Asmena	C. Semblat	R. Johnstone
1951	Neasham Belle	G. Brooke	S. Clayton
1952	Frieze	C. Elsey	E. Britt
1953	Ambiguity	J. Colling	J. Mercer
1954	Sun Cap	R. Carver	R. Johnstone
1955	Meld	C. Boyd-Rochfort	W.H. Carr
1956	Sicarelle	F. Mathet	F. Palmer
1957	Carrozza	N. Murless	L. Piggott
1958	Bella Paola	F. Mathet	M. Garcia
1959	Petite Etoile	N. Murless	L. Piggott
1960	Never Too Late	E. Pollet	R. Poincelet
1961	Sweet Solera	R. Day	W. Rickaby

YEAR	HORSE	TRAINER	JOCKEY
1962	Monade	J. Lieux	Y. Saint-Martin
1963	Noblesse	P.J. Prendergast	G. Bougoure
1964	Homeward Bound	J. Oxley	G. Starkey
1965	Long Look	M.V. O'Brien	J. Purtell
1966	Valoris	M.V. O'Brien	L. Piggott
1967	Pia	W. Elsey	E. Hide
1968	La Lagune	F. Boutin	G. Thiboeuf
1969	Sleeping Partner	D. Smith	J. Gorton
1970	Lupe	N. Murless	A. Barclay
1971	Altesse Royale	N. Murless	G. Lewis
1972	Ginevra	H. Price	A. Murray
1973	Mysterious	N. Murless	G. Lewis
1974	Polygamy	P. Walwyn	P. Eddery
1975	Juliette Marny	J. Tree	L. Piggott
1976	Pawneese	A. Penna	Y. Saint-Martin
1977	Dunfermline	W. Hern	W. Carson
1978	Fair Salinia	M. Stoute	G. Starkey
1979	Scintillate	J. Tree	P. Eddery
1980	Bireme	W. Hern	W. Carson
1981	Blue Wind	D.K. Weld	L. Piggott
1982	Time Charter	H. Candy	W. Newnes
1983	Sun Princess	W. Hern	W. Carson
1984	Circus Plume	J. Dunlop	L. Piggott
1985	Oh So Sharp	H. Cecil	S. Cauthen
1986	Midway Lady	B. Hanbury	R. Cochrane
1987	Unite	M. Stoute	W.R. Swinburn
1988	Diminuendo	H. Cecil	S. Cauthen

ENGLAND

GOLD CUP
Ascot, Berkshire: 2½ miles (4,000 m).
Three-year-olds and up. First run: 1807

YEAR	HORSE	TRAINER	JOCKEY
1930	Bosworth	Frank Butters	T. Weston
1931	Trimdon	J. Lawson	J. Childs
1932	Trimdon	J. Lawson	J. Childs
1933	Foxhunter	J. Jarvis	H. Wragg
1934	Felicitation	Frank Butters	G. Richards
1935	Tiberius	J. Lawson	T. Weston
1936	Quashed	C. Leader	R. Perryman
1937	Precipitation	C. Boyd-Rochfort	P. Beasley
1938	Flares	C. Boyd-Rochfort	R. Jones
1939	Flyon	J. Jarvis	E. Smith
1941	Finis	O. Bell	H. Wragg
1942	Owen Tudor	F. Darling	G. Richards
1943	Ujiji	J. Lawson	G. Richards
1944	Umidadd	Frank Butters	G. Richards
1945	Ocean Swell	J. Jarvis	E. Smith
1946	Caracalla II	C. Semblat	E.C. Elliott
1947	Souverain	H. Delavaud	M. Lollierou
1948	Arbar	C. Semblat	E.C. Elliott
1949	Alycidon	W. Earl	D. Smith
1950	Supertello	J. Waugh	D. Smith
1951	Pan II	E. Pollet	R. Poincelet
1952	Aquino II	F. Armstrong	G. Richards
1953	Souepi	G. Digby	E.C. Elliott
1954	Elpenor	E.C. Elliott	J. Doyasbere
1955	Botticelli	Marchese della Rocchetta	E. Camici
1956	Macip	E.C. Elliott	S. Boullenger
1957	Zarathustra	C. Boyd-Rochfort	L. Piggott
1958	Gladness	M.V. O'Brien	L. Piggott
1959	Wallaby II	P. Carter	F. Palmer
1960	Sheshoon	A. Head	G. Moore
1961	Pandofell	F. Maxwell	L. Piggott
1962	Balto	M. Bonaventure	F. Palmer
1963	Twilight Alley	N. Murless	L. Piggott
1964	No race		
1965	Fighting Charlie	F. Maxwell	L. Piggott
1966	Fighting Charlie	F. Maxwell	G. Starkey
1967	Parbury	D. Candy	J. Mercer
1968	Pardallo II	C. Bartholomew	W. Pyers
1969	Levmoss	S. McGrath	W. Williamson
1970	Precipice Wood	Mrs R. Lomax	J. Lindley
1971	Random Shot	A. Budgett	G. Lewis
1972	Erimo Hawk	G. Barling	P. Eddery
1973	Lassalle	R. Carver	J. Lindley
1974	Ragstone	J. Dunlop	R. Hutchinson
1975	Sagaro	F. Boutin	L. Piggott
1976	Sagaro	F. Boutin	L. Piggott
1977	Sagaro	F. Boutin	L. Piggott
1978	Shangamuzo	M. Stoute	G. Starkey
1979	Le Moss	H. Cecil	L. Piggott
1980	Le Moss	H. Cecil	J. Mercer
1981	Ardross	H. Cecil	L. Piggott
1982	Ardross	H. Cecil	L. Piggott
1983	Little Wolf	W. Hern	W. Carson
1984	Gildoran	B. Hills	S. Cauthen
1985	Gildoran	B. Hills	B. Thomson
1986	Longboat	W. Hern	W. Carson
1987	Paean	H. Cecil	S. Cauthen
1988	Sadeem	G. Harwood	G. Starkey

SUSSEX STAKES
Goodwood, Sussex: 1 mile (1,600 m).
Three-year-olds and up. First run: 1841

YEAR	HORSE	TRAINER	JOCKEY
1930	Paradine	J. Lawson	R. Jones
1931	Inglesant	J. Lawson	R. Jones
1932	Dastur	Frank Butters	M. Beary
1933	The Abbot	W. Jarvis	J. Childs
1934	Badruddin	Frank Butters	F. Fox
1935	Hairan	Frank Butters	R. Perryman
1936	Corpach	J. Lawson	G. Richards
1937	Pascal	F. Darling	G. Richards
1938	Faroe	C. Leader	R. Perryman
1939	Olein	B. Jarvis	T. Lowrey
1946	Radiotherapy	F. Templeman	G. Richards
1947	Combat	F. Darling	G. Richards
1948	My Babu	F. Armstrong	C. Smirke
1949	Krakatao	N. Murless	G. Richards
1950	Palestine	N. Marsh	C. Smirke
1951	Le Sage	T. Carey	G. Richards
1952	Agitator	N. Murless	G. Richards
1953	King Of The Tudors	W. Stephenson	C. Spares
1954	Landau	N. Murless	W. Snaith
1955	My Kingdom	W. Nightingall	D. Smith
1956	Lucero	H. Wragg	E. Mercer
1957	Quorum	W. Lyde	A.J. Russell
1958	Major Portion	T. Leader	E. Smith
1959	Petite Etoile	N. Murless	L. Piggott
1960	Venture VII	A. Head	G. Moore
1961	Le Levanstell	S. McGrath	G. Williamson
1962	Romulus	R. Johnson Houghton	W. Swinburn
1963	Queen's Hussar	T. Corbett	R. Hutchinson
1964	Roan Rocket	G. Todd	L. Piggott
1965	Carlemont	P.J. Prendergast	R. Hutchinson
1966	Paveh	T. Ainsworth	R. Hutchinson
1967	Reform	Sir G. Richards	A. Breasley
1968	Petingo	F. Armstrong	L. Piggott
1969	Jimmy Reppin	J. Sutcliffe	G. Lewis
1970	Humble Duty	P. Walwyn	D. Keith
1971	Brigadier Gerard	W. Hern	J. Mercer
1972	Sallust	W. Hern	J. Mercer
1973	Thatch	M.V. O'Brien	L. Piggott
1974	Ace of Spies	M. Zilber	J. Lindley
1975	Bolkonski	H. Cecil	G. Dettori
1976	Wollow	H. Cecil	G. Dettori
1977	Artaius	M.V. O'Brien	L. Piggott
1978	Jaazeiro	M.V. O'Brien	L. Piggott
1979	Kris	H. Cecil	J. Mercer
1980	Posse	J. Dunlop	P. Eddery
1981	Kings Lake	M.V. O'Brien	P. Eddery
1982	On The House	H. Wragg	J. Reid
1983	Noalcoholic	G. Pritchard-Gordon	G. Duffield
1984	Chief Singer	R. Sheather	R. Cochrane
1985	Roussillon	G. Harwood	G. Starkey
1986	Sonic Lady	M. Stoute	W.R. Swinburn
1987	Soviet Star	A. Fabre	G. Starkey
1988	Warning	G. Harwood	P. Eddery

JULY CUP
**Newmarket, Suffolk: 6 f (1,200 m).
Three-year-olds and up. First run: 1876**

YEAR	HORSE	TRAINER	JOCKEY
1930	Sir Cosmo	W. Walters	G. Swann
1931	Xandover	B. Jarvis	E.C. Elliott
1932	Concerto	O. Bell	H. Wragg
1933	Myrobella	F. Darling	G. Richards
1934	Coroado	W. Easterby	H. Gunn
1935	Bellacose	R.J. Colling	P. Beasley
1936	Bellacose	R.J. Colling	P. Beasley
1937	Mickey The Greek	H. Leach	H. Wragg
1938	Shalfleet	H. Leader	R. Perryman
1939	Portobello	R.J. Colling	T. Lowrey
1941	Comatas	O. Bell	W. Nevett
1945	Honeyway	J. Jarvis	E. Smith
1946	The Bug	H. Wellesley	C. Smirke
1947	Falls Of Clyde	E. Williams	S. Wragg
1948	Palm Vista	P. Beasley	E. Smith
1949	Abernant	N. Murless	G. Richards
1950	Abernant	N. Murless	G. Richards
1951	Hard Sauce	N. Bertie	G. Richards
1952	Set Fair	W. Nightingall	E. Smith
1953	Devon Vintage	J. Colling	G. Richards
1954	Vilmoray	B. Bullock	W. Snaith
1955	Pappa Fourway	W. Dutton	W.H. Carr
1956	Matador	J. Waugh	W. Rickaby
1957	Vigo	W. Dutton	L. Piggott
1958	Right Boy	W. Dutton	L. Piggott
1959	Right Boy	P. Rohan	L. Piggott
1960	Tin Whistle	P. Rohan	L. Piggott
1961	Galivanter	W. Hern	W.H. Carr
1962	Marsolve	R. Day	W. Rickaby
1963	Secret Step	P. Hastings-Bass	G. Lewis
1964	Daylight Robbery	A. Budgett	A. Breasley
1965	Merry Madcap	F. Maxwell	R. Hutchinson
1966	Lucasland	J. Waugh	E. Eldin
1967	Forlorn River	W.A. Stephenson	B. Raymond
1968	So Blessed	M. Jarvis	F. Durr
1969	Tudor Music	M. Jarvis	F. Durr
1970	Huntercombe	A. Budgett	A. Barclay
1971	Realm	J. Winter	B. Taylor
1972	Parsimony	R. Johnson Houghton	R. Hutchinson
1973	Thatch	M.V. O'Brien	L. Piggott
1974	Saritamer	M.V. O'Brien	L. Piggott
1975	Lianga	A. Penna	Y. Saint-Martin
1976	Lochnager	M.W. Easterby	E. Hide
1977	Gentilhombre	N. Adam	P. Cook
1978	Solinus	M.V. O'Brien	L. Piggott
1979	Thatching	M.V. O'Brien	L. Piggott
1980	Moorestyle	R. Armstrong	L. Piggott
1981	Marwell	M. Stoute	W.R. Swinburn
1982	Sharpo	J. Tree	P. Eddery
1983	Habibti	J. Dunlop	W. Carson
1984	Chief Singer	R. Sheather	R. Cochrane
1985	Never So Bold	R. Armstrong	S. Cauthen
1986	Green Desert	M. Stoute	W.R. Swinburn
1987	Ajdal	M. Stoute	W.R. Swinburn
1988	Soviet Star	A. Fabre	C. Asmussen

CORAL ECLIPSE STAKES
**Sandown Park, Surrey: 1¼ miles (2,000 m).
Three-year-olds and up. First run: 1886**

YEAR	HORSE	TRAINER	JOCKEY
1930	Rustom Pasha	R. Dawson	H. Wragg
1931	Caerleon	G. Lambton	T. Weston
1932	Miracle	J. Jarvis	H. Wragg
1933	Loaningdale	C. Boyd-Rochfort	J. Childs
1934	King Salmon	O. Bell	H. Wragg
1935	Windsor Lad	M. Marsh	C. Smirke
1936	Rhodes Scholar	J. Lawson	R. Dick
1937	Boswell	C. Boyd-Rochfort	P. Beasley
1938	Pasch	F. Darling	G. Richards
1939	Blue Peter	J. Jarvis	E. Smith
1946	Gulf Stream	W. Earl	H. Wragg
1947	Migoli	Frank Butters	C. Smirke
1948	Petition	Frank Butters	K. Gethin
1949	Djeddah	C. Semblat	E.C. Elliott
1950	Flocon	P. Carter	F. Palmer
1951	Mystery IX	P. Carter	L. Piggott
1952	Tulyar	M. Marsh	C. Smirke
1953	Argur	J. Glynn	E.C. Elliott
1954	King Of The Tudors	W. Stephenson	K. Gethin
1955	Darius	H. Wragg	L. Piggott
1956	Tropique	G. Watson	P. Blanc
1957	Arctic Explorer	N. Murless	L. Piggott
1958	Ballymoss	M.V. O'Brien	A. Breasley
1959	Saint Crespin III	A. Head	G. Moore
1960	Javelot	P. Carter	F. Palmer
1961	St Paddy	N. Murless	L. Piggott
1962	Henry The Seventh	W. Elsey	E. Hide
1963	Khalkis	P.J. Prendergast	G. Bougoure
1964	Ragusa	P.J. Prendergast	G. Bougoure
1965	Canisbay	C. Boyd-Rochfort	S. Clayton
1966	Pieces Of Eight	M.V. O'Brien	L. Piggott
1967	Busted	N. Murless	W. Rickaby
1968	Royal Palace	N. Murless	A. Barclay
1969	Wolver Hollow	H. Cecil	L. Piggott
1970	Connaught	N. Murless	A. Barclay
1971	Mill Reef	I. Balding	G. Lewis
1972	Brigadier Gerard	W. Hern	J. Mercer
1973	Scottish Rifle	J. Dunlop	R. Hutchinson
1974	Coup De Feu	D. Sasse	P. Eddery
1975	Star Appeal	T. Grieper	G. Starkey
1976	Wollow	H. Cecil	G. Dettori
1977	Artaius	M.V. O'Brien	L. Piggott
1978	Gunner B	H. Cecil	J. Mercer
1979	Dickins Hill	M.O'Toole	A. Murray
1980	Ela-Mana-Mou	W. Hern	W. Carson
1981	Master Willie	H. Candy	P. Waldron
1982	Kalaglow	G. Harwood	G. Starkey
1983	Solford	M.V. O'Brien	P. Eddery
1984	Sadler's Wells	M.V. O'Brien	P. Eddery
1985	Pebbles	C. Brittain	S. Cauthen
1986	Dancing Brave	G. Harwood	G. Starkey
1987	Mtoto	A. Steward	M. Roberts
1988	Mtoto	A. Steward	M. Roberts

FRANCE

PRIX DU JOCKEY CLUB
Chantilly: 1½ miles (2,400 m).
Three-year-olds

YEAR	HORSE	TRAINER	JOCKEY
1950	Scratch II	C. Semblat	W. Johnstone
1951	Sicambre	M. Bonaventure	P. Blanc
1952	Auriban	C.Semblat	W. Johnstone
1953	Chamant	C. Bartholomew	M. Garcia
1954	Le Petit Prince	C.Semblat	R. Bertiglia
1955	Rapace	R. Wallon	F. Palmer
1956	Philius II	C. Elliott	S. Boullenger
1957	Amber	R. Carver	M. Garcia
1958	Tamanar	J. Cunnington	J. Deforge
1959	Herbager	P. Pelat	G. Chancelier
1960	Charlottesville	A. Head	G. Moore
1961	Right Royal V	E. Pollet	R. Poincelet
1962	Val De Loir	M. Bonaventure	F. Palmer
1963	Sanctus	E. Pollet	M. Larraun
1964	Le Fabuleux	W. Head	J. Massard
1965	Reliance II	F. Mathet	Y. Saint-Martin
1966	Nelcius	M. Clement	Y. Saint-Martin
1967	Astec	A. Mieux	A. Jezequal
1968	Tapalque	F. Mathet	Y. Saint-Martin
1969	Goodly	W. Head	F. Head
1970	Sassafras	F. Mathet	Y. Saint-Martin
1971	Rheffic	F. Mathet	W. Pyers
1972	Hard To Beat	R. Carver	L. Piggott
1973	Roi Lear	A. Head	F. Head
1974	Caracolero	F. Boutin	P. Paquet
1975	Val De L'Orne	A. Head	F. Head
1976	Youth	M. Zilber	F. Head
1977	Crystal Palace	F. Mathet	G. Dubroeucq
1978	Acamas	G. Bonaventure	Y. Saint-Martin
1979	Top Ville	F. Mathet	Y. Saint-Martin
1980	Policeman	C. Millbank	W. Carson
1981	Bikala	P. Biancone	S. Gorli
1982	Assert	D. O'Brien	C. Roche
1983	Caerleon	M.V. O'Brien	P. Eddery
1984	Darshaan	A. de Royer-Dupré	Y. Saint-Martin
1985	Mouktar	A. de Royer-Dupré	Y. Saint-Martin
1986	Bering	Mme C. Head	G. Moore
1987	Natroun	A. de Royer-Dupré	Y. Saint-Martin
1988	Hours After	P. Biancone	P. Eddery

PRIX DE L'ARC DE TRIOMPHE
Longchamp, Paris: 1½ miles (2,400 m).
Three-year-olds and up. First run: 1920

YEAR	HORSE	TRAINER	JOCKEY
1920	Comrade	P.P. Gilpin	F. Bullock
1921	Ksar	W.R. Walton	G. Stern
1922	Ksar	W.R. Walton	F. Bullock
1923	Parth	J.H. Crawford	F. O'Neill
1924	Massine	E. Cunnington	A. Sharpe
1925	Priori	P. Carter	M. Allemand
1926	Biribi	J. Torterolo	D. Torterolo
1927	Mon Talisman	F. Carter	C.H. Semblat
1928	Kantar	R. Carver	A. Esling
1929	Ortello	W. Carter	P. Caprioli
1930	Motrico	M. d'Okhuysen	M. Fruhinsholtz
1931	Pearl Cap	F. Carter	C.H. Semblat
1932	Motrico	M. d'Okhuysen	C.H. Semblat
1933	Crapom	F. Regoli	P. Caprioli
1934	Brantôme	L. Robert	C. Bouillon
1935	Samos	F. Carter	W. Sibbritt
1936	Corrida	J.E. Watts	E.C. Elliott
1937	Corrida	J.E. Watts	E.C. Elliott
1938	Eclair Au Chocolat	L. Robert	C. Bouillon
1939–1940 no race			
1941	Le Pacha	J. Cunnington	P. Francolon
1942	Djebel	C.H. Semblat	J. Doyasbère
1943	Verso	C. Clout	G. Duforez
1944	Ardan	C.H. Semblat	J. Doyasbère
1945	Nikellora	R. Pelat	R. Johnstone
1946	Caracalla	C.H. Semblat	E.C. Elliott
1947	Le Paillon	W. Head	F. Rochetti
1948	Migoli	Frank Butters	C. Smirke
1949	Coronation	C.H. Semblat	R. Poincelet
1950	Tantieme	F. Mathet	J. Doyasbere
1951	Tantieme	F. Mathet	J. Doyasbere
1952	Nuccio	A. Head	R. Poincelet
1953	La Sorellina	E. Pollet	M. Larraun
1954	Sica Boy	P. Pelat	W.R. Johnstone
1955	Ribot	U. Penco	E. Camici
1956	Ribot	U. Penco	E. Camici
1957	Oroso	D. Lescalle	S. Boullenger
1958	Ballymoss	M.V. O'Brien	A. Breasley
1959	Saint Crespin	A. Head	G. Moore
1960	Puissant Chef	C. Bartholomew	M. Garcia
1961	Molvedo	A. Maggi	E. Camici
1962	Soltikoff	R. Pelat	M. Depalmas
1963	Exbury	G. Watson	J. Deforge
1964	Prince Royal	G. Bridgland	R. Poincelet
1965	Sea Bird	E. Pollet	T.P. Glennon
1966	Bon Mot	W. Head	F. Head
1967	Topyo	C. Bartholomew	W. Pyers
1968	Vaguely Noble	E. Pollet	W. Williamson
1969	Levmoss	S. McGrath	W. Williamson
1970	Sassafras	F. Mathet	Y. Saint-Martin
1971	Mill Reef	I. Balding	G. Lewis
1972	San San	A. Penna	F. Head
1973	Rheingold	B. Hills	L. Piggott
1974	Allez France	A. Penna	Y. Saint-Martin
1975	Star Appeal	T. Grieper	G. Starkey
1976	Ivanjica	A. Head	F. Head
1977	Alleged	M.V. O'Brien	L. Piggott
1978	Alleged	M.V. O'Brien	L. Piggott
1979	Three Troikas	Mme C. Head	F. Head
1980	Detroit	O. Douieb	P. Eddery
1981	Gold River	A. Head	G.W. Moore
1982	Akiyda	F. Mathet	Y. Saint-Martin
1983	All Along	P. Biancone	W.R. Swinburn
1984	Sagace	P. Biancone	Y. Saint-Martin
1985	Rainbow Quest	J. Tree	P. Eddery
1986	Dancing Brave	G. Harwood	P. Eddery
1987	Trempolino	A. Fabre	P. Eddery
1988	Tony Bin	L. Carmic	J. Reid

IRELAND

IRISH DERBY
The Curragh: 1½ miles (2,400 m).
Three-year-olds. First run: 1866

YEAR	HORSE	TRAINER	JOCKEY
1866	Selim	–	C. Maidment
1867	Golden Plover	–	C. Maidment
1868	Madeira	–	D. Wynne
1869	The Scout	–	W. Miller
1870	Billy Pitt	T. Connolly	W. Canavan
1871	Maid of Athens	P. Doucie	T. Broderick
1872	Trickstress	W. Miller	T. Moran
1873	Kyrle Daly	P. Doucie	T. Broderick
1874	Ben Battle	T. Connolly	E. Martin
1875	Innishowen	J. Toon	G. Ashworth
1876	Umpire	J. French	P. Lynch
1877	Redskin	D. Broderick	F. Wynne
1878	Madame Dubarry	F. Martin	F. Wynne
1879	Soulouque	T. Connolly	J. Connolly
1880	King Of The Bees	D. Broderick	F. Wynne
1881	Master Ned	P. Doucie	T. Broderick
1882	Sortie	P. Doucie	N. Behan
1883	Sylph	J. Dunne	J. Connolly
1884	Theologian	W. Behan	J. Connolly
1885	St Kevin	J. Dunne	H. Saunders
1886	Theodemir	G. Moore	J. Connolly
1887	Pet Fox	H.E. Linde	T. Kavanagh
1888	Theodolite	G. Moore	W. Warne
1889	Tragedy	T.G. Gordon	T. Beasley
1890	Kentish Fire	R. Meredith	M. Dawson
1891	Narraghmore	C. Archer	T. Beasley
1892	Roy Neil	R. Meredith	M. Dawson
1893	Bowline	R. Meredith	M. Dawson
1894	Blairfinde	S. Darling	W.T. Garrett
1895	Portmarnock	S.C. Jeffery	W. Clayton
1896	Gulsalberk	S.C. Jeffery	A. Aylin
1897	Wales	W.P. Cullen	T. Fiely
1898	Noble Howard	R. Exshaw	T. Moran
1899	Oppressor	S.C. Jeffery	A. Anthony
1900	Gallinaria	D. McNally	G.W. Lushington
1901	Carrigavalla	D. McNally	A. Anthony
1902	St. Brendan	M. Dawson	D. Condon
1903	Lord Rossmore	J. Fallon	J. Dillon
1904	Royal Arch	M. Dawson	F. Morgan
1905	Flax Park	J. Dunne	P. Hughes
1906	Killeagh	M. Dawson	C. Aylin
1907	Orby	F.F. MacCabe	W. Bullock
1908	Wild Bouquet	J. Dunne	P. Hughes
1909	Bachelor's Double	M. Dawson	A. Sharples
1910	Aviator	P. Behan	John Doyle
1911	Shanballymore	J. Dwyer	John Doyle
1912	Civility	B. Kirkby	D. Maher
1913	Bachelor's Wedding	H.S. Persse	S. Donoghue
1914	Land Of Song	H.S. Persse	S. Donoghue
1915	Ballaghtobin	J. Hunter	W. Barrett
1916	Furore	V. Tabor	H. Robbins
1917	First Flier	J.J. Parkinson	W. Barrett
1918	King John	P.P. Gilpin	H. Beasley
1919	Loch Lomond	J.J. Parkinson	E.M. Quirke
1920	He Goes	J. Butters	F. Templeman
1921	Ballyheron	J. Hunter	M. Wing
1922	Spike Island	P.P. Gilpin	G. Archibald
1923	Waygood	W. Halsey	M. Wing
1924	Haine	C. Davis	Jos Canty
	and Zodiac	P.P. Gilpin	G. Archibald
1925	Zionist	R.C. Dawson	H. Beasley
1926	Embargo	C. Bartholomew	S. Donoghue
1927	Knight Of The Grail	R.J. Farquharson	M. Beary
1928	Baytown	N. Scobie	F. Fox
1929	Kopi	W. Earl	F. Winter
1930	Rock Star	W. Nightingall	M. Wing
1931	Sea Serpent	P. Behan	Jos Canty
1932	Dastur	Frank Butters	M. Beary
1933	Harinero	R.C. Dawson	C. Ray
1934	Primero	R.C. Dawson	C. Ray
	and Patriot King	F.C. Pratt	G. Bezant
1935	Museum	J.T. Rogers	S. Donoghue

PHOENIX CHAMPION STAKES
Phoenix Park, Dublin: 1¼ miles (2,000 m).
Three-year-olds and up. First run: 1984

YEAR	HORSE	TRAINER	JOCKEY
1984	Sadler's Wells	M.V. O'Brien	P. Eddery
1985	Commanche Run	L. Cumani	L. Piggott
1986	Park Express	J. Bolger	J. Reid
1987	Triptych	P. Biancone	A. Cruz
1988	Indian Skimmer	H. Cecil	M. Roberts

YEAR	HORSE	TRAINER	JOCKEY
1936	Raeburn	J. Lawson	T. Burns
1937	Phideas	J.T. Rogers	S. Donoghue
1938	Rosewell	A.J. Blake	M. Wing
1939	Mondragon	Jas Canty	Jos Canty
1940	Turkhan	Frank Butters	C. Smirke
1941	Sol Oriens	A.J. Blake	G. Wells
1942	Windsor Slipper	M. Collins	M. Wing
1943	The Phoenix	F.S. Myerscough	Jos Canty
1944	Slide On	R. Fetherston-haugh	J. Moylan
1945	Piccadilly	R. Fetherston-haugh	J. Moylan
1946	Bright News	D. Rogers	M. Wing
1947	Sayajirao	F. Armstrong	E. Britt
1948	Nathoo	Frank Butters	W.R. Johnstone
1949	Hindostan	Frank Butters	W.R. Johnstone
1950	Dark Warrior	P.J. Prendergast	J.W. Thompson
1951	Fraise Du Bois	H. Wragg	C. Smirke
1952	Thirteen Of Diamonds	P.J. Prendergast	J. Mullane
1953	Chamier	M.V. O'Brien	W. Rickaby
1954	Zarathustra	M. Hurley	P. Powell
1955	Panaslipper	S. McGrath	J. Eddery
1956	Talgo	H. Wragg	E. Mercer
1957	Ballymoss	M.V. O'Brien	T.P. Burns
1958	Sindon	M. Dawson	L. Ward
1959	Fidalgo	H. Wragg	J. Mercer
1960	Chamour	A.S. O'Brien	G. Bougoure
1961	Your Highness	H. Cottrill	H. Holmes
1962	Tambourine	E. Pollet	R. Poincelet
1963	Ragusa	P.J. Prendergast	G. Bougoure
1964	Santa Claus	J.M. Rogers	W. Burke
1965	Meadow Court	P.J. Prendergast	L. Piggott
1966	Sodium	G. Todd	F. Durr
1967	Ribocco	R. Johnson Houghton	L. Piggott
1968	Ribero	R. Johnson Houghton	L. Piggott
1969	Prince Regent	E. Pollet	G. Lewis
1970	Nijinsky	M.V. O'Brien	L. Ward
1971	Irish Ball	P. Lallié	A. Gibert
1972	Steel Pulse	A. Breasley	W. Williamson
1973	Weavers' Hall	S. McGrath	G. McGrath
1974	English Prince	P. Walwyn	Y. Saint-Martin
1975	Grundy	P. Walwyn	P. Eddery
1976	Malacate	F. Boutin	P. Paquet
1977	The Minstrel	M.V. O'Brien	L. Piggott
1978	Shirley Heights	J. Dunlop	G. Starkey
1979	Troy	W. Hern	W. Carson
1980	Tyrnavos	B. Hobbs	A. Murray
1981	Shergar	M. Stoute	L. Piggott
1982	Assert	D.V. O'Brien	C. Roche
1983	Shareef Dancer	M. Stoute	W.R. Swinburn
1984	El Gran Señor	M.V. O'Brien	P. Eddery
1985	Law Society	M.V. O'Brien	P. Eddery
1986	Shahrastani	M. Stoute	W.R. Swinburn
1987	Sir Harry Lewis	B. Hills	J. Reid
1988	Kahyasi	L. Cumani	R. Cochrane

Legendary Johnny Longden has the ride here on America's 1941 Triple Crown hero, Whirlaway. Eddie Arcaro was aboard for the triumphant treble.

Preakness, after whom the famous Preakness Stakes was named, was bred at Woodburn Farm, Kentucky. He was bought by Milton H Sanford as a yearling for $2,000, in 1868.

UNITED STATES OF AMERICA

ARLINGTON MILLION
Arlington Park, Chicago*: 1¼ miles (2,000 m). Three-year-olds and up. First run: 1981

YEAR	HORSE	TRAINER	JOCKEY
1981	John Henry	R. McAnally	W. Shoemaker
1982	Perrault	C. Whittingham	L. Pincay
1983	Tolomeo	L. Cumani	P. Eddery
1984	John Henry	R. McAnally	C. McCarron
1985	Teleprompter	J.W. Watts	T. Ives
1986	Estrapade	C. Whittingham	F. Toro
1987	Manila	L. Jolley	A. Cordero
1988	Mill Native	A. Fabre	C. Asmussen

WASHINGTON INTERNATIONAL
Laurel Washington, D.C.: 1½ miles (2,400 m). Three-year-olds and up. First run: 1952

YEAR	HORSE	TRAINER	JOCKEY
1952	Wilwyn	J. Waugh	E. Mercer
1953	Worden	G. Bridgland	C. Smirke
1954	Fisherman	S. Veitch	E. Arcaro
1955	El Chama	J. Labelle	R. Bustamante
1956	Master Boeing	G. Pelet	G. Chancelier
1957	Mahan	H. Trotsek	S. Boulmetis
1958	Sailors Guide	J.B. Bond	H. Grant
1959	Bald Eagle	W. Stephens	M. Ycaza
1960	Bald Eagle	W. Stephens	M. Ycaza
1961	T V Lark	P. Parker	J. Longden
1962	Match II	F. Mathet	Y. St Martin
1963	Mongo	F.A. Bonsal	W. Chambers
1964	Kelso	C. Hanford	I. Valenzuela
1965	Diatome	G. Watson	J. Deforge
1966	Behistoun	J. Lieux	J. Deforge
1967	Fort Marcy	E. Burch	M. Ycaza
1968	Sir Ivor	M.V. O'Brien	L. Piggott
1969	Karabas	B.van Cutsem	L. Piggott
1970	Fort Marcy	E. Burch	J. Velasquez
1971	Run The Gantlet	E. Burch	P. Woodhouse
1972	Droll Role	T. Kelly	B. Baeza
1973	Dahlia	M. Zilber	W. Pyers
1974	Admetus	J. Cunnington	M. Philipperon
1975	Nobiliary	M. Zilber	S. Hawley
1976	Youth	M. Zilber	S. Hawley
1977	Johny D	M. Kay	S. Cauthen
1978	Mac Diarmida	F. Schulhofer	J. Cruguet
1979	Bowl Game	J. Graver	J. Velasquez
1980	Argument	M. Zilber	L. Piggott
1981	Providential II	C. Whittingham	A. Lequeux
1982	April Run	F. Boutin	C. Asmussen
1983	All Along	P. Biancone	W.R. Swinburn
1984	Seattle Song	F. Boutin	C. Asmussen
1985	Vanlandingham	C. McGaughey	D. MacBeth
1986	Lieutenant's Lark	H. Tesher	R. Davis
1987	Le Glorieux	R. Collet	L. Pincay
1988	Sunshine Forever	J. Veitch	A. Cordero

BELMONT STAKES
Belmont Park, NY: 1½ miles (2,400 m). *Three-year-olds*

YEAR	HORSE	TRAINER	JOCKEY	YEAR	HORSE	TRAINER	JOCKEY
1867	Ruthless	A. Minor	J. Gilpatrick	1941	Whirlaway	B. Jones	E. Arcaro
1868	General Duke	A. Thompson	R. Swim	1942	Shut Out	J. Gaver	E. Arcaro
1869	Fenian	J. Pincus	C. Miller	1943	Count Fleet	G. Cameron	J. Longden
1870	Kingfisher	R. Colston	E. Brown	1944	Bounding Home	M. Brady	G. Smith
1871	Harry Bassett	D. McDaniel	W. Miller	1945	Pavot	O. White	E. Arcaro
1872	Joe Daniels	D. McDaniel	J. Rowe	1946	Assault	M. Hirsch	W. Mehrtens
1873	Springbok	D. McDaniel	J. Rowe	1947	Phalanx	S. Veitch	R. Donoso
1874	Saxon	W. Prior	G. Barbee	1948	Citation	H. Jones	E. Arcaro
1875	Calvin	A. Anderson	R. Swim	1949	Capot	J. Gaver	T. Atkinson
1876	Algerine	T. Doswell	W. Donohoe	1950	Middleground	M. Hirsch	W. Boland
1877	Cloverbrook	J. Walden	C. Holloway	1951	Counterpoint	S. Veitch	D. Gorman
1878	Duke Of Magenta	R. Walden	W. Hughes	1952	One Count	O. White	E. Arcaro
1879	Spendthrift	T. Puryear	G. Evans	1953	Native Dancer	W. Winfrey	E. Guerin
1880	Grenada	R. Walden	T. Costello	1954	High Gun	M. Hirsch	E. Guerin
1881	Saunterer	R. Walden	T. Costello	1955	Nashua	J. Fitzsimmons	E. Arcaro
1882	Forester	L. Stuart	J. McLaughlin	1956	Needles	H. Fontaine	D. Erb
1883	George Kinney	J. Rowe	J. McLaughlin	1957	Gallant Man	J. Nerud	W. Shoemaker
1884	Panique	J. Rowe	J. McLaughlin	1958	Cavan	T. Barry	P. Anderson
1885	Tyrant	C. Claypool	P. Duffy	1959	Sword Dancer	J. Burch	W. Shoemaker
1886	Inspector B	F. McCabe	J. McLaughlin	1960	Celtic Ash	T. Barry	W. Hartack
1887	Hanover	F. McCabe	J. McLaughlin	1961	Sherluck	H. Young	B. Baeza
1888	Sir Dixon	F. McCabe	J. McLaughlin	1962	Jaipur	W. Mulholland	W. Shoemaker
1889	Eric	J. Huggins	W. Hayward	1963	Chateaugay	J. Conway	B. Baeza
1890	Burlington	A. Cooper	S. Barnes	1964	Quadrangle	J. Burch	M. Ycaza
1891	Foxford	M. Donovan	E. Garrison	1965	Hail To All	E. Yowell	J. Sellers
1892	Patron	L. Stuart	W. Hayward	1966	Amberoid	L. Laurin	W. Boland
1893	Comanche	G. Hannon	W. Simms	1967	Damascus	F. Whiteley	W. Shoemaker
1894	Henry Of Navarre	B. McClelland	W. Simms	1968	Stage Door Johnny	J. Gaver	H. Gustines
1895	Belmar	E. Feakes	F. Taral	1969	Arts And Letters	J. Burch	B. Baeza
1896	Hastings	J. Hyland	H. Griffin	1970	High Echelon	J. Jacobs	J. Rotz
1897	Scottish Chieftain	M. Byrnes	J. Scherrer	1971	Pass Catcher	E. Yowell	W. Blum
1898	Bowling Brook	R. Walden	F. Littlefield	1972	Riva Ridge	L. Laurin	R. Turcotte
1899	Jean Bereaud	S. Hildreth	R. Clawson	1973	Secretariat	L. Laurin	R. Turcotte
1900	Ildrim	H. Leigh	N. Turner	1974	Little Current	L. Rondinello	M. Rivera
1901	Commando	J. Rowe	H. Spencer	1975	Avatar	A. Doyle	W. Shoemaker
1902	Masterman	J. Hyland	J. Bullman	1976	Bold Forbes	L. Barrera	A. Cordero
1903	Africander	R. Miller	J. Bullman	1977	Seattle Slew	W. Turner	J. Cruguet
1904	Delhi	J. Rowe	G. Odom	1978	Affirmed	L. Barrera	S. Cauthen
1905	Tanya	J. Rogers	E. Hildebrand	1979	Coastal	D. Whiteley	R. Hernandez
1906	Burgomaster	J. Rogers	L. Lyne	1980	Temperance Hill	J. Cantey	E. Maple
1907	Peter Pan	J. Rowe	G. Mountain	1981	Summing	L. Barrera	G. Martens
1908	Colin	J. Rowe	J. Notter	1982	Conquistador Cielo	W. Stephens	L. Pincay
1909	Joe Madden	S. Hildreth	E. Dugan	1983	Caveat	W. Stephens	L. Pincay
1910	Sweep	J. Rowe	J. Butwell	1984	Swale	W. Stephens	L. Pincay
1911	no race			1985	Crème Fraîche	W. Stephens	E. Maple
1912	no race			1986	Danzig Connection	W. Stephens	C. McCarron
1913	Prince Eugene	J. Rowe	R. Troxler	1987	Bet Twice	W. Croft	C. Perret
1914	Luke McLuke	J. Schorr	M. Buxton	1988	Risen Star	L. Rousse	E. Delahoussaye
1915	The Finn	E. Heffner	G. Byrne				
1916	Friar Rock	S. Hildreth	E. Haynes				
1917	Hourless	S. Hildreth	J. Butwell				
1918	Johnren	A. Simons	F. Robinson				
1919	Sir Barton	H. Bedwell	J. Loftus				
1920	Man O'War	L. Feustel	C. Kummer				
1921	Grey Lag	S. Hildreth	E. Sande				
1922	Pillory	T. Healey	C. Miller				
1923	Zev	S. Hildreth	E. Sande				
1924	Mad Play	S. Hildreth	E. Sande				
1925	American Flag	G. Tompkins	A. Johnson				
1926	Crusader	G. Conway	A. Johnson				
1927	Chance Shot	P. Coyne	E. Sande				
1928	Vito	M. Hirsch	C. Kummer				
1929	Blue Larkspur	C. Hastings	M. Garner				
1930	Gallant Fox	J. Fitzsimmons	E. Sande				
1931	Twenty Grand	J. Rowe	C. Kurtsinger				
1932	Faireno	J. Fitzsimmons	T. Malley				
1933	Hurryoff	H. McDaniel	M. Garner				
1934	Peace Chance	P. Coyne	W. Wright				
1935	Omaha	J. Fitzsimmons	W. Saunders				
1936	Granville	J. Fitzsimmons	J. Stout				
1937	War Admiral	G. Conway	C. Kurtsinger				
1938	Pasteurized	G. Odom	J. Stout				
1939	Johnstown	J. Fitzsimmons	J. Stout				
1940	Bimelech	W. Hurley	F. Smith				

UNITED STATES OF AMERICA

KENTUCKY DERBY
Churchill Downs, Kentucky: 1¼ mile (2,000 m). *Three-year-olds*

YEAR	HORSE	TRAINER	JOCKEY	YEAR	HORSE	TRAINER	JOCKEY
1875	Aristedes	A. Anderson	O. Lewis	1949	Ponder	B. Jones	S. Brooks
1876	Vagrant	J. Williams	R. Swim	1950	Middleground	M. Hirsch	W. Boland
1877	Baden Baden	E. Brown	W. Walker	1951	Count Turf	S. Rutchick	C. McCreary
1878	Day Star	L. Paul	J. Carter	1952	Hill Gail	B. Jones	E. Arcaro
1879	Lord Murphy	G. Rice	C. Shauer	1953	Dark Star	E. Hayward	H. Moreno
1880	Fonso	T. Hutsell	G. Lewis	1954	Determine	W. Molter	R. York
1881	Hindoo	J. Rowe	J. McLaughlin	1955	Swaps	M. Tenney	W. Shoemaker
1882	Apollo	G. Morris	B. Hurd	1956	Needles	H. Fontaine	D. Erb
1883	Leonatus	J. McGinty	W. Donohoe	1957	Iron Liege	H. Jones	W. Hartack
1884	Buchanan	W. Bird	I. Murphy	1958	Tim Tam	H. Jones	I. Valenzuela
1885	Joe Cotton	A. Perry	E. Henderson	1959	Tomy Lee	F Childs	W. Shoemaker
1886	Ben Ali	J. Murphy	P. Duffy	1960	Venetian Way	V. Sovinski	W. Hartack
1887	Montrose	J. McGinty	I. Lewis	1961	Carry Back	J. Price	J. Sellers
1888	Macbeth	J. Campbell	G. Covington	1962	Decidedly	H. Luro	W. Hartack
1889	Spokane	J. Rodegap	T. Kiley	1963	Chateaugay	J. Conway	B. Baeza
1890	Riley	E. Corrigan	I. Murphy	1964	Northern Dancer	H. Luro	W. Hartack
1891	Kingman	D. Allen	I. Murphy	1965	Lucky Debonair	F. Catrone	W. Shoemaker
1892	Azra	J. Morris	A. Clayton	1966	Kauai King	H. Forrest	D. Brumfield
1893	Lookout	W. McDaniel	E. Kunze	1967	Proud Clarion	L. Gentry	R. Ussery
1894	Chant	E. Leigh	F. Goodale	1968	Forward Pass	H. Forrest	I. Valenzuela
1895	Halma	B. McClelland	J. Perkins	1969	Majestic Prince	J. Longden	W. Hartack
1896	Ben Brush	H. Campbell	W. Simms	1970	Dust Commander	D. Combs	M. Manganello
1897	Typhoon	J. Cahn	F. Garner	1971	Canonero	J. Arias	G. Avila
1898	Plaudit	J. Madden	W. Simms	1972	Riva Ridge	L. Laurin	R. Turcotte
1899	Manuel	R. Walden	F. Taral	1973	Secretariat	L. Laurin	R. Turcotte
1900	Lieut. Gibson	C. Hughes	J. Boland	1974	Cannonade	W. Stephens	A. Cordero
1901	His Eminence	F. Van Meter	J. Winkfield	1975	Foolish Pleasure	L. Jolley	J. Vasquez
1902	Alan-A-Dale	T. McDowell	J. Winkfield	1976	Bold Forbes	L. Barrera	A. Cordero
1903	Judge Himes	J. Mayberry	H. Booker	1977	Seattle Slew	W. Turner	J. Cruguet
1904	Elwood	C. Durnell	F. Prior	1978	Affirmed	L. Barrera	S. Cauthen
1905	Agile	R. Tucker	J. Martin	1979	Spectacular Bid	G. Delp	R. Franklin
1906	Sir Huon	P. Coyne	R. Troxler	1980	Genuine Risk	L. Jolley	J. Vasquez
1907	Pink Star	W. Fizer	A. Minder	1981	Pleasant Colony	J. Campo	J. Velasquez
1908	Stone Street	J. Hall	A. Pickens	1982	Gato Del Sol	E. Gregson	E. Delahoussaye
1909	Wintergreen	C. Mack	V. Powers	1983	Sunny's Halo	D. Cross	E. Delahoussaye
1910	Donau	G. Ham	F. Herbert	1984	Swale	W. Stephens	L. Pincay
1911	Meridian	A. Ewing	G. Archibald	1985	Spend A Buck	C. Gambolati	A. Cordero
1912	Worth	F. Taylor	C. Shilling	1986	Ferdinand	C. Whittingham	W. Shoemaker
1913	Donerail	T. Hayes	R. Goose	1987	Alysheba	J. Van Berg	C. McCarron
1914	Old Rosebud	F. Weir	J. McCabe	1988	Winning Colours	D. W. Lucas	G. Stevens
1915	Regret	J. Rowe	J. Notter				
1916	George Smith	H. Hughes	J. Loftus				
1917	Omar Khayyam	C. Patterson	C. Borel				
1918	Exterminator	H. McDaniel	W. Knapp				
1919	Sir Barton	H. Bedwell	J. Loftus				
1920	Paul Jones	W. Garth	T. Rice				
1921	Behave Yourself	H. Thompson	C. Thompson				
1922	Morvich	F. Burlew	A. Johnson				
1923	Zev	D. Leary	E. Sande				
1924	Black Gold	H. Webb	J. Mooney				
1925	Flying Ebony	W. Duke	E. Sande				
1926	Bubbling Over	H. Thompson	A. Johnson				
1927	Whiskery	F. Hopkins	L. McAtee				
1928	Reigh Count	B. Mitchell	C. Lang				
1929	Clyde Van Dusen	C. Van Dusen	L. McAtee				
1930	Gallant Fox	J. Fitzsimmons	W. Saunders				
1931	Twenty Grand	J. Rowe	C. Kurtsinger				
1932	Burgoo King	H. Thompson	E. James				
1933	Brokers Tip	H. Thompson	D. Meade				
1934	Cavalcade	R. Smith	M. Garner				
1935	Omaha	J. Fitzsimmons	W. Saunders				
1936	Bold Venture	M. Hirsch	I. Hanford				
1937	War Admiral	G. Conway	C. Kurtsinger				
1938	Lawrin	B. Jones	E. Arcaro				
1939	Johnstown	J. Fitzsimmons	J. Stout				
1940	Gallahadion	R. Waldron	C. Bierman				
1941	Whirlaway	B. Jones	E. Arcaro				
1942	Shut Out	J. Gaver	W. Wright				
1943	Count Fleet	G. Cameron	J. Longden				
1944	Pensive	B. Jones	C. McCreary				
1945	Hoop Jr	I. Parke	E. Arcaro				
1946	Assault	M. Hirsch	W. Mehrtens				
1947	Jet Pilot	T. Smith	E. Guerin				
1948	Citation	B. Jones	E. Arcaro				

PREAKNESS STAKES
Pimlico, Maryland: 1 mile 1½ f (1,900 m). *Three-year-olds*

YEAR	HORSE	TRAINER	JOCKEY	YEAR	HORSE	TRAINER	JOCKEY
1873	Survivor	A. Pryor	G. Barbee	1948	Citation	H. Jones	E. Arcaro
1874	Culpepper	H. Gaffney	M. Donohoe	1949	Capot	J. Gaver	T. Atkinson
1875	Tom Ochiltree	R. Walden	L. Hughes	1950	Hill Prince	J. Hayes	E. Arcaro
1876	Shirley	W. Brown	G. Barbee	1951	Bold	P. Burch	E. Arcaro
1877	Cloverbrook	J. Walden	C. Holloway	1952	Blue Man	W. Stephens	C. McCreary
1878	Duke Of Magenta	R. Walden	C. Holloway	1953	Native Dancer	W. Winfrey	E. Guerin
1879	Harold	R. Walden	L. Hughes	1954	Hasty Road	H. Trotsek	J. Adams
1880	Grenada	R. Walden	L. Hughes	1955	Nashua	J. Fitzsimmons	E. Arcaro
1881	Saunterer	R. Walden	T. Costello	1956	Fabius	H. Jones	W. Hartack
1882	Vanguard	R. Walden	T. Costello	1957	Bold Ruler	J. Fitzsimmons	E. Arcaro
1883	Jacobus	R. Dwyer	G. Barbee	1958	Tim Tam	H. Jones	I. Valenzuela
1884	Knight Of Ellerslie	T. Doswell	S. Fisher	1959	Royal Orbit	R. Cornell	W. Harmatz
1885	Tecumseh	C. Littlefield	J. McLaughlin	1960	Bally Ache	H. Pitt	R. Ussery
1886	The Bard	J. Huggins	S. Fisher	1961	Carry Back	J. Price	J. Sellers
1887	Dunboyne	W. Jennings	W. Donohoe	1962	Greek Money	V. Raines	J. Rotz
1888	Refund	R. Walden	F. Littlefield	1963	Candy Spots	M. Tenney	W. Shoemaker
1889	Buddhist	J. Rogers	W. Anderson	1964	Northern Dancer	H. Luro	W. Hartack
1890	no race			1965	Tom Rolfe	F. Whiteley	R. Turcotte
–93				1966	Kauai King	H. Forrest	D. Brumfield
1894	Assignee	W. Lakeland	F. Taral	1967	Damascus	F. Whiteley	W. Shoemaker
1895	Belmar	E. Feakes	F. Taral	1968	Forward Pass	H. Forrest	I. Valenzuela
1896	Margrave	B. McClelland	H. Griffin	1969	Majestic Prince	J. Longden	W. Hartack
1897	Paul Kauvar	T. Hayes	C. Thorpe	1970	Personality	J. Jacobs	E. Belmonte
1898	Sly Fox	H. Campbell	W. Simms	1971	Canonero	J. Arias	G. Avila
1899	Half Time	F. McCabe	R. Clawson	1972	Bee Bee Bee	D. Carroll	E. Nelson
1900	Hindus	J. Morris	H. Spencer	1973	Secretariat	L. Laurin	R. Turcotte
1901	The Parader	T. Healey	F. Landry	1974	Little Current	L. Rondinello	M. Rivera
1902	Old England	G. Morris	L. Jackson	1975	Master Derby	W. Adams	D. McHargue
1903	Flocarline	H. Riddle	W. Gannon	1976	Elocutionist	P. Adwell	J. Lively
1904	Bryn Mawr	W. Presgrave	E. Hildebrand	1977	Seattle Slew	W. Turner	J. Cruguet
1905	Cairngorm	A. Joyner	W. Davis	1978	Affirmed	L. Barrera	S. Cauthen
1906	Whimsical	T. Gaynor	W. Miller	1979	Spectacular Bid	G. Delp	R. Franklin
1907	Don Enrique	J. Whalen	G. Mountain	1980	Codex	D. Lukas	A. Cordero
1908	Royal Tourist	A. Joyner	E. Dugan	1981	Pleasant Colony	J. Campo	J. Velasquez
1909	Effendi	F. Frisbee	W. Doyle	1982	Aloma's Ruler	J. Lenzini	J. Kaenel
1910	Layminster	J. Healy	R. Estep	1983	Disputed Testimony	W. Boniface	D. Miller
1911	Watervale	J. Whalen	E. Dugan	1984	Gate Dancer	J. Van Berg	A. Cordero
1912	Colonel Holloway	D. Woodford	C. Turner	1985	Tank's Prospect	D. Lukas	P. Day
1913	Buskin	J. Whalen	J. Butwell	1986	Snow Chief	M. Stute	A. Solis
1914	Holiday	J. Healy	A. Schuttinger	1987	Alysheba	J. Van Berg	C. McCarron
1915	Rhine Maiden	F. Devers	D. Hoffman	1988	Risen Star	L. Roussel	E. Delahoussaye
1916	Damrosch	A. Weston	L. McAtee				
1917	Kalitan	W. Hurley	E. Haynes				
1918	War Cloud	W. Jennings	J. Loftus				
	and Jack Hare Jr*	F. Weir	C. Peak				
1919	Sir Barton	H. Bedwell	J. Loftus				
1920	Man O'War	L. Feustel	C. Kummer				
1921	Broomspun	J. Rowe	F. Coltiletti				
1922	Pillory	T. Healey	L. Morris				
1923	Vigil	T. Healey	B. Marinelli				
1924	Nellie Morse	A. Gordon	J. Merimee				
1925	Coventry	W. Duke	C. Kummer				
1926	Display	T. Healey	J. Maiben				
1927	Bostonian	F. Hopkins	A. Abel				
1928	Victorian	J. Rowe	R. Workman				
1929	Dr Freeland	T. Healey	L. Schaefer				
1930	Gallant Fox	J. Fitzsimmons	E. Sande				
1931	Mate	J. Healey	G. Ellis				
1932	Burgoo King	H. Thompson	E. James				
1933	Head Play	T. Hayes	C. Kurtsinger				
1934	High Quest	R. Smith	R. Jones				
1935	Omaha	J. Fitzsimmons	W. Saunders				
1936	Bold Venture	H. Hirsch	G. Woolf				
1937	War Admiral	G. Conway	C. Kurtsinger				
1938	Dauber	R. Handlen	M. Peters				
1939	Challedon	L. Schaefer	G. Seabo				
1940	Bimelech	H. Hurley	F. Smith				
1941	Whirlaway	B. Jones	E. Arcaro				
1942	Alsab	A. Swenke	B. James				
1943	Count Fleet	G. Cameron	J. Longden				
1944	Pensive	B. Jones	C. McCreary				
1945	Polynesian	M. Dixon	W. Wright				
1946	Assault	M. Hirsch	W. Mehrtens				
1947	Faultless	H. Jones	D. Dodson				

* 1918: run in two divisions.

251

UNITED STATES OF AMERICA

JOCKEY CLUB GOLD CUP
Belmont Park, New York: 1½ miles (2,400 m)*. *Three-year-olds and up. First run: 1919*

YEAR	HORSE	TRAINER	JOCKEY	YEAR	HORSE	TRAINER	JOCKEY
1919	Purchase	–	C. Kummer	1968	Quicken Tree	W. Canney	W. Hartack
1920	Man O'War	–	C. Kummer	1969	Arts And Letters	E. Burch	B. Baeza
1921	Mad Hatter	–	E. Sande	1970	Shuvee	W. Freeman	R. Turcotte
1922	Mad Hatter	–	E. Sande	1971	Shuvee	W. Freeman	J. Velaquez
1923	Homestretch	–	C. Lang	1972	Autobiography	F. Martin	A. Cordero
1924	My Play	–	A. Schuttinger	1973	Prove Out	H. Jerkens	J. Velasquez
1925	Altawood	–	E. Sande	1974	Forego	S. ward	H. Gustines
1926	Crusader	–	J. Maiben	1975	Group Plan	H. Jerkens	J. Velasquez
1927	Chance Play	–	E. Sande	1976	Great Contractor	R. Laurin	P. Day
1928	Reigh Count	–	C. Lang	1977	On The Sly	M. Gross	C. McCarron
1929	Diavolo	–	J Maiben	1978	Exceller	C. Whittingham	W. Shoemaker
1930	Gallant Fox	–	E. Sande	1979	Affirmed	L. Barrera	L. Pincay
1931	Twenty Grand	–	C. Kurtsinger	1980	Temperance Hill	J. Contey	E. Maple
1932	Gusty	–	B. Hanford	1981	John Henry	R. McAnally	W. Shoemaker
1933	Dark Secret	–	H. Mills	1982	Lemhi Gold	L. Barrera	C. McCarron
1934	Dark Secret	–	C. Kurtsinger	1983	Slew O'Gold	S. Watters	A. Cordero
1935	Firethorn	–	E. Arcaro	1984	Slew O'Gold	J. Hertler	A. Cordero
1936	Count Arthur	–	J. Stout	1985	Vanlandingham	C. McGaughey	P. Day
1937	Firethorn	–	H. Richards	1986	Crème Fraîche	W. Stephens	R. Romero
1938	War Admiral	–	W.D. Wright	1987	Crème Fraîche	W. Stephens	L. Pincay
1939	Cravat	–	B. James	1988	Waquoit	G. Federico	J. Santos
1940	Fenelon	–	J. Stout				
1941	Market Wise	–	B. James				
1942	Whirlaway	–	G. Woolf				
1943	Princequillo	–	C. McCreary				
1944	Bollingbroke	–	R. Permane				
1945	Pot O'Luck	–	D. Dodson				
1946	Pavot	–	E. Arcaro				
1947	Phalanx	–	R. Donoso				
1948	Citation	–	E. Arcaro				
1949	Ponder	–	S. Brooks				
1950	Hill Prince	J. Hayes	E. Arcaro				
1951	Counterpoint	S. Veitch	D. Gorman				
1952	One Count	O. White	D. Gorman				
1953	Level Lea	M. Hirsch	W. Boland				
1954	High Gun	M. Hirsch	E.Arcaro				
1955	Nashua	J. Fitzsimmons	E. Arcaro				
1956	Nashua	J. Fitzsimmons	E. Arcaro				
1957	Gallant Man	J. Nerud	W. Shoemaker				
1958	Inside Tract	J. Weipert	C. McCreery				
1959	Sword Dancer	J. Burch	E. Arcaro				
1960	Kelso	C. Hanford	E. Arcaro				
1961	Kelso	C. Hanford	E. Arcaro				
1962	Kelso	C. Hanford	I. Valenzuela				
1963	Kelso	C. Hanford	I. Valenzuela				
1964	Kelso	C. Hanford	I. Valenzuela				
1965	Roman Brother	B. Parke	B. Baeza				
1966	Buckpasser	E. Neloy	B. Baeza				
1967	Damascus	F. Whiteley	W. Shoemaker				

* To 1976: 2 miles (3,200 m)

BREEDERS' CUP
Hollywood Park: *1984, 1987*; **Aqueduct, New York**: *1985*; **Santa Anita, California**: *1986*; **Churchill Downs,**

BREEDERS' CUP TURF
1½ miles (2,400 m). *Three-year-olds and up*

YEAR	HORSE	TRAINER	JOCKEY
1984	Lashkari	A. de Royer-Dupré	Y. Saint-Martin
1985	Pebbles	C. Brittain	P. Eddery
1986	Manila	L. Jolley	J. Santaos
1987	Theaatrical	W. Mott	P. Day
1988	Great Communicator	T. Ackel	R. Sibille

BREEDERS' CUP CLASSIC
1¼ miles (2,000 m). *Three-year-olds and up*

YEAR	HORSE	TRAINER	JOCKEY
1984	Wild Again	V. Timphony	P. Day
1985	Proud Truth	J. Veitch	J. Velasquez
1986	Skywalker	M. Whittingham	L. Pincay
1987	Ferdinand	C. Whittingham	W. Shoemaker
1988	Alysheba	J. Van Bers	C. McCarron

Fabulous French filly Miesque gives jockey Freddie Head a jubilant moment of triumph in the 1987 Breeders' Cup Mile.

MARLBORO CUP
Belmont Park, New York: 1¼ mile (2,000 m). Three-year-olds. Run: 1973—87

YEAR	HORSE	TRAINER	JOCKEY	YEAR	HORSE	TRAINER	JOCKEY
1973	Secretariat	L. Laurin	R. Turcotte	1985	Chief's Crown	R. Laurin	D. MacBeth
1974	Big Spruce	V. Nickerson	M. Hole	1986	Turkoman	G. Jones	G. Stevens
1975	Wajima	S. Di Mauro	B. Baeza	1987	Java Gold	M. Miller	P. Day
1976	Forego	F. Whiteley	W. Shoemaker				
1977	Proud Birdie	J. Maloney	J. Vasquez				
1978	Seattle Slew	D. Peterson	A. Cordero				
1979	Spectacular Bid	G. Delp	W. Shoemaker				
1980	Winter's Tale	M. Miller	J. Fell				
1981	Noble Naskra	J. Martin	R. Hernandez				
1982	Lemhi Gold	L. Barrera	J. Vasquez				
1983	Highland Blade	D. Whiteley	J. Vasquez				
1984	Slew O'Gold	J. Hertler	A. Cordero				

Kentucky: 1988

BREEDERS' CUP MILE
1 mile (1,600 m). Three-year-olds and up

YEAR	HORSE	TRAINER	JOCKEY
1984	Royal Heroine	J. Gosden	F. Toro
1985	Cozzene	J. Nerud	W. Guerra
1986	Last Tycoon	R. Collet	Y. Saint-Martin
1987	Miesque	F. Boutin	F. Head
1988	Miesque	F. Boutin	F. Head

BREEDERS' CUP SPRINT
6 f (1,200 m). Three-year-olds and up

YEAR	HORSE	TRAINER	JOCKEY
1984	Eillo	B. Lepman	C. Perret
1985	Precisionist	L. Fenstermaker	C. McCarron
1986	Smile	F. Schulhofer	J. Vasquez
1987	Very Subtle	M. Stute	P. Valenzuela
1988	Gulch	D. W. Lukas	A. Cordero

Index

Page numbers in *italics* refer to illustration captions.
Those in **bold** refer to main entries.

Acknowledgements

The publishers wish to thank the following contributors to the text of Trainers and Training, Famous Racecourses and The Great Jockeys: Jules Bedford (Italy), Colin Cameron (South America), David Connolly-Smith (Germany), Robert Garner (South Africa), Reg Green (Aintree), John Holloway and J A McGrath (Australia), Dorothy Laird (Ascot and Goodwood), Tom McCormack (Ireland), Richard Onslow (Newmarket), Janet Slade (France), Larry Stratton (New Zealand), with special thanks to The Racing Hall of Fame, USA and The Racing Hall of Fame, Canada.

Bibliography

Mortimer, Roger: *The History of the Derby Stakes* Michael Joseph
Mortimer, Roger: *The Epsom Derby* Michael Joseph
Pollard, Jack: *The Pictorial History of Australian Horse Racing* Paul Hamlyn
Smyly, Patricia: *The Encyclopedia of Steeplechasing* Robert Hale
Wright, Howard: *The Encyclopedia of Flat Racing* Robert Hale

Picture credits

Allsport: 54, 55, 61, 63, 68, 77, 78, 90, 103, 111, 117, 135, 136, 138, 139, 146, 148, 152, 156, 157, 158, 160, 162, 163, 165, 166, 175, 176/7, 194, 196/7, 210/1, 243, 253. Associated Press: 42, 51, 60/1, 67, 118, 121, 127, 154. Associated Sports Photography: 40, 47, 62, 92/3, 94/5, 120, 143, 151. Bridgeman Art Library: 199, 220/1. Colorsport: 45, 58, 80, 84, 86, 96/7, 101, 153, 159, 183, 184, 219, 226, 228. Gerry Cranham: 22, 29, 69, 70, 73, 77, 79, 81, 104/5, 106/7, 108, 114/5, 172/3, 180, 181, 182. Mary Evans Picture Library: 6/7, 9, 66, 140/1, 142, 150, 161, 170, 171, 177, 178, 186/7, 202. Fores Ltd: 16/7. French Government Tourist Office: 72, 91. Michael Holford: 8. Hong Kong Tourist Board: 102. Kit Houghton: 26, 39, 41, 46, 89, 109, 112, 112/3, 195, 218. Hulton Deutsch Collection: 10, 18, 19, 24/5, 27, 31, 37, 38, 52, 53, 57, 126, 143, 145, 149, 155, 167, 189, 190, 191, 192, 200, 201, 205, 208, 209, 215. The Hutchison Library: 15. Illustrated London News: 213. Alan Johnson: 2, 64/5, 82/3, 116, 117, 123, 124, 125, 134, 241. Bob Langrish: 4/5, 32/3, 34, 46, 74/5, 87, 100, 110. Mansell Collection: 11, 12, 14, 21. Peter Newark's Historical Pictures: 13, 248. Ontario Jockey Club: 35, 36. Popperfoto: 30, 56, 119, 137, 219, 230. Press Association: 59. Rex Features: 122. W. W. Rouch: 23, 193, 204, 206, 212. Frank Spooner Pictures/Gamma: 133. Sport & General: 51, 132, 157, 168, 169, 207. Sporting Life: 48, 49, 205. Sporting Pictures (UK) Ltd: 44, 147.

Artwork credits

Simon Roulstone: 128, 129, 130, 131.